40°E

URAL MTS.

Torneälven

FINLAND
(Sweden)

Gulf of Bothnia

Umeälven

Lake
Onega

Lake
Ladoga

Åbo

Vyborg

Helsingfors

St. Petersburg

Stockholm

Volkhov

Saaremaa

Lake
Vänern

Gotland

Volga

Öland

Moscow

RUSSIAN
EMPIRE

Baltic
Sea

Dvina

olm
(Denmark)

Neman

Danzig (Poland)

Minsk

USSIA

Vistula

POLAND

Warsaw

Bug

Silesia

Oder

Kiev

Dnieper

Galicia

Don

Carpathian Mts.

Southern Bug

Donets

Volga

via

Dniester

HABSBURG
POSSESSIONS

Prut

Moldavia

anna

Buda   Pest

Tisza

Maros (Mureş)

Transylvania

Siret

Kuban'

Hungary

Drava

Sava

Wallachia

Caspian
Sea

Belgrade

Bucharest

Morava

Danube

Black Sea

CAUCASUS MTS.

nnaric Alps

Balkan Mts.

CE

Maritsa

RAGUSA

MONTENEGRO

Vardar

Constantinople

OTTOMAN EMPIRE

ASIA

APLES

Sea of
Marmara

Aegean
Sea

Ionian
Sea

Athens

N

Crete
(Ottoman Empire)

Cyprus

| 0 | | 200 | | 400 mi. |
| 0 | | 200 | | 400 km |

EUROPE
1789 TO 1914
ENCYCLOPEDIA OF THE
AGE OF INDUSTRY AND EMPIRE

EDITORIAL BOARD

SCRIBNER LIBRARY OF MODERN EUROPE

EUROPE
1789 TO 1914
ENCYCLOPEDIA OF THE
AGE OF INDUSTRY AND EMPIRE

Volume 5

Talleyrand to Zollverein; Index

John Merriman and Jay Winter

EDITORS IN CHIEF

CHARLES SCRIBNER'S SONS

An imprint of Thomson Gale, a part of The Thomson Corporation

THOMSON

—★—

GALE

Detroit • New York • San Francisco • San Diego • New Haven, Conn. • Waterville, Maine • London • Munich

Europe 1789 to 1914: Encyclopedia of the Age of Industry and Empire

John Merriman
Jay Winter
Editors in Chief

LIBRARY OF CONGRESS CATALOGING-IN-PUBLICATION DATA

Europe 1789 to 1914 : encyclopedia of the age of industry and empire / edited by John Merriman and Jay Winter.
    p. cm. — (Scribner library of modern Europe)
    Includes bibliographical references and index.
    ISBN 0-684-31359-6 (set : alk. paper) — ISBN 0-684-31360-X (v. 1 : alk. paper) — ISBN 0-684-31361-8 (v. 2 : alk. paper) — ISBN 0-684-31362-6 (v. 3 : alk. paper) — ISBN 0-684-31363-4 (v. 4 : alk. paper) — ISBN 0-684-31364-2 (v. 5 : alk. paper) — ISBN 0-684-31496-7 (ebook)
    1. Europe–History–1789-1900–Encyclopedias. 2. Europe–History–1871-1918–Encyclopedias. 3. Europe–Civilization–19th century–Encyclopedias. 4. Europe–Civilization–20th century–Encyclopedias. I. Merriman, John M. II. Winter, J. M.
    D299.E735 2006
    940.2'8–dc22   2006007335

This title is also available as an e-book and as a ten-volume set with
Europe since 1914: Encyclopedia of the Age of War and Reconstruction.
E-book ISBN 0-684-31496-7
Ten-volume set ISBN 0-684-31530-0
Contact your Gale sales representative for ordering information.

Printed in the United States of America
10 9 8 7 6 5 4 3 2 1

CONTENTS OF THIS VOLUME

CONTENTS OF OTHER VOLUMES

C

MAPS OF EUROPE, 1789 TO 1914

The maps on the following pages show the changes in European national boundaries from 1789 to 1914, including the unification of Italy and of Germany.

Europe, 1789
— International border
• City

0   100   200 mi.
0 100 200 km

N

Norwegian Sea

Faroe Islands

Shetland Islands

SWEDEN

FINLAND (Sweden)

Helsingfors

St. Petersburg

Gulf of Bothnia

Gulf of Finland

NORWAY (Denmark)

• Christiania

Stockholm •

Moscow •

Orkney Islands

North Sea

Baltic Sea

RUSSIA

Scotland

Edinburgh •

DENMARK   • Copenhagen

Königsberg •

Ireland

GREAT BRITAIN

Dublin •

PRUSSIA

POLAND

• Berlin

Warsaw •

Wales   England

Hanover

Amsterdam •

London •

NETH.

Hanover

HOLY ROMAN EMPIRE

Saxony

Bohemia

GALICIA

Brussels •

Austrian Netherlands

Moravia

HABSBURG POSSESSIONS

ATLANTIC OCEAN

• Paris

Bavaria

Austria

Vienna •

Buda • • Pest

Moldavia

Munich •

HUNGARY

TRANSYLVANIA

FRANCE

SWISS CONFED.

Tyrol

Wallachia

Black Sea

Bay of Biscay

Milan VENICE

Venice •

PIEDMONT

Genoa •

Florence •

VENICE

RAGUSA

MONTENEGRO

Constantinople •

TUSCANY

PAPAL STATES

Adriatic Sea

OTTOMAN EMPIRE

ANDORRA

Corsica (France)

Rome •

PORTUGAL

• Madrid

Minorca (Great Britain)

SARDINIA

Naples • NAPLES

Athens •

Lisbon •

SPAIN

Iviza (Spain)

Majorca (Spain)

Tyrrhenian Sea

Sicily

Ionian Sea

Algiers •

Tunis •

Malta

Crete (Ottoman Empire)

OTTOMAN EMPIRE

Mediterranean Sea

France in 1789

--- International border
• City

GREAT BRITAIN

English Channel

Flanders

• Lille

AUSTRIAN NETHERLANDS

GERMAN STATES

N

• Rouen

Île de France

Seine River

Normandy

• Nancy

Lorraine

Alsace

Rhine River

• Paris

Brittany

Franche Comté

NEUCHÂTEL

Loire River

F R A N C E

SWISS CONFEDERATION

• Nantes

ATLANTIC OCEAN

Burgundy

• Geneva

Poitou

• La Rochelle

• Lyon

KINGDOM OF SARDINIA

Rhône River

Bay of Biscay

• Bordeaux

Garonne River

AVIGNON

REPUBLIC OF GENOA

Guyenne and Gascony

Provence

NICE

• Toulouse

Languedoc

• Marseille

0   50   100 mi.
0   50   100 km

ANDORRA

Corsica

S P A I N

Mediterranean Sea

Europe, 1815

— Boundary of the German Confederation, 1815

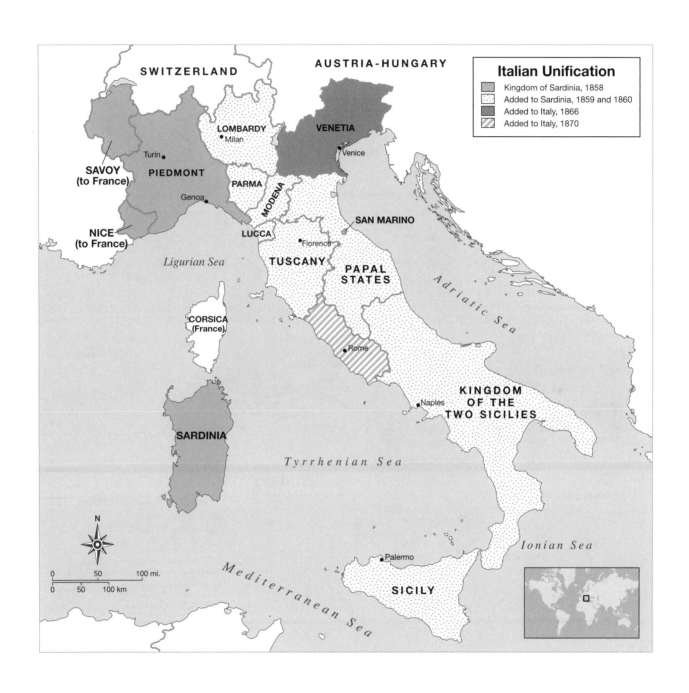

Italian Unification
- Kingdom of Sardinia, 1858
- Added to Sardinia, 1859 and 1860
- Added to Italy, 1866
- Added to Italy, 1870

SWITZERLAND

AUSTRIA-HUNGARY

LOMBARDY
• Milan

VENETIA

• Venice

SAVOY
(to France)

Turin •

PIEDMONT

PARMA

MODENA

Genoa •

SAN MARINO

NICE
(to France)

LUCCA

• Florence

Ligurian Sea

TUSCANY

PAPAL
STATES

Adriatic Sea

CORSICA
(France)

• Rome

KINGDOM
OF THE
TWO SICILIES

• Naples

SARDINIA

Tyrrhenian Sea

Ionian Sea

N

0   50   100 mi.
0   50   100 km

• Palermo

Mediterranean Sea

SICILY

SWEDEN

DENMARK

North Sea

Baltic Sea

N

Schleswig

Holstein

Mecklenburg

East Prussia

Hamburg

Hanover

Pomerania

West Prussia

A

S

NETHERLANDS

Brandenburg

Berlin

Posen

Vistula R.

RUSSIA

Westphalia

P

R

U

S

BELGIUM

Rhine R.

Ems

Thuringia

Saxony

Elbe R.

Oder R.

Silesia

Sedan

LUX.

Frankfurt

Prague

Sadowa

To Paris

Metz

Main R.

Lorraine

Bavaria

AUSTRIA-HUNGARY

FRANCE

Württemberg

Danube R.

Alsace

Baden

Hohenzollern

Munich

Vienna

SWITZERLAND

German Unification

- Prussia, 1865
- Added to Prussia, 1866
- Added to form North German Confederation, 1867
- Added to form German empire, 1871
- Boundary of German empire, 1871
- Route of Prussian armies in Austro-Prussian War
- Route of German armies in Franco-Prussian War
- ✴ Battle sites

0   50   100 mi.

0   50   100 km

Europe, 1914

International border

ICELAND

ATLANTIC OCEAN

NORWAY

SWEDEN

North Sea

Baltic Sea

DENMARK

UNITED KINGDOM

NETH.

BELG.

LUX.

GERMANY

RUSSIA

Caspian Sea

FRANCE

SWITZ.

AUSTRIA-HUNGARY

ROMANIA

Black Sea

ITALY

SERBIA

MONT.

BULGARIA

ALBANIA

PORTUGAL

ANDORRA

SPAIN

GREECE

OTTOMAN EMPIRE

PERSIA

Spanish Morocco

Tunisia (Fr.)

Mediterranean Sea

Morocco (Fr.)

Algeria (Fr.)

Libya (It.)

Egypt (Br.)

N

0   250   500 mi.

0   250   500 km

TALLEYRAND, CHARLES MAURICE DE (1754–1838), arguably the most famous diplomat that France ever produced.

Charles Maurice de Talleyrand-Périgord was born in Paris on 2 February, the son of a noble army officer. Neglected by his parents, as a young boy he sustained a foot injury that gave him a limp for the rest of his life, thus ruling out the possibility of a military career. Instead he trained for the priesthood, was ordained a Roman Catholic priest in December 1779, but then led a very secular life in Paris aristocratic society, openly consorting with his mistress Adelaide Filleul, the Countess of Flahaut, by whom he had an illegitimate son. Nevertheless, his aristocratic credentials secured his appointment as bishop of Autun in 1788.

In April 1789, Talleyrand was elected a deputy of the clergy of Autun to the Estates General. On 10 October 1789 in the National Assembly, the successor to the Estates General, he proposed that all Church property should be confiscated to solve the continuing financial crisis. The acceptance of this proposal in November deprived the Roman Catholic Church in France of nearly all its wealth and led to its radical restructuring in the Civil Constitution of the Clergy (July 1790). Talleyrand was one of only four bishops to swear an oath of loyalty to this Constitution, and as a "constitutional bishop" on 14 July 1790 he officiated at the Feast of the Federation, the national ceremony in Paris to commemorate the first anniversary of the storming of the Bastille. In January 1791,

Talleyrand resigned his bishopric. His diplomatic career began in 1792 when he was sent on a mission to London to improve relations between France and Britain. Expelled from Britain in February 1794, he moved to the United States, where he settled in Philadelphia. There he traveled quite extensively, made money from property speculations, and frequented a circle of fellow French émigrés.

Allowed to return to France, he arrived in Paris in September 1796 and resumed a relationship with Anne-Louise-Germaine de Staël (1766–1817). Partly due to her influence, Talleyrand was appointed minister of foreign affairs by the Directory in July 1797. In December 1797, he met Napoleon Bonaparte for the first time and soon began planning with him the expedition to Egypt, which set sail from France in May 1798. Meanwhile, Talleyrand had acquired a new mistress, the wife of Charles Delacroix, Talleyrand's predecessor as minister of foreign affairs. By her he had another illegitimate son, Eugène Delacroix (1798–1863), who became a famous Romantic artist. Talleyrand resigned as minister of foreign affairs in July 1799 and soon began plotting a coup d'état to remove the Directory with Joseph Fouché (1759–1820, the minister of police) and Napoleon Bonaparte (who had returned from Egypt in October 1799).

Following the coup d'état of 10 November 1799, Napoleon reappointed Talleyrand minister of foreign affairs. Talleyrand negotiated the Treaty of Lunéville with Austria (9 February 1801) and supported Napoleon's policies of reconciliation with royalists and Roman Catholics, but he was soon disagreeing with the First Consul over the severity of the Treaty of Amiens with Britain (27 March 1802), the annexation of Piedmont to France (21 September 1802), and the declaration of war against Britain (18 May 1803). Nevertheless, Talleyrand was, at the very least, a passive accomplice in the execution of Louis-Antoine-Henri de Bourbon-Condé, the Duke of Enghien (20 March 1804). When Napoleon assumed the imperial title (2 December 1804), Talleyrand became Imperial Grand Chamberlain.

Whereas Napoleon sought to impose French domination over Europe, Talleyrand believed in the balance of power and unsuccessfully urged moderation on Napoleon after the successive defeats of Austria, Prussia, and Russia. In August 1807, Talleyrand resigned as foreign minister and from 1808 publicly criticized Napoleon's policies, at a time when Napoleon was at the height of his success. While Talleyrand supported Napoleon's marriage to Marie-Louise (1791–1847) of Austria, he bitterly opposed the invasion of Russia in 1812. Thus, although Napoleon had made Talleyrand a prince and extremely rich, Talleyrand deserted him in 1814 to play a leading role in the restoration of the Bourbons. In April 1814, Talleyrand persuaded Alexander I (1777–1825) of Russia to accept the return of the Bourbons and the French Senate to depose Napoleon and offer the French throne to Louis XVIII (1755–1824).

Once more the minister of foreign affairs (13 May 1814), Talleyrand represented France at the Congress of Vienna. Brilliantly exploiting the principle of legitimacy that the Allies claimed to uphold, Talleyrand secured for France remarkably favorable terms. However, the Hundred Days episode resulted in harsher treatment of France by the Second Treaty of Paris (20 November 1815). Forced to resign in September 1815, Talleyrand retired to his country estate, Valençay.

During the late 1820s, Talleyrand actively supported the liberal opposition to Charles X (1757–1836); in the Revolution of 1830, he contributed to the accession of Louis Philippe (1773–1850) as king of the French. As a reward, he was appointed French ambassador in London (September 1830–November 1834), when he helped to negotiate the separation of Belgium from the Netherlands. He died on 17 May 1838. To his critics he was the serial betrayer of the Roman Catholic Church, the Directory, Napoleon I, and Charles X, and the personification of corruption and vice. To his admirers he was the consummate politician and diplomat, who always sought the true interests of France.

See also **Concert of Europe; Congress of Vienna; France; French Revolution; Napoleonic Empire; Restoration; Revolutions of 1830.**

BIBLIOGRAPHY

Primary Sources

Talleyrand-Périgord, Charles-Maurice de. *Memoirs of Talleyrand.* Edited by the Duke of Broglie. 5 vols. New York, 1891.

Secondary Sources

Bernard, Jack F. *Talleyrand: A Biography.* New York, 1973.

Brinton, Crane. *The Lives of Talleyrand.* New York, 1936.

Dwyer, Philip G. *Charles-Maurice de Talleyrand, 1754–1838: A Bibliography.* Westport, Conn., 1996.

WILLIAM FORTESCUE

TCHAIKOVSKY, PETER (1840–1893), Russian composer.

Peter Ilyich Tchaikovsky was born in Votkinsk, Russia. His father worked as a superintendent of state mines; his mother, who was half French, insisted on hiring French servants to attend to her son. Even as a child, Tchaikovsky was introspective and neurotic. By age thirteen, his homosexuality had become obvious. At fourteen he lost his only true friend, his mother, to cholera. He felt no closeness to any of his other relatives, nor was he interested in communicating with any of his peers. After a short period as a student in a government law school, which he despised, he left to study with the composer and pianist Anton Rubinstein, the founder of the St. Petersburg Conservatory of Music. Several years thereafter, he accepted an offer to teach harmony and was also invited by several western and southern European countries to appear as a guest conductor in major concert halls, as well as at his home base, the Moscow Conservatory. He resigned from his professorship in 1878.

Tchaikovsky was one of the innovators of Russian Romanticism, but he also considered it his duty to introduce Russian patriotism and nationalism into his music. His vast output included piano and violin concertos, choral works, symphonies, chamber music, and church music. His most creative works were in genres that included fantasies, overtures such as "Romeo and Juliet," choral works, and piano-and-violin concertos. In western Europe, Tchaikovsky's music was well received, and in Russia he was considered to be the most Romantic and patriotic of composers. The literary giants of his time were Fyodor Dostoyevsky and Leo Tolstoy, yet controversy exists over whether Tchaikovsky ever made the time or had the desire to meet either of them.

In 1888 Tchaikovsky took a significant tour to Leipzig, Germany, to meet with Edvard Grieg and Johannes Brahms. He also visited London, Paris, and Prague. His labors on Symphony No. 5 in E Minor became increasingly intense and emotional, which fed his neurotic despair. Nevertheless, he insisted on continuing his travels. He went to the United States and to England, where he was awarded an honorary doctorate of music at Cambridge.

Tchaikovsky's attempts to masquerade as heterosexual were obvious to all. The only woman he ever truly loved was his mother. He spent one night with Desire Artot, a singer and prima donna of a visiting Italian troupe, but refused to comment on it. In the 1870s he visited Georgia and other Russian territories. A former student of his, Antonia Milyukova, talked him into marrying her but the marriage did not last long. Beginning in 1876 he was subsidized by the wealthy widow Nadezhda von Meck, who gave him the means to survive. In 1885 he bought a house in Maidanovo, near Moscow and lived there until a year before his death.

Despite his successes, his mental condition deteriorated, and this was aggravated when Nadezhda von Meck stopped supporting him, both financially and socially. By then he was no longer in need of her money, but the psychological damage was noticeable. On his deathbed, he repeated her name over and over. He had just completed his last symphony, the *Pathetique*, which he rightfully considered his masterpiece. Several historians have claimed that he wanted to poison himself after having allegedly been accused of involvement with a male member of the British imperial family.

Tchaikovsky's major works include the operas *Undine*, 1869; *Mazepa*, 1884; *Pathetique*, 1893; *Queen of Spades*, 1890; and *Eugene Onegin*, 1879; the ballets *The Nutcracker Suite*, 1892; *The Sleeping Beauty*, 1890; and *Swan Lake*, 1877; the symphonies No. 4 in F Minor, No. 5 in E Minor, and No. 6 in B Minor (*Pathetique*); the Piano Concerto No. 1 in B-Flat Minor; and the Americanized Russian vocals "None but the Lonely Heart"; "Why Did I Dream of You"; and "Don Juan's Serenade"; as well as chamber and instrumental music.

See also **Diaghilev, Sergei; Music; Mussorgsky, Modest; Rimsky-Korsakov, Nikolai.**

BIBLIOGRAPHY

Abraham, Gerald, ed. *Tchaikovsky: A Symposium*. London, 1945.

Brown, David. *Tchaikovsky*. 4 vols. New York, 1978–1992.

Garden, Edward. *Tchaikovsky*. New York, 1973.

Strutte, Wilson. *Tchaikovsky: His Life and Times*. Speldhurst, U.K., 1979.

Tchaikovsky, Peter Ilich. *The Diaries of Tchaikovsky*. Translated by Wladimir Lakond. New York, 1945.

Volkoff, Vladimir. *Tchaikovsky: A Self-Portrait*. Boston, 1975.

Warrack, John.Hamilton *Tchaikovsky*. London, 1973.

LEO HECHT

TELEGRAPH. *See* **Science and Technology.**

TELEPHONES. Private enterprise, operating under government-granted concessions, initiated urban telephone service in most European countries (except Germany) in the late 1880s, though virtually all were nationalized in the 1880s and 1890s. The government-operated post and telegraph (and later, telephone) administrations (PTT) then often restricted telephone network development to protect their earlier telegraph investments. As a result, by 1914 the telephone was far more developed in the United States (which had nearly two-thirds of the world's telephones, or nearly ten for every one hundred people) than anywhere in Europe.

Telephone devices patented by Alexander Graham Bell (1847–1922) were first demonstrated in London and several continental cities in 1877–78. The inception of regular telephone service varied across European capitals, from London and Paris in 1879; followed by Stockholm, Copenhagen, and Christiania, Norway, in 1880; Berlin, Vienna, and several Italian cities in 1881; Helsinki and Lisbon in 1882; Brussels, Moscow, and St. Petersburg in 1883; Luxembourg City in 1885; and finally various Spanish cities in 1886–87. As these dates suggest, early telephone development concentrated in urban areas with many potential users, providing little interconnection among them and little or no service to small communities and rural areas. Virtually all switching of calls required manual operation using male, and later female, operators. Women operators were required to be single (and to resign upon marrying) in Britain, Switzerland, Norway, and Sweden.

Local pricing of telephone service varied. Most subscriber charges were based on per use with some reflection of the distance carried or (more rarely) a flat charge for a given period of use. There was considerable variation in the prices charged by different PTTs. By the mid-1880s, the International Telegraph Bureau in Bern, Switzerland, began to collect and publish statistics on telephone availability and use. By 1887, Germany's PTT had 123 exchanges and more than 22,000 subscribers, while Sweden's privately owned operation (with 148 exchanges and nearly 13,000 subscribers) was second. Other nations fell far behind.

The growing need to interconnect service across national boundaries raised similar questions as had the telegraph decades earlier: the need for some means of setting and interconnecting varied technical standards, as well as melding different currencies and means of paying for telephone service—and determining how to divide revenues across the telephone systems involved. Among the earliest international links were landlines connecting such European cities as Brussels and Paris. Over-water routes took longer: the first was London to Paris in 1891, and Britain to Ireland by means of an undersea cable from Scotland two years later.

The telephone was occasionally applied to deliver concert music and stage entertainment—for example, in Budapest (the Telefon Hirmondo operated by the Puskas brothers in 1893), Paris (the Theatrophone), and in London. The first European automatic telephone exchange (using strowger devices developed in the United States) began operation in Berlin in 1899, but most European nations relied on (often high-capacity) manual switches to the eve of World War I. The first pay telephone kiosks appeared in Britain by 1904, and soon in other nations.

Europe fell far behind U.S. rates of telephone system growth and technical developments from 1890 to 1914, chiefly because of PTT monopoly control of telephone services across Europe. This usually meant that insufficient capital was made available for system expansion (telephones had low priority in national budgets), telephone rates were held to artificially low levels by national parliaments (thus financially starving the systems even more), and telephone administrators generally were subordinate to those directing telegraph and postal services. Further, and with few exceptions, there was virtually no overall system planning or policy and very little study of either rates charged or traffic carried. On the other hand, German and Swiss PTTs stood out for their effective operation of telephone networks, and the three Scandinavian nations retained private ownership and thus a strong commercial impetus to expand telephone availability. This shows up in some statistics: by 1914, a third of British telephones were in London, but the city still had but 3.5 telephones per 100 people, while Stockholm had 24; Copenhagen, 9; Berlin, 6.6; and Paris, 3.2.

As had been the case earlier in the United States, telephone use was limited for the first several decades to government officials, businesses, and the wealthy who could afford the equipment and service charges. Only very slowly—and barely so by 1914—was telephone service made more widely available to and affordable by the general public, at first with phones in public places and pay stations, and later in individual homes.

See also **Science and Technology; Transportation and Communications.**

BIBLIOGRAPHY

Baldwin, F. G. C. *The History of the Telephone in the United Kingdom.* London, 1925.

Bennett, Alfred Rosling. *The Telephone Systems of the Continent of Europe.* London, 1895. Reprint, New York, 1974.

Chapuis, Robert J. *100 Years of Telephone Switching (1878–1978).* Amsterdam, 1982.

Holcomb, A. N. *Public Ownership of Telephones on the Continent of Europe.* Boston, 1911.

Webb, Herbert Laws. *The Development of the Telephone in Europe.* London, 1911. Reprint, New York, 1974.

CHRISTOPHER H. STERLING

TEMPERANCE. *See* **Alcohol and Temperance.**

TENNYSON, ALFRED (1809–1892), English poet and the leading representative of Victorian verse.

Born in Somersby, Lincolnshire, Alfred, Lord Tennyson was a precocious child who wrote poems after the styles of John Milton (1608–1674) and the British Romantics.

In November 1827 Tennyson entered Trinity College, Cambridge, where his standing as a poet grew and in June 1829 he won the chancellor's gold medal for his poem, *Timbuctoo.* The death of his father in March 1831 revealed his family's deep financial indebtedness, and Tennyson left Cambridge without taking a degree.

In 1832 Tennyson published *Poems,* a volume that included "The Lotos-Eaters" and "The Lady of Shalott." Reviewers' attacks deeply distressed the self-critical Tennyson, but he continued to revise his old poems and compose new ones.

In September 1833, Tennyson's close Cambridge friend Arthur Hallam died suddenly. The loss of Hallam, recently engaged to marry Tennyson's sister Cecilia, dealt a serious blow to Tennyson. He soon drafted "Ulysses," "Morte d'Arthur" and "Tithonus"—three poems prompted by the death, but all with strong classical echoes that spoke to his expressly modern and personal sentiments.

Between 1832 and 1842 Tennyson published no new volumes, but he edited and wrote much during this melancholic period, initiating *In Memoriam,* which celebrated Hallam, "The Two Voices" (originally entitled "Thoughts of a Suicide") and his "English Idylls." In 1842 Tennyson published *Poems* to unfavorable reviews. The volume included "Morte d'Arthur," "Locksley Hall," and "The Vision of Sin." That same year the prime minister, Sir Robert Peel (1788–1850), granted him a pension of £200 for life, easing his financial burden. In 1847 Tennyson published his first long poem, *The Princess,* a conservative view of university education for women.

On 13 June 1850, Tennyson married Emily Sellwood, after a very long and uncertain courtship, due in part to her father's early disapproval of Tennyson's unorthodox lifestyle and liberal religious views.

The year 1850 also marked a professional turning point. Tennyson anonymously published *In Memoriam,* which enjoyed tremendous success and won him the favor of Queen Victoria (r. 1837–1901), who helped bring about his appointment as poet laureate that same year. Tennyson had finally secured his reputation and finances.

A massive poem, *In Memoriam* captured the public imagination, highlighting many concerns of the Victorian age as the author searched for the meaning of life and death and tried to come to terms with the loss of his friend. The poem struggles with religious doubt and faith, weighing spiritual belief in immortality against emerging scientific theories of evolution, astronomy, and modern geology. Tennyson cemented his position as national poet with his *Ode on the Death of the Duke of Wellington* (1852) and a poem about the 25 October 1855 Charge of the Light Brigade at Balaklava in the Crimea in *Maud and Other Poems* (1855).

In 1859 Tennyson published the first four parts of *Idylls of the King,* a series of twelve connected poems that reviewed the legend of King Arthur, in whom he held a lifelong interest. He held Arthur up as an exemplar of human spirituality, while the poems infused elements of traditional romance with middle class Victorian morality. The poems were an immediate success and thrust upon

Tennyson an undesired public fame, which rose with further publications, such as *Enoch Arden* (1864).

In September 1883 Tennyson accepted a peerage as First Baron and took his seat in the House of Lords in March 1884. In 1886 he published a new volume containing "Locksley Hall Sixty Years After," which assaulted modern decadence and liberalism and retracted the earlier poem's belief in inevitable human progress.

In the last two decades of his life Tennyson also turned to poetic drama, though his plays proved only moderate successes, broadcasting his growing disapproval of the religious, moral, and political tendencies of the age. His poem "The Ancient Sage," published in *Tiresias and Other Poems* (1885), aired a more hopeful suggestion of eternal life.

Tennyson remained productive well into old age. He wrote the elegy "Crossing the Bar" in October 1889 while crossing the Isle of Wight. Despite ill health, he finished his last volume, *The Death of Oenone, Akbar's Dream, and Other Poems* in 1892. He died on 6 October 1892 in Aldworth, Surrey, aged eighty-four.

Tennyson's fame was challenged during his own lifetime, when poets Robert Browning (1812–1889) and Algernon Charles Swinburne (1837–1909) emerged as rivals. Early twentieth-century critics, who held aloft the modernist approaches of such poets as William Butler Yeats (1859–1939) and T. S. Eliot (1888–1965) and celebrated the rediscovery of poets John Donne (1572–1631) and Gerard Manley Hopkins (1844–1889), further eroded Tennyson's reputation. Around the turn of the twenty-first century, appreciation for the abundance and variety of Tennyson's sweeping lyricism reemerged, most especially for his *In Memoriam,* "Crossing the Bar," and "Ulysses."

See also **Carlyle, Thomas; Romanticism.**

BIBLIOGRAPHY

Martin, Robert Bernard. *Tennyson: The Unquiet Heart.* Oxford, U.K., 1980.

Ormond, Leonée. *Alfred Tennyson: A Literary Life.* New York, 1993.

Richardson, Joanna. *Pre-eminent Victorian, A Study of Tennyson.* London, 1962.

Ricks, Christopher B. *Tennyson.* New York, 1972.

Tennyson, Charles. *Alfred Tennyson.* New York, 1949.

STEPHEN VELLA

TERROR, THE. *See* **Reign of Terror.**

THIERS, LOUIS-ADOLPHE (1797–1877), one of the founders of the Third Republic in France.

Adolphe Thiers was born in Marseilles on 15 April 1797. He overcame birth outside wedlock, desertion by his father, relative poverty, and a stature of just five feet and two inches with his ambition, intelligence, and industry. A pupil at the lycée in Marseilles, he went on to study law at the University of Aix-en-Provence. Although his family had suffered financially during the Revolution, Thiers embraced liberal political ideas after 1815, and following graduation chose journalism, not law.

Moving to Paris in 1821, he joined the leading liberal newspaper, *Le Constitutionnel.* Thiers also embarked on a major historical work, his *History of the Revolution* (ten volumes, 1823–1827), which provided a liberal interpretation of the Revolution and a rational explanation for the Jacobin Terror. In January 1830, a new Paris liberal newspaper was founded, *Le National,* and, with François-Auguste-Marie Mignet (1796–1884) and Jean-Baptiste Nicolas Armand Carrel (1800–1836), Thiers became one of its three editors. *Le National* argued that the king's ministers had to have a majority in the Chamber of Deputies, supported opposition candidates in parliamentary elections, attacked the Jules Armand Polignac (1780–1847) ministry, and opposed the four ordinances of 26 July 1830. Thiers was one of the principal authors of a protest against the ordinances drawn up on 26 July and signed by forty-four journalists. He also played a leading role in persuading Louis-Philippe (1773–1850), Duke of Orleans, to succeed King Charles X (1757–1836) after the latter's abdication.

On 21 October 1830, Thiers was elected deputy for Aix-en-Provence. He served as minister of the interior from October 1832 to January 1833, and then as minister of commerce and public works. Minister of the interior once more, Thiers was blamed for the massacre of the Rue Transnonain (13 April 1834), when several innocent civilians were killed in a shoot-out between republican militants and soldiers and guardsmen. Nevertheless, Louis-Philippe appointed him to head a ministry from February to August 1836, and again from 1 March 1840. In his second ministry, Thiers apparently threatened a war between France and the other European powers over Egypt and Syria. Alarmed, Louis-Philippe eventually dismissed Thiers (22 October 1840).

Out of government office for the rest of the July Monarchy, Thiers began his mammoth *History of the Consulate and Empire* (twenty volumes, 1845–1862). This long and detailed narrative history portrayed Napoleon I (r. 1804–1814/15) as a Romantic hero and successful military commander. After Louis-Philippe had dismissed François-Pierre-Guillaume Guizot (1787–1874) on 23 February 1848, he invited Thiers to form a ministry, but by then it was too late to save the July Monarchy.

Elected to the National Assembly on 4 June 1848, Thiers backed Napoleon III (1808–1873) in the presidential election of 10 December 1848. Yet Thiers did not accept ministerial office and became increasingly critical of the Prince-President. Briefly imprisoned after the coup d'état of 2 December 1851, Thiers then led a life of exile in Brussels, London, and Switzerland until allowed to return to France in August 1852. In May 1863, he gained election to the Legislative Body, where he joined the opposition while remaining separate from the republican Left. He campaigned for liberal freedoms (though not free trade), opposed the Mexican expedition, and warned against the expansion of Prussian power in Germany. In July 1870 he desperately tried to discourage war with Prussia. Once the war had begun, he urged the concentration of French troops in the Paris area. He refused to serve as a minister under Empress Eugénie or in the provisional government formed after 4 September 1870, but he did agree to accept a diplomatic mission to seek foreign assistance for France.

In the National Assembly elections of 8 February 1871, following the armistice with Germany of 28 January, twenty-six departments elected Thiers. This remarkable indication of his popularity ensured his election in Bordeaux as "Chief of the Executive Power" (13 February 1871). Thiers then had to accept the harsh terms of the Treaty of Frankfurt (10 May 1871)—the payment of a large indemnity and the loss of Alsace and Lorraine. Meanwhile, by ordering the removal of cannon from Paris on 17 March 1871, Thiers had provoked the outbreak of the Paris Commune. The defeat of the Paris Commune temporarily crushed the radical Left, while the opposition of Thiers to a monarchical restoration helped to check the royalist Right. Instead, Thiers presided over the emergence of a conservative Republic. By the time of his resignation (24 May 1873), he had achieved financial stability, the full payment of the indemnity owed to Germany, and the ending of German military occupation of French territory. Thiers continued to be a deputy, but took little part in parliamentary debates.

Thiers died on 3 September 1877. His exceptionally long career, from the 1820s to the 1870s, indicates the political continuities in this period, despite four changes of regime, and the close connections between journalism, historical writing, and politics common in nineteenth-century France. His political legacy, a combination of patriotism, liberalism, and conservatism, had a profound effect on the Third Republic.

See also **France; Guizot, François; Liberalism; Paris Commune; Restoration; Revolutions of 1830; Revolutions of 1848.**

BIBLIOGRAPHY

Primary Sources

Thiers, Louis-Adolphe. *Discours parlementaires de M. Thiers.* Edited by M. Calmon. 16 vols. Paris, 1879–89.

———. *Notes et souvenirs de M. Thiers: 1848: Révolution du 24 février.* Paris, 1902.

Secondary Sources

Bury, J. P. T., and R. P. Tombs. *Thiers, 1797–1877.* London, 1986.

Guiral, Pierre. *Adolphe Thiers, ou, De la nécessité en politique.* Paris, 1986.

WILLIAM FORTESCUE

TIRPITZ, ALFRED VON (1849–1930), Prussian admiral.

Alfred Peter Friedrich Tirpitz (who was ennobled in 1900) was born on 19 March 1849 in the small town of Küstrin in the eastern part of Prussia. The son of a judge, he joined the Prussian Navy in 1865 and soon made a brilliant career. In the 1880s he was responsible for the development of the new torpedo weapon. In 1891 he became chief of staff of the Baltic naval station. He also quickly attracted the attention of the new kaiser, William II, himself a naval enthusiast, for unlike many of his elder comrades Tirpitz had a clear concept of both naval policy and naval strategy.

Although the extent of the influence of Admiral Alfred Thayer Mahan on Tirpitz is difficult to measure, their concepts were similar. Mahan believed that the Roman Empire was shaped by its control of the sea; Tirpitz was deeply convinced that history had proven sea power to be a prerequisite to the German Empire's power, prestige, welfare, and social stability in the twentieth century. Accordingly, he developed a plan to achieve these aims by building a battle fleet that he believed would be able to gain command of the sea.

Appointed commanding admiral of the German East Asian Squadron in 1896, he was called back in June 1897 to become secretary of the Imperial Navy Office. Supported by the new secretary for foreign affairs, Bernhard von Bülow, and using modern methods of propaganda to influence both parties in the Reichstag as well as the public, he began to realize what historians later were to call the Tirpitz Plan, which aimed at securing "a place in the sun" for Germany. For the advocates of this policy, it seemed inevitable that Germany would challenge Britain's supremacy in the world and on the seas. In June 1898 the Reichstag passed the First Navy Law, which established a battle fleet consisting of two battle squadrons and, most importantly, ensured continuous fleet building. Only two years later, this fleet was doubled. Although Tirpitz finally gave up the idea of demanding two more battle squadrons in 1905, he added six armoured cruisers for service on foreign stations to the existing fleet in 1906. More important, he decided to follow Britain's example and start building battleships of the Dreadnought type, armed with large guns. Thus he openly challenged the Royal Navy, which as a result quickly lost its margin of superiority in modern vessels. By reducing the age of replacement of older ships in 1908, he further accelerated the tempo of German battleship building. Contrary to his own expectations, this step was the beginning both of an arms race and the decline of his plan. After the failure in 1908 of British attempts to induce the German government to reduce its building program, the Royal Navy started to outbuild its German rival in 1909. At the same time, Tirpitz began to lose support within the government as well as with the public. Steadily increasing costs and Germany's isolation among the great powers seemed to require a change in German foreign and naval policy. Supported by the Kaiser, Tirpitz was, however, still strong enough to thwart the attempts of Theobald von Bethmann Hollweg, appointed chancellor in July 1909, to negotiate a naval agreement. Moreover, Bethmann Hollweg's fiasco in the Moroccan crisis in 1911 offered Tirpitz an opportunity to once again increase the navy. Tirpitz eventually pushed through a new naval bill in 1912, stabilizing a building rate of 3 capital ships a year. The Imperial Navy now consisted of 61 capital ships, 40 light cruisers, 144 torpedo boats, and 72 submarines.

In spite of this success, his influence on German politics was diminishing. The Moroccan crisis, the Balkan Wars in 1912 to 1913, and the threat of a world war on the Continent strengthened the position of the army, which was enlarged twice in 1912 and 1913. Moreover, in early 1914 even Tirpitz realized that his policy was on the verge of bankruptcy due to financial constraints and rising costs on the one hand and Britain's determination to preserve its naval supremacy on the other. His policy's obvious lack of success did not harm his popularity, however. Members of the German Right were convinced that he was the ideal candidate to replace Bethmann Hollweg, who seemed too weak to break the iron ring around Germany.

Tirpitz was not involved in the decisions that led to the outbreak of war in August 1914. However, afraid of a humiliating diplomatic defeat, he did not plead for moderation. The war soon proved disastrous for Tirpitz's navy. Bottled in the German Bight, it was unable to successfully challenge the

Grand Fleet. Raids on the British east coast were costly and dangerous, and the battle of Jutland in May 1916 was no strategic breakthrough. Only unrestricted submarine warfare, advocated by Tirpitz since 1915, seemed to offer a way out of a strategic deadlock but at a high price: it brought the United States into the war in 1917. Having lost the confidence of the kaiser, Tirpitz was forced to resign in March 1916 after one of several disputes with the chancellor about submarine warfare. However, he did not refrain from interfering in politics. In September 1917 he became chairman of the German Fatherland Party, a right-wing organization demanding far-reaching annexations and rejecting all domestic reforms.

After the war he quickly became the *eminence gris* (gray eminence) of the German Right, and he was involved in a number of attempts to overthrow the republican government. In 1925 he was one of the main architects of Field Marshall Paul von Hindenburg's candidacy for president. At the same time, he exerted great influence on the navy, whose members still regarded him as their master. Still actively involved in antirepublican intrigues, the father of the German battle fleet died on 6 March 1930.

See also **Balkan Wars; Germany; Moroccan Crises; Naval Rivalry (Anglo-German).**

BIBLIOGRAPHY

Primary Sources

Tirpitz, Alfred von. *My Memoirs.* 2 vols. New York, 1919.

Secondary Sources

Berghahn, Volker R. *Der Tirpitz-Plan: Genesis und Verfall einer innenpolitischen Krisenstrategie unter Wilhelm II.* Dusseldorf, Germany, 1971.

Halpern, Paul G. *A Naval History of World War I.* Annapolis, Md., 1994.

Herwig, Holger H. *"Luxury Fleet": The Imperial German Navy, 1888–1918.* London, 1980.

Hobson, Rolf. *Imperialism at Sea: Naval Strategic Thought, the Ideology of Sea Power, and the Tirpitz Plan, 1875–1914.* Boston, 2002.

Lambi, Ivo N. *The Navy and German Power Politics, 1862–1914.* Boston, 1984.

Scheck, Raphael. *Alfred von Tirpitz and German Right-Wing Politics, 1914–1930.* Atlantic Highlands, N.J., 1998.

Steinberg, Jonathan. *Yesterday's Deterrent: Tirpitz and the Birth of the German Battle Fleet.* London, 1968.

MICHAEL EPKENHANS

TOBACCO. On the eve of the French Revolution, some 250 years after its introduction from the Americas, tobacco (*Nicotiana tabacum*) was used as a recreational stimulant throughout Europe. It was an important article of trade between Europe and the rest of the world and a significant source of income for many European governments. In Spain, France, Portugal, and Austria the supply of tobacco was subject to a government monopoly; in every other European country its import, processing, or sale was controlled by some form of fiscal legislation.

State control of the tobacco supply was challenged at various times during the period, notably in France, where both taxation and the government monopoly were abolished during the Revolution (although both were subsequently reinstated); in Berlin in 1848, when the right to smoke in public places was a demand of and concession made to the revolutionaries; and in Italy in 1848, where protests against an Austrian monopoly led to open revolt in Lombardy, Venice, and Piedmont.

The principal source of tobacco was the Americas, with the United States the largest supplier followed by Brazil and Cuba. Tobacco was also imported to Europe from Sri Lanka and the Philippines in the Far East and Egypt and the Ottoman Empire in the Near East. Tobacco cultivation was banned in many European countries, including Great Britain, in order to protect national monopolies or customs revenues. However, it was grown on a commercial scale in Russia, the Netherlands, and a number of Germany principalities.

SOCIAL ASPECTS

At the beginning of the nineteenth century the usual way in which tobacco was consumed throughout Europe was as snuff—dried, flavored, powdered tobacco, sniffed by the pinch as a stimulant. Over the next half-century, as a general trend across the Continent, snuffing was replaced by smoking. In some countries such as Great Britain and Holland the trend was a revival, but in others, such as Prussia, the habit was new. The switch from snuff taking to smoking commenced in the Napoleonic Wars, when the British soldiers who served in Spain during the Peninsula campaign were introduced to cigars, hitherto a Spanish or South American method of tobacco consumption, and brought the habit home with them, where it quickly spread: in 1800 Britain imported twenty-six pounds of cigars; in 1830, two hundred fifty thousand pounds. Contemporaneously with the introduction of cigars, Britain also witnessed a revival of pipe smoking, which had been the principal form of tobacco use in the sixteenth and seventeenth centuries. The revival, however, was accompanied by new social attitudes to smoking and a new etiquette for smokers. It was accepted that the smell of tobacco smoke might cause offense, and so space was dedicated, in both private houses and public institutions, to the creation of smoking rooms. Moreover, while snuff had been used by both sexes at every level of society, smoking was considered to be a masculine habit, and except among the poor, women who smoked were the subjects of moral opprobrium (although perhaps not in "bohemian" circles).

The pan-European drift toward smoking was uneven: the first year in which more tobacco was sold in France for smoking rather than snuffing was 1830, whereas in Venice the change did not occur until 1860. As a consequence, a variety of tobacco habits coexisted side by side in many European countries, and the particular habit any individual possessed often reflected his or her social class. The ability to determine a person's background by how they used tobacco was employed by novelists as an aid to characterization: Charles Dickens in Great Britain and Honoré de Balzac in France were both careful to specify the tobacco habits of their characters. In Britain, in particular, clear literary conventions were established: the amoral or ostentatious rich smoked cigars; the dependable middle class and intellectuals enjoyed pipes; old people and mill workers took snuff. Tobacco and smoking were also the subject of artistic works in their own right. For instance, Charles Baudelaire included a poem dedicated to his pipe in *Les Fleurs du Mal* (1857).

Attitudes toward tobacco generally were very positive. It was associated with thinking as well as relaxation and considered to be a mental stimulant. Among the poor it was used to suppress appetite. Despite advances in chemistry and the isolation, in 1828 in Heidelberg, of the alkaloid nicotine—the chemical soul of tobacco—which was found to be highly toxic, neither smoking nor snuffing were thought to be injurious. Criticism usually focused on sanitary matters (the odor of tobacco smoke tainted clothes) or safety: in Prussia, wire cigar guards were employed to protect smokers and their surroundings from ash and burning embers. Opposition to tobacco use gained some momentum in Great Britain with the advent of the temperance movement, which attacked smoking as being godless and wasteful. However such sentiments were rare and were contrary to received opinion.

CIGARETTES AND INDUSTRIALIZATION

Although tobacco was mass consumed, for much of the nineteenth century its conversion into a consumer product was unsophisticated: it was processed rather than manufactured, and the principal cost of production in every European country was labor. The Royal Tobacco Factory in Seville, Spain, was the largest industrial building in Europe at the beginning of the period, yet it lacked all but the most rudimentary of machinery. The snuff, cigars, and loose tobacco it produced were handmade by a largely female workforce. The loose tobacco was destined for the urban poor, who smoked it rolled in scraps of paper. This manner of smoking was adopted by French travelers who carried it to Paris, where the little hand-rolled paper and tobacco cigar was named the "cigarette" by the writer Théophile Gautier in 1833. Cigarettes acquired romantic associations in France. Works such as Prosper Mérimée's *Carmen* (1845) put them into the mouths of tempting young women and the men who wished to seduce them. In response to evident demand, the French tobacco monopoly started manufacturing cigarettes by hand in 1845.

In Great Britain, by contrast, cigarettes were a luxury item and their consumption was thought to be effete. They had been introduced to the country in 1856 by a veteran of the Crimean War, were produced in limited quantities by exclusive tobacconists such as Philip Morris of Bond Street, and

An 1824 print captioned "Tis very good! (indeed)" depicts women enjoying snuff.
© HULTON-DEUTSCH COLLECTION/CORBIS

were smoked by people of equivocal social standing such as the playwright Oscar Wilde. Matters changed in 1883 with the introduction of mechanization, which enabled British suppliers to produce a cheap and uniform product. Machine-made cigarettes did not displace existing tobacco products but rather created their own market. Unlike pipes they were simple to use, in contrast to cigars they were mild to smoke, and above all, they were consistent in quality. Such attributes made cigarettes appealing to the ever-increasing number of clerical workers; they were also attractive to women and to minors.

Cigarettes inspired the first popular opposition to smoking in Great Britain. It was perceived that such cheap branded products were irresistible to children, and in 1908 the Children and Young Persons Act was passed, which made it illegal to sell tobacco to those under sixteen years of age—an implicit acknowledgment that tobacco use might pose a risk to health. Notwithstanding such reservations, tobacco rations were supplied to British troops and to the soldiers of every other one of the principal combatant nations at the outbreak of World War I, and tobacco consumption throughout Europe ended the period on a rising trend.

See also Alcohol and Temperance; Drugs.

BIBLIOGRAPHY

Barrie, J. M. *My Lady Nicotine*. London, 1890.

Gately, Iain. *Tobacco—A Cultural History of How an Exotic Plant Seduced Civilization*. New York, 2002.

Goodman, Jordan. *Tobacco in History*. London, 1993.

Hilton, Matthew. *Smoking in British Popular Culture, 1800–2000*. Manchester, U.K., 2000.

IAIN GATELY

TOCQUEVILLE, ALEXIS DE (1805–1859), French political theorist, historian, and political liberal.

Alexis de Tocqueville remains best known as the author of two classics: *De la démocratie en Amérique* (1835 and 1840; *Democracy in America*) and *L'ancien régime et la révolution* (1856; *The Old Regime and the Revolution*).

Tocqueville was born on 29 July 1805 into an old Norman aristocratic family that had suffered severely from the French Revolution. His life was dedicated to understanding the origins and implications of that upheaval for his nation and the larger world. Despite a frail voice in a fragile body he chose a career in politics. In preparation for that career he was strongly influenced by the lectures of the historian and statesman François-Pierre-Guillaume Guizot (1787–1874), who traced the decline of aristocratic privilege over the centuries preceding the French Revolution. At the same time Tocqueville became deeply interested in the Anglo-American world, which was to become his major source for a lifetime of comparisons with developments in his own country.

The July Revolution of 1830 was a turning point for the young Alexis. The Bourbon dynasty, to which his family was closely tied, was displaced by the "citizen king," Louis-Philippe (r. 1830–1848). The revolution confirmed Tocqueville's conviction that France was moving rapidly and inevitably toward "equality of conditions." Breaking with the perspective of the older generation's liberals epitomized by Guizot, Tocqueville looked toward America rather than aristocratic Great Britain as a potential model for the democratic future. Because of his family's continued loyalty to the exiled Bourbons, Tocqueville's political position had also become precarious. He and his close friend and fellow liberal, Gustave-Auguste de Beaumont de la Bonnière, formulated a plan to obtain official permission to study prison reform in America. In doing so they also hoped to establish a reputation for themselves as experts on the new political order, which would qualify them to participate in building France's political future.

DEMOCRACY IN AMERICA

The two young men traveled through the United States for nine months in 1831–1832. The first-fruits of their journey was a joint report in fulfillment of their official mission: *Du système pénitentiaire aux États-Unis* (1833; *On the Penitentiary System in the United States and Its Application to France*). On the basis of his observations and further readings Tocqueville attempted to lay bare the essential components of political society in the United States. He focused on those aspects of America most relevant to his own liberal philosophy and political ambitions. The vitality, the limitations, the excesses, and the potential future of democracy became the themes of *Democracy in America*.

The period immediately following the publication of *Democracy* was probably the happiest in Tocqueville's life. The book instantly won him an international reputation as a judicious political scientist. It was soon translated and published in Great Britain, the United States, Belgium, Germany, Spain, Hungary, Denmark, and Sweden. A voyage to England and Ireland in 1835 solidified lifelong friendships with the British elite, a bond that was reinforced that same year by his marriage to an Englishwoman, Marie Mottley. As a source of comparisons and intellectual exchange, England became, in Tocqueville's words, his second country.

Returning to France, Tocqueville began a sequel to his *Democracy,* now focusing on democratic ideas, beliefs, and mores in America. The second *Democracy* took longer to write and took Tocqueville further afield than its author had anticipated. Although published in 1840 under the same title as the earlier work, it ended up being as much about democracy in France and Europe as in the United States. Tocqueville's observations on the continuing bureaucratization of the French state and the progressive diminution of French political life during the late 1830s caused him to envision a new threat to democracy. Centralization and apathetic individualism made egalitarian societies vulnerable to a new form of despotism. Tocqueville's theme, as he wrote to John Stuart Mill, had become less America than "the influence of equality on the ideas and the sentiments of men." The ambiguities created by chapters on this new theme, interspersed with others more directly focused on America, accounted for some confusion among readers, and for the more muted reception of the 1840 volume in France.

Just as he completed his second *Democracy,* Tocqueville fulfilled his youthful ambition to step into the political arena. He was elected to the Chamber of Deputies in 1839 from Valognes. Tocqueville's need for uncompromising dignity and independence, however, deprived him of the influence to which he aspired in the legislature of the July Monarchy. For the next eight years he remained only a well-respected spokesman for legislative committees. On nonpartisan issues such as prison reform and colonial policy, he put his familiarity with American and British examples to good use.

The Revolution of 1848 presented Tocqueville with new threats and new opportunities. France was immediately faced with militant working-class demands for extensive and even revolutionary social reforms. Tocqueville was determined to combat what he viewed as the combined danger of increased state power and a proletarian attack on the basic principle of private property. France's electoral system also changed dramatically in 1848. The provisional government called for a new national constituent assembly based on universal male suffrage. Tocqueville's own voting constituency therefore suddenly expanded from several hundred to 160,000. In his campaigns for reelection in the Second French Republic, Tocqueville made the transition so well that he became the most successful vote getter in his department of La Manche. He subsequently opposed all radical social reform and joined the National Assembly in crushing a working-class uprising in 1848. The following year he briefly served the Republic as foreign minister, from June to October 1849. During a long period of illness in 1850 Tocqueville began a memoir on the Revolution of 1848. It was published posthumously, in 1893, under the title *Souvenirs* (1896; *Recollections*).

When the Republic was overthrown on 2 December 1851 by President Louis Napoleon Bonaparte (later Napoleon III; r. 1852–1871), Tocqueville refused to take an oath to the new regime and withdrew from politics. Seeking to sustain his liberal mission by other means, Tocqueville reverted to the strategy of the 1830s, touching on his fundamental concern with the relation of liberty to equality. He sought to trace the origins of France's entrapment in cycles of despotism and revolution by investigating the two centuries preceding the French Revolution. After four years of intensive archival research the *Old Regime and the Revolution* was published in 1856. Tocqueville located the deep structural sources of France's alterations of upheaval and despotism in the long-term evolution of the prerevolutionary monarchy and society. At the same time he offered his readers a counterpoint to his pessimistic analysis of French political instability by continuous comparisons with the Anglo-American world. The acclaim from liberal sympathizers in France and abroad that greeted his new history dispelled some of the gloom of his last years.

INFLUENCE

In the midst of writing his sequel to the *Old Regime,* Tocqueville died on 16 April 1859 at Cannes. Although he quickly became the posthumous leader of French liberalism, his reputation in France languished at the end of the nineteenth century. In the following century the totalitarian challenges to the survival of liberal democratic institutions helped to stimulate a "Tocqueville renaissance." After World War II the revival of his *Democracy* was fostered by the emergence of the United States as a world power. The expansion of political democracy in Eastern Europe after 1989 sustained that momentum. Tocqueville's *The Old Regime* became the foundational text for a revision of the prevailing Marxist interpretation of the Revolution in France itself.

However, the revival of interest in Tocqueville has not been based only on a sequence of events. A major change in the scholarly attention to Tocqueville's writings emerged during the late twentieth century. There was a broadening consensus on the relevance of his thought to democracy on a global scale. This growing encounter with Tocqueville's major writings is evidenced by an explosion of international scholarship. That scholarship has given us a rich sense of Tocqueville's complex dialogues with himself and his contemporaries and with the challenges faced by the world of the early twenty-first century. Some have sought to demonstrate that Tocqueville was entrapped by the limitations of his own time and background. Others have argued that he ultimately despaired of his hopes for political liberty in an egalitarian world. Yet a majority of historians and social scientists find in his thought a deeper affirmation of the resilience of democratic liberal institutions and mores. Tocqueville's sensitivity to civil society as a determinative of institutional success or failure has been echoed by contemporary students of political thought. Tocqueville's cumulative legacy is evidence of his unparalleled power to bring contemporary political concerns into sharper focus even where consensus on fundamentals remains difficult to achieve.

See also **French Revolution; Marx, Karl; Michelet, Jules; Napoleon III; Revolutions of 1830; Revolutions of 1848.**

BIBLIOGRAPHY

Drescher, Seymour. *Tocqueville and England*. Cambridge, Mass., 1964. Assesses the influence of England on Tocqueville's life and thought.

Jardin, André. *Tocqueville: A Biography*. Translated by Lydia Davis with Robert Hemenway. New York, 1988. The most recent and detailed narrative of Tocqueville's life.

Lamberti, Jean-Claude. *Tocqueville and the Two Democracies*. Cambridge, Mass., 1989. Stresses changes in Tocqueville's view of democracy between the 1835 and 1840 volumes.

Mélonio, Françoise. *Tocqueville and the French*. Translated by Beth G. Raps. Charlottesville, Va., 1998. An account of French attitudes toward Tocqueville and his works during the nineteenth and twentieth centuries.

Schleifer, James T. *The Making of Tocqueville's Democracy in America*. Indianapolis, 2000. An abundantly documented reconstruction of the major concepts in *Democracy*, using Tocqueville's extensive notes and drafts. Schleifer stresses the unity of the two books, published in 1835 and 1840.

Tocqueville, Alexis de. *The Tocqueville Reader: A Life in Letters and Politics*. Edited by Olivier Zunz and Alan S. Kahan. Oxford, U.K., 2002.

Welch, Cheryl B. *De Tocqueville*. Oxford, U.K., 2001. A synthesis of Tocqueville's political thought from the perspective of political science.

SEYMOUR DRESCHER

TOLSTOY, LEO (in Russian, Lev Nikolayevich Tolstoy; 1828–1910), Russian novelist and moral philosopher.

Leo Tolstoy, a Russian nobleman, was born at his family's estate, Yasnaya Polyana ("clear glade"), on 9 September (28 August, old style) 1828. Orphaned by age ten, he was raised by close relatives. While at Kazan University, he read Jean-Jacques Rousseau's *Confessions*, which exerted a profound and lifelong influence on him. Rejecting what he perceived as a trivial education, Tolstoy broke off his studies and eventually followed his brother Nikolai to the Crimea to serve in the elite artillery corps.

LIFE AND WORKS

In the Crimea Tolstoy's literary career began in earnest, with the publication of the autobiographical trilogy *Childhood* (1852), *Boyhood* (1854), and *Youth* (1857), and the remarkable *Sevastopol Stories* (1855–1856). In late 1859, contemptuous of the vagaries of the writer's life, Tolstoy returned to Yasnaya Polyana intent on bettering the lives of his own peasants. He married Sophia Andreyevna Bers in 1862; they had thirteen children. Tolstoy wrote *The Cossacks* (1863), and then began his stupendous historical novel *War and Peace*, written and published between 1865 and 1869. It provoked lively and heated critical debate. He followed it with a tale of modern society, *Anna Karenina*

(1875–1877), which was published serially to good reviews.

In the late 1870s, seized by a profound feeling of hopelessness in the face of the eventuality of death, Tolstoy embarked on a religious transformation detailed in the profound and controversial *Confession* (1879). The essential elements of Tolstoy's new religious ideas can be found in a trilogy: *An Investigation of Dogmatic Theology* (1880), *A Translation and Harmony of the Four Gospels* (1882–1884), and *What I Believe* (1884). *The Kingdom of God Is Within You* (1894) details Tolstoy's doctrine of pacifism. Tolstoy's crisis was both aesthetic and moral, so his literary works took on a more overtly didactic tone. Masterful stories of this period include "The Death of Ivan Ilych" (1886), "How Much Land Does a Man Need?" (1886), and "The Kreutzer Sonata" (1891). *Master and Man* (1895) portrays a man's deathbed conversion. The less successful *Resurrection* (1899) concerns an impassioned search for justice. Tolstoy's famous work of literary criticism, *What Is Art?* (1898), vituperatively condemns much of world literature—Tolstoy's own contribution as well as William Shakespeare's—as elitist and corrupting. Art, he argued, should not seduce for the sake of enjoyment, but should edify the masses by infecting them with sympathetic feelings.

Tolstoy's outspoken repudiation of government and church responses to social crises contributed to his excommunication from the Russian Orthodox Church in 1901. His masterful novel *Hadji Murat* (1904) concerns a protracted war between Caucasian mountaineers and the Russians. Seeking to free himself of the wealth, privilege, and fame that overwhelmed him, Tolstoy left home and died at Astapovo railway station on 20 November (7 November, old style) 1910. At the time of his death Tolstoy was a figure of world renown and an ambivalent leader of his own religious movement. Thousands of Russian peasants accompanied his funeral procession, and the demise of this giant of a man was felt by many to be the passing of a whole era.

CONTRIBUTIONS TO LITERATURE

Tolstoy discovered new forms for the novel. Set during the Napoleonic Wars, *War and Peace* depicts the lives of three families. Compared by

Leo Tolstoy c. 1900–1910. ©MICHAEL NICHOLSON/CORBIS

Tolstoy himself to Homer's *Iliad*, the subject of the novel is "life itself," conveyed by Tolstoy through precise detail and sweeping description. *Anna Karenina,* lauded as one of the world's greatest novels, contrasts the eponymous heroine's adulterous relationship with two other, more or less ideal, marriages. Even upon the publication of *Childhood,* however, Tolstoy was heralded as a great new literary talent for his extraordinary ability to convey every nuance of conscious thought. His works are rife with luminous moments where the individual's existence melds harmoniously with all creation, as when Levin is mowing hay in *Anna Karenina,* or Prince Andrei lies dying on the battlefield in *War and Peace.* Also central to Tolstoy's thought is a strain of anti-individualism that intensifies with time. It manifests itself in his critique of the "great men" theory of historical causation.

For Tolstoy, there exists an eternal truth that is the same for all people in all times. One merely needs to discover what that truth is and live in complete harmony with it. Through most of Tolstoy's literary career, apprehension of the truth occurs through aesthetic means, most insistently through defamiliarization (*ostranenie*), a method that exposes society's conventions by making them "strange." This device is famously employed in *War and Peace,* for example, in the scene in which Natasha attends the opera for the first time. Tolstoy also employs repetition, enumeration, and logical sequencing. He effects narrative shifts in point of view that are held together by an omniscient narrator who as often as not contains a measure of the personality of Tolstoy himself. In his postconversion works the aesthetic element is often dominated by social and political commentary, although the best works, such as *Hadji Murat,* achieve universal clarity.

CONTRIBUTIONS TO SOCIAL, POLITICAL, AND RELIGIOUS THOUGHT

While at times sympathetic to radicals, liberals, and conservatives, Tolstoy largely remained at odds with the main currents of nineteenth-century Russian intellectual thought. Akin to an eighteenth-century philosophe, Tolstoy, a fierce believer in the equality of all people, envisioned and put into practice at times utopian social and educational reforms. Although he eventually came to a wholesale rejection of his class's way of life, in less dogmatic moments he believed that with privilege came the responsibility to educate those less fortunate than oneself.

After his moral crisis of 1880, Tolstoy came to embrace Christian anarchism. He interpreted Christ's injunction to turn the other cheek as a summons to nonviolent protest against injustice. Tolstoy tended to follow any idea through to its logical conclusions, even if that led him to extreme, even contradictory, positions. For example, he spoke out not against revolutionaries' violent tactics, but against the government's execution of the revolutionaries. He used his notoriety to rail against the legal system, the prisons, private property, the bureaucracy, marriage, education, and agriculture. Tolstoy's pacifism had a profound influence on Mahatma Gandhi, spiritual and political leader of India.

See also **Chekhov, Anton; Dostoyevsky, Fyodor; Pacifism; Russia; Turgenev, Ivan.**

BIBLIOGRAPHY

Primary Sources

Tolstoy, Leo. *Polnoe sobranie sochenenii.* Edited by V. G. Chertkov. 90 vols. Moscow, 1928–1958. Definitive Russian edition of Tolstoy's works.

——. *Tolstoy Centenary Edition.* Translated by Louise and Aylmer Maude. 21 vols. London, 1929–1937. Comprehensive, though incomplete, set of translations.

——. *Anna Karenina.* Translated by Constance Garnett. Edited and translation revised by Leonard J. Kent and Nina Berberova. New York, 1965. Reprint, 1993.

——. *Great Short Works of Leo Tolstoy.* Translated by Louise and Aylmer Maude. New York, 1967.

——. *War and Peace.* Translated by Ann Dunnigan. New York, 1968. Reprint, 1993.

Secondary Sources

Bloom, Harold, ed. *Leo Tolstoy: Modern Critical Views.* New York, 1986. Excellent articles by distinguished scholars on key aspects of Tolstoy's work.

Orwin, Donna Tussing. *Tolstoy's Art and Thought, 1847–1880.* Princeton, N.J., 1993. Brilliant study of the ideas that led Tolstoy to write his masterpieces.

Steiner, George. *Tolstoy or Dostoevsky: An Essay in the Old Criticism.* 2nd ed. New Haven, Conn., 1996. Good overall interpretation of Tolstoy's works.

The Tolstoy Studies Journal. Toronto, 1998–. Good source for contemporary scholarly articles on Tolstoy.

SARAH A. KRIVE

TORIES. On 14 July 1789, when the Bastille was attacked by a revolutionary mob, there were, save perhaps for James Boswell (1740–1795) and a few politically eccentric High Church clergymen, few individuals in Great Britain who would have identified themselves as Tories. None would have considered themselves as members of a "Conservative Party," as that was an expression of 1830. The term *Tory* had first come into widespread usage in the 1670s and came to denote thereafter English and Welsh politicians and their supporters who placed a great deal of emphasis on the royal prerogative and the virtues of the established Church of England; were well able to restrain their enthusiasm for Protestant Dissenters (Baptists, Quakers, Presbyterians, Unitarians, Congregationalists); were, at best, wobbly in their passion for the Glorious Revolution of 1688 and the subsequent settlement of the English, Scottish, and Irish crowns on the German Lutheran electors of Hanover; and who tended, as a generally landed and country party, to mistrust the accoutrements (national banks, national debts, stock exchanges) of commercial capitalism.

By the 1760s and 1770s, the term *Tory* was fast becoming an anachronism owned up to by few and utilized chiefly by Whigs as a cudgel with which to beat up political opponents. Most members of the political nation of 1789, including those "fathers of conservatism," Edmund Burke (1729–1797) and William Pitt (1759–1806), would have considered themselves as Whigs of one form or another.

GOVERNING PARTY

William Pitt the Younger had been prime minister since 1783 as leader of a post–American war coalition, usually termed "Pittite," whose distinguishing characteristic was loyalty to George III (r. 1760–1820). They were widely credited with the ability to provide sound and efficient government. Indeed, from the perspective of 1750 or of 1850, there was, save for this pragmatic loyalty to the king, nothing particularly "Tory" about Pitt or his government. Pitt tended to be broadly sympathetic to the Irish Catholics, to limited parliamentary reform, and to the cultivation of at least reasonable relations with the Protestant Dissenters. This Pittite moderation changed with the increasing radicalization of the French Revolution. What could arguably be called the bible of modern conservatism, Edmund Burke's clarion call for resistance to the French explosion, *Reflections on the Revolution in France,* was published in 1790. Burke, like Pitt, with a background replete with parliamentary opposition to the American war and, in a qualified way, to British imperialism in India, was no Tory, but a Foxite Whig. Yet it was Pitt and Burke, old enemies and never very cordial colleagues, who in the 1790s stitched together a governing coalition of Pittites and former Foxite Whigs that became, even more than the papacy or the Russian monarchy, the centerpiece of European opposition to the Revolution and to Napoleon

Bonaparte. This coalition, save for a brief time in 1806 and 1807, remained in power from 1794 to 1830. It was the nucleus of a revived Tory Party, though most of its members, at least until the 1820s, wore the Tory label most uncomfortably.

The Tories, who oversaw the great victories over the French Empire in 1814 and 1815, and the establishment thereafter of a Pax Britannica over the sea lanes of the world, and who attempted in the 1820s to liberalize the rigors of traditional mercantilism, were smashed by the Catholic issue after 1827. Many of the leading lights of the coalition, the Pitts, the Burkes, the Cannings, the Castlereaghs, were supporters of Catholic emancipation, allowing the Catholics of the United Kingdom, who were, of course, the vast majority in Ireland, access to the imperial parliament in London. The backwoodsmen of the party, in this reflecting, most probably, the wider views of the British people, did not support emancipation. When Arthur Wellesley, the Duke of Wellington (1769–1852), an anti-Catholic of long standing, became prime minister in 1828, he decided, not for the last time in the history of his party, to trump ideology with pragmatism and give in to the demands of the Catholic Irish and their leader, Daniel O'Connell (1775–1847). The result was the death knell of the Pittite-Burkeite coalition at the general election of 1830. The victorious Whigs and Liberals then proceeded to institute a reformation of the voting system for the House of Commons in the interest, most generally, of their middle class supporters.

OPPOSITION PARTY

The Tory Party, used to running the country and the empire since 1783 or 1794, found themselves in 1830 in the unfamiliar terrain of opposition. It was, alas for the Tories, to be a too familiar terrain over the bulk of the nineteenth century, the liberal century of British politics. Between 1830 and 1885, the Tories only once won the majority of votes cast at a general election, in 1841, and otherwise only won in 1874. They lost to some sort of Liberal-Whig coalition at thirteen general elections during the time period. Contrast this to their years of triumph between 1783 and 1829, when only one general election was lost and nine were won!

The Tories in the early 1830s rechristened themselves "the Conservative Party" and developed or refined their old Pittite principles into what many hoped would be a coherent political ideology called "Conservatism." This new ideology was trumpeted in newspapers, magazines, and speeches on the hustings and in Parliament. It basically endorsed the idea of a confessional (Anglican) party and denounced the works and pomps of those forces of economic and social modernity that the Conservatives held responsible for their electoral defeats: the classical political economists, the factory owners, the New Poor Law reformers, and those free traders who advocated the ending of protective duties on agriculture. That the Conservative leadership in Parliament, the Wellingtons, the Peels, the Grahams, were enthused by this agenda is unlikely. Sir Robert Peel (1788–1850) in the Tamworth Manifesto of 1834 presented a more moderate Conservatism, accepting of much of the Liberal reforms of 1830–1834. But it may have been the more undiluted conservatism of the church and the newspapers that orchestrated Peel's great victory of 1841.

Peel's 1841–1846 administration showed the great disconnect that existed between the party leadership and the rank and file. Little was done for the church, the New Poor Law was not repealed, economic modernity was not repudiated, and agricultural protection was not retained. In 1846, Peel, William Ewart Gladstone, Sir James Graham, and other party notables began the trek away from conservatism toward the wider shores of liberalism, leaving their former party a rump. This secession of the Tory generals forms the background for the emergence of a witty, talented parliamentarian, Benjamin Disraeli (1804–1881), a baptized Jew with numerous personal quirks not normally congenial to a conservative-minded club, nor to the party leadership in the House of Commons.

The Tory Party came to power, if briefly, in 1852, 1858, and 1866, and, for a longer time, in 1874, not because the voting public wanted them but because the dominant Liberals fell out among themselves. And the Tories (and Disraeli) played the Liberal game to stay in power. They jettisoned protection and their confessional leanings, supported Jewish emancipation, enfranchised the urban working class, and adopted a high imperialist foreign policy. None of this seemed to matter greatly, and the Liberal machine, chastened by its periodic loss of power, picked itself up, won elections, and moved on. What changed this idiom more than the political skill and eccentric wisdom of Disraeli or the iron pragmatism of Disraeli's successor, Lord Salisbury (Robert Arthur Talbot Gascoyne-Cecil, 1803–1903), was the destruction of the nineteenth-century Liberal paradigm by its own leader, Gladstone. In 1885 and 1886, by suddenly embracing the Irish leader Charles Stewart Parnell's vision of Home Rule for Ireland, Gladstone ended the Liberal era in British politics as savagely as in 1829 the Duke of Wellington and Robert Peel, by supporting Catholic emancipation, had ended the Tory one. The Conservatives now found themselves in an anti–Home Rule governmental alliance with the relatively congenial whiggish Right of the Liberal Party and the not so congenial collectivistic Left, led by Joseph Chamberlain (1836–1914).

"UNIONIST PARTY"

Between 1886 and the official formation of a "Unionist Party" in 1895, the two sides (or three sides) of the new coalition learned to tolerate and support each other. For twenty years after 1886, led by Salisbury and then by his nephew Arthur James Balfour (1848–1930), the Conservatives (or Unionists) won three general elections and were in unaccustomed power for all but three years. The dominant figure of the party, however, probably more than Salisbury and certainly more than Balfour, was Chamberlain. As Winston Churchill said of him, he made the weather. He also made trouble for the future, by too aggressively promoting African imperialism and by suddenly jettisoning sixty years of a general free trade consensus in favor of massive protection. The divided Unionists, then, lost three general elections between 1905 and 1914.

In 1914 the great men of British politics, Herbert Henry Asquith, David Lloyd George, and Winston Churchill, were Liberals. Liberalism seemed more than Unionism (or Conservatism) to have captured the public mood on foreign, imperial, and domestic issues. On 4 August 1914, the day that the German army invaded Belgium, few would have predicted that the Unionist and Conservative Party would be the most formidable political machine in Europe during the twentieth century.

See also **Conservatism; Great Britain; Whigs.**

BIBLIOGRAPHY

Primary Sources

Burke, Edmund. *Reflections on the Revolution in France.* Edited by J. C. D. Clark. Stanford, Calif., 2001.

Secondary Sources

Bentley, Michael. *Lord Salisbury's World: Conservative Environments in Late-Victorian Britain.* Cambridge, U.K., 2001.

Colley, Linda. *Britons: Forging the Nation, 1707–1837.* New Haven, Conn., 1992.

Dangerfield, George. *The Strange Death of Liberal England.* New York, 1935.

Gash, Norman. *Reaction and Reconstruction in English Politics, 1832–1852.* Oxford, U.K., 1965.

Marsh, Peter T. *Joseph Chamberlain: Entrepreneur in Politics.* New Haven, Conn., 1994.

Sack, James J. *From Jacobite to Conservative: Reaction and Orthodoxy in Britain, 1760–1832.* Cambridge, U.K., 1993.

Smith, Paul. *Disraeli: A Brief Life.* New York, 1996.

JAMES J. SACK

TOULOUSE-LAUTREC, HENRI DE

(1864–1901), French artist best known for portrayals of Paris life.

Henri de Toulouse-Lautrec belonged to no theoretical school, but is now sometimes classified as postimpressionist. His primary focus was unsentimental evocations of personalities and social mores in working-class, cabaret, circus, and brothel scenes. Toulouse-Lautrec's greatest contemporary impact came with the thirty posters done between 1891 and 1901 that transformed the aesthetics of poster art.

BACKGROUND AND ARTISTIC TRAINING

A heritage of wealth, artistic talent, and a rare genetic disorder defined Toulouse-Lautrec. Born in Albi, France, as the child of a first-cousin marriage between aristocrats, Henri Marie Raymond de Toulouse-Lautrec Montfa inherited a rare form of dwarfism that left him deformed and crippled. During an otherwise normal childhood, he suffered from increasingly severe bone pain. At age thirteen in 1878, a minor fall broke his left femur or thighbone. In 1879, a second fall broke the right femur. His growth stopped at 152 cm (about 4' 11") tall. Controversies surrounding the causes of his disability include rumors he fell from a horse or received incompetent medical treatment. It is sometimes claimed that he had pycnodysostosis (a genetic disorder of the bones), but in photographs he does not appear to have several of its identifying symptoms. His exact malady remains undiagnosed.

His childhood was marked by conflicts between his parents. Consequently the primary family unit became the artist and his mother. The child Toulouse-Lautrec often drew and painted alongside his father or one of his uncles, all talented amateur artists; he used art to tolerate long convalescences. His uncle, Charles de Toulouse-Lautrec (1840–1915), and deaf-mute artist René Princeteau (1844–1914), who specialized in horses, provided early art training. In 1882 at age seventeen, with parental approval, he began art study in Paris, receiving training from Léon-Joseph-Florentin Bonnat (1833–1922) and Fernand Cormon (1845–1924). Toulouse-Lautrec kept studios in Montmartre, influenced by neighboring artists Edgar Degas (1834–1917) and Jean-Louis Forain (1852–1931). Friends included close relatives, fellow aristocrats, prostitutes, circus performers, and artists Vincent Van Gogh (1853–1890), Pierre Bonnard (1867–1947), and Edouard Vuillard (1868–1940). Much of his art portrayed dance halls and cabarets like the Moulin de la Galette, the Moulin Rouge, and the Mirliton, where, after dining at his mother's, he drank nightly.

ART AND LIFE

By age twenty-two, Toulouse-Lautrec was an accomplished artist and a hopeless alcoholic. Rejecting the hypocrisy and sentimentality he believed corrupted all human relations, he flaunted his physical handicaps, with a veneer of self-mockery and outrageous public misbehavior. Many works make reference to his disabilities, ranging from cruel caricatures of himself and others to "nostril view" portraits, and figure studies with legs, arms,

Poster for the Moulin Rouge by Toulouse-Lautrec, 1891. Toulouse-Lautrec depicts La Goulue, one of the most popular and risqué dancers at the Moulin Rouge. THE ART ARCHIVE

and in one case, head cut off by the frame, symbolically handicapping his models as he was himself. He became iconoclastic, resolutely destroying others' pretensions with a sharp word or a slash of pencil on paper. Against his father's wishes, he decided to sign with the family name: H. T-Lautrec.

ARTISTIC PROCESS

Toulouse-Lautrec prepared a final work by proceeding through a variety of media. First he did many sketches, sometimes using carbon and tracing paper to preserve images he liked. He at length distilled an expression or gesture into a single evocative, sometimes caricatural line. Obsessed with technical innovation and being "modern," he sometimes used photographs to fix a pose or scene, while making a painted portrait. His paintings are virtually always in oil, usually greatly thinned with turpentine, painted on an absorbent surface such as bare canvas, wood panel, or cardboard. He typically used tiny brushes to make subtle and detailed facial studies, sketching in the rest of the scene in quick strokes with larger brushes.

Toulouse-Lautrec's paintings are striking for the revealing expressions and body language of his models and for his staging of social narratives via costume and location. Finished paintings in turn sometimes served as preliminary studies for a color lithograph or poster. However, the image in the final print was pared down, simplified, and abstracted into a work whose emphasis was on areas of color and repeated shapes, containing virtually none of the psychological impact of the oil. It was in his multiples that Toulouse-Lautrec most showed the influence of Japanese art. He experimented with superimposed layers of color on the lithographic print, a variety of spatter techniques, and other technological inventions, but it was above all his understanding of the guiding principles of the advertising poster that revolutionized the art form. He created striking trademark images whose message was immediately understandable, rendering his subjects so memorable that they are still recognizable to the early-twenty-first-century viewer.

Both notoriety and success came quickly to Toulouse-Lautrec. In spite of his irregular and distracting lifestyle, he was remarkably productive. By age twenty-one he was selling drawings to magazines and newspapers, illustrating books, song sheets, menus, and theater programs. Acclaimed by the avant-garde, he exhibited constantly. Although his work sold well, and his monthly allowance from his parents (around 15,000 francs per year) was perfectly adequate, he had extravagant tastes and lavish generosity. Virtually every letter home said, "Send money!"

He was institutionalized for several months in 1899 for treatment of psychological symptoms caused by organic deterioration certainly from advanced alcoholism, and possibly from tertiary syphilis. He died two months before his thirty-seventh birthday. In a career lasting only twenty years, he produced a phenomenal amount of art: 737 canvases, 275 watercolors, 368 prints and posters, and 5,084 drawings, not to mention lost works, an occasional book binding, ceramic, or stained-glass window. Some 300 works are pornographic.

Toulouse-Lautrec's art remains so popular that it has become a commonplace, reproduced on coffee mugs, dish towels, and shopping bags. Research and criticism have traditionally centered on its art historical, biographical, or social context. More recent studies focus on Toulouse-Lautrec's distinctive, repetitive artistic characteristics: fleeting impressions, transparency, layering, visual narrative, jokes and puns, homages to and pastiches of other artists. These traits reveal subtlety and complexity that are increasingly appreciated by other artists, scholars, and the public at large.

See also **Fin de Siècle; France; Impressionism; Paris; Posters.**

BIBLIOGRAPHY

Primary Sources

Carlton Lake Collection, Harry Ransom Center, University of Texas. Austin, Tex. Unpublished original letters by Toulouse-Lautrec and members of his family, most written between 1864 and 1894.

Dortu, M. G. *Toulouse-Lautrec et son oeuvre.* 6 vols. New York, 1971. Only catalog of all works credibly attributed to Toulouse-Lautrec. A huge effort, but contains many errors in dating and some in attribution.

Musée Toulouse-Lautrec Collection. Albi, France. Originals and/or copies of all possible documentation on Toulouse-Lautrec, including letters, photographs, schoolbooks, clippings, etc.

Wittrock, Wolfgang, ed. *Toulouse-Lautrec: The Complete Prints.* 2 vols. London, 1985. Reproduces and documents each known state of Toulouse-Lautrec's prints. Worthwhile articles by several critics.

Secondary Sources

Bibliotheque Nationale and Queensland Art Gallery. *The Lautrecs of Lautrec.* Brisbane, 1991. Exhibition catalog. Notable for interesting articles and entries.

Castleman, Riva, and Wolfgang Wittrock, eds. *Henri de Toulouse-Lautrec, Images of the 1890s.* New York, 1985. Exhibition catalog. Reproduces evolution of artistic choices through preparatory and finished works.

Cate, Phillip Dennis, and Patricia Eckert Boyer. *The Circle of Toulouse-Lautrec: An Exhibition of the Work of the Artist and of his Close Associates.* New Brunswick, N.J., 1985. Exhibition catalog. Artists who were Toulouse-Lautrec's friends and contemporaries.

Denvir, Bernard. *Toulouse-Lautrec.* London, 1991. Excellent overall analysis of the artist's relation to his work.

Devynck, Daniele. *Toulouse-Lautrec: The Posters, Collection of the Musée Toulouse-Lautrec.* Graulhet, 2001. Thorough, serious study of Toulouse-Lautrec's poster art.

Frey, Julia. *Toulouse-Lautrec: A Life.* London, 1994. Only complete biography. Based on contemporaneous letters and documents.

Heller, Reinhold. "Rediscovering Henri de Toulouse-Lautrec's *At the Moulin Rouge.*" *Art Institute of Chicago Museum Studies* 12, no. 2 (1986): 114–135. Examines the cutting and re-stitching of a section of the famous oil, theorizing possible intent.

Murray, Gale B. *Toulouse-Lautrec: The Formative Years, 1878–1891.* Oxford, U.K., 1991. Study of Toulouse-Lautrec's early work with focus on dating and artistic influences.

Schimmel, Herbert, ed. *The Letters of Henri de Toulouse-Lautrec.* Oxford, U.K., 1991. Translates (sometimes badly) many if not all Toulouse-Lautrec's existing letters.

Thomson, Richard, et al. *Toulouse-Lautrec.* London, 1977. Exhibition catalog. Some interesting critical articles. Excellent chronology.

Thomson, Richard, Phillip Dennis Cate, and Mary Weaver Chapin. *Toulouse-Lautrec and Montmartre.* Washington, D.C., 2005. Exhibition catalog.

JULIA FREY

TOURISM. Until the late twentieth century, the history of tourism was not a serious subject for historical inquiry. Before the advent of social history, political historians duly noted where decisions and pronouncements were made, and the place of leisure travel becomes obvious only in retrospect: French Emperor Napoleon III met Count Cavour (Camillo Benso) in the comfortable French spa town of Plombières to plot what turned out to be a war of Italian unification against the Austrians; and King William of Prussia had been taking the waters at Ems when the Ems dispatch was issued in 1870, provoking the French to declare war. Even the emergence of social history initially left the history of tourism at the margins. Careful analysis of workers, peasants, the bourgeoisie, and eventually women, that is, specific social groups, eventually made room for analysis of cultural practices besides work, such as tourism. The neglect was unfortunate because the history of tourism has revealed just how much various social groups used travel to set themselves off from others

THE MICHELIN RED GUIDE: AUTOMOBILE TOURISM AND GENDER ROLES

In 1900, Michelin published the first *Guide Michelin* to France. In the preface, Michelin noted that "this work desires to give all information that can be useful to a driver traveling in France, to supply [the needs of] his automobile, to repair it, and to permit him to find a place to stay and eat, and to correspond by mail, telegraph, or telephone" (p. 5). Offering this new red guide free of charge, the company recognized that by encouraging automobile travel it fostered the consumption of tires. In essence, the guide offered knowledge about tires and about French towns, thus providing a sort of informational infrastructure for early automobile tourists.

Interestingly, the red guide and advertisements for it reinforced societal assumptions about sexual difference in early twentieth-century Europe. In an age when many wealthy men did not even drive their own cars, they were still portrayed as in charge in their planning of trips and management of the chauffeur. Women, by contrast, were presumed to be flighty, hopefully attractive, and concerned with maintaining their beauty.

Advertisements for the red guides played on the idea that men, the providers, needed to supply a comfortable place to stay for women, the presumed consumers. In one case, Michelin recounted the tale of newlyweds traveling without a red guide. After the chauffeur informed them that a mechanical breakdown would leave them stranded overnight, the Viscount René de la Ribaudière (a name suggesting bawdiness as well as aristocratic origins) and Giselle, his new wife (the text notes that "she was not yet [really] the countess"), got a room in a hotel that was, according to the owner, "the best in the region." After retiring to their room, they found a bat, and

it took a quarter of an hour and all of the eloquence that M. de la Ribaudière had in order to calm down Giselle. However, the little viscount did not waste any time, and he quickly addressed his very imminent wife the most legitimate compliments on the beauty of her legs and the finesse of her ankles, when suddenly he cried out in distress. "Ah! my God, what is the matter?" Giselle asked him. [He replied,] "my darling, where did you get this bit of red on your shoulder which was so white a moment ago?" The same exclamation came out of both of their mouths, "Bed bugs." They killed 10, then 100, then 577; they could not have fought off the yellow invasion with more ardor. Finally, overtaken by sleep, Giselle resigned herself to stretching out on her uncomfortable and hard bed. And the viscount wanted to begin the conversation again. "Oh, no, my dear," she told him. . . . When the sun rose, Giselle was still not yet Madame de la Ribaudière, though she looked like cream with strawberries [that is, her cream-colored skin had many red marks resembling strawberries]. ("Lundi de Michelin," *Le Journal*, 6 July 1908, p. 5)

By playing on the notion of consummation of the marriage, Michelin suggested that the viscount, however desperately he may have tried, did not get to have sex with his new wife because he had not ordered a copy of the red guide, so he did not realize there was a fine hotel nearby. Having not fulfilled his role as good provider, the viscount could not fulfill his role as a husband in the act of sex. Thus, marketing of the red guide—which began ostensibly as a list of mechanics and places to buy gas—could assert assumptions about the appropriate behavior of men and women: men were supposed to take care of the practical details while traveling, by buying a red guide, and women were to worry about their appearance.

and thus to construct differences of class and gender as "natural" social divides. In fact, tourism, like other forms of consumption, was as much a defining characteristic of social position as the work with which it was often contrasted.

THE GRAND TOUR

In the eighteenth century, the British had been predominant as early tourists. Before the French Revolutionary and Napoleonic Wars, many aristo-

cratic and wealthy British families sent their sons on a Grand Tour of Europe. To have done a Grand Tour set a young English man apart from his contemporaries, not to mention his social inferiors. For the growing upper middle class, a tour of classical ruins was construed as cultural training, not unlike attending university. Lasting for several months, a tour usually included Paris and often other major European capitals and was almost always dominated by the Italian cities. Venice,

Florence, Rome (including the digs at Pompeii), and sometimes Naples were must-sees, while Genoa and Turin usually figured as stopping points en route from the Alpine crossing to the south. Art collections, architecture, classical ruins, and brothels were the main attractions.

The French Revolutionary and Napoleonic Wars interrupted much international tourism, particularly by the British, until 1815. However, in the course of the nineteenth century, the idea of the Grand Tour remained an important image as the numbers of Europeans with the time and financial resources to travel grew. Napoleon's road building across France and through the Alps facilitated access by reducing travel times. Museums opened their doors, following the example of the Louvre, which became public during the Revolution. The populations capable of affording a tour grew. In addition, the number of women traveling, escorted by female family members, servants, and friends—and sometimes husbands and fathers—steadily increased.

Both evolving aesthetics and accessibility changed the destinations and the perceptions of early nineteenth-century tourists. The Alps, long considered a mere untamed obstacle en route to Italy, became a destination in their own right and an important stop on many a Grand Tour. Mountain climbing for the few and hiking for the many became primary attractions. Romantic sensibilities also led to interest in Gothic cathedrals along with the classical monuments. The few travelers to Greece in the nineteenth century, which seemed more accessible after its independence from the Ottoman Empire in 1832, were in search of classical ruins overrun by vegetation and partially destroyed by time; here Lord George Gordon Byron's poetry was an obvious inspiration. During the period from 1792 to 1815, a heyday of early Romanticism, the British Lake Counties so dear to William Wordsworth became primary alternatives for wealthy British tourists unable to tour the Continent. With a volume of Wordsworth in hand, visitors sought the uncontrolled nature he had described.

TAKING THE WATERS: SPAS AND SEASIDES

Named for Spa, a well-known spring of mineral water in what would after 1830 be known as Belgium, spas had long existed in Europe. The Romans had established baths filled with spring water, and some of those same baths remained in operation throughout the Middle Ages, attracting both local inhabitants and the infirm from farther away. In Hungary, baths experienced a boom in the eighteenth century. Improved roads and coach service made the baths more accessible, and towns such as Bath in western England, Vichy in south-central France, and Baden-Baden in the southwestern German state of Baden became important destinations.

Until the late eighteenth and early nineteenth centuries, baths frequently remained large pools in the open air, situated within the towns and open, without charge, to all who wished to bathe. Although only scattered evidence has survived, it appears that in the early modern period bathers of both sexes of all social groups wore little clothing, frolicking in the baths. By the early nineteenth century, as bourgeois usage grew dramatically, so too did the expectations for regulation of access. In France, the open-air pools largely disappeared, replaced by individual bathing compartments where a bather would not come in contact with anyone but spa staff. At least in France, the strict separation of the sexes and careful attention to appropriate attire resulted in part from women's complaints of men's behavior at the baths, so the institution of new norms of propriety may have resulted as much from women's increased presence as from a desire for social control on the part of the bourgeoisie in general. Nevertheless, a clear segmentation by social class clearly took place. The poor and working poor found themselves excluded from many of the baths, and an array of new hospitals for the poor requiring hydrotherapy segregated them from the wealthy bathers.

In the nineteenth century, doctors largely controlled access to the baths. Doctors developed a complement of hydrotherapeutic techniques, including hot and cold pressurized showers, hot mud packs for the body, and individualized boxes for prescribed steam baths. During an average three-week course of treatment, the majority of a patient's time was often not spent in the bathing pools themselves. Even when patients were in the bath, the duration of daily treatments was closely controlled by the spa's staff.

Social stratification was a defining characteristic of spa towns. Locals worked in the baths, in the hotels, and in the newly organized casinos. In towns such as Vichy and Aix-les-Bains (in Savoy), service to wealthy travelers was the primary employment for local residents. While the wealthy travelers registered their names, addresses, professions, and the number of accompanying servants— all markers of social station in the nineteenth century—before going off to the baths for their cures, locals lost their earlier (nonmedical) access to the baths. Spa employees and larger municipal police forces further kept the homeless and begging poor out of the casinos and off the important promenades, where their presence was assumed to damage the appeal of the spa town.

After 1750, first in Britain and then on the Continent, the aristocracy and increasingly the middle classes also began to flock to the seaside, spurring the development of resorts. In many parts of Europe, though sources are comparatively scarce, there is evidence of swimming or playing in sea water on the Atlantic and the Mediterranean. As bourgeois interest in the seaside grew, so too did municipal regulations governing use of the beaches. In the first half of the nineteenth century, nude bathing was banned on most beaches, which were also usually segregated by sex. Although access to the sea remained open to people of all social classes, the primary beachfront connected to resort towns was largely reserved for wealthy travelers whose expenditures supported local economies.

Although Romantic interest in the sea as untamed nature was not unlike the "discovery" of the Alps, the motivation for travel to the seaside, as in the case of spas, was also ostensibly medical. For skin and particularly pulmonary ailments, especially tuberculosis, doctors often advised an extended stay on the coast. By the early nineteenth century, doctors also began to regulate immersion in the water. Doctors offered careful instructions as to the preparation, duration, and necessary movements during daily baths in sea water.

Doctors and bathers made an important distinction between men and women. While women in particular were prescribed strict guidelines, carried out by attendants who manned the individualized bathing boxes ostensibly for the preservation of female modesty, doctors exercised comparatively little control over men, who customarily treated jumping into the waves as a sort of male rite of passage, a proof of their virility. The medicalized control established at the seaside was thus inseparable from a broader social control of women's movements and their bodies in the nineteenth century.

RIDING THE RAILS AND READING THE GUIDEBOOKS

Although the network of European roads and coach services improved steadily in the eighteenth and early nineteenth centuries, facilitating tourism among wealthy Europeans, the development of the railroad allowed faster and considerably cheaper transportation, dramatically increasing the number of people who could afford to travel. The greater accessibility made possible by the railroad did not erase social distinctions but rather altered their contours; just as the railroad had first-class, second-class, third-class, and even fourth-class carriage, tourist destinations changed to accommodate both greater social diversity but also the desire for social differentiation by those who could afford better.

The railroad had an ironic effect on established tourist destinations. For example, on the southern coast of England, Brighton had been a favored destination of the English nobility and royalty in the eighteenth century. However, when the railroad connected Brighton to nearby London, the middle and lower middle class of the city began to make day trips to Brighton. The royal family and social elite relocated their social season to the north, placing themselves outside the logistical and financial reach of these new tourists. In France, where the warm and more desirable seasides were in the south, the railroad made it possible for the wealthy of Paris and of Europe to easily make a journey impractical for those of limited means. The empress Eugénie, wife of Napoleon III of France, made Biarritz on the southwestern French coast a sought-after resort town once the railroad line was established. On the Riviera, the French annexation of Nice in 1860 facilitated the development of a French railway line from Paris. Nice expanded rapidly and its wintertime (the social season on the Riviera) population exploded as the international social elite swarmed in.

More tourists with more destinations sought ever more information about where to go, what to see, and how to get there most easily. Because tourists on land were by mid-century traveling almost exclusively by railroad, guidebooks adopted railway itineraries as their organizational framework. In Britain, John Murray published little red guides to sights and hotels of Europe, in a format quickly adopted by Karl Baedeker in Germany. With guides in several European languages covering western, northern, and southern Europe by 1914, Baedeker and his successors built a veritable empire of guidebooks, directing tourists where to go and what to see. In France, Adolphe Joanne launched a similar series published by Hachette, which had a monopolistic control of bookstores in French rail stations.

The Murray, Baedeker, and Joanne guidebooks, like their eventual competitors, offered practical information about the quality and prices of hotels, admission prices to museums, train schedules, detailed information about the sights a dutiful tourist should not miss, and even advice about appropriate behavior. In short, the guidebooks attempted to instruct the novice tourist in how to travel. By providing abundant information updated in frequent re-editions, guidebooks took some of the uncertainty out of travel, but arrangements remained entirely in the hands of individual tourists, who needed to negotiate not only with hotels but also with the multitude of different train companies even within a given country.

For the lower middle class and skilled workers with limited means, less time, and little familiarity with the profusion of train schedules and fares, Thomas Cook offered both greater certainty and moderate prices. A British cabinetmaker and minister, Cook organized his first tour by railroad for working men and women attending a Temperance meeting in 1841. In 1851 he negotiated prices with the railroads and lined up accommodations for some 165,000 British men and women who traveled to the see the Grand Exhibition in London (some 3 percent of visitors). By the 1860s, as railroad fares declined within Britain, often obviating the need for his services, Cook focused on tours of the Continent, beginning with Paris (1861), then Switzerland (1863), Italy (1864), and Spain (1872). In several respects, Cook and his competitors opened up touring to social groups that had not traveled in the past. Initially, "workingmen," usually skilled artisans or lower middle-class tradesmen on day trips, formed the primary travelers. Without this early group being abandoned, as the destination increasingly became the Continent, Cook's tourists also came from a broad spectrum of the middle class; not only doctors, lawyers, and salaried employees but also teachers and ministers, who had time but limited incomes, were a primary constituency.

Cook's tour came to embody the increased access to travel in nineteenth-century Europe. As a result, those travelers who could afford longer, slower, and more costly trips ridiculed the month-long Cook's tours to Continental Europe as offering no time for the real appreciation of the monuments, museums, and landscapes seen in a blur. The perceptions of social distinction shifted; for the modest, touring offered status, but for the wealthy the fact of touring the Continent often became less important than in what company and how one did.

The most obvious social change among tourists became in the nineteenth century the increased presence of women. Although a few women had done the Grand Tour or had taken the waters in the eighteenth century, in the course of the nineteenth century tourism by women unaccompanied by men became standard. The railroads and guidebooks (which were often, as in the case of the Baedeker, downright sexist even by nineteenth-century standards) facilitated travel, making it easier for women to travel without the company of men. In Cook's tours both single women and women traveling in groups were actually more heavily represented than men. While ease of transport was clearly one reason, the broader cultural changes in nineteenth-century Europe were another. Whereas men had been the primary collectors of art early in the century, women increasingly became connoisseurs of art, music, and culture generally, though the remunerated professions of artist, curator, or academic remained the preserve of men. Bourgeois women's predominance in the church was also a factor; in largely Protestant Britain women had an important role in the Temperance movement, sometimes necessitating travel by train, and in Catholic areas women were proportionately better represented in the organized group tours to

Egyptian guides help tourists climb the Great Pyramid at Cheops c. 1900. ©CORBIS

Morocco were sometimes destinations. While traveling outside Europe, Europeans could congratulate themselves on their own national—in having a grander empire they could be superior to other Europeans—and racial superiority, presumably manifest in the vast material divide between them and indigenous peoples.

BICYCLE AND AUTOMOBILE TOURISM
While the overwhelming majority of travelers in the early twentieth century continued to use the railroad, technological innovations of the late nineteenth and early twentieth centuries placed renewed emphasis on traveling by road as well as rail. The "safety" bicycle with two wheels of the same size became a fashionable rage for sportsmen rich enough to buy one in the 1890s. In the first decade of the twentieth century, the automobile began to rival the bicycle among sportsmen, and it quickly became a means of tourist transportation for aristocrats and bourgeois Europeans. The automobile's price and extremely high maintenance costs made it a socially exclusive mode of transportation. An automobile allowed wealthy men, accompanied by women and usually a mechanic/driver, to make long trips, veritable adventures given the poor reliability of automobiles when compared to trains.

Both bicycle and automobile tourism necessitated a new infrastructure eventually provided by local and national authorities. Well-maintained, eventually paved roads with road signs became the subject of important lobbying efforts by tourists enamored of the new forms of transport. An array of nonprofit organizations emerged across Europe to advocate the interests of first cyclists then motorists. Inspired by the British Cyclist Touring Club, "touring clubs" funded by members' contributions and often public subsidies, worked with local and national governments to provide an infrastructure for all forms of tourism, though cycling received pride of place in the 1890s. After 1900, touring clubs, working alongside more socially exclusive automobile clubs, also argued for roadway improvements necessary for automobiles. In several countries, the touring clubs, while overwhelmingly bourgeois, were among the largest of associations. The Touring Club de France, founded in 1890, had nearly 100,000 members in

pilgrimage sites, such as the spring at Lourdes in the Pyrenees mountains.

By the end of the nineteenth century, growing nationalist and imperialist sentiment, laced with Social Darwinism, was also reflected in well-off Europeans' travel. Guidebooks could be quite nationalistic. In the 1860s, the Baedeker guides in the German language fervently claimed that French-held Alsace-Lorraine should in fact be part of united Germany. British guides frequently deplored the supposedly inadequate hygiene on the Continent, especially the absence of toilets flushed with water. In countries with expanding empires, most notably Britain and France, trips to the colonies gained in popularity among the wealthy. Although their numbers remained small, Britons and to a lesser extent other Europeans, very often under the auspices of a Cook's tour down the Nile, traveled to Egypt in search of cultural exoticism; by the 1880s they were reassured by the British protectorate. Britons also went to Palestine to visit the "Holy Land." Among the French, the colonies of Algeria and later

1914. The Touring Club Ciclistico Italiano, founded in 1894, dropped "cycling" from its name in 1900 and itself grew to 450,000 members in the interwar years.

CONCLUSION: TOURISM AND SOCIAL DISTINCTIONS

Before the 1790s, when the English term *tourist,* itself derived from the French term *tour,* first emerged in the English language, *traveler* was the primary designation used for what one might call the "leisure traveler." In the course of the nineteenth century, most European languages acquired a term equivalent to the English tourist. Since the nineteenth century, tourists and social observers have often distinguished between travelers and tourists. Late-nineteenth-century travelers condemned Cook's tourists as superficial. Travelers supposedly appreciated what they saw and experienced whereas tourists completed a list of things that "needed to be seen." Many historians and other writers have often accepted the distinction at face value, stressing the difference between the old bourgeois, aristocratic, and educated travelers and the late nineteenth- and twentieth-century hordes who supposedly understood little besides how to have a good time.

In fact, the terms reveal more about the people employing them to reinforce social difference than about any real difference between leisure travelers and tourists. Many middle-class travelers in the nineteenth century, even "Cook's tourists," could be far more interested in European art and architecture, which also offered them the possibility of a sort of cultural capital upon returning home, than the fabulously wealthy who spent much of their time simply enjoying themselves in the company of their compatriots. In short, the distinction that some have made between travelers and tourists, like the distinctions that post–World War II tourists often make between themselves and other, presumably less knowledgeable and culturally sensitive tourists, are not "real," measurable differences.

In the nineteenth century, social distinctions made between those who could afford to take the tour, take the waters in a spa, or go to the beach and those who could not mirrored the social segmentation of European society as a whole. Similarly, the prescribed roles for women and men further reflected widespread assumptions about the "natural" differences between the sexes. Tourism, having afforded some people the occasion to join their presumed cohorts and set themselves off from other people, thus provides a fascinating glimpse at the social hierarchies that characterized nineteenth-century Europe.

See also **Automobile; Cycling; Popular and Elite Culture; Railroads; Transportation and Communications.**

BIBLIOGRAPHY

Baranowski, Shelley O., and Ellen Furlough, eds. *Being Elsewhere: Tourism, Consumer Culture, and Identity in Modern Europe and North America.* Ann Arbor, Mich., 2001.

Bertho Lavenir, Catherine. *La roue et le style: Comment nous sommes devenus touristes.* Paris, 1999.

Bosworth, R. J. B. "The Touring Club Italiano and the Nationalization of the Italian Bourgeoisie." *European History Quarterly* 27, no. 3 (July 1997): 371–410.

Buzard, James. *The Beaten Track: European Tourism, Literature, and the Ways to Culture, 1800–1918.* New York, 1993.

Corbin, Alain. *The Lure of the Sea: The Discovery of the Seaside, 1750–1840.* Translated by Jocelyn Phelps. New York, 1994.

Grewal, Inderpal. *Home and Harem: Nation, Gender, Empire, and Cultures of Travel.* Durham, N.C., 1996.

Harp, Stephen L. *Marketing Michelin: Advertising and Cultural Identity in Twentieth-Century France.* Baltimore, 2001.

Haug, C. James. *Leisure and Urbanism in Nineteenth Century Nice.* Lawrence, Kansas, 1982.

Koshar, Rudy. "'What Ought to Be Seen': Tourists' Guidebooks and National Identities in Modern Germany and Europe." *Journal of Contemporary History* 33, no. 3 (1998): 323–340.

Koshar, Rudy, ed. *Histories of Leisure.* New York, 2002.

Levenstein, Harvey. *Seductive Journey: American Tourists in France from Jefferson to the Jazz Age.* Chicago, 1998.

Löfgren, Orvar. *On Holiday: A History of Vacationing.* Berkeley, Calif., 1999.

MacCannell, Dean. *The Tourist: A New Theory of the Leisure Class.* Berkeley, Calif., 1999.

Mackaman, Douglas Peter. *Leisure Settings: Bourgeois Culture, Medicine, and the Spa in Modern France.* Chicago, 1998.

Nordman, Daniel. "Les Guides-Joanne." In vol. 2, *Lieux de mémoire,* edited by Pierre Nora, 1035–1072. Paris, 1997.

Pemble, John. *The Mediterranean Passion: Victorians and Edwardians in the South.* Oxford, U.K., 1987.

Rauch, André. *Vacances et pratiques corporelles: La naissances des morales du dépaysement.* Paris, 1988.

———. *Vacances en France de 1830 à nos jours.* Paris, 1996.

Swinglehurst, Edmund. *Cook's Tours: The Story of Popular Travel.* Poole, Dorset, U.K., 1982.

Tissot, Laurent. *Naissance d'une industrie touristique: Les Anglais et la Suisse au XIXe siècle.* Lausanne, Switzerland, 2000.

Towner, John. *An Historical Geography of Recreation and Tourism in the Western World, 1540–1940.* Chichester, U.K., and New York, 1996.

Walton, John K. *The English Seaside Resort: A Social History, 1750–1914.* Leicester, U.K., and New York, 1983.

Withey, Lynne. *Grand Tours and Cook's Tours: A History of Leisure Travel, 1750–1915.* New York, 1997.

STEPHEN L. HARP

TOUSSAINT LOUVERTURE (c. 1743–1803), French general and Haitian political leader.

Legends maintain that on *Toussaint* (All Saint's Day), 1 November 1745, at a plantation owned by the Comte de Bréda, a first son was born to a former African king. In Catholic Saint-Domingue (as Haiti was known during the French colonial period), the slave child was christened François Dominique Toussaint. François Antoine Bayon de Libertat, the plantation overseer, saw only potential in the small, frail boy, and in a striking departure from convention, ensured that he became literate and solidly grounded in the Catholic faith. While Toussaint's equestrian skills earned him the exclusive position of driver and master of horses at Bréda, he also gained wide recognition among his fellow slaves as a master practitioner of herbal medicine—felicitous skills that would serve Toussaint well during the convulsions that lay ahead.

Battles for primacy between the white social classes and mulattoes characterized the French Revolution in Saint-Domingue, until the night of 22 August 1791, when tens of thousands of slaves throughout the colony's great northern plain revolted, torching cane fields and plantations, and

"I am Toussaint Louverture, my name is perhaps known to you. I have undertaken vengeance. I want liberty and equality to reign in Saint-Domingue. I work to make them exist." (Toussaint to his "brothers and friends" in Saint-Domingue, 29 August 1793)

"By defeating me, one has only cut the trunk of the tree of Negro liberty in Saint-Domingue; it will rise again by its roots, for they are numerous and deep." (Toussaint from his cell in Fort de Joux)

massacring nearly every non-black they could find. After helping the Bayon de Libertat family to safety, Toussaint joined the rebellion, and by early 1793 was among the thousands of rebel slaves who had crossed into neighboring Santo Domingo, where the Spanish king offered freedom and promotion for black (and white) fugitives who would take up arms against French Republicans. Starting as physician and key advisor to slave leader Georges Biassou, Toussaint eventually attained the rank of brigadier with an independent command of more than 4,000 black troops—irregulars that he drilled into an extraordinarily competent fighting force. Throughout 1793, Toussaint's military talent became so well established that by August, he composed a general call to arms to the slaves of Saint-Domingue in which he referred to himself for the first time as "Louverture"—the opening.

For reasons that remain unclear, on 6 May 1794, Toussaint renounced his allegiance to Spain, declared for France, and quickly amassed a series of victories against his former Spanish and British confederates. In 1796, Toussaint rescued French Governor General Étienne Laveaux from imprisonment by disaffected mulattos; Laveaux reciprocated by appointing Toussaint lieutenant governor general of the colony. France's Directory followed suit, officially promoting Toussaint to division general, and naming him lieutenant governor general and commander in chief of armies of Saint-Domingue (2 May 1797). By November 1800, Toussaint was complete master of Saint-Domingue. He annexed Santo Domingo in February 1801, and in May, promulgated the island's first

Toussaint Louverture meets with defeated generals. Nineteenth-century engraving commemorating Toussaint Louverture's defeat of British troops in Haiti, 1798. ©BETTMANN/CORBIS

constitution—a document that named him governor general for life.

Acknowledged as a protector to anyone, regardless of color, who would support his designs for a stable, resurgent Saint-Domingue, Toussaint exercised his authority to rebuild the devastated colony. He encouraged the return of émigré French planters and enforced labor decrees through martial law, but ensured that former slaves were compensated for their labor with one-third of the crops they helped produce. However, Toussaint's regime barely had time to accrue measurable successes before the colony was once again at war.

In December 1801, Napoleon I (r. 1804–1814/15) dispatched to Toussaint his most respectful greetings, along with a 21,000-man invasion force under the command of his brother-in-law, Captain-General Charles-Victor-Emmanuel Leclerc (1772–1802). Leclerc's secret instructions from Napoleon included orders to conciliate Toussaint and his leaders (promising anything in order to take possession of the colony), disarm the blacks, and then force their return to slavery. Ferocious fighting ensued until Toussaint and Leclerc concluded an armistice during which the black general was allowed to retire under protection to his estate. This reprieve was only a ruse; Toussaint and his family soon were abducted from their home and spirited away to France, where Napoleon had the general barbarously incarcerated in the dungeons of Fort de Joux in France's eastern Jura Mountains. Toussaint died the following year from exposure and neglect, while his wife and children simply disappeared. Fighting in Saint-Domingue continued until November 1803 when, abandoned by Napoleon and decimated by yellow fever and malaria, the pitiful remnants of the Army of Saint-Domingue surrendered to General Jean-Jacques Dessalines (1758–1806).

As the result of Napoleon's ill-advised treatment of Toussaint and Saint-Domingue, France not only lost any chance to regain meaningful influence over its most lucrative former overseas possession, but also a potential staging base for regaining control of the Louisiana Territory. The impact on Haiti, however, was tragic. Minus Toussaint's unifying leadership, Haiti devolved into the 200 years of internecine fighting and corrupt administrations that characterize the country into the twenty-first century.

See also **Caribbean; Colonies; French Revolutionary Wars and Napoleonic Wars; Haiti.**

BIBLIOGRAPHY

Fick, Carolyn E. *The Making of Haiti: The Saint Domingue Revolution from Below.* Knoxville, Tenn., 1990.

Heinl, Robert Debs, Jr., and Nancy Gordon Heinl. *Written in Blood: The Story of the Haitian People, 1492–1971.* Boston, 1978.

James, Cyril Lionel Robert. *The Black Jacobins: Toussaint L'Ouverture and the San Domingo Revolution.* Rev. ed. New York, 1963.

JAMES L. HAYNSWORTH

TRADE AND ECONOMIC GROWTH. Since Adam Smith (1723–1790) and David Ricardo (1772–1823), trade and economic growth have been regarded as interconnected, and "Smithian growth" has become a fixed term in economic growth analysis. The connection is obvious: if previously nonintegrated regions and countries have cost advantages in different types of products, trade will benefit both sides. For example, Polish grain farmers can produce wheat at a lower cost than English farmers, whereas English workers can produce textiles more cheaply than Polish workers. The "comparative advantages" of the English textile sector furthermore imply that even if an English worker could in principle produce grain at a lower cost than even a Polish laborer, that worker can only spend his time either with grain or with textile production. If the cost advantage in textiles is relatively larger, the worker should thus continue to produce textiles and eat imported wheat.

Smith and Ricardo were convinced that the effects of trade are positive. However, international trade has also been the target of hostile criticism, and the debates on how beneficial the effects of trade were in nineteenth-century Europe are relevant for the contemporary world. The debates focused on the following four hypotheses:

1. Growing imports have always provoked counter-measures, or attempted countermeasures, from interest groups who were afraid of losing income and social status when faced with competition from imported labor or goods. For example, British landowners lobbied for and benefited from protectionism in the early nineteenth century while continental European textile man-ufactures flourished when Napoleon I (r. 1804–1814/15) closed the French ports to British manufactures.

2. While market integration had mostly beneficial effects on purchasing power, it is less clear that the contribution to the overall growth of welfare was always positive. For example, integration might in some situations have detrimental effects on health or longevity for parts of the population, which might adversely affect living standards. The "Human Development Index" of the United Nations includes measures such as life expectancy and education, whereas others have used human height as a proxy for the so-called Biological Standard of Living. During the nineteenth century in Europe, height in some cases even declined in some previously remote and nonintegrated regions of Europe.

3. It has been argued that trade not only promoted direct growth in ways that Adam Smith had predicted but that it also influenced the development of institutions. Daron Acemoglu, Simon Johnson, and James Robinson have argued that trading cities on the Atlantic coast benefited particularly from the development of institutions that transmitted information more easily and protected and defined property rights. Although their study concentrates on the early modern period, the influence of greater institutional efficiency might have continued well into the nineteenth century. Another indirect effect might also have been the formation of physical and financial capital through the reinvestment of a produced surplus, as is implied by Douglass North's theory of "export-led growth."

4. The indirect growth effects of trade may influence income inequality. Eli F. Heckscher and Bertil Gotthard Ohlin have argued that an increased import of goods produced primarily with unskilled labor will reduce unskilled wages, thereby increasing inequality. The opposite holds for the increased export of goods "containing" unskilled labor inputs. Yet while increasing inequality may imply more investments by the rich (because poorer people do not invest much), inequality can also lead to a lack of schooling and human capital formation among the poor, in addition to negative health and crime effects, or even upheaval and social conflict.

These four hypotheses about the relationship between trade and economic growth will be discussed in more detail below. Before addressing them, however, the trade structure of Europe in the nineteenth century needs to be addressed: Which countries concentrated on which export staples? How large were the net exports of particular items that can inform us about the country's growth prospects? Which imports and exports restored the trade balance (taking into account that national deficits were modest in nineteenth-century Europe, at least if we interpret colonial military activities as "service exports," which is surely debatable)?

India House, Sale Room. Engraving by Pugin and Rowlandson, 1808. Buyers gather to bid on the rich cargoes brought into London by the East India Company. ©Historical Picture Archive/Corbis

FLOWS OF TRADE IN NINETEENTH-CENTURY EUROPE: GRAIN, MACHINERY, AND OTHER GOODS

Who traded which commodities in nineteenth-century Europe? To answer this question, we must concentrate on a small number of commodities, and only the principal exporters and importers can be taken into account. A German survey published by the German Imperial Statistical Yearbook (1915) gives an overview of trade in the pre–World War I period. Two commodities, or rather commodity groups, are particularly interesting for European trade history: "grain" (more precisely: grain, rice, and flour) and machinery.

Grain had been a major trading commodity from the Middle Ages onward. It is self-evident that grain, rice, and flour are crucial for human nutrition. In the nineteenth century, grain imports were responsible for sustaining the extremely high population density of some of Europe's rapidly developing regions. The biggest exporters of grain, rice, and flour in 1913 were Russia, the United States, and British India (which included today's Pakistan, Bangladesh, and Burma). Much smaller quantities were exported in 1913 by Canada, Romania, and Australia. Especially Romania, with a population of less than one tenth of the Russian population, exported remarkable quantities per capita. Argentina was also an important grain exporter.

Not surprisingly, the biggest importer of grain was the United Kingdom. Britain was thus not only the workshop of the world but also consumed most of the traded grain. The second-largest importer was Germany, whose export of industrial goods was growing strongly at the time. However, the German East (and the Polish parts of the empire) were long-established grain exporters, so that Germany's grain-trade statistics were more balanced in effect, with internal trade playing an important role as well. We also need to take into account that the United Kingdom and Germany had the largest populations among the large grain consumers. On a per capita basis, imports were in fact very high in the Netherlands and Belgium as well. Italy imported a substantial total amount of grain, but not as much per capita. Other modest grain importers were Switzerland, France, Denmark, and Norway. Most of these importing countries were among the early industrializers, whereas most exporters tended to be late developers (except for the United States). Interestingly, there were also a number of net grain importers among the less developed countries (LDCs) in 1913, such as China, Sri Lanka ("Ceylon" at the time), and Indonesia. The same applies to Japan and the British Straits Settlement (mostly Singapore and Melaka), which counted as LDCs in 1913.

During the period following the "grain invasion," a term coined by Kevin O'Rourke, the dramatic decline of transportation costs for grain from the New World and Black Sea area caused enormous shifts in production and land revenues. The New World and Russia now accounted for a large share of the total grain trade, whereas a much larger amount had been produced locally before.

Net export values of machinery are important to examine because machinery was one of the most human capital–intensive (that is, skill-intensive) commodities being traded at large quantities during the period. The United Kingdom remained the world's export champion in the prewar period, with 6.4 million Marks of net exports. Germany had heavily reduced the United Kingdom's lead in the decade before and almost reached its competitor with 6.0 million Marks in machinery exports. In a similar vein, the United States had made its mark as a strong new force producing machinery for many different purposes. Switzerland—with its much smaller population—reached only about 5 percent of the net export value of each of the big three machinery exporters. It is also interesting to look at the principal importers of machinery because those countries were using imports to

build up a physical capital stock during the period. The world's leading importer of machinery was the Russian Empire. Canada and France had approximately half of the volume of Russia's imports, making them also significant importers at the time. Next followed Australia and Austria-Hungary, whereas the net machinery imports of Italy, Mexico, and Belgium were only modest in 1913.

To summarize, the United Kingdom, Germany, and the United States were the leading exporters of machinery in the nineteenth century. In contrast, the major importers were spread more evenly among the richer and developing nations in 1913. Grain imports tended to be the mirror image of machinery exports, with the important exception of the United States, which exported both grain and machinery in substantial quantities.

This discussion has concentrated on the two commodities that are of particular interest for assessing economic development. What has not been discussed, however, is the value of the most important import and export goods. By far the most valuable export commodity in 1913 was cotton from the United States, which accounted for 23 million Marks, or about three times the value of U.S. net grain exports. In second place came British coal, with Brazilian coffee ranking third. Of course, these goods were much more dependent on natural conditions such as resources and climate than were grain and machinery, which could in principle be produced in any location that had sufficient population density and skill levels.

TRADE DEVELOPMENTS IN THE EUROPEAN NORTH AND SOUTH

The major European trading nations were undoubtedly Great Britain, Germany, France, and other northwest European countries. Yet the development of trade also played an important role for countries in the far north and south, and it was only in the eastern European regions that lacked access to rivers or coasts that international trade might have been somewhat less important.

The grain exports of the Russian Empire, eastern Germany (including today's Poland), and Romania have already been discussed. In addition, wood and butter exports played an important role for the far north of Europe, whereas fruit, olive oil, and other horticultural exports came from the

Mediterranean. Similar to the grain invasion that shook all of Europe, important globalization events occurred in the South, as José Morilla Critz, Alan Olmstead, and Paul W. Rhode have argued: during the 1880s Mediterranean fruit exports dominated European and U.S. markets, but fruit production in California, Florida, and similar regions of the New World started to become competitive in the following three decades. California farmers first captured large slices of their home market, aided by U.S. protectionist policies and natural disasters in Europe such as the phylloxera plague that destroyed two-thirds of the European grape production in the second half of the nineteenth century. By the end of the century, U.S. products were even competing with Mediterranean fruits in northern Europe. In the 1870s, for example, the important Spanish raisin exporting area of Málaga exported nearly 60 percent of its production to the United States. In the 1890s, this share had fallen to 10 percent. Initially, this decline was caused by phylloxera, but later on, the market opportunities that had been lost to the California competitors played the major role. Since the Málaga region also had the highest emigration rates in Spain, some authors have concluded that a causal relationship existed between lost export markets and emigration.

In contrast to raisins, citrus exports were in general a success story for Mediterranean agriculture. Oranges from Spain and lemons from Italy became famous in many parts of the world. However, American competition grew in these fruit markets as well, and U.S. protectionism posed further problems. In the case of lemons in particular, the Italians had to redirect their trade to northern Europe, after performing vast advertising campaigns there. In 1907–1913, Germany and Austria-Hungary became the most important recipients of Italian citrus fruits.

Greek exporters specialized in currants and even benefited from the phylloxera catastrophe at first, since they could sell their produce to French winemakers, who used it as a temporary substitute for their own grape production. After the recovery of grape production, however, the French government in 1892 imposed high tariffs, which had disastrous consequences for the Greek economy. The plum and prune exports of Serbia and of Bosnia and Herzegovina, as well as the fig and raisin exports of the Turkish west coast, experienced a similar development: a promising start, followed by a struggle against protectionism and competition with California and other New World regions (such as Australia).

What is particularly interesting about this phenomenon is that we would not expect high-wage areas in the New World to be able to compete successfully with the low-wage areas of southern Europe in the seemingly labor-intensive horticulture. Critz, Olmstead, and Rhode, on whose research this section draws heavily, report that one acre of land requires only 9 man-hours of labor to grow wheat, whereas 286 hours are required to grow lemons, for instance. The output value varies drastically as well, of course. The authors have calculated that the value of output per man-hour on U.S. fruit farms was in fact very similar to that of other U.S. farms in the early twentieth century. Moreover, California farmers were quite successful in using modern packing techniques, brand names, and scientific techniques to overcome blue mold and similar production problems. In this way, they were able to outbalance higher labor and transportation costs compared with their major competitors.

The effects on southern European exports were sometimes dramatic. More successful development of the fruit markets could have resulted in dynamic, export-led growth engines in many southern European regions, as well as in the reinvestment of profits into those poor regions. This remains true even when considering that the total value of production of horticultural goods was certainly lower than that of other agricultural goods (mainly for the domestic market). Another important point here is that the majority of consumers clearly benefited from the increased competition.

Nonetheless, two of the three markets discussed in more detail above share some common characteristics that suggest some answers to our initial question: Why was there opposition to trade, if trade increased welfare? In both the European grain market and the Mediterranean fruit market, decisive changes occurred in the nineteenth century. The "grain invasion" and the "fruit invasion" produced a substantial number of losers who tended to be politically well-organized. Even if on average, the growth in trade surely added to European prosperity, the fate of the fruit farmers of the Mediterranean and the eastern German grain-farming nobility gave rise to political forces that influenced the economic history of their respective countries in crucial ways.

TRADE AND GROWTH

What follows is an empirical discussion of Smith's and Ricardo's expectation that trade would trigger economic growth in nineteenth-century Europe. This issue is difficult to resolve because comparative evidence on trade shares in the early nineteenth century still contains a large margin of error. Moreover, convergence effects must be taken into account, since a country with a high initial trade share (such as the Netherlands) would probably increase its trade shares at a lower rate than any newcomer. In addition, a thorough analysis would require taking into consideration all other potential growth determinants such as human and physical capital growth, institutional design, geography, and political development as well as alternatives to commodity trade, for example, the exchange of capital (foreign investment) and population (migration). Here, our aims are more modest. We have taken Paul Bairoch's rough estimates of export shares for the early and late nineteenth century and compared them with Maddison's GDP estimates for 1820 and 1913, combined with an investigation of individual cases. In the following, we distinguish trade shares (imports plus exports per GDP) from export shares (only exports per GDP).

Even with all those caveats, some important facts emerge clearly. First, the Netherlands exported the highest share of their GDP in 1840, followed by a number of relatively small countries such as Norway and Denmark. Smaller countries often had larger trade shares because country-size is negatively correlated with the amount of production items passing borders. However, in early-nineteenth-century Europe, there were also many smaller countries with low trade shares while the United Kingdom displayed one of the highest shares.

Between the early and late nineteenth century, export shares grew for all countries. Overall, they ranged between about 1 and 9 percentage points higher in 1910 than in 1840, with typical values of 1 to 3 percent. At the same time, GDP per capita grew substantially in all countries. Even the inhabitants of slowly growing economies such as Portugal, Russia, and Greece had become richer by roughly

$500–1000 per year before World War I (measured in 1990 Geary-Khamis Dollars, a standard measure for making purchasing power comparable across time). In many cases, this meant a doubling or tripling of real incomes within less than a century. Lastly, the Swiss population had acquired four times more purchasing power in 1913 than in 1820.

Based on those numbers, it is not implausible to assume that nineteenth-century growth was caused to a large extent by "Smithian" trade effects. Yet was it the case that countries with higher integration into trading networks also achieved more growth? As the example of the Netherlands, with a high export level but only slightly above-average growth rates indicates, export levels probably had no impact on subsequent growth performance. Even if additional explanatory variables were taken into account, this result would not change significantly.

It is clear that countries with disproportionately large export shares at the end of the period (i.e., irrespective of the initial level) also experienced much higher increases in national income per capita. Belgium, the United Kingdom, Denmark, Switzerland, France, and Germany were examples of the strong and positive development of both variables. On the other hand, the small export-share increases of Portugal, Russia, and Greece went hand in hand with an only modest increase in income. Again, we would like to emphasize that we are not looking at growth rates in percentages here. Moreover, this analysis cannot reveal the direction of the causality involved: Did increasing trade shares cause income growth, or did increasing per capita–production (which equals income per capita) correlate with the need to export a higher share of production? Hence, from this descriptive analysis, we can only conclude that a higher export share correlates empirically with higher additional income. Overall, both export shares and income per capita grew in all European countries over the nineteenth century, yet while the increase was most significant in Belgium and the United Kingdom, it was much less so in southern and eastern Europe.

TRADE POLICY

Bairoch, O'Rourke, and Jeffrey Williamson have given excellent overviews of trade policy. They

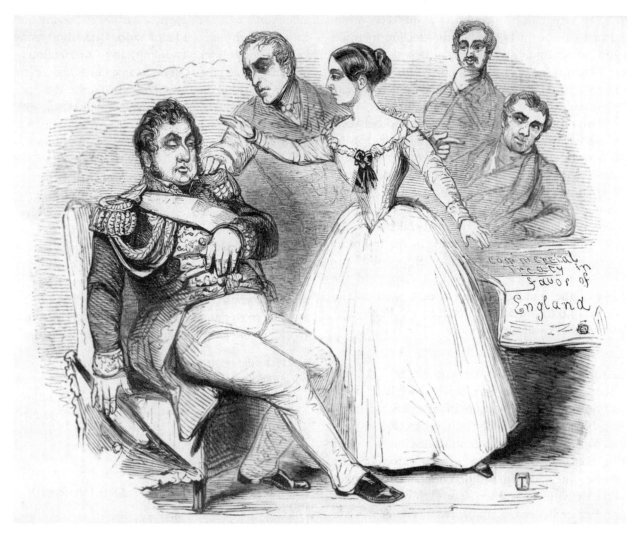

Victoria Mesmerises. Illustration from *Punch,* 1843. The young Queen Victoria made her first visit to France in 1843, meeting with French king Louis-Philippe and helping to overturn the adversarial relations that had long persisted between Great Britain and France. Trade issues were very much on the minds of the British, as opposition to the Corn Laws grew dramatically. The cartoonist here suggests that the queen dominated the negotiations by hypnotizing the seventy-year-old Louis-Philippe. MARY EVANS PICTURE LIBRARY

describe in detail the history of ideas that influenced the debate about free-trade versus protectionist policies. What they found was that most countries were certainly not free-traders in the early nineteenth century, except for perhaps the Netherlands, Denmark, Switzerland, and Portugal. In England, an intensive discussion was waged before midcentury on whether the country should abolish its protectionist policies against grain imports. Over time, free-traders influenced by Ricardo and the "Manchester" liberals convinced enough political decision-makers in their favor, so that the famous protectionist Corn Laws were finally dropped in the 1840s (after having been gradually reduced

earlier). Subsequent negotiations between the United Kingdom and France, as well as the general economic upturn of the 1860s led to a wave of free-trade policies in the 1860s and 1870s. However, the dramatic decline in transportation costs and the high productivity of New World farmers stimulated a rebound in protectionism in many continental European countries against grain imports while the United States acted in a strongly protectionist manner against industrial imports. However, protectionist measures were not strong enough to hinder the international integration of many markets. The fall in transportation costs simply outweighed most such measures.

The integration of commodity markets within Europe can be measured by the decline in price gaps. For example, the price gap between Odessa in Ukraine (one of the major grain exporting regions) and London decreased from 40 percent to virtually 0 percent between 1870 and 1906. Similarly, the price gap of Swedish wood between its country of origin and England fell from 155 to 70 percent. In general, O'Rourke and Williamson found that the strong increase in commerce and trade in the nineteenth century was mainly the result of declining transportation costs and only to a much lesser extent of more liberal trade policies. This stands in sharp contrast to the boom in international trade in the second half of the twentieth century, when trade policies accounted for most of the trade-generating effects, whereas the decline of transportation costs due to technological improvement was only modest.

TARIFFS AND ECONOMIC GROWTH

The expansion of export shares correlated with additional per capita income in nineteenth-century Europe. Does this imply that protectionism was bad for growth? To answer this question, we must first consider that neither protectionism nor its inverse, the "openness" of countries, correlates perfectly with trade shares. For example, Germany and France became grain protectionists in the late nineteenth century, yet their export shares still continued to increase substantially, since economic forces were simply much stronger than the respective political countermeasures.

The growth effects of protection (as opposed to free trade) have been studied in great detail for the contemporary world. Free-traders expect welfare effects if the external effects (i.e., side effects) of protection are not important. However, if "infant industries" cannot develop because the industries of industrialized countries have already achieved specific knowledge and cost-efficient production methods, then the protection of those industries on the side of the newcomers could stimulate growth. Empirically, most studies for the late twentieth century concur with Jeffrey D. Sachs's conclusions that free trade rather then protectionism was a successful device for growth. However, for the late nineteenth century, O'Rourke found that protective tariffs in fact had a positive influence on growth rates, even after allowing for changes in the capital-labor ratio, land-labor ratio, initial income level, schooling, and other country-specific characteristics. His analysis included seven European countries, the United States, Australia, and Canada for 1870–1913 and indicates that the protectionist United States grew fast, whereas the free-trading United Kingdom grew only modestly during the period under consideration. In addition, O'Rourke found that Germany was not as protectionist as studies focusing particularly on the grain trade have suggested. Even if the United States and the United Kingdom are omitted as extreme cases, the positive relationship between protectionism and growth is confirmed for the nineteenth century. A possible causal mechanism, O'Rourke suggests, was that tariffs caused a declining share of the labor force to be employed in agriculture, especially in the New World, where tariffs benefited industrial production.

It should be noted, however, that our comparison of export shares and GDP growth refers to long-term growth over almost a century, whereas O'Rourke's study explores the effect of protection levels on annual growth rates in the period 1875–1913, controlling for a number of other variables as well.

INTERNAL TRADE: DIRECT AND INDIRECT EFFECTS

So far we have concentrated mainly on international trade, since external exchange always attracts the highest attention from policy makers and the general public. More important in terms of value, however, was internal trade that did not cross national boundaries in nineteenth-century Europe. Trade within countries increased dramatically at the time because transportation facilities experienced a veritable revolution. The railway network not only grew dramatically in size, but the railway system also became ever more refined. Moreover, toward the very end of the nineteenth century, refrigeration wagons allowed the transportation of perishable goods. For the first time in human history, it became possible to provide large urban populations with food that was as healthy as the food consumed in the countryside. Milk, for example, had previously not been transportable to large urban agglomerations at reasonable costs, although urban centers were in dire need of protein in particular because of the high rates of disease. Before the

The Battle of Trafalgar. Painting by John Callow, 1875. ©Fine Art Photographic Library/Corbis

problem of putting paid to Villeneuve once and for all. His intention was to let the allied fleet sortie, then attack it not in an orthodox line of battle formation but in two columns, splitting his enemy and bringing about a no-holds-barred melee. Conventional wisdom argued such an action could not be controlled. Nelson was confident in the quality of his crews and captains—and not least in an improved signal system facilitating transmission of orders even in close action.

Under orders from Napoleon to engage, Villeneuve set sail on 19 October. Fearing to frighten his opponent back to port, Nelson stalked him until the morning of the twenty-first. The subsequent jockeying for position only highlighted Franco-Spanish navigational shortcomings. Nothing was wrong with their courage—but as the British came to close quarters the Royal Navy's gunnery and ship-handling created a debacle. Twenty-two allied ships out of thirty-three were lost when the final tally was taken. No British ship was sunk, though most were badly battered.

Nelson fell to a musket shot, his place among the great admirals assured for all time.

Trafalgar was the most important naval engagement of the Napoleonic Wars. It put an end to Napoleon's hopes of invading England, and decided as well an Anglo-French struggle for naval mastery dating back to the mid-seventeenth century. Nelson's victory secured a British mastery of the high seas that endured for more than a century.

See also **French Revolutionary Wars and Napoleonic Wars; Military Tactics; Napoleon; Nelson, Horatio.**

BIBLIOGRAPHY

Howarth, David. *Trafalgar: The Nelson Touch*. London, 1969. Reprint, London, 2003.

Lambert, Andrew. *Nelson: Britannia's God of War*. London, 2004. Excellent alike on Nelson's history and mythology.

Schom, Alan. *Trafalgar: Countdown to Battle, 1803–1805*. New York, 1990.

DENNIS SHOWALTER

TRANSPORTATION AND COMMUNICATIONS.

Over centuries, roads evolved in response to the movement of goods and people. They included narrow tracks linking farms to fields and those linking villages to each other and to local and regional markets; links between market towns and regional administrative and commercial centers; and major routes radiating from national capitals toward these regional centers and the frontiers. Differing natural conditions meant that the physical condition and carrying capacity of these routes varied considerably, as did the priorities and resources accorded to their maintenance by local users as well as administrative bodies. Everywhere, however, users incurred substantial "transaction costs" as a result of slow movement, dependent on horse traction. Furthermore, irregularity and the resulting need to maintain stocks of foodstuffs and essential raw materials, which were susceptible to spoilage, added to costs.

ROADS AND WATERWAYS

In response to growing demand, from at least the beginning of the eighteenth century, increasingly efforts were made to improve road construction techniques, provide paved surfaces, and introduce more regular maintenance. The timing and nature of the decisions taken are intelligible only within particular geographical, political, social, institutional, and cultural contexts. Thus in Britain, improvement was to be funded primarily through private initiative by means of the creation of turnpike trusts—of which there were 1,037 by 1834—and the introduction of tolls. Elsewhere, classification of routes, the ordering of priorities, and supervision of construction by state engineers were more likely, with resources provided by a mixture of tolls, taxation, and obligatory labor service. With better road surfaces, carts and carriages could move more rapidly and carry heavier loads, with less wear and tear on both beasts and vehicles. Certainly less strain was imposed on the horses. Carefully selected for their particular functions, they represented a substantial investment. In an expansive economic situation, improved roads were a major factor in sustaining growth. Government interest was also encouraged by the desire to reinforce political centralization. Additionally, improved

roads promoted changing perceptions of time and space as well as more positive attitudes toward travel. For official use, as well as for the convenience of the small minority who could afford to use the mail coach or a private carriage and able to take advantage of relays of horses, travel was becoming increasingly rapid. In France, where technical improvements in road construction and maintenance largely followed British models, the most effective road system in Continental Europe was created during the eighteenth century. Subsequently, with the exception of strategic routes, roads were neglected during the long and destructive wars of the revolution and empire until, with the coming of peace, work was resumed.

While these improvements were certainly welcomed, travelers continued to complain, especially about the marked deterioration in conditions once they moved away from privileged axes. In the uplands steep gradients frequently required the use of packhorses rather than carts. Although times varied considerably according to the season and weather, in 1827 it was still likely to take twenty-five days to transport goods from Paris to Marseilles at a cost of 14.50 francs a metric ton, even on relatively good roads. For somewhere between 32 and 36 francs "accelerated" transport might reduce the time taken to thirteen days. The range of transport services included large enterprises with heavy wagons and large teams of horses and offering regular departures; local carriers providing links with nearby market towns; and the hosts of peasants engaged in transporting their own produce or, during the agricultural quiet season, offering their services, together with horses or oxen, to whomever needed a cart and generally at very low cost.

There was a clear division of function between road and waterway transport. Road transport was generally preferred for innumerable short-distance movements, in the absence of navigable water, or else as a feeder to the waterways. In general it was more rapid and reliable and certainly offered greater flexibility than did carriage by water. High-value goods, which could bear the cost of transport, would be transported by road. However, waterways offered the only economic means of transporting such bulky products as cereals, coal,

A stagecoach on a mountain road. The use of horse-drawn vehicles for transportation and tourism increased early in the nineteenth century due to improved roadways and more comfortable coaches. In this photograph, passengers riding a stagecoach through the scenic Furka Pass in the Swiss Alps admire the view. ©HULTON-DEUTSCH COLLECTION/CORBIS

and building materials as well as finished textiles and metallurgical products, glass, and pottery. Britain, an island penetrated by numerous waterways, and the Low Countries thus enjoyed considerable advantages. Nevertheless, conditions on the waterways and transport costs were extremely diverse. In part this reflected seasonal variations in the depth of water and in the strength of the current, whether movement was with or against the current, and, on the larger rivers and at sea, the direction of the prevailing winds. The existence of obstacles (including rocks, shifting sandbanks, bridges, and mill weirs) was another key factor. Transshipment was frequently necessary. Even minor rivers might be employed at least downriver and when water levels were high. On faster-flowing streams, where downriver movement alone was possible, boats were likely to be broken up on reaching their destination. As a result of differences in the conditions for navigation, the structure and capacity of boats varied considerably. Rivers were also the means of floating downriver the wood that served as the

essential construction material and as a major source of fuel. In addition to numerous barges coming downriver, regions accessible to the sea attracted ships active in long-distance international trade and also played host to the numerous small coasters plying their trade between the large number of mostly tiny harbors.

In response to growing demand, the construction of canals offered a means of bypassing obstacles and of linking the various river basins in order to create more extensive networks. The excavation of reservoirs to improve water supply, the construction of locks to overcome gradients, and the provision of towpaths to make it easier to use horses to tow barges, all represented means of improving canal navigation. In France, where the rivers Seine, Loire, Saône, and Rhône carried the most traffic, much of the canal construction, beginning in the seventeenth century, was directed toward improving links between these river basins. In the south the Canal du Midi linked the Garonne River at

Toulouse with the Mediterranean at Sète, transporting cereals from upper Languedoc, an area of surplus, to lower Languedoc, where deficits were common. Considered to be a technological marvel when under construction between 1665 and 1681, it ran for some 240 kilometers and included 74 locks. By 1840 Paris was linked to central France by the upper Seine and its tributaries and by the canals of Bourgogne and the Centre, with the east by the Marne-Rhine canal, with the coal fields of Belgium and the north by the Canal de Saint-Quentin and the Oise, and by the lower Seine to the sea. Lyon, at the confluence of the rivers Rhône and Saône, served as the second major node in the French transport system. As late as 1829, with steam locomotion already in its early stages but with an uncertain future, the Becquey Plan assumed that economic change would continue to depend on substantial investment in the canalization of rivers and in canal construction.

In practice the waterways continued to suffer from major shortcomings. As a senior French government engineer pointed out: "the utility of canals is recognised along their length, but extends itself for only short distances from their banks. Immediately the merchandise transported by boats has to be re-loaded into carts, the unloading, the reloading and carting eliminates the economies offered by water transport" (quoted in Price, p. 45). Every lock represented a bottleneck. Propulsion, prior to the development of small and inexpensive steam engines, depended on horse or sail and in some cases even on human power and represented a major problem, especially against the current. The upper reaches of the Rhine were thus used primarily by downriver traffic, with the most active stretch of the river that between Mainz and Cologne. Gradually, in the early nineteenth century efforts were made to abolish the tolls charged by various cities along its banks and to clear the riverbed; from the late 1820s steamers were introduced to carry passengers and from midcentury tugs to tow barges. In northern Germany the Weser, Elbe, and Oder were used mainly by local traffic, while farther east the Vistula, even if closed by freezing for some three months each year, made possible substantial transports of rye and wheat. In both Germany and Russia the north-south flow of the major rivers limited their impact on both internal and international trade. By 1850 the various German states had constructed only 750 kilometers of canals to link the major river systems, while the navigable link established from the 1820s between the Baltic and Black Seas was often interrupted by adverse water conditions. Nevertheless, ports like Hamburg, Lübeck, Danzig, and the Russian Baltic port of Riga at the mouths of these rivers made important contributions to the export trades in grain, timber, flax, and hemp. In Italy the river Po and the Tiber below Rome carried substantial traffic; in Spain the Guadalquivir and the lower reaches of the Tagus, Duero, and Ebro were also used for navigation. Topography represented an insurmountable obstacle to significant canal construction, however. In much of Scandinavia slow construction of what would in any case be a low-density rail network would ensure that coastal shipping remained important throughout the nineteenth century.

In spite of the expense and frequent difficulty of movement by both road and water the gradual increase in the efficiency of the transport system reduced the cost and improved access to potential markets, as well as increasing the efficiency with which marketplace information was diffused. Thus, although they provided few of the "backward" linkages to industry—which, for example, would be created by railway demand for metallurgical products—improved road/water transport would have a substantial impact on economic conditions. Reductions in transport costs, and in effect of the prices paid by consumers, stimulated the expansion of demand for manufactured goods and the greater commercialization of agriculture, particularly in the already relatively favored areas of valley and plain. Urban centers at nodal points in communications networks, which performed key commercial functions, could be supplied more easily with the raw materials and foodstuffs necessary to their further development. Central to regional communications systems themselves, they were also the key elements in interregional and international trade. Even in the more isolated areas growing numbers of middlemen were active in the host of markets and fairs still made necessary by the slow and expensive communications that limited the zone of attraction of most small markets to something like a circumference of fifteen kilometers. Nevertheless, they drew in peasant farmers anxious to sell their produce and increasingly able to make purchases. Information on the prices of such key commodities as cereals and coal suggests that a gradual and piecemeal process of market integration was underway but also points at the continued fragmentation that remained a predominant characteristic of pre-rail economies. The survival of numerous dispersed small-scale iron producers was a further indication of the difficulties of access to both raw materials and markets, of poor diffusion of technical as well as market information, and the weakness of competitive pressures to innovate. In such situations railway construction would represent a response to the bottlenecks emerging within road/water transport systems as the economic development, to a large degree stimulated by their improvement, resulted in a further growth in the demand for transport facilities. Just to take one example, the Thames below, and especially in, London, was increasingly packed with colliers bringing coal from the northeast while nearby streets were congested with horses and carts.

RAILWAYS AND STEAM-POWERED WATER TRANSPORT

A technical solution to these problems was being developed, however. Like the canals, the first railways were constructed as adjuncts to river systems and as means of replacing costly road transport. However, it rapidly became evident that in spite of considerable investment in the improvement of roads and waterways and substantial pre-rail reductions in the cost of transport, the railways offered considerable further advantages in terms of cost, speed, and regularity. This was especially welcomed in those areas that had previously lacked easy access to waterways or the sea. Rail construction would have a substantial market-widening impact. The cost reductions they allowed stimulated demand for a wide range of products. The growing integration of space would also result in greater regional specialization as the more resourceful producers benefited from comparative advantage. Together with the intensification of competition, they promoted the more efficient diffusion of information and stimulated technical innovation. Long-distance passenger transport moved virtually entirely to the railways, which offered cheaper, far more rapid, and more comfortable transport. The time taken for the

coach journey from Paris to Lille in northern France had already been reduced from forty-eight hours in 1815 to twenty in 1845 as a result of road improvements and better coach design and horse breeding. Clearly more positive attitudes toward traveling had developed as a result. However, there were limits to what could be achieved by horse traction, and by 1855 the rail journey took only four hours and fifty minutes. The greater concentration of manufacturing processes also led to the deindustrialization of less well-endowed areas and to a process of ruralization as dispersed handicraft manufacture collapsed.

The injection of this new technology into the communications system had a substantial impact on road and waterway traffic, which underwent a relative decline in importance. The schematic model drawn by Norman J. G. Pounds (*An Historical Geography of Europe, 1800–1914,* Cambridge, U.K., and New York, 1985, figure 9.1, p. 428) provides an effective representation of these trends. The statistical information available is extremely fragmentary, however, particularly for road and waterway transport. Table 1 therefore provides only an additional impression of trends.

Although the pre-rail forms of transport continued to move similar or even slightly greater volumes of freight, their share dropped considerably. Between 1851 and 1876, while the tonnage carried by French railways increased by around 1,590 percent, that carried by water and road rose by 18 and 19 percent respectively. In general traffic declined on waterways and roads running parallel to the railways while rising substantially on roads providing access to railway stations. It also needs to be borne in mind that rail construction was extended over at least a half-century, affecting repeated local and regional changes in road use.

Waterway transport of bulky commodities was also threatened. Operating in an area with relatively efficient waterborne transport, the Nord railway company in France nevertheless proved able, by means of competitive pricing, to attract a substantial part of the traffic in coal coming from Belgium and the departments of the Nord and Pas-de-Calais. This represented 44 percent of its goods traffic in the period from 1873 to 1884. Major coal

TABLE 1

Transport of commodities in France, 1830–1914 (in thousand millions of metric ton-kilometer)

Period	Road	Canal	Rail	Sea (coaster)	Total
1830	2.0	0.5	—	0.6	3.5
1841–1844	2.3	0.8	0.06	0.7	3.9
1845–1854	2.6	1.2	0.46	0.7	5.0
1855–1864	2.7	1.4	3.00	0.7	7.8
1865–1874	2.8	1.3	6.30	0.6	11.0
1875–1884	2.6	1.5	9.40	0.6	14.1
1885–1894	2.7	2.3	10.90	0.8	16.7
1895–1904	2.8	3.2	14.90	1.1	22.0
1905–1914	2.9	3.8	21.00	1.1	28.8

SOURCE: J.-C.Toutain, *Les transports en France de 1830 à 1965* (Paris: Presses Universitaires de France, 1968), p. 252

mining and metallurgical enterprises constructed both internal rail systems and spurs linking them to the external railway network. In the case of seaborne trade the railway was either complementary, in providing a means of penetration inland for seaborne people and goods, or else competitive, particularly with coastal traffic. International and especially transatlantic trade grew substantially in volume, reflecting both rising prosperity and substantial reductions in maritime freight costs resulting from improvements in the design and construction of both sailing and steam ships. Gradually, from the 1820s and 1830s, steamers entered coastal trade and from midcentury into longer-distance transport. Although as late as 1870 only 24 percent of British merchant tonnage and around 9 percent of that of France, Germany, and Italy was steam powered, the speed and carrying capacity of sailing ships was improved considerably. Increasingly, however, especially from the 1870s and 1880s and in long-distance trade, steam propulsion replaced sail, especially as more reliable and efficient engines reduced fuel consumption and larger iron—then steel—ships were constructed offering more cargo space. This growing maritime trade—and the shipbuilding that made it possible—was increasingly concentrated in the major ports, where infrastructure investment in docks, quays, and cranes had improved turnaround times for ships and which furthermore benefited from efficient rail links to wide hinterlands as well as rail tariff policies that sought to maximize traffic. There was intense competition between such ports as Le Havre, Antwerp, and Hamburg for a lucrative transit trade. The massive imports of raw materials

and foodstuffs did much to keep down both the price of manufactured goods and the cost of living and thus to stimulate consumer demand.

From the 1860s through 1880s, on a selective basis, substantial investments also took place in the improvement of conditions for navigation on such major rivers as the lower Seine, Meuse, Rhine, Elbe, and even the Danube (where natural obstacles continued to deter users) as well as in the widening and deepening of canals, designed to allow the constant movement of high-capacity barges. Between 1873 and 1914 the length of canals and canalized rivers in Germany almost doubled, to 6,600 kilometers. In France and Germany governments favored this as a means of countering rail monopoly by providing an even cheaper means of transport for bulky commodities like coal and iron ore. Between the mid-1880s and 1905 the tonnage carried on French waterways grew by 73 percent, on Belgian by 114 percent, and on German by 274 percent. In the French case the relative decline in the significance of inland waterways was reversed as their share in goods traffic, which had fallen from 37 percent to 15 percent between 1851 and 1882, rose again to 21 percent by 1903. In less economically dynamic regions or where natural conditions made the cost of improvement prohibitive, waterways like the Loire or Vistula were largely abandoned and river ports decayed rapidly.

REVIVAL OF THE ROAD: BICYCLES AND MOTORCARS

As had been the case with the development of the railway system, the revival of the road as a means of

A group of shipbuilders in their shipyard. Late-nineteenth-century photograph. The use of steel for shipbuilding allowed for the construction of much larger vessels and greatly enlarged the fortunes of shipping magnates. ©Hulton-Deutsch Collection/Corbis

transport was a response to the perceived short-comings of existing rail/road transport facilities. The introduction of the bicycle and then of the motorcar were once again to transform transport conditions. Substantial investment in road improvement had continued because of roads' central importance to short-distance transport and in providing access to the railways.

In 1867, a Parisian blacksmith called Pierre Michaux probably produced the first commercial bicycle. By 1885 the modern safety bicycle had been developed. From the late 1880s its use rapidly spread as its cost fell. The bicycle offered both a means of getting to work and a leisure activity that enhanced personal liberty. By 1890 some five hundred thousand were in use in Britain. Michelin's

invention of the detachable, inflatable tire in 1888 provided for a more comfortable ride. Typically, large numbers of producers entered the new industry before competition and overproduction eliminated the weakest.

Even more significant was the development of the internal combustion engine, invented independently by Karl Benz and Gottlieb Daimler in the 1870s and 1880s. This provided a more compact, fuel-efficient power technology than that provided by steam and allowed the construction of lighter vehicles no longer dependent on rails. The automobile offered a flexible and rapid means of personal transport to luxury consumers anxious to escape from crowded, more "democratic" forms of transport. Initially, customized cars were

TABLE 2

Annual expenditure on roads in France, 1815–1913 (in millions of francs)	
Period	Expenditure
1815–1819	58.2
1820–1829	65.0
1830–1839	110.3
1840–1849	170.6
1850–1859	176.8
1860–1869	220.7
1870–1879	223.7
1880–1889	243.9
1890–1899	231.9
1900–1909	234.2
1910–1913	249.0

assembled by skilled artisans in hundreds of metal-working and carriage-building workshops, some of which, like Peugeot, were pushed into diversification by intense competition among bicycle manufacturers. Again, only a small minority of these companies, including Peugeot, Opel, and Fiat, would survive growing competitive pressures. By 1907 there were some 150,000 vehicles in use throughout Europe, increasing to 600,000 by 1914. In France 91,000 vehicles were in use in 1913; in Germany there were 61,000 private cars and 9,700 commercial vehicles. Public transport was also affected. Thus, whereas in London in 1903 11,000 hansom and hackney cabs and 1 motor cab plied their trade, by 1913 there were already 8,000 motor cabs, and the number of horse-drawn cabs had declined to 1,900. Trucks and motorbuses were also making an appearance. As a result of better automobile design and the improvement of road surfaces, the reliability of vehicles and their capacity for long-distance movement also increased rapidly. A major new industry was in the making. In Europe's fragmented markets assembly-line production was slower to develop than in the United States. In 1914 Peugeot, the largest European producer, turned out only around 2 percent of the cars produced by Ford. Even at this stage, however, the burgeoning new industry substantially increased demand for aluminum, high-quality steels and alloys, and rubber and oil. Renault, Panhard et Levassor, and others were also already moving into the production of aircraft engines. In France by 1914 some 100,000 were employed in making cars and espe-

cially in related activities in garages and road maintenance. Soon World War I would provide a massive stimulus to production that heralded the postwar rebirth of road transport and, because motor vehicles offered greater convenience and flexibility at a competitive price, the gradual but accelerating decline of the railway. Although the process would take decades, particularly in the countryside, the age of the horse was also coming to an end.

See also **Airplanes; Automobile; Cycling; Industrial Revolution, First; Industrial Revolution, Second; Railroads; Trade and Economic Growth.**

BIBLIOGRAPHY

Laux, James Michael. *In First Gear: The French Automobile Industry to 1914.* Liverpool, U.K., 1976.

Livet, Georges. *Histoire des routes et des transports en Europe.* Strasbourg, France, 2003.

Price, Roger. *The Modernization of Rural France: Communications Networks and Agricultural Market Structures in Nineteenth-Century France.* London, 1983.

Szostak, Rick. *The Role of Transportation in the Industrial Revolution: A Comparison of England and France.* Montreal, 1991.

Ville, Simon P. *Transport and the Development of the European Economy, 1750–1918.* London, 1990.

———. "Transport and Communications." In *The European Economy, 1750–1914: A Thematic Approach,* edited by Derek H. Aldcroft and Simon P. Ville. Manchester, U.K., 1994.

ROGER PRICE

TREITSCHKE, HEINRICH VON
(1834–1896), German nationalist.

Born on 15 September 1834 in Dresden, the future champion of Prussian-led German unification Heinrich von Treitschke grew up in the aristocratic, conservative, and provincial atmosphere of the capital of the kingdom of Saxony. The son of an army officer who eventually rose to the rank of general and a mother who descended from a venerable Saxon noble family, Treitschke became interested at an early age in German nationalism, convinced as early as 1848 that only the Prussian monarchy could unite the Germans states. Prevented from becoming an officer due

Ponte Rosso on the Grand Canal, Trieste. Photograph by Giuseppe Wulz c. 1890. The church of Sant'Antonio can be seen in the background. ALINARI/ART RESOURCE

Archduke Ferdinand Maximilian, the younger brother of the emperor Francis Joseph and supreme commander of the Imperial Austrian Navy, began construction of his royal palace Miramare. Ferdinand died in 1867 in an ill-advised attempt to rule as the emperor of Mexico, but construction of the castle continued, and by 1871 the completed royal residence stood as a symbol of Habsburg authority.

By the mid-nineteenth century, under Habsburg tutelage, Trieste's trade position was enhanced. The Südbahn rail connection, completed in 1857, formed a direct link to Vienna. Although the Adriatic route could never match the northern German port route in terms of efficiency and economy, Trieste grew as a cosmopolitan port city serving international commercial interests. In the 1860s the convergence of Austria's loss of Venice to Italy, Habsburg suspicions of German states unifying under a "small German" model, and the monarchy's compromise of 1867 that split the empire into two parts served to focus Austrian energies on the development of Trieste. The Adriatic port served as an alternative to lost Venetian routes and politically unreliable networks through Bismarck's Germany.

In 1891 the monarchy abrogated Trieste's free-port status, but Habsburg monopolies, subsidies, and commercial advantages continued to feed economic growth. In 1913 trade with imperial regions accounted for over 80 percent of Triestine commercial rail traffic.

COSMOPOLITAN PORT AND CULTURE

From the Habsburg perspective, Trieste rested in the hands of commercial elites of a variety of ethnic and cultural backgrounds, whose allegiance lay with the monarchy and whose focus was on economic concerns. The urban environment had an Italian character due to reliance on an Italian dialect as the lingua franca and general adherence to Italian customs. However, the city was reputed to be cosmopolitan, with a climate heavily influenced by diverse groups of immigrants, including Greeks, Ottomans, Jews, and English and Swiss Protestants. At the same time, a strong civic identity grew out of the city's pretensions to economic importance and autonomy within the Habsburg Empire. Writers in Trieste captured the contradictions of the "cosmopolitan" and "municipal" identities and the clash between economic internationalism and nationalist particularism. They also emphasized the psychoanalytic perspective, filtering to the port from Freud's circle in Vienna. The Irish writer James Joyce spent several years before World War I teaching English in Trieste and is reputed to have drawn inspiration for many of his characters, including Leopold Bloom in *Ulysses,* from the Triestines. Best known among the psychoanalytically inspired works is the novel *Zeno's Conscience* by Triestine native Italo Svevo.

Cultural networks and literary circles embracing diversity remained intact on the eve of World War I, but political bifurcation went hand in hand with the emergence of ethnic antagonisms that increasingly pit Italians against Slavs in the second half of the nineteenth century. By the 1880s, the increasing wealth of Trieste had quickened the pace of immigration to the urban center, altering the ethnic and political landscape. The migration of workers from nearby rural districts in Italy, Istria, and Slovene and Croatian Adriatic provinces and the changes wrought by rapid urbanization set the stage for the opposition between socialists and national liberals.

NATIONALIST/ETHNIC DEBATE

Nationalist or ethnic antagonism in Trieste had its roots in the upheavals of 1848. In 1848 local civilian and military leaders, recognizing the port's reliance on Vienna, generally maintained calm in Trieste. The monarchy rewarded the city's loyalty by transferring the seat of the Austrian navy from revolutionary Venice. Nonetheless, the city's role as a port serving Germanic Austria increasingly clashed with the aspirations and ambitions of nationalist groups, in particular irredentist Italians, who wished to integrate all Italian-speaking territories into the new Italian state.

The 1860s were critical in the emergence of ethnic and nationalist politics in the northeastern Adriatic lands. Italian unification, particularly the inclusion of Lombardy and Venetia, former Habsburg holdings, in the new state of Italy, exacerbated tensions over the fate of the Italian-speaking populations of the Adriatic littoral. The Austro-Hungarian Compromise of 1867 brought nationalist questions to the fore. It excited Slavic interests in autonomy and, by the turn of the century, spurred proposals for a third, Slavic component to the monarchy.

The most famous local nationalist incident occurred in 1882 and involved Guglielmo Oberdan (or Oberdank) and a plan to assassinate the Austrian monarch Francis Joseph, visiting Trieste to honor the five-hundredth anniversary of the city's adhesion to Austria. Officials uncovered Oberdan's plot, and he was hanged for treason. The execution furnished the irredentist movement with a local martyr for the Italian cause.

By the turn of the twentieth century, Trieste's municipal council rested squarely in the hands of Italian nationalists who controlled local matters. Heightening sensitivities to ethnic and cultural differences fueled nationalist antagonisms throughout the empire. In the northeastern Adriatic provinces, Slavs and Italians began to struggle against one another and against Austrian (considered Germanic) officials. The fever pitch of the prewar debate between factions favoring international commerce under the oversight of Austria and those with Italian irredentist aspirations was evident in 1912 in the firestorm that erupted over the publication of Angelo Vivante's *Irredentismo adriatico* (Adriatic irredentism). Irredentists expected Vivante, a respected member of an Italian Triestine bourgeois family, to support pro-Italian factions. Instead, he emphasized Trieste's dependence on Austria and painted irredentist schemes as "utopian" dreams, emphasizing the "antithesis between the economic element and the national one" as "the guiding thread of all Triestine history" (Vivante, p. 221).

At the end of World War I, victorious Italy's incorporation of Trieste into the liberal state could be counted an Italian nationalist triumph. However, Vivante's antithesis could not be reconciled. Italy's victory proved Pyrrhic. Italy was frustrated at the inability to annex other coveted territories in the eastern Adriatic; nationalists and socialists clashed; the port city, due to the ravages of war and political separation from hinterlands in central Europe, entered into a period of decline. Economic crisis and political and ethnic antagonisms set the stage for the well-known, bitter twentieth-century contests over the fate of Trieste.

See also **Austria-Hungary; Italy; Vienna.**

BIBLIOGRAPHY

Primary Sources

Slataper, Scipio. *Lettere triestine: Col seguito di attri scritti vociani di polemica su Trieste.* Trieste, 1988.

Svevo, Italo. *Zeno's Conscience.* Translated by William Weaver. New York, 2001. Translation of *Coscienza di Zeno* (1923).

Vivante, Angelo. *Irredentismo adriatico.* Trieste, 1984.

Secondary Sources

Dubin, Lois C. *The Port Jews of Habsburg Trieste: Absolutist Politics and Enlightenment Culture.* Stanford, Calif., 1999.

McCourt, John. *The Years of Bloom: James Joyce in Trieste, 1904–1920.* Dublin, 2000.

Pizzi, Katia. *A City in Search of an Author: The Literary Identity of Trieste.* London, 2001.

Schächter, Elizabeth. *Origin and Identity: Essays on Svevo and Trieste.* Leeds, U.K., 2000.

Sondhaus, Lawrence. *In the Service of the Emperor: Italians in the Austrian Armed Forces, 1814–1918.* New York, 1990.

MAURA E. HAMETZ

TRISTAN, FLORA (1803–1844), French feminist and socialist.

Flore-Célestine-Thérèse-Henriette Tristan Moscoso, who called herself Flora Tristan, was born in Paris. Her French mother had met her father, a Peruvian-born nobleman of Spanish ancestry, in Bilbao (Spain) during the French Revolution. Their religious marriage was not recognized under Revolutionary law, making Flora and her younger brother Pio technically illegitimate. They did not inherit on their father's sudden death in 1807, and grew up in modest circumstances in the countryside near Paris.

Little is known of Tristan's life until she returned to Paris in 1818 and found work coloring designs in the engraving workshop of André Chazal. She married him shortly before her eighteenth birthday, but the marriage was violent and Tristan left her husband in 1825. With two sons to support and pregnant with her third child, she had difficulty finding work. Following the birth of her daughter in October 1825, she left her children in her mother's care and became a "lady's maid," traveling throughout Europe with her employers. She then made contact with her father's family and visited Peru in 1832–1833 in an unsuccessful attempt to claim her inheritance. This voyage provided the basis for her first major publication, *Peregrinations of a Pariah* (1838), and for a career as a writer. Her account of her unhappy marriage also sparked renewed conflict with her estranged husband, who was jailed after attempting to kill her in 1838.

Tristan's travels opened her eyes to the extent of social injustice and transformed her from a disillusioned wife pursuing her own rights into a political activist. In the 1830s she signed petitions for the legalization of divorce and against capital punishment, and published a pamphlet on the plight of single women. She became interested in the socialist theories of Charles Fourier (1772–1837), Robert Owen (1771–1858), the Saint-Simonians, and Étienne Cabet (1788–1856), but found none of them satisfactory. Tristan began to publish her own proposals in both fiction and nonfiction. The hero of her 1838 novel *Méphis,* a self-proclaimed "proletarian," fought oppression by aristocrats and Jesuits with his lover, the Andalusian Maréquita (a character based partly on Tristan herself). The novel ends with the birth of their daughter, Mary, a female savior destined to complete the redemption of the proletariat.

Following a fourth trip to England in 1839, Tristan published a report on the plight of workers in the nation at the forefront of industrialization

Flora Tristan. Nineteenth-century lithograph portrait.
BIBLIOTHÈQUE MARGUERITE DURAND, PARIS, FRANCE/BRIDGEMAN ART
LIBRARY/ARCHIVES CHARMET

(*Promenades dans Londres* [Walks in London], 1840). She cited a range of investigations and reports to give her work credibility. Her preface warned French workers that they faced similar problems as industrialization spread. Her links with militant French workers from 1843 and her investigation of French workers' lives sharpened her conviction that the political mobilization of the "largest and most useful class" was the key to social transformation. She promoted this idea in her best-known book, *Workers' Union* (1843). It emphasized the need for workers to form a "union" with a broad membership, superseding craft-based associations, if they were to become a political force. Unskilled workers and women needed to be included. She argued that women's oppression underpinned the oppression of workers and that workers should lead the way in recognizing women's rights. While on a speaking tour to promote this book, Tristan died at Bordeaux of suspected typhoid fever on 14 November 1844.

A monument to Tristan, funded by French workers, was erected at Bordeaux in October 1848. It was inscribed: "In memory of Madame Flora Tristan, author of the *Workers' Union*, with the workers' gratitude. Liberty—Equality—Fraternity—Solidarity." This acknowledged her dedication to the workers' cause. Nevertheless, her relationships with workers were sometimes difficult. She remained an outsider, defining herself as one of the "enlightened bourgeoisie." Her messianic vision and her claim to be the "mother of the workers" also emphasized her own leadership, creating some resentment. Tristan's approach reflected both the religious currents within Romantic socialism, and the prominence of middle-class figures within socialist organizations at that time.

Tristan's feminist legacy is also complex. She did not form alliances with other feminists of her day, desiring to lead rather than follow. But she articulated the concerns shared by feminists in this period about discriminatory marriage laws, education, employment, and personal autonomy for women. Tristan's reputation as one of the most significant feminists and socialists of her day is well deserved, and her life illustrates that these two sets of ideas were intimately connected in the early nineteenth century.

See also **Feminism; France; Socialism.**

BIBLIOGRAPHY

Primary Sources

The London Journal of Flora Tristan. Translated, annotated, and introduced by Jean Hawkes. London, 1982.

The Workers' Union. Translated with an introduction by Beverly Livingston. Champaign, Ill., 1983.

Flora Tristan, Utopian Feminist: Her Travel Diaries and Personal Crusade. Selected, translated, and with an introduction to her life by Doris Beik and Paul Beik. Bloomington, Ind., 1993.

Flora Tristan's Diary: The Tour of France, 1843–1844. Translated, annotated, and introduced by Máire Fedelma Cross. Oxford, U.K., and New York, 2002.

Secondary Sources

Bloch-Dano, Evelyne. *Flora Tristan: La femme-messie.* Paris, 2001. The best recent biography in French.

Cross, Máire, and Tim Gray. *The Feminism of Flora Tristan.* Oxford, U.K., and Providence, R.I., 1992.

Grogan, Susan K. *Flora Tristan: Life Stories*. London, 1998. Explores Tristan's life through the variety of self-images she created.

Puech, Jules-L. *La vie et l'oeuvre de Flora Tristan, 1803–1844*. Paris, 1925. This first biography remains invaluable.

SUSAN K. FOLEY

TUBERCULOSIS. The symptoms of tuberculosis, more often called consumption or phthisis in the nineteenth century, have been known in Europe for many hundreds of years. A Dublin physician described consumption of the lungs in 1772 in much the same way as modern medical treatises do—as an obstinate cough, inclination to vomit, oppression of the chest, habitual fever that increases after eating, general paleness, high pulse, night sweats, loss of weight, and coughing up of blood. Infection with the tubercle bacillus was widespread in Europe; some calculations for the early twentieth century suggest an almost 100 percent rate of infection. But though not all who were infected went on to develop the full-blown disease, mortality was high. At the height of the epidemic possibly at least two-thirds to three-quarters of those who had the disease died, most commonly from respiratory failure. Even among the recovered, tuberculosis could return in later life.

Some historians see the high rates of tuberculosis in Europe in the eighteenth and nineteenth centuries as the downward curve of an epidemic that had reached its peak several hundred years before. Others argue that a deteriorating urban environment caused an increased incidence in the early nineteenth century. All agree that in most European countries—Ireland and Norway were the exception—tuberculosis was on the decline in the late nineteenth century. Nonetheless, of all the infectious diseases, tuberculosis was the most important contributor to mortality in the nineteenth century and, while its decline continued into the twentieth, it was still the leading cause of death among young adults. Tuberculosis was more prevalent in the cities and towns. There is some evidence that in the nineteenth century, with important exceptions, mortality from tuberculosis was higher among women than men in rural areas, whereas the reverse was true for the towns; no definitive explanation for this variation is known in the early twenty-first century.

MODERN CONCEPTS OF TUBERCULOSIS
Modern concepts of the causes of tuberculosis date from 1882, when the German scientist Robert Koch identified the bacteria responsible for the disease. Before then only two significant developments had taken place that affected the understanding of tuberculosis. One was the refinement around 1816 by the French scientist René-Théophile-Hyacinthe Laennec of the stethoscope, which aided better diagnosis; the other was the microscope, which enabled the identification of the characteristic lesions or "tubercles" that were present in the infected organs of sufferers. This established that, although consumption of the lungs was the most prevalent form of the disease, it could be found in other parts of the human body. It also gave the disease its modern name—tuberculosis.

Before Koch it was not known whether tuberculosis was infectious, though some doctors suspected it was. It was widely believed to be hereditary, and this led to families concealing the disease. Innumerable cures were offered in the early nineteenth century, all in retrospect valueless, including inhalation of iodine, a diet rich in fat, water cures, and even starvation. Some doctors attributed its incidence to overindulgence. By the middle of the nineteenth century, climate was considered to be an important influence on tuberculosis, and medical journals of the period are full of investigations of the incidence of tuberculosis in different climates around the world. This led sufferers to take tours or voyages in search of a climate they hoped would improve their health. A significant number of immigrants from Europe to the New World and the colonies were tuberculosis sufferers.

The lingering nature of death from consumption of the lungs and the fact that it seemed to strike the young in their prime led to a romantic iconography growing up around the disease in the nineteenth century. Some symptoms—flushed cheeks, glittering eyes—were considered to enhance beauty. The febrile excitement that sufferers often displayed in their psychological reaction to their illness led to an association between susceptibility to tuberculosis and emotional and artistic temperaments. Thus in operas, novels, and art, death from tuberculosis was used as the climax of a tragic

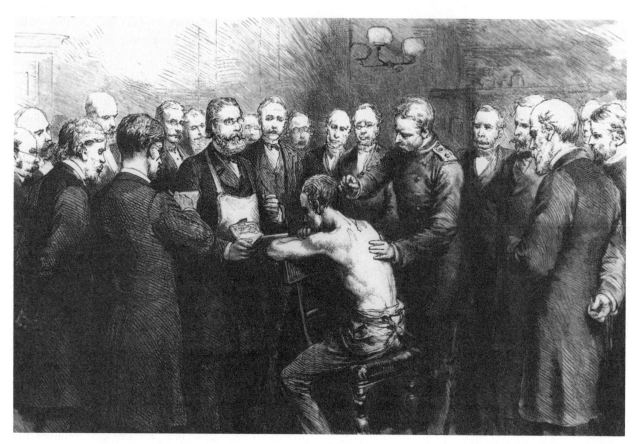

Dr. Koch's Treatment for Consumption at the Royal Hospital, Berlin. English engraving, late nineteenth century. Following his discovery of the bacterium that causes tuberculosis in 1882, Robert Koch attempted to develop treatments for the disease. He was awarded the Nobel Prize in 1905 for his discoveries. PRIVATE COLLECTION/BRIDGEMAN ART LIBRARY

narrative of unfulfilled promise and youthful hopes dashed. Most famously the theme appears in the death of Mimi in Giacomo Puccini's opera *La Bohème* (1896), based on Henri Murger's novel of 1849. However, there are many examples in real life of the impact of tuberculosis on promise. The disease claimed the composer Frédéric Chopin at thirty-nine; the Brontë sisters Emily, Anne, and Charlotte at ages thirty, twenty-nine, and thirty-eight respectively; and the playwright Anton Chekhov at forty-four and the poet John Keats at age twenty-five.

TREATMENT

The belief that fresh, uncontaminated air was good for the tuberculosis sufferer gained ground in the nineteenth century and came to dominate treatment of the disease. One product of this was the specialized tuberculosis hospital or sanatorium situated in an area chosen for climate and fresh air. The most famous example was the hospital in the German Black Forest opened by Dr. Otto Walther in 1888, which combined bed rest, medical attendance, and exposure to the air. Sanatoriums based on similar principles, catering initially to the private patient, opened throughout Europe. Isolated mountain retreats in Europe, brought within reach by the railway, experienced burgeoning local economies built on the provision of sanatoriums for the tubercular. The sanatorium led to the development of a specialized form of hospital architecture and to a literature based on the patient's experience. Every European country produced novels of sanatorium life, most now forgotten. However, the most famous is the German novelist Thomas Mann's *The Magic Mountain*, published in 1924. This was the year that the writer Franz Kafka, whose life and work was also overshadowed by the disease, died from tuberculosis in an Austrian sanatorium.

The late nineteenth century saw a dramatic change in attitudes toward tuberculosis. Koch's discovery of the infectious nature of tuberculosis opened up the possibility that it could be susceptible to the kind of public health measures that had once been used to combat the "fevers"—the epidemic diseases such as cholera, typhus, and smallpox. These included notification, isolation, and decontamination. Between 1890 and 1914 nongovernmental organizations emerged in Europe, usually initiated and led by medical professionals. They raised consciousness of the disease among the public, advocated hygiene, and strove to bring the benefits of the sanatorium within reach of the poor. The principle they operated under was that the disease could be prevented, contained, and perhaps even cured. Thus tuberculosis became a focus for private charitable and eventually government action. A series of international conferences acted as a vector for the spread of ideas about its treatment across Europe. They encouraged comparisons between national tuberculosis rates, though the figures these comparisons were based on were notoriously unreliable. Nonetheless, this helped to make lowering the national tuberculosis rate a matter of patriotic duty.

There were national styles in the public health treatment of tuberculosis. Germany was the country with strongest adherence to the sanatorium; France to the outpatient clinic dealing exclusively with tuberculosis—the tuberculosis dispensary. Some countries had a system of compulsory notification of sufferers, others resisted. Two significant disparities in tuberculosis policy concerned the use of the antituberculosis vaccine BCG and the treatment of bovine tuberculosis. Koch's discoveries had encouraged the search for a vaccine against tuberculosis and in 1921 two French scientists Albert-Léon-Charles Calmette and Camille Guérin announced the discovery of BCG. By the 1930s it was in use in France and Scandinavian countries but elsewhere, particularly in Britain, its value as a preventative measure was questioned. By the 1940s, however, the use of BCG, particularly for children, had become widespread in Europe.

The second was treatment of bovine tuberculosis. Tubercles similar to those seen in humans were observed in animals, and the bacteria Koch found in affected humans was also present in animals. But he doubted, incorrectly, that tuberculosis could be transmitted between animals and humans. In the first decade of the twentieth century experimental proof that it could be so transmitted was available and generally accepted. The chief vector was in the milk and meat of infected animals, primarily cattle. Tuberculosis transmitted by milk affected the bones and internal organs of children in particular. This led to another familiar figure of the nineteenth century—the severely crippled child. Improved agricultural practices and pasteurization of milk eventually led to decline in tuberculosis of bovine origin, but the politics of agriculture intervened in some countries to slow down reform.

See also **Disease; Public Health.**

BIBLIOGRAPHY

Barnes, David. *The Making of a Social Disease: Tuberculosis in Nineteenth-Century France.* Berkeley, Calif., 1995.

Bryder, Lynda. *Below the Magic Mountain: A Social History of Tuberculosis in Twentieth-Century Britain.* Oxford, U.K., 1988.

Dormandy, Thomas. *"The White Death": A History of Tuberculosis.* London, 1999.

Jones, Greta. *"Captain of All These Men of Death": The History of Tuberculosis in Nineteenth and Twentieth Century Ireland.* New York and Amsterdam, 2001.

Smith, Francis Barrymore. *The Retreat of Tuberculosis, 1850–1960.* London, 1988.

GRETA JONES

TUNISIA. The history of Tunisia during the long nineteenth century really begins with the advent of Ottoman suzerainty in the late sixteenth century. In 1574 Sinan Pasha took control of Tunis on behalf of the Ottomans and put an end to the Hafsid dynasty that had ruled Tunisia since 1229. For the Ottomans, this victory represented a strategic success that complemented their conquest of Egypt-Syria (1516–1517) and their capture of Algiers (1525) and Tripoli, Libya (1551). In North Africa, only Morocco would escape Ottoman dominance. In the race to control the southern Mediterranean coast in the sixteenth century, the Ottomans emerged as victors against their Spanish rivals.

The administration of Tunisia was vested in the appointment of a pasha and the stationing of a contingent of Janissaries (elite Turkish soldiers) to ensure the continuance of Ottoman rule. Next to the pasha, the bey was responsible for internal affairs (mostly keeping the local tribes in check) and for the collection of taxes. By 1591 a rebellion of the Janissaries propelled their junior commanders, each bearing the title of dey, to the forefront of the provincial administration. This date marked the ascendancy of the power of the deys in Tunisia. The dey relied on the allegiance of fellow officers and on the discipline of the Janissaries while the bey had authority over the indigenous members of the *Mahalla* (the "fiscal" troops). For most of the seventeenth century the position of bey rose to the detriment of its rival after Murad Bey (d. 1631), a Corsican of origin, founded the hereditary Muradid dynasty that would last until 1702, when its last ruler was assassinated. By 1705 a bey, al-Husayn ibn Ali (whose father was of Greek origin) succeeded in repelling an invasion from Algiers and took control of Tunisia, hence founding the Husaynid dynasty that would rule the country until 1957, when the Tunisian republic was declared. He was a *Kuloğlu* (Turkish for "son of a slave"), a term generally applied to someone issued from the union of a member of the Turkish military and a local woman. This dynasty was granted hereditary succession by the Ottomans and acknowledged nominal Ottoman suzerainty. In the eighteenth century, the Husaynid rulers successfully faced the challenge posed by the expansionist aims of the deys of Algiers. Economically, they encouraged the creation of new crafts (weaving and textiles), imposed a state monopoly over the export of the main agricultural products (particularly olive oil and cereals), and tolerated corsair activity from their ports. By the end of the century, the rule of Hammuda Pasha (r. 1782–1814) witnessed added prosperity as a result of the fiscal reform and the abolition of the state monopoly on agriculture, known as *Mushtara,* which victimized the farmers and the peasantry. This last measure was repealed by his successor.

A turning point in the history of this dynasty came in 1830, with the French occupation of Algeria. Although France rid the Husaynid beys of a bellicose neighbor against whom they had fought many wars, its military presence in Algeria represented a greater threat to their rule, because this allowed France to flex its military muscle toward achieving its imperialist designs over the region. Barely a month after the fall of Algiers, France was able to impose a treaty on Tunisia's Husayn Bey (r. 1824–1835) that stipulated the lifting of the state monopoly over agricultural exports, the establishment of a system of capitulations similar to the one maintained with the Ottomans, and the suppression of piracy by the Barbary corsairs. With regard to the last issue, an identical demand had been made by France and Britain in 1819 in the name of the European powers following the Congress of Aix-la-Chapelle but was met with the procrastination of the beys.

The nineteenth century witnessed the implementation of modernist reforms in the Ottoman Empire, Egypt, and Iran. In the case of Tunisia, the rule of Ahmad Bey (r. 1837–1855) was the beginning of such a trend. The crux of the reform was the common model adopted by the other three countries, namely the concentration on building a modern army along European lines. To this effect, the bey established a military school at Bardo, a suburb of Tunis, using Italian instructors who were soon replaced with Frenchmen. A visit to Paris in 1846 whetted Ahmad Bey's appetite for palace building, and the mounting expenditures led to higher taxation, monopolistic policies, and financial ruin. His successors had to deal with internal unrest, such as the 1864 revolt in the south led by Ali bin Ghadahum, and with the need to meet the state's expenditures. With regard to the latter, Tunisia borrowed from European banks. Unable to repay the debt on schedule, it declared bankruptcy in 1869 and had to agree to the formation of an International Financial Commission (made up of representatives of Tunisia, France, Britain, and Italy) to oversee its revenues. This commission controlled Tunisian finances until 1884, when France assumed the Tunisian debt three years after the establishment of its protectorate over the country.

Despite the bleak financial situation, Tunisia undertook a number of reforms. Under European pressure, slavery was abolished (1846) and the bey issued the Fundamental Pact (*Ahd al-Aman,* September 1857) guaranteeing the rights of minorities, equal justice, and freedom of commerce. In 1861 a constitution (the first of its kind in the

Arab and Islamic worlds) reiterated the principles of the Fundamental Pact and created a grand council whose members were selected by the bey. The reformer Khayr al-Din assumed the presidency of the council, but this last experiment was short lived, and in 1864 the constitution was suspended. In the realm of education, the Sadiqi college, founded in 1875, was the first establishment to offer a modern and secular instruction and would play a role in the formation of the future Tunisian intelligentsia.

Tunisia had to deal with the competing interests of three European powers: France, Britain, and Italy. Of these, France exploited its position of strength to further its own interests in Tunisia and to outmaneuver its main European rivals. At the Congress of Berlin (1878), it reached an understanding with Great Britain regarding their respective colonial designs in the Mediterranean. Three years later, French land and naval forces swiftly took control of the Tunisian capital and imposed the Treaty of Bardo (12 May 1881) on Muhammad al-Sadiq Bey (r. 1859–1882), a year before British troops landed in Egypt (1882) and thirty years before the Italian occupation of Libya (1911). This treaty, together with the subsequent Convention of al-Marsa (8 June 1883) established the French protectorate over Tunisia. The bey was reduced to a figurehead, and real power was concentrated in the hands of the French resident-minister, a title that changed in 1885 to resident-general. French citizens were offered incentives to settle in Tunisia and own farmland at symbolic prices. By 1893 the military draft was extended to the Tunisians, thus giving France the opportunity to count on the added manpower to maintain order in its colonies or to fight its wars. As a result, over sixty thousand Tunisians served in the French army in World War I.

See also **Algeria; Colonialism; Egypt; France; Imperialism.**

BIBLIOGRAPHY

Abun-Nasr, Jamil M. *A History of the Maghrib in the Islamic Period.* Cambridge, U.K., 1987.

Brown, Carl L. *The Tunisia of Ahmad Bey, 1837–1855.* Princeton, N.J., 1974. An excellent study of Tunisian society in the period under study.

Ganiage, Jean. *Les origines du protectorat français en Tunisie, 1861–1881.* 2nd ed. Tunis, 1968.

Green, Arnold H. *The Tunisian Ulama, 1873–1915: Social Structure and Response to Ideological Currents.* Leiden, Netherlands, 1978.

Kraïem, Mustapha. *La Tunisie précoloniale.* 2 vols. Tunis, 1973. A documentary survey of the period.

Krieken, G. S. van. *Khayr al-Dîn et la Tunisie, 1850–1881.* Leiden, Netherlands, 1976.

Mahjoubi, Ali. *L'établissement du protectorat français en Tunisie.* Tunis, 1977.

Perkins, Kenneth J. *Historical Dictionary of Tunisia.* 2nd ed. Lanham, Md., 1997. Contains an extensive bibliography.

Tlili, Béchir. *Les rapports culturels et idéologiques entre l'Orient et l'Occident, en Tunisie au XIXème siècle (1830–1880).* Tunis, 1974.

ADEL ALLOUCHE

TURATI, FILIPPO (1857–1932), Italian socialist.

Filippo Turati was the most significant Italian Socialist leader before the Fascist era. Turati passed from his conservative and Catholic family traditions to positivism and finally to socialism. In the 1880s Turati began to write for *La plebe,* an early socialist newspaper, and in 1885 he met the Russian socialist Anna Kuliscioff. This relationship was to be the most important on a personal and intellectual level in his life and lasted until Kuliscioff's death in 1925. In the late 1880s Turati began to read Karl Marx, whose theories he combined with his original positivism and democratic faith. However, Turati was never tied to ideology as an end in itself, but was much more drawn to practical results. In 1889 he founded the Milanese Socialist League and two years later launched the influential journal *Critica sociale.*

In 1892 Turati played a key role in creating the Italian Socialist Party (PSI). He was elected to the Chamber of Deputies for the first time in 1896. However, during the repression that followed the popular protests of May 1898, he was stripped of his parliamentary immunity and imprisoned. The experience of martial law and prison convinced Turati that a fundamental step to a socialist society was the democratization of Italy. He accepted the overtures of Giovanni Giolitti and Giuseppe

Zanadelli to collaborate with more democratic liberals in a defense of the rights of Parliament. In 1901 Turati, Leonida Bissolati, and Claudio Treves formed the core of a reformist group that engineered a favorable vote from the Socialist deputies for the Zanardelli-Giolitti government. Giolitti, as interior minister, allowed the Socialist trade unions greater scope to organize industrial and peasant labor and to conduct strikes in the private sector.

Turati's relationship with Giolitti proved to be a complicated one. In 1903, when Giolitti succeeded Zanardelli as prime minister, he offered a position in the government to Turati. The reformist leader rejected the offer. Two issues drove a wedge between the two men. Turati was identified with the unionization of state workers, which Giolitti did not accept. More importantly, it became apparent that Giolitti's program did not entail major social and economic reforms.

Turati's control over the Socialist Party was also tenuous. His strength was in the parliamentary delegation, not in the base of the party. In 1904 the party took a turn to the left; Turati's reformist faction did not regain full control of the party until 1908. That year the Socialists adopted a program that called for fundamental reforms of the taxation system and the introduction of universal manhood suffrage. Turati never embraced universal suffrage and in 1910 accepted a more limited voting rights bill from the government of Luigi Luzzatti. When Luzzatti's government fell in March 1911 and Giolitti returned to office on a program of nationalization of the insurance industry and universal manhood suffrage, the time seemed to be right for a renewed alliance between Giolitti and the Socialist reformists. The new prime minister offered a position in the cabinet to Leonida Bissolati, a leading moderate. This time, Turati, fearing that the more radical party militants would not accept participation in a non-Socialist government, weighed in to persuade Bissolati to reject the offer. Soon after, relations between Turati and Giolitti turned sour when the government decided to conquer Libya in September 1911. Although Turati passed into opposition, more revolutionary leaders, including Benito Mussolini, took control of the party in 1912. Turati never again regained a majority, nor was his relationship with Giolitti ever fully repaired.

The years after 1914 would be frustrating ones for Turati as he sought to find a constructive role. The 1917 Bolshevik Revolution radicalized the Italian Socialist Party and blocked Turati's hopes that the PSI might cooperate with other democratic movements in a campaign for a new constitution and a democratic republic. Turati was in the minority at the 1919 party congress when the leadership set its sights on joining the new Communist International. Although the PSI won 156 seats in the November 1919 elections, Turati was blocked by party policy from using this strength constructively. Turati remained in a party that frittered away its opportunities and opened the door to Fascist reaction; only in October 1922, when the Socialist Party was completely irrelevant, did Turati's reformist faction finally break off to form the Unitary Socialist Party (PSU).

Turati watched helplessly as the Fascist dictatorship took hold in Italy. In December 1925 Anna Kuliscioff died; the next year a group of young socialists organized Turati's escape from Italy to France. Turati became active in exile politics, supporting the movement to reunify the PSI and PSU, which took place in July 1930. He died in Paris in March 1932.

See also **Giolitti, Giovanni; Italy; Kuliscioff, Anna; Socialism.**

BIBLIOGRAPHY

Di Scala, Spencer. *Dilemmas of Italian Socialism: The Politics of Filippo Turati.* Boston, 1980.

Miller, James Edward. *From Elite to Mass Politics: Italian Socialist in the Giolittian Era, 1900–1914.* Kent, Ohio, 1990.

ALEXANDER DE GRAND

TURGENEV, IVAN (1818–1883), Russian novelist, poet, and playwright.

Ivan Sergeyevich Turgenev, a Russian nobleman, was born on 9 November (28 October, old style) 1818 and grew up on his mother's vast estate, Spasskoye, in Russia's Orel Province. Both witness and recipient of his mother's arbitrary beatings, Turgenev grew to abhor tyrannical systems and violence of all kinds. He was graduated from St. Petersburg University in 1837. A subsequent momentous period of study at the University of Berlin solidified his belief that progress lay along the path of Westernization begun during the reign of Peter I (r. 1682–1725), rather than with purely Russian social forms as stipulated by the adherents of its countercurrent in Russian thought, Slavophilism. In Europe he also became acquainted with many future Russian intellectual leaders. Back in St. Petersburg, he published a long poem, *Parasha* (1843). In this same year he became acquainted with Pauline Viardot-Garcia, an operatic star who was married, and with whom he soon began a lifelong, probably unconsummated, liaison. Quitting the civil service to devote himself to literature, Turgenev published the long story, "Diary of a Superfluous Man" (1847), which, in a manner that was to be rather uncharacteristic of his work as a whole, depicted a self-deprecating, proto-Dostoyevskian type. Turgenev's play *A Month in the Country* (1850) influenced the development of Russian theater, in particular the dramatic art of Anton Chekhov.

"Diary" marks the beginning of Turgenev's literary focus on the intellectual debates of the Russian intelligentsia. In 1852 he was arrested for the publication of an obituary on Nikolai Gogol. Turgenev spent a month in police detention, then more than a year under house arrest. Perennially interested in social and political problems, he achieved notoriety for the publication—first serially in the journal *The Contemporary*—of a collection of sympathetic, realistic depictions of the peasantry titled *A Sportsman's Sketches*. The first, "Khor and Kalinich," sensitively contrasts two peasants' attitudes toward life, and its successful reception emboldened Turgenev to continue in this vein. Among the sketches, "Bezhin Meadow" epitomizes Turgenev's lyrical description of the natural world. *Sketches* was the first work to reveal the plight of the peasant class in Russia, and they contributed to Tsar Alexander II's decision to emancipate the serfs in 1861. In the 1850s Turgenev also wrote three novels, each of which reflects both important social issues of the period and Turgenev's ambivalent nostalgia for the romanticism of his youth. The well-received *Rudin* (1856) depicts a man of Turgenev's own genera-

tion; *A Nest of the Gentry* (1859) conveys an outsider's unsettling effect on a family; and *On the Eve* (1860) offers a portrait of a revolutionary hero. Also in 1860 Turgenev published an influential essay, "Hamlet and Don Quixote," whose literary typology divides heroes into two types: the self-conscious, introspective, and ironic Hamlets, and the idealistic Don Quixotes, who selflessly devote themselves to abolishing oppression. Two remarkably evocative love stories of this period are "Asya" (1858) and "First Love" (1860).

Turgenev's artistically accomplished but politically controversial novel *Fathers and Children* (1862; *Otsi i deti*)—sometimes translated into English as *Fathers and Sons*—unsentimentally depicts the conflict between the young generation of radicals and their conservative, Slavophile-leaning elders. By the 1860s, moderate Westernizers such as Turgenev were losing sway to a rising class of men who were neither nobles nor peasants. These so-called men of various classes (*raznochintsi*) were agitating—some with increasing violence—for social reforms. Credited with bringing the term *nihilism* into wide usage, *Fathers and Children* was rejected by liberals because it seemed to ridicule their cause, and by conservatives because it oversympathized with the radicals. The work's hostile reception shocked Turgenev, leading him to leave Russia permanently and settle in western Europe, first in Baden-Baden, then in Paris. Despite or perhaps because of his physical distance from his homeland, Turgenev's last novels, *Smoke* (1867) and *Virgin Soil* (1877), continued to reflect particularly Russian social problems. His final novel, *The Torrents of Spring* (1872), achieves poignant clarity, while the pessimistic *Poems in Prose* (1883) presages modernist stylistic innovations.

Turgenev became the first Russian writer to gain a wide reputation in Europe. He was a well-known figure in Parisian literary circles, where he had connections with Gustave Flaubert and Émile Zola. Warmly received by Anglophone society, Turgenev received an honorary degree at Oxford University, and exerted a strong influence on Henry James. *Virgin Soil*'s sympathetic treatment of the populist movement lifted Turgenev's reputation at home one last time. After a triumphant return to Moscow in 1880 for the unveiling of the monument to Alexander Pushkin, he returned to France and died in Bougival, near Paris, on 3 September (22 August, old style) 1883. Generally considered masterful evocations of nineteenth-century life, Turgenev's works remain widely read in Russia today.

See also **Chekhov, Anton; Dostoyevsky, Fyodor; Flaubert, Gustave; Gogol, Nikolai; Tolstoy, Leo; Westernizers; Zola, Émile.**

BIBLIOGRAPHY

Primary Sources

Beaumont, Barbara, ed. *Flaubert and Turgenev: A Friendship in Letters; The Complete Correspondence.* New York, 1985.

Turgenev, Ivan. *Polnoe sobranie sochinenii i pisem.* 28 vols. Moscow, 1960–1968. Definitive Russian edition of Turgenev's works.

———. *The Essential Turgenev.* Edited by Elizabeth Cheresh Allen. Evanston, Ill., 1994. Contains translations of *Rudin, A Nest of Gentry, Fathers and Sons,* and *First Love;* selections from *Sportsman's Sketches;* seven short stories; and fifteen prose poems. Also contains samples of the author's nonfiction drawn from autobiographical sketches, memoirs, public speeches, the essay "Hamlet and Don Quixote," and correspondence with Fyodor Dostoyevsky and Leo Tolstoy.

Secondary Sources

Allen, Elizabeth Cheresh. *Beyond Realism: Turgenev's Poetics of Secular Salvation.* Stanford, Calif., 1992.

Freeborn, Richard H. *Turgenev: The Novelist's Novelist.* London, 1960. Reprint, Westport, Conn., 1978.

Kagan-Kans, Eva. *Hamlet and Don Quixote: Turgenev's Ambivalent Vision.* The Hague, Netherlands, 1975.

Moser, Charles A. *Ivan Turgenev.* New York, 1972.

Waddington, Patrick. *Turgenev and England.* London, 1980.

SARAH A. KRIVE

TURNER, J. M. W. (1775–1851), English painter.

Born in London in 1775, the landscape and history painter J. M. W. Turner had a long, productive, and highly successful career, which evolved against a background of tumultuous political and social change in Europe. The son of a barber, Turner received little formal education but embarked on his career at a precociously young age, entering the Royal Academy Schools in 1789 and making his exhibition debut there in 1796, at the age of twenty-one, with his painting *Fishermen at Sea.* Despite his reclusive tendencies, Turner played an important role in the artistic politics of the period and participated actively in the institutional and social life of the Royal Academy, holding the post of professor of perspective between 1807 and 1837. Secretive about his working methods and private life, he never had pupils but was often generous with advice to his fellow artists.

Turner traveled extensively in Britain and the Continent, documenting with an acute eye both scenes of everyday life and events of broader political significance. Although patriotic and intensely interested in contemporary events, Turner rarely articulated his views on politics and seldom addressed controversial issues directly in his work, perhaps in order not to alienate his patrons. He preferred subtle allusion, often literary in nature, over overt reference. His extensive body of work nonetheless constitutes a penetrating chronicle of the political and social landscape of Europe during the first half of the nineteenth century and an eloquent articulation of contemporary ideas of nationhood.

The wars with Napoleon (1793–1815) played a crucial role both in the development of Turner's career and in the evolution of British landscape art. Between 1799 and 1815, recreational travel on the Continent was highly restricted and Turner was forced to delay his visit to Italy, which was regarded as an essential component of an artist's education, until the cessation of hostilities. He eventually embarked on the trip in 1819, when he was over forty. In 1802, the year he was elected as a full member of the Royal Academy, Turner took advantage of the respite offered by the short-lived Peace of Amiens and traveled to France and Switzerland. In Paris he made sketches and detailed notes of Old Master paintings looted by Napoleon and exhibited in the Louvre.

In Britain during the Napoleonic Wars, necessity and patriotism created a renewed interest in the indigenous landscape. Turner undertook a series of sketching tours of Britain, which provided raw

The Burning of the Houses of Lords and Commons, October 16, 1834. Painting by J. M. W. Turner, 1834.

material for a large output of paintings and water-colors, many of which were engraved and published. His designs for *Picturesque Views on the Southern Coast of England* (1814–1826), a series of line-engravings focusing on the area of the country most vulnerable to French attack, celebrate the nation's military and economic strength, containing references to the forestry, ship-building, and sail-making industries.

Turner shared his contemporaries' fascination with Napoleon, whose extraordinary career spoke to his preoccupation with the theme of rise and fall of civilizations. In 1812, the year of Napoleon's retreat from Moscow, Turner exhibited his monumental painting *Snow Storm: Hannibal and His Army Crossing the Alps,* drawing parallels between ancient history and contemporary events. Following the British victory at Waterloo

on 18 June 1815, many artists made pilgrimages to the battleground. Turner was forced by pressure of work to delay his visit until 1817, but the site made a profound impression on him. His 1818 painting *The Field of Waterloo* is a profound and unequivocally antiheroic response to the subject, depicting the relatives of the fallen common soldiers searching for their loved ones in the aftermath of battle.

Although Turner's political affiliations remain unclear, one of his closest friends, Walter Fawkes (1769–1825), was an ardent Whig, and libertarian sympathies, albeit often expressed through the filter of historical subject matter, seem to inform works such as *Dolbadern Castle, North Wales,* and *Northampton,* the latter implying support of the controversial bill for electoral reform spearheaded by the Whigs and passed in 1832. Turner was sometimes moved to comment more overtly on acts of inhumanity. His unexhibited canvas *Disaster at Sea* responded to the destruction of the female convict-ship *Amphitrite* in a storm on 1 September 1833, in which the entire cargo of 125 women and children, bound for Botany Bay, perished less than a mile from the French shore when the ship's captain rejected offers of assistance. In 1840, perhaps stimulated by the abolition of the slave trade in the British colonies in 1833, Turner exhibited his spectacular critique of empire and the slave trade, *Slavers Throwing Overboard the Dead and Dying: Typhoon Coming On.*

Turner lived and worked in London all his life, yet representations of the metropolis and references to its political life are surprisingly rare in his oeuvre, even though he witnessed there and depicted some of the most momentous events of his era, including the return of the *Victory,* bearing Nelson's body, after the Battle of Trafalgar in 1805, and the burning of the Houses of Parliament on 16 October 1834.

Of all the British landscape artists of the period, Turner was most fascinated by modernity. Alert to the aesthetic possibilities offered by industrial sites and aerial pollution, many of his acutely observed images, such as his 1816 watercolor of *Leeds* and *Keelmen Heaving Coals by Night* (1835), chart Britain's troubled transition from an agrarian to an industrial society. Turner was particularly interested in steamboats, which enabled him to travel more quickly and widely than was previously possible. Intellectually curious (as his fellow painter John Constable noted, he had "a wonderful range of mind"), Turner's eclectic range of scientific interests included meteorology, geology, perspective, and color theory, and his use of pigments was highly experimental.

Although his often arcane choice of subject matter and unconventional handling of paint often attracted adverse criticism, Turner was nonetheless regarded as the most significant painter of his time, and his work continues to exert an enduring influence, both in Europe and North America.

See also **Constable, John; French Revolutionary Wars and Napoleonic Wars; Romanticism; Slavery.**

BIBLIOGRAPHY

Bailey, Anthony. *Standing in the Sun: A Life of J. M. W. Turner.* London and New York, 1997. An excellent and readable biography.

Butlin, Martin, and Evelyn Joll. *The Paintings of J. M. W. Turner.* 2 vols. New Haven, Conn., and London, 1984. An exemplary catalog *raisonné* of exhibited and unexhibited paintings.

Gage, John. *J. M. W. Turner: A Wonderful Range of Mind.* New Haven, Conn., and London, 1987. A groundbreaking study, demonstrating the breadth and depth of Turner's intellectual interests.

Hamilton, James. *Turner's Britain.* London, 2003. An exhibition catalog exploring Turner's profound engagement with the social, political, and physical landscape of Britain.

Joll, Evelyn, Martin Butlin, and Luke Herrman, eds. *The Oxford Companion to J. M. W. Turner.* Oxford, U.K., 2001. An exemplary reference book written by team of distinguished Turner scholars; particularly relevant are articles on Chartism, the Napoleonic Wars, politics, and slavery.

Rodner, William S. *J. M. W. Turner: Romantic Painter of the Industrial Revolution.* Berkeley, Calif., 1997. A comprehensive account of Turner's concern with industry and technology.

Venning, Barry. *Turner.* London and New York, 2003. An insightful and readable introduction to Turner's life and work, situating the artist within his political, social, and artistic contexts.

GILLIAN FORRESTER

U

UKRAINE. The history of Ukraine begins with Kiev (Kyïv). In the Early Middle Ages, Kiev was the center of Kievan Rus, a trading domain that became an Orthodox Slavic state. Its civilizational base was the Old Church Slavonic language, written in Cyrillic characters, and a law code recorded in a modified form of that language. By the time the Mongols arrived in 1241, Kievan Rus had already been divided into competing principalities. In the fourteenth century the Grand Duchy of Lithuania absorbed most of the territories now known as Belarus and Ukraine. Lithuania became a largely Orthodox country, and Orthodox culture and law migrated from Kiev to Vilnius. Galicia, a western duchy of Rus, was annexed by Poland in the 1340s. Poland and Lithuania established a personal union in 1386. In 1569, when Poland and Lithuania established a Commonwealth, Ukrainian lands were transferred from the Grand Duchy of Lithuania to the kingdom of Poland. This created a new boundary among the lands that had once been Rus, between Belarus (which remained in Lithuania) and Ukraine (now in Poland).

THE COMMONWEALTH AND THE COSSACKS

Between 1569 and 1648 Polish rule animated Ukrainian civilization, but also provoked Ukrainian opposition. Reacting to the Reformation and Counter-Reformation, Ukrainian clerics published books and established academies, most importantly in Kiev. Ukrainian and Belarusian bishops initially supported the Union of Brest of 1596, which was designed to preserve the Eastern Christian rite within the Catholic Church. The church thus established was known as Uniate, and later Greek Catholic. This transformation was incomprehensible to the peasantry, which was increasingly exploited by a "second serfdom." The Cossacks, a native Ukrainian group of free warriors and fighters, constituted an important segment of the Polish army. As they were not noble, they could not take part as equals in the Polish-Lithuanian Commonwealth, a republic of nobles. In 1648 one of their number, Bohdan Khmelnytsky organized a rebellion against Polish rule. Cossacks and peasants murdered Poles and Jews, and Ukrainian peasants were murdered in their turn by Polish landlords.

As the war turned against the Cossacks, Khmelnytsky solicited help from Muscovy at Pereyaslav in 1654. Ukrainian Cossacks then fought with Muscovite armies against the Polish-Lithuanian Commonwealth, beginning the period in Polish history known as the Deluge. The Commonwealth conceded to Muscovy left-bank Ukraine (east of the Dnieper [Dnipro] River) and the city of Kiev, in a peace accord of 1667. Whereas Kiev had shared its medieval Christian achievements with Vilnius, it now imparted its renaissance and baroque attainments to Moscow. Kievan churchmen provided the reservoir of learning and ambition for Tsar Peter's reform of the Orthodox Church and spread European learning in Muscovy. The Cossacks, having freed themselves from Polish rule, tried to assert Polish-style rights for themselves within the Russian Empire. They also wished to preserve their own administration, known as the hetmanate, in left-bank Ukraine. Their ideas of reform clashed with those of Catherine II (r. 1762–1796), who wished to create a uniform state. She abolished the hetmanate in 1764.

The Cossacks made their case in Catherine the Great's legislative commission (1767–1768), referring as ever to the traditional rights of nobles in the Polish-Lithuanian Commonwealth. Yet Catherine had little need for groups of warriors living in an ill-defined relationship to central authorities. Military victories over the Ottoman Empire and the Russian annexation of the Crimea revealed that the Cossacks were of relatively little importance in war. The Zaporozhian Cossacks, free men living to the east of the old hetmanate, were eliminated by a Russian surprise attack in 1775. In 1781 Ukraine was divided, along with the rest of the empire, into provinces. In 1786 Ukrainian Orthodox dioceses were secularized, as were Russian dioceses before them. The Kiev Academy, which had taught a classical curriculum in Polish and Latin, was abruptly made into a theological school with Russian as the language of instruction. Conscription was introduced in 1789, ending any possibility for the creation of local fighting forces.

Catherine's state building, despite appearances, had much to offer the Cossack elite. Cossack officers became members of the Russian *dvorianstvo* (according to the 1785 Charter to the Nobility). As such they were able to press claims to own land and peasants. Ukrainian peasants became serfs, and the Jews were expelled from Kiev. With the creation of a state administration Cossack officers and their descendants found new opportunities for careers in the provincial capitals and indeed in St. Petersburg. In the last three decades of the eighteenth century, Ukrainian families filled the ranks of the Russian civil service and essentially dominated the (nonforeign) intellectual classes. They arrived in the Russian capital as Russia was partitioning Poland out of existence, in 1772, 1793, and 1795. The partitions brought right-bank Ukraine, west of the river Dnieper, into the Russian Empire. Of the old lands of Kievan Rus, only Galicia remained outside Russia, annexed in the partitions by Austria. As the nineteenth century began, almost the entirety of Ukraine was part of the Russian Empire.

EMPIRE AND NATIONS

As in Europe as a whole, so in Russia the extension of imperial rule coincided with the emergence of local patriotism. Kharkov University, founded in 1805, was intended to anchor Ukraine in Russia and transmit European scholarship throughout the empire. It served this purpose, but with the French Enlightenment it also brought German philosophy. Kharkov, perhaps the most important Ukrainian city at this time, was east of the old hetmanate, and can in no way be seen as directly transmitting Cossack traditions. Instead, scholars and students sought, like Romantics throughout Europe, to seize upon what was local and authentic, counterposing implicitly or explicitly tradition to progress. Taras Shevchenko (1814–1861), the greatest Ukrainian Romantic poet, drew from Polish and Russian models as he created a uniquely Ukrainian idiom. In 1846 the publication of the *Istoriia Rusov* (History of the Rus people) revealed the potential political implications of Romanticism. It treated the Cossacks, not Muscovy, as the true people of Rus, and the Russian Empire as an interloper in the heartland of the Slavs.

In the nineteenth century, left-bank and right-bank Ukraine were very different. In right-bank Ukraine, west of the Dnieper, Polish nobles remained the dominant class, despite the destruction of Poland itself. It was precisely in right-bank Ukraine that the early modern Polish system revealed itself in its most extreme form: a small number of Roman Catholic landlords owned vast estates and huge numbers of serfs. In some cases Polish families owned territories as large as small countries, and hundreds of thousands of serfs. In this system, Jews mediated between those who owned the land and those who worked it, between Polish lords and Ukrainian serfs. Although there were far more landless Polish nobles than there were great lords, and many more Polish peasants, those who stood atop the system were Poles. Precisely because this arrangement was so profitable, relatively few important Polish families joined in the Polish uprising of 1830 to 1831 against Russian rule.

Polish nobles in right-bank Ukraine nevertheless confronted a harsher Russian policy once the uprising had been defeated. The Commission on National Education, which had organized Polish-language schooling, was liquidated. The famous lycée in Krzemieniec was closed, its priceless library of thirty-four thousand volumes (which included the collections of the Royal Palace in Warsaw) sent to Kiev. About two-thirds of the Roman Catholic monasteries in left-bank Ukraine were liquidated after 1831. In 1840 the Lithuanian Statute was annulled, on the grounds that it was alien to Russian traditions. Here was the great irony of modernization. The first Lithuanian Statute (1529) flowed from the traditions of Kievan Rus. In form and in content, in language and in law, it represented an unbroken tradition of the Eastern Slavs. The Russian Empire, which claimed to be the inheritor of such traditions, liquidated them instead.

In left-bank Ukraine, St. Petersburg had confronted for decades the problem of "surplus" Polish nobles, men without means who clung nevertheless to their noble status. In the old Polish-Lithuanian Commonwealth, some very high percentage of the population, perhaps 10 percent, had been noble. Noble status required neither the ownership of land nor service to the state. Like the Cossacks of the right bank a few decades before, the petty nobles of the left bank referred to ancient rights, with the distinction that they and their families had indeed enjoyed such rights under the Commonwealth. After 1831, Russia moved to eliminate this troublesome group, which so ill fit the Russian notion of nobility. In the two decades after 1831, some 340,000 nobles were "declassified," leaving a total of perhaps 70,000 Polish nobles in left-bank Ukraine. Of these, only about 7,000 possessed great estates. Russian policy thus distorted further an already extremely exploitative society. Polish landholders then used Russian property law to expel poorer brethren from land they had tilled for centuries.

In their own way, these few Polish landlords preserved Polishness in these terrains, although it was an image of Polishness that denied all modern democratic ideas and could only provoke the local peasantry. St. Petersburg occasionally tried to use the Ukrainian peasantry against Polish landlords. Peasants who were encouraged by imperial promises, however, then had to be quelled by imperial soldiers. The abolition of serfdom in 1861 was received differently by Ukrainian peasants than by those in Russia: the Ukrainian peasants wished to receive their own individual plots. They did not in any case receive enough land to truly prosper, and did not understand that land reform would also mean the loss of rights to traditional use of common land. Polish landlords held their own against this pressure and against others. They circumvented Russian legislation banning the sale of land to Poles by leasing it to Jews. They deterred Russians from settling by humiliating them socially. They began small-scale industrial projects such as sugar beet refineries.

Over the course of the nineteenth century Kiev became a center of Ukrainian national society and Ukrainian intellectual life. The annexation of the right bank placed Kiev squarely between Russia's eastern and western Ukrainian territories. Kiev was a provincial capital, and increasingly a port of call for traders. It was a city that spoke Russian, Polish, and Yiddish rather than Ukrainian, but it was the center of hopes for those who began to think of Ukraine as a future political home. Like other university towns in imperial Russia, it became the center of a populist movement. In Ukraine, however, populism took on a particularly national character. Populists of Polish and Russian origin, when they "went to the people," realized that Ukrainian culture could not be reduced to Polish or Russian models. Some Polish students felt that their families had subjected peasants to both social and national exploitation. Some of them, such as the populist historian Volodymyr Antonovych, took up a Ukrainian identity themselves.

Especially after the Polish uprising of 1863 to 1864, Russian authorities assimilated the Ukrainian national question to a Polish plot. When the publication of books in Ukrainian and the use of the Ukrainian language were banned in the 1860s, this was a response to a perceived Polish threat. Ukrainian intellectuals, obviously, bore the brunt of this repression. Important scholars chose immigration, thereby transferring the ideas of Kharkov and Kiev farther west. In this way, in the 1870s, Ukrainian populist scholars animated a Ukrainian national movement in Austria, in the eastern portion of Austria's province of Galicia. Antonovych's student Mykhailo Hrushevsky, for example, was hired by Austrian authorities to teach east European history at the university in Lemberg in 1894. In Austria, starting in 1898, he published his

Ukrainian peasants at a market, Mukacheve, Ukraine, c. 1908–1914. ©SCHEUFLER COLLECTION/CORBIS

ten-volume masterpiece, *A History of Ukraine-Rus.* This foundational work of Ukrainian history was based on ideas developed and research completed in the Russian Empire, but could be published only beyond its boundaries. At the end of the nineteenth century Austria became the center of the Ukrainian national movement.

THE GALICIAN REVIVAL

The eastern half of Austrian Galicia was perhaps 65 percent Ukrainian in population, but such numbers mattered only when church and secular leaders began to attend to the peasantry. The most important institution of the Ukrainian national revival in Galicia, the Greek Catholic Church, was designed to serve entirely different purposes. The Greek

Catholic Church was the old Uniate Church, created in 1596 at Brest by Orthodox bishops who wished to preserve their Eastern rite in an institutional union with Rome. Although the Uniate solution never supplanted traditional Orthodoxy, the Uniate Church survived (paradoxically) as a separate institution. The partitions of Poland left most Uniate believers in the Russian Empire, but a considerable number in Austrian Galicia. While St. Petersburg merged the Uniate Church with the Russian Orthodox Church, Vienna preserved the church but changed its name to the Greek Catholic Church. Austrian Empress Maria Theresa meant to underline thereby that the church was the equal of the Roman and Armenian Catholic Churches in Galicia, and emphasize the distinction from Orthodoxy.

Until the middle of the nineteenth century, the Greek Catholic Church was loyal to the Habsburgs and faithful to traditions of Polish high culture. While a few of its priests experimented with Ukrainian lexicons and folklore, the church itself was hostile to such undertakings. In 1848 Austrian authorities called upon the Greek Catholic Church to help quell the revolution, in which Poles were taking part. Ukrainian peasants, dominant in numbers, were to frighten Polish nobles who requested home rule. This achieved, Vienna ignored the Greek Catholic hierarchy, which was disappointed to find the loyalty of its flock unrewarded. A fascination with Russia ensued, because Russia could present itself as an alternative to both Austria and Poland. After Polish nobles succeeded in gaining autonomy for themselves in Galicia in the late 1860s, the attraction of Russia as a counterweight increased. Greek Catholic Russophiles developed an ideology of themselves as a member of the family of Russian nations, writing in a mixture of Ukrainian, Old Church Slavonic, and Russian.

In the last decades of the nineteenth century, the reform of the Austrian electoral system rewarded those who could communicate directly with voters in their own language. The secular sons and daughters of priests realized that democracy required new kinds of political organization. Ukrainian populism imported from Russia played an important role in the articulation of a new secular politics. Ivan Franko, the most important of the new generation of activists, was greatly influenced by Mykhailo Drahomanov, a Ukrainian populist who had lost his professorship in Kiev. As in Russia, some of the important figures were converts from the Polish nation. Andrii Sheptytsky, the Ukrainian who turned the Greek Catholic Church into a popular national institution, was born a Pole and a Roman Catholic. He ascended to the metropolitan see of Galicia in 1900. In the early years of the twentieth century, Ukrainian national activists competed with Polish nationalists and socialists for political influence in a Galicia that was governed by the Polish nobility on behalf of the Habsburg dynasty.

The successive enlargement of the franchise and the freedom to publish in national languages favored the development of a Ukrainian-Polish national competition, one that sharpened skills and sensitivities on both sides in the early years of the twentieth century. Ukrainian parties that allied with Polish or Jewish rivals for tactical reasons displayed the experience gained from sophisticated national politics. Nothing similar could take place in the Russian Empire of the early twentieth century. During the Russian Revolution of 1905, Ukrainian demands were limited to autonomy. Before World War I, very few Ukrainians in the Russian Empire advocated national independence. Galician Ukrainian activists regarded "Great Ukraine," the lands to the east in Russia, as part of a future united state. The Russian census had revealed to them the vast domains of the Ukrainian population to their east. Their goal was national unity, as achieved earlier by the Italians and the Germans, as planned for also by the Poles. Galicia was seen as the first and crucial land of a general national revival.

See also **Austria-Hungary; Cossacks; Nationalism; Peasants; Poland; Russia.**

BIBLIOGRAPHY

Beauvois, Daniel. *Le noble, le serf, et le revizor: La noblesse polonaise entre le tsarisme et les masses ukrainiennes, 1831–1863.* Paris, 1985.

———. *La bataille de la terre en Ukraine, 1863–1914: Les Polonais et les conflits socio-ethniques.* Lille, France, 1993.

———. *Pouvoir russe et noblesse polonaise en Ukraine, 1793–1830.* Paris, 2003.

Hrycak, Jarosław (Hrytsak, Iaroslav). *Historia Ukrainy, 1772–1999: Narodziny nowoczesnego narodu.* Lublin, Poland, 2000.

Kappelar, Andreas. *Russland als Vielvölkerreich: Entstehung, Geschichte, Zerfall.* Munich, 1992.

Markovits, Andrei S., and Frank E. Sysyn, eds. *Nationbuilding and the Politics of Nationalism: Essays on Austrian Galicia.* Cambridge, Mass., 1982.

Miller, Alexei. *The Ukrainian Question: The Russian Empire and Nationalism in the Nineteenth Century.* Budapest, 2003.

Rudnytsky, Ivan L. *Essays in Modern Ukrainian History.* Edmonton, Alta., Canada, 1987.

Saunders, David. *The Ukrainian Impact on Russian Culture, 1750–1850.* Edmonton, Alta., Canada, 1985.

TIMOTHY SNYDER

ULM, BATTLE OF. The Battle of Ulm (September–October 1805) was the opening round of the War of 1805, fought between Napoleon I and the Third Coalition of Austria, Russia, Britain, and Sweden. The conflict arose primarily from conflicts between Napoleon, Russia, and Austria over measures Napoleon had taken both to secure his own position in France and to strike at Great Britain, with which he had been at war since March 1803. The immediate sources of conflict in 1805 were in Italy, a fact that played an important role in shaping the military campaign.

The allied war plan for the late summer of 1805 involved a coordinated effort: vast armies attacking France from the Adriatic to the North Sea. The largest Austrian army, commanded by Archduke Charles, would attack in Italy. Another Austrian force, nominally commanded by Archduke Ferdinand but actually controlled by its quartermaster general, Baron Karl von Mack, would seize Bavaria and await the arrival of Russian reinforcements commanded by General Mikhail Kutuzov before invading France via Switzerland. Still other forces were to make landings in Naples and Hanover, while large Russian armies attempted to compel Prussia to join the coalition as well.

Napoleon did not initially recognize the gathering storm clouds. He was intent upon his plans for the invasion of England and the final preparations of the Army of the Channel at Boulogne with which he intended to destroy his ancient nemesis. The emperor also believed that he had sufficiently cowed Austria during the War of the Second Coalition (1798–1801) that he need not fear it in 1805. When he learned in late August that the French fleet would not be able to seize the English Channel to permit his invasion of England, Napoleon decided to strike the coalition instead, hoping that by punishing Austria he could gain time to renew his war with "perfidious Albion."

He therefore directed the bulk of the newly rechristened "Grande Armée" to race from its camps along the Channel to the Rhine, while the corps of Marshal Jean-Baptiste Bernadotte, which was occupying the British territory of Hanover, would rush south, through Prussian territory, toward the Upper Danube. At first, Napoleon did not know what the Allies' intentions were. He sought only to drive into Bavaria as rapidly as possible to protect or, if necessary, restore his ally, Maximilian I, the elector of Bavaria, to his threatened throne. The emperor's initial war plan, therefore, would have precipitated a head-on collision with the advancing Austrian army. As the Grande Armée approached its final positions on the Rhine in late September, however, Napoleon realized that Mack's Austrian army had advanced all the way to the Iller River, far to the west. He saw a corresponding opportunity to drive into Mack's rear and cut his army off from its lines of communication and retreat. Adjusting his plans of movement accordingly, Napoleon enveloped Mack's right flank.

The success of that maneuver hinged on the movement of Bernadotte's corps (and two others) through the Prussian territory of Ansbach, while the Prussians had declared themselves in a state of armed neutrality. Mack did not expect or believe that Napoleon would violate Prussian neutrality, and thereby risk bringing more than 200,000 first-rate troops into the field against him. Mack had therefore taken no steps to guard his right wing, enabling Napoleon's forces to drive rapidly into Mack's rear and force the Austrians back toward Ulm in a series of confused battles along the Danube. By 14 October, the Austrians were sealed in the dilapidated fortress of Ulm itself, ringed by French troops and with no hope of escape. Mack agreed on 17 October to surrender his army by the twenty-fifth, although the date was subsequently moved up to the twentieth at Mack's request.

Napoleon's violation of Prussian territory had, in the meantime, had the effect of bringing Prussia into the war. At Potsdam in early November, King Frederick William III signed an agreement with Tsar Alexander I of Russia to strike Napoleon's exposed army along its flanks and rear. The Prussians began a rapid mobilization and deployment to effect this plan, which was suspended by the Treaty of Schönbrunn signed by Prussian co-foreign minister, Count Christian von Haugwitz, on 15 December, thirteen days after the Battle of Austerlitz at which Alexander and his remaining Austrian allies were defeated.

The Battle of Ulm was not a masterpiece of prior planning and skillful deception, as it is sometimes made out, but rather a masterpiece of skillful and decisive adaptation to changing circumstances. Napoleon's initial plans were to do more or less what Mack expected him to do, although with much greater force. He devised the plan for the final, brilliant maneuver only after he had seen the Austrian deployment. He thereby seized an opportunity that a confused enemy had presented to him. Moreover, Napoleon was able to do so only by sacrificing the future security of his army. He had not reckoned on Prussian hostility following the violation of Ansbach, and so did not understand the full danger to which he exposed his army at a strategic level in order to gain an operational advantage over the enemy at hand.

See also **Armies; Austerlitz; French Revolutionary Wars and Napoleonic Wars; Napoleon.**

BIBLIOGRAPHY

Duffy, Christopher. *Austerlitz, 1805.* London, 1977.

FREDERICK W. KAGAN

ULRICHS, KARL HEINRICH (1825–1895), German homosexual emancipationist, lawyer, journalist, and author.

In the written and spoken word, Karl Heinrich Ulrichs was the first person to demand not just the decriminalization of homosexual practices but also the complete legal equality of homosexuals and heterosexuals. A man ahead of his time, he came out publicly as a homosexual in 1867 and envisioned a political and sociocultural movement of homosexuals organized to demand their rights as an oppressed minority. Unable to rally any substantial solidarity among the homosexuals of his era, he left Germany for voluntary exile in Italy.

Ulrichs's ability to imagine homosexual emancipation and his maverick willingness to challenge authority was surely in part a matter of individual temperament but may also have derived from his family heritage in Frisia, the coastal region straddling Holland, Germany, and Denmark that is the only part of Germany that remained free of feudalism in the Middle Ages. He was born on 28 August 1825 in Aurich, the foremost Frisian city, as the son of an architect in the civil service of the king-

dom of Hanover. Following the study of law at the Universities of Göttingen and Berlin, Ulrichs began a promising judicial career in Hanover in 1848. Six years later, however, his homosexual proclivities came to light, and he chose to resign from the civil service rather than face certain dismissal. He moved to Frankfurt am Main, where he worked as a newspaper journalist and as an administrative assistant for a delegate to the German Confederation.

In 1864 Ulrichs published the first of a series of twelve small books that appeared under the collective title *Investigations into the Riddle of Man-Manly Love.* In language that was closely reasoned and legalistic but at times also impassioned and immediately accessible, this wide-ranging set of books surveyed the domains of law, religion, medicine, history, literature, and current events in an almost encyclopedic effort to assemble all available information on homosexuality, challenge homophobic prejudice, and muster support among homosexuals themselves. These books—the first five appeared in 1864 and 1865—led to a far-flung correspondence with homosexuals throughout Germany and abroad, and they document Ulrichs's own growing knowledge about homosexuality, drawing on data and leads he received from his correspondents.

THE "THIRD SEX" THEORY

Ulrichs began with the assumption that virtually all homosexuals shared his delicate features, which he himself described as feminine, as well as his boyhood interest in girls' pastimes and their colorful clothing, which contrasted vividly with the increasingly drab men's dress of his era. His first awareness of homosexual interests came at age fifteen, followed by a full recognition of his orientation at twenty-one, and he frankly described his erotic fascination with laborers clad in working-class garb and soldiers decked out in colorful uniforms. His contacts with his contemporaries soon convinced him, however, that beyond effeminate homosexuals of his own stripe there were fully masculine ones as well as butch and femme lesbians, and he eventually came to recognize bisexuality as a valid sexual category.

Despite his acknowledgment of a panoply of sexual orientations and types, Ulrichs basically maintained his "third sex" theory of homosexuality, according to which gay men are endowed at birth with a female anima (which might be translated as spirit, psyche, or soul) and lesbians are endowed with a male one. He coined the word *Urning* for a homosexual, drawing on the speech by Pausanias in Plato's *Symposium* in which the origins of same-sex and opposite-sex love are attributed to the two avatars of the love goddess, one being the motherless daughter of Uranus, and the other the daughter of Zeus and Dione (thus *Dioning* was Ulrichs's name for heterosexuals). The term *Urning*, occasionally rendered in English as *Uranian*, had some European-wide currency for a few decades but was ultimately edged aside by adoption of the term *homosexual*, which was likewise coined in the 1860s. Ulrichs argued that the natural, innate quality of homosexuality meant that it was unjust and pointless to punish it, and he compared the persecution of homosexuals with that of witches in earlier centuries, confident that growing enlightenment would ultimately lead to homosexual equality.

ANTI-PRUSSIAN ACTIVISM

Ulrichs's publication series was halted by the wars of German unification spearheaded by Otto von Bismarck. A local patriot, Ulrichs was twice imprisoned in 1866 for opposing the Prussian invasion and annexation of Hanover. His house was searched and his papers, including a manuscript collection of homosexual poetry, were confiscated. Shortly after his second release from prison, he traveled to Munich to deliver an address on homosexual rights at the 1867 Congress of German Jurists. His call for the repeal of sodomy statutes in the various German states was roundly shouted down by the entire outraged audience.

Following his aborted speech in Munich, Ulrichs resolved to come out publicly as a homosexual to the entire German nation. "As Urnings, we should and must present ourselves without a mask. Only then will we conquer ground to stand on in human society; otherwise, never" (Ulrichs, vol. 1, p. 123). Whereas his first five books had appeared under the pseudonym Numa Numantius, his sixth, published in 1868, was published under his own name, as were his six subsequent volumes on homosexuality that appeared between 1869 and 1879. Banned from Hanover, Ulrichs moved initially to southern Germany. These books documented a growing international network of homosexuals

and an increasing knowledge of the homosexual subculture, including the slang and practices of his era in Germany, England, and elsewhere. He criticized the homophobia of the majority but also lamented the cowardice of his fellow homosexuals.

Ulrichs was bitterly disappointed when Prussia, with its harsh antisodomy statute, became the foremost state following national unification in 1871, which led in the following year to the imposition of Prussia's criminal code throughout Germany. Ulrichs left Germany for voluntary exile in Italy in 1880, and here he spent the last fifteen years of his life cultivating the revival of Latin as a universal language. His grave is in Aquila, Italy, where he died on 14 July 1895.

In Aquila, Ulrichs was visited by John Addington Symonds (1840–1893), who provided a sympathetic portrait of Ulrichs as an individual along with a useful précis of his third-sex theory in *A Problem in Modern Ethics* (1881). In Germany, Richard von Krafft-Ebing (1840–1902) credited Ulrichs with first drawing his attention to homosexuals, these "stepchildren of nature" (Ulrichs, vol. 2, p. 512), and Sigmund Freud (1856–1939) commented, albeit disparagingly, on Ulrichs's theory in his *Three Essays on Sexuality* (1905). Magnus Hirschfeld (1868–1935) admiringly noted that Ulrichs single-handedly developed virtually the entire platform of the homosexual emancipation movement that finally came into being at the close of the nineteenth century, including proposals of a homosexual journal, a national petition to repeal the antisodomy statute, and even a "bond of love" or civil union "analogous to" heterosexual marriage (vol. 1, p. 234). In their private correspondence, Karl Marx (1818–1883) and Friedrich Engels (1820–1895) commented on Ulrichs's writings, remarking that "the pederasts" were beginning to count themselves and to notice that they formed an organizable minority.

Although he estimated that homosexuals constituted just 0.2 to 0.4 percent of the German adult male population, Ulrichs indeed recognized that homosexuals constituted a minority that could demand its "inalienable . . . civil rights" from "despotic majorities" (vol. 2, pp. 605, 547). He fully anticipated the identity politics of the late twentieth century by placing homosexuals on a par with other oppressed minorities and reminding his fellow homosexuals of their duty to practice solidarity "on the side of the victims of violence and abuse: whether they are called Poles, Hanoverians, Jews, Catholics" (vol. 2, p. 547). By the early twenty-first century, German homosexual activists had successfully lobbied to have streets in Aurich, Hanover, Bremen, and Munich named in his honor.

See also **Freud, Sigmund; Hirschfeld, Magnus; Homosexuality and Lesbianism; Krafft-Ebing, Richard von; Symonds, John Addington.**

BIBLIOGRAPHY

Primary Sources

Ulrichs, Karl Heinrich. *The Riddle of "Man-Manly" Love: The Pioneering Work on Male Homosexuality.* 2 vols. Translated by Michael A. Lombardi-Nash. Buffalo, N.Y., 1994.

Secondary Sources

Kennedy, Hubert. "Karl Heinrich Ulrichs: First Theorist of Homosexuality." In *Science and Homosexualities,* edited by Vernon A. Rosario, 26–45. New York, 1997.

———. *Karl Heinrich Ulrichs: Pioneer of the Modern Gay Movement.* 2nd ed. San Francisco, 2005.

JAMES D. STEAKLEY

UMBERTO I (1844–1900; ruled 1878–1900), king of Italy.

Born 14 March 1844, Umberto received the rank of captain on his fourteenth birthday. He held a series of military commands beginning in October 1862 and saw action at Custoza against Austria in 1866. He married his cousin Margherita, daughter of Ferdinand, the duke of Genoa, on 22 April 1863. Umberto became king of Italy when his father, Victor Emmanuel II, died on 9 January 1878. Departing from his father's example, he ignored the legacy of the House of Savoy and took the title Umberto I rather than Umberto IV. Just ten months after he assumed the throne, the anarchist Giovanni Passanante tried to stab him (17 November 1878). Umberto escaped unscathed, but twenty-two years later another anarchist succeeded in killing him.

King Umberto inherited the challenges of establishing the infrastructure, laws, and institutions for the newly united Italian state and of securing its place among the powers of Europe. Political factionalism and the strains of economic modernization produced increasing tension and tumult during his reign. To popularize the monarchy, Umberto traveled widely in Italy, and he regularly visited the sites of earthquakes, floods, and epidemics to comfort the victims. His efforts to connect with the people earned him the label "the good king." But Umberto did not limit his duties to ceremony. He played a role in turning Italy away from France and toward an alliance with Germany and Austria-Hungary, using his personal ties with fellow monarchs to smooth the way. He also encouraged Italy's imperialist ambitions in Africa.

The king's role in domestic politics produced controversy at the time and in historical assessments of his reign. He accepted a series of weak cabinets directed by prime ministers of the left, including Agostino Depretis, Benedetto Cairoli, and Francesco Crispi. In the 1890s these governments faced agrarian and urban discontent and the growing power of the Socialists. Alarmed industrialists and landowners supported the suspension of constitutional guarantees to enforce public order. In a context of rapidly fluctuating majorities and weak cabinets, Umberto allowed prime ministers to legislate by royal decree. The persistent weakness of parliament caused influential lawmakers such as Sidney Sonnino to call for the return to even stronger royal authority.

In 1898 high bread prices intensified popular agitation, and in May an insurrection broke out in Milan. The government imposed martial law and General Fiorenzo Bava Beccaris restored order, with considerable loss of civilian life. Despite the outrage of socialists, republicans, and anarchists, on 9 June 1898 the king proclaimed his gratitude to the soldiers, decorated Bava Beccaris for merit, and named him senator (16 June). Hoping for a firm government, he then appointed a military man, General Luigi Pelloux, prime minister. Pelloux ended martial law and presented to parliament proposals curbing freedom of press, meeting, and association. When deputies of the left tried to obstruct their passage, Pelloux suspended the parliamentary session (22 June 1899) and imposed the public order laws by decree (28 June 1899). The following year the courts nullified the decrees, and new elections (3 June and 10 June 1900) returned a majority favorable to the government. Pelloux resigned anyway, and the king appointed the moderate Giuseppe Saracco to replace him.

This "liberal about face" ended conservative efforts to bypass parliament and to revitalize government by reinforcing royal power. In the view of some historians, Umberto had endorsed what amounted to a legal coup d'etat during the turn-of-the-century crisis. Others criticize his passivity in the face of parliamentary weakness and the autocratic initiatives of politicians such as Crispi. When he inaugurated the new parliament on 16 June 1900, Umberto underscored his intention to maintain the commitment with which he had begun his reign: the defense of constitutional liberties. Six weeks later, on 29 July 1900, Gaetano Bresci, a silk worker and anarchist, killed Umberto at Monza, proclaiming that renewing Italy began with eliminating its symbolic head. Judgments of Umberto vary, and while few credit him with saving the monarchy or accuse him of destroying it, most concur that his actions caused serious discussion of its merits.

See also **Italy; Victor Emmanuel II.**

BIBLIOGRAPHY

Primary Sources

Farini, Domenico. *Diario di fine secolo.* Edited by Emilia Morelli. Rome, 1961. Provides an inside look at political life from a close advisor of King Umberto.

Secondary Sources

Alfassio Grimaldi, Ugoberto. *Il re "buono": La vita di Umberto I e la sua epoca in un'esemplare ricostruzione.* 5th ed. Milan, 1973.

Mack Smith, Denis. *Italy and Its Monarchy.* New Haven, Conn., 1989.

SUSAN A. ASHLEY

UNIFICATION, ITALIAN. *See* **Risorgimento (Italian Unification).**

UNITED KINGDOM. *See* **Great Britain.**

UNIVERSITIES. In the first half of the nineteenth century, higher education in Europe underwent changes that resulted in the establishment of divergent institutional systems. Beginning in the 1870s, however, a new consensus began to emerge, based on an ideal that combined teaching and research that accelerated the exchange of knowledge, teachers, and students across the Continent.

CHANGES IN THE MAP OF EUROPEAN UNIVERSITIES

In 1790 there were 143 active universities in Europe. As the century came to a close, and over the first half of the nineteenth century, major changes started to occur that, to begin with, affected Germany, France, and Russia.

Germany, France, and Russia: Revolution in the university   Of the thirty-five German universities existing in 1789, with a total of seventy-nine hundred students, eighteen disappeared during the Revolutionary period. On the other hand, three new institutions were founded, in Berlin (1810), Breslau (1811), and Bonn (1818). Prussia hoped that these would help buttress the control it recovered after 1815 over extremely heterogeneous lands now stretching from part of conquered Poland to the Catholic Rhineland.

The French university landscape was even more radically altered. A string of revolutionary laws and decrees issued between 22 December 1789, when universities were subordinated to the départements, and 7 Ventôse Year III (25 February 1795) quite simply swept away colleges and faculties of theology, medicine, the arts, or law founded in the Middle Ages. Under the Consulate (1799–1804) and Empire (1804–1814), French higher education was integrated into a highly restrictive central administrative framework from which all local institutional autonomy was completely absent. Professional faculties (three of medicine and three of law for the whole empire in 1804) and academic faculties (of arts and letters and of science) were all brought under the authority of a central administration known as the "Imperial University." Fortunately, the Napoleonic regime spared certain major institutions considered to be genuine seedbeds of scientific innovation. Some of these dated from the *ancien régime*, such as the

Jardin du Roi, turned into a museum in 1793, and the Collège de France; some had been founded during the Revolutionary period, such as the Conservatoire des Arts et Métiers, the Institut de France, and the School of Oriental Languages; and others were long-established elite training establishments such as the École Polytechnique for civil and military engineers, the Saint-Cyr military academy, and the École Normale for the training of university teachers.

In Russia too the transformation of the university system was rapid and carried out from above. Moscow University itself was founded early on, in 1755. Between 1803 and 1819, however, as many as five Russian universities came into being: Kazan (1804); Kharkov (1805); Dorpat (Tartu), formerly a German institution, became Russian in 1802; Vilna (1803), transferred to Kiev in 1835; and St. Petersburg (1819). In the second half of the nineteenth century, universities in Odessa (1865), Tomsk (1888), and Saratov (1909) were established. To these institutions should be added very many higher technical schools, chiefly in Moscow.

Elsewhere in Europe, however, the growth of universities was far slower.

Slow progress in northwestern and southern Europe The British Isles were especially conservative. In 1800 there was one university in Ireland, namely Trinity College in Dublin; four in Scotland; and two—the University of Oxford and the University of Cambridge—in England. This deficit was gradually mitigated by local endeavors with no overarching plan: by 1901, Durham (1832), London (1828; reincorporated 1836), Manchester (1851), and twelve other "civic universities" had gradually been established in the larger English cities. And, thanks to reforms made in Scotland in 1858 and at Oxford and Cambridge in 1877, it is possible to say that a real university system, rather than the isolated colleges of an earlier time, had come into existence in Great Britain before 1914.

As for the Mediterranean region and northern and eastern Europe, it is hard to blame traditionalism for the delayed progress of higher education. Governments in these areas tended to create new, more functional institutions as a response to social and political pressures, the result being a highly unbalanced distribution of facilities. Before 1871,

the Italian states as a whole possessed twenty-one establishments of higher learning, but these varied dramatically in size and were distributed in a way that failed to reflect real needs: northern and central areas were overserved, whereas from the academic standpoint the south was a near-desert utterly dominated by the giant University of Naples.

By contrast, a centralized country such as Spain was able to rationalize its university map gradually during the nineteenth century. A number of the institutions of the old regime were simply closed down between 1807 and 1845, with no attempt being made to revitalize them. Just ten universities remained, each covering a district conceived on the model of France's "circumscriptions." After the transfer of the main institution from Alcalá de Henares to Madrid in 1836, the nationwide network suffered, just like that of France, from the crushing weight and privileges of what in the official terminology was called the "Central University."

Smaller countries also, notably the Netherlands, Belgium, Switzerland, and to a lesser degree the countries of Scandinavia, met with much difficulty in their attempts to bring a measure of rationality to their university systems. As in the modern period, religious traditions and national, even regional, rivalries meant that these sparsely populated states had a disproportionate number of institutions relative to their actual needs. In the wake of Belgium's independence, two new universities were founded, a liberal and secular one in Brussels and a Catholic one in Malines (both in 1834). The reorganization of 1835, however, left the country with just four universities: two state institutions, in Ghent and Liège, an independent university in Brussels, and a Catholic one in Louvain.

The map of Scandinavian universities went through analogous revisions in response to political changes and the requirements of scientific innovation. The achievement of autonomy, and then independence, by such new states as Norway and Finland enabled them to develop systems of higher education clearly distinct from those of their former protectors, Denmark and Russia, respectively. The ancient universities in Scandinavia were Copenhagen, founded in 1479, and, in Sweden, Uppsala (1477) and Lund (1666). To these was added the University of Christiania (Oslo); founded in 1811, six years after Norway became independent of Denmark, it was to be the center of Norwegian nationalism. Similarly, the elevation of Finland to the status of a grand duchy dependent on the Russian Empire was followed by the transfer of the University of Turku to Helsinki (1828).

Change in the university and political change in central and eastern Europe

In the early modern period, central and eastern Europe was a region with little in the way of a university system. This traditional pattern, however, was gradually transformed by virtue of the expanding national and liberal movement, the training of local elites in western Europe, the birth of new states, religious and ethnic rivalries, and a growing desire to catch up with the more developed parts of Europe. A few signs of intellectual subordination or archaism nevertheless survived until after World War I, as witness the continuing flow of students sent to Germany and France from most of these new nations.

The western part of the Austrian Empire (Cisleithania) was undoubtedly the best served region, with six ancient universities at the beginning of the nineteenth century, to which almost as many advanced technical schools were added in the first half of that century. This picture underwent very few modifications thereafter, except for the division of the University of Prague into two autonomous institutions, one Czech and the other German, in 1882; the creation of the University of Agram (Zagreb) in Croatia in 1874, with philosophy, theology, and law faculties; and the founding of the University of Czernowitz (now Chernivtsi, Ukraine) in 1875.

As for the eastern portion of the empire, Transleithania, its sole university was founded in Nagyszombat (now Trnava, Slovakia) in 1635 then moved to Buda in 1775 and then to Pest in 1784. The university could award doctorates but offered only partial programs of technical instruction and specialized law and theology courses. New universities were eventually established around the turn of the nineteenth century, as was consistent with the country's development.

A very different path was taken by higher education in partitioned Poland, which would not regain its independence until 1918. Throughout the nineteenth century, Polish elites were educated for the most part in foreign universities. Students from the Prussian province of Posen (Poznán) attended the universities of Berlin and Breslau and, being barred from administrative posts, tended to take up Catholic theology. In Austrian Galicia, however, there were two predominantly Polish university towns, Kraków and Lemberg (now L'viv, Ukraine). The most repressive university system was in the Russian-dominated "Congress Kingdom of Poland." From 1831 to 1862, the University of Warsaw was in effect closed in reprisal for the 1830 uprising. During those years, Polish students were thus obliged to go to Russia—to Kiev or St. Petersburg. After 1864 the University of Warsaw was Russified, becoming in effect a sort of private free university. This institution had to struggle to survive, and indeed it lost all autonomy in 1869. In the latter part of the nineteenth century, Polish elites preferred to educate their young people abroad, in clandestine establishments or, more and more, in the Polish-speaking and relatively independent Galician universities. The most oppressed group of all were Jews aspiring to higher education but confronted by both Russian and Polish anti-Semitism.

On the fringes of Europe, Greece, Bulgaria, and Romania provide examples of the simultaneous emergence of the modern university and the modern nation under strong foreign influence—Bavarian or German for the first two, French for the third. In such small rural countries the founding of a university in the capital was one of the chief symbols of an independence eventually won after long centuries of cultural oppression. From the outset, the new kingdom of Greece, with Otto, son of the king of Bavaria, at its head, sought to buttress its national identity by establishing a university in Athens. Inaugurated on 3 May 1837, it was to serve for the rest of the century as a rallying point for the Greek diaspora living under the Ottoman Empire (more than 40 percent of students at the University of Athens were born outside Greece's borders).

In Romania, the creation of the University of Iași (1860) through the expansion of an academy dating from 1835 was followed in 1864 by the founding of the University of Bucharest on the basis of three preexisting faculties (arts, sciences, and law); a medical school was added in 1869 and a department of theology in 1884. These two institutions reflected the desire of the Moldo-Wallachian elites to emancipate themselves from dependence on ancient centers of learning abroad that had trained the ruling class until that time. As a small country speaking a romance language, however, Romania maintained its links to France, and most of its future university teachers and a significant proportion of its students, especially in law and medicine, continued to complete their education in Paris.

EUROPEAN UNIVERSITY SYSTEMS

The first seventy-five years of the nineteenth century thus saw the rise of university systems in Europe that differed greatly according to their location. This may be explained in part by the upheavals and reorganizing already mentioned, and in part, too, by the survival of long-standing cultural traditions. The two most radically distinct approaches, which for the sake of convenience are referred to here as the "Napoleonic" and "Humboldtian" systems, were instituted almost simultaneously and represented opposing responses both to critical historical contingencies and to the intellectual and pedagogical debates of the Enlightenment.

The Napoleonic system Though constructed almost from scratch, the Napoleonic system of higher education extended certain eighteenth-century innovations (the vocational schools) while rejecting the universalizing ambitions and new departures of the radical phase of the French Revolution. The intent was to endow the state and postrevolutionary society with the framework needed to stabilize a country turned upside down, to exercise a tight control over education in accordance with the new social order, and to prevent the emergence of a sphere of intellectual freedom too large and dangerous for the state to handle. This enlightened despotism accounts for the predominance of the "school" model (even when the term *faculty* was used), the tyranny of state diplomas governing the right to exercise a specific function or profession, the importance placed on grading and competition even in courses of study that did not necessarily call for them, the regimentation of curricula, and the conferment of degrees by the state alone. The system implied a strict division of labor among faculties and a high measure of educational specialization. In consequence all essential

research and innovation was confined to the large establishments—to a few departments of the Sorbonne or the Collège de France or to the academies and learned societies. This explains the chief shortcoming of French higher education, namely the overconcentration of resources and manpower in Paris.

This unegalitarian logic was also reflected in the hierarchical relations among teachers: because a portion of their remuneration was in the form of examination rights, teachers in the vocational schools with their large intake and those in Paris with its abundance of candidates had unfair advantages. This inequity was exacerbated by the ability of professionals, notably teachers of law and medicine, to supplement their incomes through extramural activity. Professors of arts and science subjects, meanwhile, often sought to increase their revenue by cumulating teaching or administrative functions, which had an exploitative effect on substitutes and adjuncts.

The Humboldtian system The new university system promoted by Wilhelm von Humboldt (1767–1835) was conceived in explicit opposition to the Napoleonic approach. Under its sway the philosophy faculty was assigned equal if not superior status to other departments. The philosopher Friedrich Schleiermacher (1768–1834) defined the university in this context as that place where masters and fellow students assemble between *school* (in the sense of secondary education, viewed as a coming together of masters and apprentices) and *academy* (meaning an assembly of masters among themselves).

This ambitious intellectual ideal explains the categorical rejection of French-style vocational and specialized schools, which turn their back on what the German model considered the true purpose of the university, namely to awaken the individual to knowledge, to adopt an encyclopedic approach, and to offer a free choice of studies (*Lernfreiheit*). Nevertheless, even though the organization of the University of Berlin was certainly influenced by these ideas, it would be an error to assume that its structure conformed strictly to the myth of the "Humboldtian system" as later constructed by German academia.

To begin with, research played a distinctly subordinate role in the new system, and the particular relationship between teaching and research that was subsequently deemed one of the chief distinguishing features of the Prussian approach came into being only slowly and in an uneven manner depending on place and discipline. As for another hallmark of the German system, much admired by foreign observers, namely the use of the *privatdocent* (an assistant professor who gives lectures to students without being tenured and is directly paid by them) in the training of future teachers, it should be pointed out that this arrangement was by no means as widespread as is often assumed. The real basis of the dynamism of the German system (or more accurately systems) was perhaps that, being less rigid than any other, it was able to benefit from nineteenth-century intellectual and social advances. Decentralization indeed allowed for local initiatives that might later, imitated or imported, spread to other universities. Student mobility obliged institutions to adapt according to demand, and this created a process of emulation that was by definition absent from unified and centralized states such as France. All these features are primarily the result not of any concerted approach but of a history based on the division of Germany into several different states.

Nor should one overlook the persistence of older traditions (differing religious practices according to region, the continuing subordination of philosophy departments in southern Catholic states such as Bavaria) or the enduring wish of the sovereign of the German states to retain political control over "their" universities. In 1819, for example, the conference of German states in Karlsbad decided that the universities should be subject to political surveillance in view of a growing liberal student movement, the *Burschenschaft*. The concern of the states was only increased by the degree of student participation in the 1848 movement for German unification. The supposed competitiveness of the academic market within a multipolar system unique in Europe was nonetheless vulnerable to corruption through persistent nepotism in recruitment, especially in the smaller universities. Inasmuch as the state, in order to meet the demand for teachers, resorted to the creation of extraordinary, low-paying and nontenured positions for teachers or *privatdocenten*, this arguably served as a spur to

young researchers whose work had to be truly distinguished if they were to join the professoriate. On the other hand, the appointment process remained prone to biases of a social kind into the twentieth century; in the conservative Protestant states, for instance, Catholics, teachers considered too liberal, and—a fortiori—Jews were persistently discriminated against or even excluded from the academy.

The vocational crisis of the German system

During the latter part of the nineteenth century, when the German university system was being imitated across Europe and elsewhere in the world, the system itself was undergoing a crisis. This reflected several problems related to social and intellectual changes: the difficulty of incorporating the most modern scientific and technical culture, the aristocratic corporatism of the teachers, the lagging professionalization of certain career paths, and so on. This was a crisis of growth—and a crisis in the academy's sense of vocation.

After stagnating between 1830 and the mid-1860s, the German student population had multiplied by a factor of five (to sixty-one thousand) by 1914. In the main, this growth benefited the smaller universities and the philosophy faculties. For the first time the number of arts and science students surpassed that of law students, while the tally of theology students in 1914 was a full half lower than in 1830. Higher education was changing, shifting its emphasis from traditional avenues such as the clergy or the civil service to more modern careers such as college teaching, scientific research, engineering, and the technical professions. In parallel to the universities a network of *Technische Hochschulen* (polytechnics) was set up—ten in all by the beginning of the twentieth century. Their student population more than tripled from five thousand in 1871–1872 to seventeen thousand in 1903; university enrollment doubled during the same period. These technical colleges were disparaged by those in traditional universities, and it was only thanks to the intervention of Emperor William II in 1899 that they obtained the right to bestow doctorates.

The new generation of students tended to be drawn from less middle-class, less cultivated backgrounds than its predecessors, and student attitudes were more pragmatic. Students were now less taken with the Humboldtian ideal, for they were seeking an education tailored to very precise career goals, and this often gave rise to misunderstandings with teaching staff who for their part were increasingly specialized, detached from the surrounding society, and prone to indulging nostalgia for a Germany that was no more.

The burgeoning student population alarmed conservatives fearful of the rise of what Otto von Bismarck called a "proletariat of bachelors." The absence of regulation with regard to enrollment probably did produce numbers of students in law, medicine, and arts and sciences that at some point became disproportionate to the society's needs.

As for the system's vocational crisis, it was an even more pointed threat to the German approach than uncontrolled expansion, because it precipitated an internal dislocation of the universities. The Humboldtian ideal was meant to help educate distinguished young men of the solid bourgeoisie or nobility. But once the universities were populated in the majority by young people (including, from the early nineteenth century on, young women and foreign students) whose concern was to maximize the future profitability of their university careers, the orientation of higher education was bound to veer toward utility and specialization. After 1871 the governments of German states gradually accepted this tendency, structuring their institutions and courses of study in accordance with the new needs of an industrial society. They also fostered ties between scientific research and the economy. These new priorities were bound to throw the earlier German ideal model of the university into question.

The crisis also affected those supposed to embody and uphold the Humboldtian ideal, the university professors themselves. The untenured were often in the majority, notably in the sciences and in medicine, but they did not always participate in collective faculty decisions. This imbalance made career advancement slower and more arduous and fed a discontent that erupted before World War I in the movement of the *Nicht-Ordinarien*. The proliferation of untenured teachers cannot be explained solely by the financial advantage governments stood to reap from the availability of lower-paid employees. It was related also to the increasing prestige of professorships, which were more and

more eagerly sought after, and to the growing specialization of disciplines, whose new branches would typically be entrusted to young untenured teachers. These factors accelerated innovation, but they were also a source of intellectual frustration. They meant, for one thing, that new entrants to the system needed to dispose of private means while waiting for promotion or occupying lower-level positions.

Meanwhile, institutional autonomy was increasingly jeopardized by state intervention in appointments and even more by the growing financial dependence of the universities on public funding for the equipment needs of scientific and medical research and even for research grants and library resources in the humanities. The "freedom and solitude" of the ideal Humboldtian professor had scant prospect of survival in institutes where collective projects held sway or in universities collaborating closely with captains of industry.

Austro-Hungarian exceptionalism Austro-Hungarian higher education presented a far more traditional aspect than the German universities. After the expulsion of the Jesuits in 1773, the central government administered the entire system, including the non-German-speaking parts, under the *Ratio educationis* law of 1777. Remnants of medieval tradition, such as "student nations" and the "assembly of the doctors," and the survival of absolutist tendencies into the 1850s, also impeded the introduction of German-style reforms. The university system thus had a strictly functional goal, namely the provision of the human cogs—priests, functionaries, or teachers—needed by a heterogeneous empire. Education was thus governed in every detail from above, in sharp contrast to the pedagogical freedom gradually spreading in Germany. With the exception of the Vienna Faculty of Medicine, Austrian universities were scientifically backward. The 1848 revolution, in which Viennese and Hungarian students were very active participants, obliged the authorities to experiment with the Prussian model (Count Leo Thun Von Hohenstien's reform), albeit in an authoritarian version that remained in place until around 1860. Under this arrangement higher education was extended by two years, while students in the preparatory years no longer entered institutions of higher education until they had passed a "maturity examination" (or baccalaureate). The philosophy faculty thus achieved parity with other departments, as in Germany. The government eliminated student nations and associated teachers' remuneration with the number of students enrolling in their courses. The opening up of the academic market through the hiring of more *privatdocenten* and the recruitment of teachers from Germany created a competitive situation that over time raised scientific teaching standards.

The chief peculiarity of the Austro-Hungarian system lay, however, in the obstinate survival up until World War I of professional (and especially law) faculties: 45.7 percent of Viennese students in 1860 and as many as 53.8 percent in 1909 were law students; in Hungary the proportion was close to 60 percent.

British systems It makes little sense to speak of a single university "system" in the British Isles. The characteristics of English universities on the one hand and Scottish on the other were the product less of any state plan than of compromises between centuries-old traditions and long-postponed reforms. To this picture must be added new institutions, privately or locally conceived, that addressed shortcomings in the existing establishments and were thus governed by the logic of local conditions rather than by an overarching idea, as in France or Germany.

For most of the nineteenth century, a clear distinction has to be drawn between the Scottish universities and the two ancient English universities of Oxford and Cambridge. The Scottish institutions were much more closely akin to universities on the Continent because they depended on the state for most of their financial support. Their doors were open to students from modest backgrounds, they imposed neither residence nor the tutorial system, and they were far more concerned with teacher training than the "colleges" of their English counterparts. Reformed before the English universities by virtue of two royal commissions (1826 and 1876) and two acts of Parliament (1858 and 1889), the Scottish universities took the lead in educating students in the new disciplines and preparing them for professions other than the clergy. As early as the 1820s, their total student population was large, totaling 4,250, whereas Oxford and Cambridge together had less than one thousand undergraduates. The reason was twofold: the simultaneous presence within the Scottish universities of adolescents of fourteen or fifteen, "lads o'parts" drawn directly from parochial schools, and young men of twenty or thirty years of age; and a generous scholarship system. The flexibility of curricula and attendance even made it possible to combine studies with work. While a humanist culture continued to dominate at Oxford and Cambridge and while vocational training in England, as a practical matter, was provided outside university walls, the Scottish universities, like those of most European countries, combined the two functions.

At the start of the nineteenth century, Oxford and Cambridge differed in every particular from the Scottish universities. They had barely emerged from a long period of stagnation stretching over the best part of the previous century. By about 1829, with 840 admissions annually, they had returned to their seventeenth-century level. The requirement that students reside in the colleges, the high cost of enrollment, the absence of vocational preparation other than clerical, and the refusal of admission to non-Anglicans placed further limits on expansion. The gradual introduction of formal examinations (the Tripos), especially at Cambridge, produced a corresponding improvement in the quality both of the teaching and of the students. The complete independence of these ancient universities vis-à-vis the state was founded on their vast landholdings and on their close relationship with the Church of England. Their ideal of an educated man was still that of a well-rounded *honnête homme* (honest man), and moral context continued to count as much as scholarly content. Thus the teacher–student ratio was kept much higher than in continental Europe. At Oxford, for example, there was a teacher for every nineteen students in 1814 and for every sixteen students in 1900. It is true that competition for "honors" introduced a kind of meritocracy and bestowed social markers, so to speak, of future success.

Even before religious restrictions were lifted, dissidents got around them in 1828 by instituting the first non-Anglican college in London, namely University College, destined to become one of the core components of the University of London. The

Protest against the admission of women to Cambridge University c. 1880. Separate women's colleges had been established at Cambridge in 1869 and 1872, and women were granted academic degrees after 1880, despite protests such as the one pictured here. ©HULTON-DEUTSCH COLLECTION/CORBIS

Anglicans of the capital responded in 1831 by founding King's College. The Whig government recognized both colleges in 1836 in setting up the University of London, licensed to deliver degrees on students in London institutions. As early as 1850, two hundred candidates took advantage of this method of circumventing the constraints of the traditional universities. The new university thus introduced another level of heterogeneity into British higher education, for London was not residential like Oxford and Cambridge ("Oxbridge"), nor was it unified like the Scottish establishments.

A third phase in the evolution of the British higher education system was constituted by the creation of the "civic universities" mentioned earlier, which had purely practical goals and philanthropical or local funding, and by the long-deferred reform of the ancient universities, where a few features of the German system were eventually introduced.

Russia between Humboldt and Napoleon In Russia, the beginning of the nineteenth century saw the establishment of a system of secondary and higher education. The new universities were modeled on the German system. The first teachers were in fact Germans or Russians trained in Germany, notably at Göttingen. The most contradictory aspect of the new system, an aspect that would endure as long as the Russian Empire itself, was that these institutions, devoted in principle to science and theoretically rather autonomous, were nevertheless assigned the task, after the fashion of France's *grandes écoles*, of training civil servants. This ambiguity was reflected in an alternation between liberal periods facilitating Westernization and the politicizing of student youth and periods of repression and militarization precipitated whenever the authorities felt they had been too permissive.

The first such reactionary moment came in the 1830s in response to the European and Polish revolutionary events of 1830 to 1832. The statute of 1835 obliged students to wear uniforms and follow regimented curricula while teachers were forced to defend the Orthodox religion, autocracy, and nationalism. The tumult of 1848 in Europe sparked a new militarization of the Russian universities. Rectors were now to be appointed, the teaching staff was purged, the content of courses became liable to prior vetting, enrollment fees were increased so as to reduce the number of students, and students were subjected to military training and strict pedagogical control. Disciplines perceived as dangerous (such as constitutional law and philosophy) were eliminated. By the early 1860s, however, the return to a more liberal administration had begun.

Initially intended as they were to train a nobility integrated into the state, the Russian universities accepted but a small proportion of poorer students. In Moscow in 1862, 71 percent of students were children of the nobility or of eminent functionaries—actually up from the 65.9 percent estimated for 1831.

In theory at least, the teaching system was very rigorous, calling for twenty hours of obligatory course work per week, a pass-or-fail yearly examination, and a maximum of six years of study to finish the nominal four-year program. Selection was not very strict in practice, however: more than two-thirds of students were graduated and received the title of *kandidat*.

TRANSFORMATIONS AND CONVERGENCE OF EUROPEAN UNIVERSITY SYSTEMS

Sociologists and historians of education have described the period from 1860 to 1914 as one of diversification, expansion, and professionalization of higher education. These three tendencies were accompanied by the growing influence of the German system as a model for reform in countries whose universities had remained traditional. Convergence was nevertheless only partly realized because of the persistence of national and regional particularities.

France: Incomplete reform (1868–1904)

In France during these years two main concerns, the need to develop the research function within the faculties, as in the German system, and the

need to restore balance to a vastly overcentralized structure, joined forces with a mood of intense national self-examination prompted by the defeat of the Franco-Prussian War (1870–1871) to spur on the movement for reform.

In 1868 the first concern was addressed when Victor Duruy (1811–1894) founded the four sections of the École pratique des hautes études, so creating teaching laboratories and a place where knowledge was transmitted by means of specialized seminars that broke from formal courses intended for a wide audience (the main form of teaching in the faculties). The second concern, the need for decentralization, took longer to address. A solution required local support from the provincial cities, a new inflow of teachers (teaching positions nearly tripled between 1865 and 1919), and much increased financial resources (faculty budgets more than tripled between 1875 and 1913). Most universities were reorganized or expanded during this time. An improved balance was achieved, too, between vocational and academic faculties, bringing things closer to the German model in this regard. The greatest challenge was the administrative reform embodied in the law of 1896 that grouped faculties together as universities. As was consonant with their status as civil institutions, these new entities had elected governing councils, controlled a portion of their budgets, and were empowered to create and eliminate professorial posts and to receive endowments. In a word, they could innovate.

Convergence with the German system was nevertheless incomplete. The decentralization failed to impinge seriously on the dominance of Paris: 43 percent of all French faculty students were still to be found in Paris in 1914, as compared with 55 percent in 1876. Paradoxically, the decision finally taken to transform all groups of faculties into universities, even in small towns, prevented the emergence of major regional centers capable of competing with Paris.

All the same, the reform must be credited with the diversification of the subjects on offer and a reduction in the average age of teachers, who now fell into several different categories.

The university reform was less successful in the vocational faculties, and it failed to challenge the enduring hold of an elite system of higher education over recruitment to top technical and administrative positions. So far from losing their importance, the schools of this system multiplied, keeping most of their privileges. After 1870 they were reinforced by commercial schools, as well as new engineering schools and schools of administration. Catholic faculties created after 1875 also developed vocational training opportunities.

The development of the British universities

This period was also decisive for British universities, which experienced their most radical reforms since the Middle Ages. England's two ancient universities were obliged by parliamentary action to adapt to the modern world: non-Anglican, female, and foreign students were at last admitted in the 1870s, when they were permitted to enroll outside the college system. Meanwhile college fellows were gradually given permission to marry. From this point on, therefore, a genuine academic career became a possibility, because university teaching was no longer merely a stepping-stone to the clergy or to the liberal professions. In consequence the population of Oxford and Cambridge grew considerably. The range of subjects taught, still confined at midcentury to the classics and to mathematics, opened up now to the sciences, history, law, and foreign languages. Research too now had a place, especially at Cambridge, after a gift from the Duke of Devonshire made it possible in 1871 to create the Cavendish Laboratory, where part of the future British scientific elite would be trained.

The most significant changes in the British academic landscape nevertheless occurred outside Oxbridge, as the new civic universities grew in number in the provincial cities, their purpose being to train the new managers needed by an industrial and urban society. Until these universities were granted full independence by royal charter, their students received their degrees through the University of London, an establishment that itself expanded very greatly as more and more specialized institutions were federated under its aegis in a somewhat abstract manner. The resulting "exploded" university obtained its real charter only in 1898.

The other change that underlined the break with the Middle Ages was the state's ever-increasing financial stake in institutions that had hitherto subsisted either on their inherited wealth (Oxbridge) or on the support of private or municipal benefactors (the provincial universities). This departure was initiated in 1889, and by 1906 state aid had already reached £100,000, a by no means negligible sum, albeit much inferior to university apportionments on the Continent (from the 1890s on, for example, France disbursed four times as much to its fifteen groups of faculties).

The Scottish universities depended even more on the state. They were granted £72,000 yearly from 1892, to which were added funds for building, endowments from local businesspeople to create chairs of practical interest, and, beginning in 1901, a gift worth £100,000 per annum from the Scottish-born American industrialist and philanthropist Andrew Carnegie.

The social background of university entrants continued to reflect great elitism at Oxbridge, but for the new universities and above all for the Scottish institutions the picture was considerably more egalitarian, and thus closer to the continental pattern. In 1910, for instance, 24 percent of university entrants at the University of Glasgow were children of manual workers, and 20 percent those of small shopkeepers, artisans, and office workers; at Oxford these two categories together accounted for a mere 10 percent of student intake, although they constituted 90 percent of the active population in Britain. This discrepancy in the level of social discrimination between the two kinds of universities had a financial underpinning: in Scotland, fees were low, scholarships plentiful, and the primary and secondary education network well developed; in England, by contrast, Oxbridge students continued to be drawn mostly from the high-fee public (i.e., private) schools, while some two hundred pounds per annum, roughly equivalent to the entire income of a middle-class family, was needed to fund an Oxbridge student. And in 1910 no more than 7 percent of English students received scholarships (predominantly young people supported by local municipalities interested in their pursuing technical careers).

Austria-Hungary: The attraction of Germany

It was during the second half of the nineteenth century, too, that the Austro-Hungarian Empire and the newly developing Balkan nations began in their turn to feel the gravitational pull of the

German model. Their universities belonged in a sense to two worlds: they were modern, and close to the German academy, inasmuch as German-speaking teachers and students were continually circulating through the western part of the empire and even reaching Budapest; but at the same time they were still archaic in many ways, still characterized by the backwardness of largely rural countries where careers for professionals lay in the civil-service, judicial, ecclesiastical, or medical spheres far more often than in the scientific or literary ones. The eighteenth century's enlightened despotism had left a concrete legacy in the shape of many well-established advanced technical schools. But the whole system was subject to unusual stress on account of the national and religious origins of its students, drawn as they were from populations of great diversity. Another difficulty arose from the pressure, strongest in the east, for students to migrate westward to Vienna, to the German or Swiss universities, or even, in the latter part of the period, to Paris, a trend that deprived many new institutions of the most highly motivated individuals.

The universities of the Austro-Hungarian Empire gradually won the right to teach in national languages. They thus became seedbeds of national freedom movements, which naturally tended to block convergence with the German system and with international intellectual life.

The Hungarian universities had a number of special traits, notably the predominance of law studies, a privileged avenue so favored by the ruling class that Hungary was dubbed "a nation of lawyers." The explanation for this lies in the development of a Magyar bureaucracy after the Compromise of 1867 and by the new prominence of the legal profession in a liberal economy. The petty and middle-level Hungarian nobility, with its land rents in decline, used law training as a way of monopolizing positions in the state apparatus. By the end of the century this monopoly was being challenged by commoners, especially by Jews who were able to take advantage of bloated university law schools where rather easy requirements made it possible to combine legal studies with other activities. By the same token, such easy access to law courses facilitated the assimilation of Germans and Slavs into the dominant ethnic group.

Switzerland: Gradual expansion During this period Switzerland slowly developed an approach to higher education that was unique in three respects. In the first place, there was no nationwide university system, because each establishment depended on a particular canton that had a free hand with respect to education. Second, because the canton authorities were directly involved in the governance of the university, institutions were immediately affected by political developments. Third, the independence of cantons notwithstanding, the nearness of Swiss university towns to one another meant that competition always had to be reckoned with when striving to attract students from a single linguistic catchment area; rather as in the German system, this was a powerful spur to productive rivalries. An original—albeit almost unavoidable—way to fund the conversion of the old Swiss academies created by the Reformation into true universities (including research facilities), was the opening of the door to foreign students and (unusually early) to young women. Even before 1914, female students constituted a fifth of the total Swiss student population, more than twice their proportion in France at that time. As for foreign students, their percentage in Geneva was very high: 44 percent in 1880 and 80 percent in 1910; for all Swiss universities their numbers were not much lower: 47 percent in 1900 and 53 percent in 1910. All these rather unusual characteristics made Switzerland's small universities into innovators when compared with peer institutions in neighboring countries.

Italy and Spain: The difficulty of reform Reform in the Italian university system proceeded alongside the construction of the national state. It was particularly elusive inasmuch as modern and medieval traditions weighed heavily on the system, while the unique role played by the Catholic Church in Italian society meant that any attempt at modernization meant contesting clerical privileges. The Casati Law of 1859 sought to centralize higher education after the fashion of the French system. It excluded the church from higher education but failed to eliminate small local universities inherited from medieval times.

With its seventeen complete or incomplete groups of faculties, post-unification Italy at the end of the nineteenth century seemed overendowed by comparison with France (fifteen groups) or Germany (twenty universities), especially since Italy's population was smaller and its territory only half as large. In addition, the Italian network was very unevenly organized: in the 1890s, for instance, eight universities had fewer than five hundred students among them, while in the following decade the student body at Naples alone numbered more than four thousand. The only notable reform, motivated by anticlericalism, was the abolition of theology faculties in 1873.

At the turn of the century, despite German influence, the system's long-standing defects remained, among them the predominance of law studies, the lack of independence for the smaller university centers, and hidebound teaching methods. The archaic character of the degree courses was at the root of significant unemployment among brainworkers and a predilection for civil-service posts that worked to the detriment of the sort of advanced technical training needed by a modern economy.

In the early 1900s, however, this last tendency was significantly reversed, thanks largely to private-sector initiatives. In response to the new industrial Italy's need for managers, business leaders, and technicians, public business schools sprang up, the private Bocconi University was founded in Milan (1902), and engineering schools were established in Milan (1863), Naples (1868), and Turin (1859). But teachers were still badly paid, precipitating a continual search for other sources of income—especially in law departments, often a springboard to politics.

Spain, like other Mediterranean countries, saw its higher education system fall dramatically behind that of the more advanced northern European nations in the latter half of the nineteenth century. Until 1900 the Spanish universities were plagued by some of the same problems as the French but in an even more chronic way. Those problems included overcentralization, skeletal staffing, bureaucratic administration, and lifeless teachers given to rote methods. The law faculties monopolized the majority of students. The central university of Madrid dominated the whole system because it alone could confer doctorates and because its teachers were better paid. Advanced technical schools supplemented the very traditional degree courses offered in the faculties.

Though overshadowed by the technical schools, the Spanish universities were very slow to welcome academic and modern disciplines. Two-thirds of teachers were underpaid and to ensure their futures were obliged to seek additional work or hope for transfer to Madrid.

The movement for reform was started by a modest group of teachers at Oviedo, the smallest university in Spain. They were inspired by measures taken from 1900 on by a new minister of public education, among them the opening up of faculties of arts and sciences to new disciplines, the introduction of the social sciences into law departments, and the establishment of scholarships. Chronic shortages of funds, however, limited such advances. The necessity of modernizing course content and attracting students from new sectors was addressed by adopting the English system of university extensions; this solution was initiated in the shape of public courses at the University of Saragossa in 1893, and later spread to other Spanish universities.

Russia: The impossibility of liberalization
Russian higher education during this period was inhabited by contradictory tendencies. On the one hand, in accordance with the Russian tradition of benevolent despotism, the state was striving to make the system into an integral part of the modernization and Westernization of the country. On the other hand, the reactionary tendencies of the autocracy reemerged from time to time in response to endemic revolutionary agitation, enforcing authoritarian measures designed to reassert control over universities viewed as hotbeds of subversive ideas and a threat to the social order.

The expansion in the student population during the period is even more striking in view of the very low initial tally: a total of five thousand students in nine universities in 1860 swelled to thirty-seven thousand students fifty years later. That this trend was unstoppable, despite restrictive measures (including quotas for Jews and those of modest means) passed in the wake of the assassination of Tsar Alexander II in 1881, is accounted for by the appeal of higher education in a society in which bureaucratic positions were the most prestigious of all. Aside from the study of law, which led to such positions, medicine also exerted a growing attraction in view of the country's immense health care needs and the perception that science was the prime weapon in the fight against poverty and ignorance. As a result of the rise of social aspirations in the middle and lower socioeconomic strata, the proportion of students of noble background dropped between 1865 and 1914 from 67 percent to 35 percent in the technical schools and from 55 percent to 25 percent in the universities. Meanwhile, aspirants from petty bourgeois, middle-class, or Jewish families who failed to enter higher education because of obstacles placed in their way by official policies were quick to go abroad, and indeed in great numbers, to obtain degrees. Thus Paris, Berlin, and the Swiss universities acquired large communities of Russian students whose number should really be added to the empire's official figures.

It was during this period too that women entered the Russian student population in force: in 1914–1915, women constituted 30 percent of all students in Russian higher education as compared with an almost negligible proportion in 1900.

Political agitation among students did not end with the century; rather, it continued to reflect the failure of the Russian system to adapt to the emerging modern society. The growth of student militancy was a response to the refusal of the authorities to recognize student associations and their recurrent reassertion of the most authoritarian regulations. The high point of student agitation was reached with the Revolution of 1905, when the universities served as centers of the mobilization that led to the general strike of October.

The growing inadequacy of the Russian university system was reflected in the fact that teachers in higher education, though drawn in the majority from privileged backgrounds (39 percent of them were nobles as late as 1904), inclined overall toward liberalism and reform. Their ideals were Humboldtian, even as tsarism continued to bar the way to the scientific freedom indispensable to progress. But both the statute of 1884, which sought to bring the universities back under control following the assassination of Alexander II, and an orientation toward vocational rather than scholarly and scientific goals were gradually brought into question in actual practice. The institution of *privatdocenten* in the German mold failed to produce the desired effect absent an adequate pool of

teachers. Mediocre remuneration and the difficulty of obtaining a post made an academic career unappealing. Between 1900 and 1914, the situation in the Russian universities deteriorated sharply for lack of revenues (the state met only 60 percent of the budget, the remainder coming from fees) and because the creation of teaching positions failed to keep pace with student enrollment. Ever-growing internal and external tensions (between tenured and untenured teachers, between teachers, students, and the authorities, and so forth) further contributed to the disorganization of a system that, despite a government commission set up in 1902, shrank in fear from any idea of reform.

CONCLUSION: A EUROPEAN SYSTEM?

Despite the multiplicity of university systems and the persistence of national and cultural differences, the last years of the nineteenth century saw the birth of a truly "European" university, albeit a university that was invisible and without institutional boundaries. Its basis was the incessant and ever-increasing movement not just of students but also of teachers between different cultural environments. For students such migrations represented ways of escape from the political and institutional obstacles that faced them in "backward" or oppressive countries, mostly in eastern and southern Europe. Teachers for their part traveled a good deal between the main centers, attending congresses, joining scientific associations, and setting up exchange programs. This invisible academy realized the Humboldtian ideal inasmuch as it was based on a true desire for knowledge, despite geographical or institutional obstacles, and on the freedom to teach and learn outside official curricula. The fact that students could choose between competing university centers was one index among others of the intellectual reach of those institutions, and hence of their capacity for innovation and excellence in particular disciplines. As for teacher exchanges, they attested to the intensity of intellectual relations between different linguistic and cultural regions, and to the strong influence of this country or that in a particular branch of learning. Even though it issued into the most murderous explosion of nationalism in European history, this period nevertheless suggested the possible shape of a reconstructed academic Europe firmly linked to the most ancient medieval traditions.

See also **Education; Humboldt, Alexander and Wilhelm von; Intellectuals; Intelligentsia; Professions; Schleiermacher, Friedrich.**

BIBLIOGRAPHY

Charle, Christophe, and Jacques Verger. *Histoire des universités.* Paris, 1994.

Jarausch, Konrad H., ed. *The Transformation of Higher Learning, 1860–1930: Expansion, Diversification, Social Opening, and Professionalization in England, Germany, Russia, and the United States.* Stuttgart, Germany, 1982.

Ringer, Fritz K. *Education and Society in Modern Europe.* Bloomington, Ind., 1979.

Rothblatt, Sheldon, and Björn Wittrock, eds. *The European and American University since 1800: Historical and Sociological Essays.* Cambridge, U.K., 1993.

Rüegg, Walter, ed. *A History of the University in Europe.* Vol. 3: *Universities in the Nineteenth and Early Twentieth Centuries (1800–1945).* Cambridge, U.K., 2004.

Schriewer, Jürgen, Christophe Charle, and Edwin Keiner, eds. *Sozialer Raum und akademische Kulturen: Studien zur europäischen Hochschul- und Wissenschaftsgeschichte im 19. und 20. Jahrhundert/A la recherche de l'espace universitaire européen: Études sur l'enseignement supérieur aux XIXe et XXe siècles.* Frankfurt am Main, 1993.

Schubring, Gert, ed. *"Einsamkeit und Freiheit" neu besichtigt: Universitätsreformen und Disziplinenbildung in Preussen als Modell für Wissenschaftspolitik im Europa des 19. Jahrhunderts.* Stuttgart, Germany, 1991.

Stone, Lawrence, ed. *The University in Society.* 2 vols. Princeton, N.J., 1974.

CHRISTOPHE CHARLE

UNKIAR-SKELESSI, TREATY OF.

On 8 July 1833, representatives of the Russian and Ottoman governments signed a "treaty of defensive alliance" in Unkiar-Skelessi (Hunkar Iskelesi), a suburb of Constantinople. The treaty consisted of two parts, a section of six articles in addition to a secret "separate article." The first section recorded the signatories' pledge of common defense and mutual aid "against all attack," in addition to consultation and cooperation in matters affecting each empire's "tranquility and safety." Unkiar-Skelessi confirmed the terms of the 1829 Treaty of Adrianople, which had concluded the Russo-Turkish conflict arising from the War of Greek Independence.

Now, Russian emperor Nicholas I (r. 1825–1855) promised to provide, when requested by the Sublime Porte (the Ottoman government), such forces as necessary to maintain Turkey's independence. For its part, the Ottoman government of Sultan Mahmud II (r. 1808–1839) would pay for provisioning these forces. The empires' representatives agreed that the treaty's terms would last for eight years, at which time they would discuss renewal. The treaty's "separate" and secret article modified the terms of the public document by stating that, to spare the expense of direct aid to Russia when the latter came under attack, the Sublime Porte would instead close the Dardanelles to any foreign warships "under any pretext whatsoever."

Unkiar-Skelessi closed one phase and began another in the history of the "Eastern Question"—that is, the international complications stemming from the Ottoman Empire's chronic weakness. The Greek revolution had inspired the Ottoman governor of Egypt, Mehmet Ali (1769–1849), to mount his own rebellion. In 1831, his French-trained troops invaded Syria under the command of his son Ibrahim Pasha (1789–1848). By the spring of 1833, Ibrahim's armies had seized Syria and were advancing on Constantinople. Unable to turn to Great Britain—where the government was embroiled in debates over the Reform Bill—the sultan reluctantly accepted Russian offers of military support, remarking that a drowning man would even cling to a serpent. In April 1833, 10,000 Russian troops landed on the Asian shore of the Bosphorus Straits. In May, Mahmud II and Mehmet Ali concluded a peace at Kutahia; the sultan ceded Egypt, Syria, Cyprus, and Adana to his vassal's control. Faced with the continuing presence of Russian troops, and amid potential tension created by the arrival in the Straits of French and British naval vessels, Mahmud II accepted the offer of an alliance extended by Nicholas I's emissary Count A. F. Orlov. The day following the treaty's signature, Russian troops received orders to withdraw, as Ibrahim Pasha's armies had returned to their new territories.

The treaty signaled a triumph for Russia's ideological and strategic interests, but provoked contention with Great Britain and France over the fate of the "sick man," as contemporaries called the Ottoman Empire. Nicholas and his advisors believed that they had protected a legitimate ruler against the forces of disorder, in keeping with their conservative view of international relations. Unkiar-Skelessi also assured Russia's ability to intervene in Ottoman affairs, in support of Nicholas I's wish to maintain a weak but unified neighbor on Russia's southern flank. These principles served as the basis of an agreement with Austria, signed at Münchengrätz in September 1833, thus resurrecting a Holy Alliance broken by the events in Greece. Russia's new dominance in Turkey also excited suspicions in London and Paris, especially after the terms of the treaty appeared in the British press in August 1833. British officials, particularly Foreign Secretary John Henry Temple, Lord Palmerston (1784–1865), feared Russia's larger designs, as well as the security of the route to India. French statesmen sought to bolster the position of their protégé Mehmet Ali.

The Eastern Question re-emerged with new urgency in April 1839, when Mahmud II sought revenge from Mehmet Ali by invading Syria. Within months his armies were routed, his fleet defected to Egypt; Mahmud II himself died, leaving the throne to his adolescent son Abdul Mejid (1823–1861). The new crisis led to an Anglo-Russian rapprochement arising from two missions to London by Russian diplomat Ernst Brunnow (Brunnov), who offered to allow the lapse of Unkiar-Skelessi and other concessions. This turn allowed for an international intervention in support of Ottoman integrity and an end to the conflict by late 1840. In July 1841, Unkiar-Skelessi was replaced by a convention on the Straits signed in London by Russia, Britain, France, Prussia, and Austria. The new convention stipulated that in peacetime the sultan would admit no foreign warships into the Straits. It also brought a temporary pause to Anglo-Russian tensions over Ottoman affairs.

See also **Eastern Question; Holy Alliance; Metternich, Clemens von; Münchengrätz, Treaty of; Ottoman Empire; Russo-Turkish War.**

BIBLIOGRAPHY

Florinsky, Michael T. *Russia: A History and an Interpretation.* New York, 1953.

Hertslet, Edward, Sir. "Treaty of Unkiar-Skelessi." In *Map of Europe by Treaty*, vol. 2, 925–928. London, 1875–1891.

Marriott, J. A. R. *The Eastern Question: An Historical Study in European Diplomacy.* Oxford, U.K., 1917.

Rich, Norman. *Great Power Diplomacy, 1814–1914.* New York, 1992.

Schroeder, Paul W. *The Transformation of European Politics, 1763–1848.* Oxford, U.K., 1994.

DAVID M. McDONALD

UTILITARIANISM.

One of the foundational doctrines of modern ethics in relation to political philosophy and public administration, utilitarianism has since the late eighteenth century pursued the implications of a number of interconnected ideas. These include the claim that the promotion of pleasure and avoidance of pain are the chief springs of human action, from which it was thought to follow, allowing for considerable complexities of measurement, that the concept of *utility* could be defined for each individual as the maximization of his or her happiness. The function of governments aiming to enhance public utility, it was argued, thus consisted in promoting "the greatest happiness of the greatest number." Since such propositions were believed to accord with psychology, utilitarians contended that their doctrine was superior to classical, Christian, and natural law conceptions of virtue or duty, which were articulated only as abstract ideals. In putting forward policies they held to be beneficial and expedient, utilitarians judged that what should be done required assessments of human conduct's tangible consequences and less attention than had been given by other thinkers to its arcane motives. Their ethics therefore placed greater emphasis on manifest standards of the good than on presumed notions of what was intrinsically right.

EIGHTEENTH-CENTURY ORIGINS

These beliefs, as articulated by Jeremy Bentham (1748–1832), James Mill (1773–1836), and John Stuart Mill (1806–1873), owed much to both ancient and modern sources, including Greek sophists' denial of the existence of moral absolutes on the grounds that man is the measure of all things, as well as Epicurean portraits of our species' hedonism, Hobbesian conceptions of felicity, and French empiricist and materialist accounts of human nature's malleability. It was only in the late eighteenth and early nineteenth century, however, that utilitarianism came to be developed as a systematic doctrine amenable to implementation by progressive rulers and radical political movements alike. This was partly because it was in this period of European intellectual history that admirers of the seventeenth-century scientific revolution undertook to extend its scope from natural phenomena to human affairs, endeavoring to formulate a science of man that also included a science of ethics and government. Utilitarianism served that purpose admirably. It was designed to promote strategies of public policy based on an empirical understanding of human nature, to derive values from facts and to dispose of all prescriptions that masqueraded prejudice and intuition as truth. To define both individual and public utility it required no strictures of Christian altruism nor, apparently, any suppression of men's and women's actual ambitions.

If in these respects it seemed to provide a more democratic ethos than any competing philosophy and was hence suitable for an age of self-government, it in fact took root in the public domain in the late eighteenth century largely because progressively minded kings and queens embraced it. Although utilitarianism was to achieve its apotheosis in England in the course of the nineteenth century, many of its principles, and especially its commitment to legislative reforms designed to promote public happiness, were first adopted in regimes already at the time portrayed as examples of enlightened despotism. Frederick II of Prussia's (r. 1740–1786) prohibition of torture and Joseph II's (Holy Roman emperor, 1765–1790; and Habsburg ruler of Austria, 1780–1790) abolition of serfdom were each inspired by utilitarian doctrines as interpreted by German and Austrian proponents of *cameralism* who, like Bentham and his followers in England, sought to reorganize government's structures and functions to make it more rational and accountable to the public interest. In France physiocratic ministers and advisors of King Louis XVI (r. 1774–1792) likewise set themselves the task of reforming feudal systems of agriculture and trade, to avert an already perceptible crisis of the old regime that would in time provoke the French Revolution of 1789.

In both theory and practice eighteenth-century utilitarianism was perhaps more concerned with alleviating suffering than with securing happiness in a positive way, its chief proponents of the period addressing their attention above all to the criminal law. Cesare Beccaria (1738–1794) made the distinction between crime and sin and the insusceptibility of religious beliefs to political enforcement central pillars of his tract of 1764, *On Crimes and Punishment,* where the expression "the greatest happiness of the greatest number," makes its first printed appearance (in Italian) in a work of political theory, although it had been anticipated by Francis Hutcheson (1694–1746) in 1725 in his *Inquiry into the Original of Our Ideas of Beauty and Virtue.* Torture, argued Beccaria, served no rational purpose in the affairs of a civilized state, since it could not deter future crimes and only managed to brutalize its victims, propositions soon taken to heart by Voltaire (François-Marie Arouet; 1694–1778) in his own denunciations of the violence of religious bigotry sanctioned against Protestants by the Catholic Church in France.

In his *Fragment on Government* of 1776 Bentham invoked Hutcheson's and Beccaria's formulation of the expression that would come to be regarded as his legacy and to encapsulate utilitarianism's meaning, by this time given currency as well in Joseph Priestley's *Essay on the First Principles of Government* of 1768. In 1789, in his *Introduction to the Principles of Morals and Legislation,* Bentham elaborated his conception of utility at greater length. Like Beccaria, he was initially most concerned with policies warranting the minimization of pain. In the late 1780s and early 1790s he developed a scheme for the reform of Britain's prison system through a strategy of benign surveillance, termed *Panopticon,* whose disciplinary character in the absence of physical violence would come to be regarded by Michel Foucault (1926–1984) as one of the modern state's insidious bureaucratic trappings. While most utilitarians after Bentham have been committed to liberal ideals, they have often been charged with inconsistency on the grounds that their principle of aggregating benefits for "the greatest number" is inescapably hostile to individual freedom.

NINETEENTH-CENTURY UTILITARIANISM
Bentham welcomed the French Revolution and was eventually nominated a citizen of France, but he at first sought reform through philanthropy and

not democracy and remarked that he would only agree to become a republican in Paris if permitted to remain a Royalist in London. In England it was less through his own endeavors than the influence of his chief and far more radical acolyte, James Mill, that utilitarianism became a potent political force. Under Mill's guidance Bentham began early in the nineteenth century to campaign for major constitutional and social reform in England by way of such instruments as a free press, a parliament more manifestly accountable to the British electorate, and, eventually, universal suffrage. His *Plan of Parliamentary Reform* of 1818, together with Mill's essays "Education" and "Government" for the *Encyclopaedia Britannica* and the *Westminster Review*, a political journal that the two men founded in 1824, were to make the philosophy of English utilitarianism, by now described as philosophic radicalism, one of the principal motors of British constitutional change that was to culminate in the great Reform Act of 1832 and the transformation around this time of the old Whigs into the modern Liberal Party. Other currents of English radicalism, including the Chartist movement, also contributed to these developments, but none sprang from so deep a source of reflection on human nature in general or, thanks above all to Mill, from its by now tributary doctrine of political representation.

Mill's son was to prove Britain's preeminent, or at least most famous, political philosopher of the nineteenth century, less for his writings on utilitarianism than for his *System of Logic* and his essay *On Liberty*, still today liberalism's chief manifesto. That Benthamite utilitarianism was an insufficient foundation for ethics seemed plain to John Stuart Mill for much of his life, and in essays on Bentham and Samuel Taylor Coleridge (1772–1834) dating from the late 1830s he held that this doctrine, for all its admirable deconstruction of purely abstract ideals and blind intuitions, offered a defense of empiricism that lacked depth, subtlety, or any appreciation of aesthetic delight or the merits of received opinion. Utilitarianism as Bentham conceived it was a pragmatic and critical philosophy that had come to be compellingly radicalized, but it had never been informed by the terrors and passions of real experience, Mill remarked. In his essay *Utilitarianism*,

dating from 1861, he continued to defend the principles of a philosophy he had mastered from his father, but he also set himself the task of distinguishing individuals' higher from their lower pleasures, insisting, contrary to Bentham's own scheme, that some kinds of pleasure, particularly of the mind, are more desirable and valuable than others.

Henry Sidgwick (1838–1900), in his *Methods of Ethics,* first published in 1874, developed Mill's objections to pure utilitarianism by way of contrasting both its virtues and faults from those of egoism and intuitionism, with which it competed for pride of place among other ethical doctrines. According to Sidgwick, each of these approaches taken separately was ultimately at variance with the more complex conceptions of reasonable conduct that did not admit of the formal definitions of the concepts of obligation and duty advocated by their proponents. To Sidgwick's analysis in particular moral philosophers of the past century have owed many of their distinctions between consequentialist and duty-based or deontological moral philosophies, and between Benthamite consequentialism and the deontology of Immanuel Kant (1724–1804) in particular, some of which were already anticipated by Kant himself in his treatment of empiricism and the philosophy of David Hume (1711–1776).

See also **Bentham, Jeremy; Coleridge, Samuel Taylor; Dickens, Charles; Great Britain; Liberalism; Mill, James; Mill, John Stuart.**

BIBLIOGRAPHY

Primary Sources

Bentham, Jeremy. *An Introduction to the Principles of Morals and Legislation.* London, 1789.

Mill, John Stuart. *Utilitarianism.* London, 1863.

Sidgwick, Henry. *The Methods of Ethics.* London, 1874.

Secondary Sources

Halévy, Elie. *The Growth of Philosophic Radicalism.* Translated by Mary Morris. With a preface by A. D. Lindsay. London, 1928.

Plamenatz, John Petrov. *The English Utilitarians.* Oxford, U.K., 1949.

Thomas, William. *The Philosophic Radicals.* Oxford, U.K., 1979.

ROBERT WOKLER

UTOPIAN SOCIALISM. The term *utopian socialism* was first given currency by Friedrich Engels in his pamphlet "Socialism: Utopian and Scientific" (1880). For Engels the term referred to a group of early-nineteenth-century social theories and movements that criticized nascent capitalism and contrasted to it visions of an ideal society of plenty and social harmony. The three principal utopian socialists were the Frenchmen Henri de Saint-Simon (1760–1825) and Charles Fourier (1772–1837) and the British factory owner Robert Owen (1771–1858). Although these thinkers differed in significant ways—only Fourier was in any strict sense a utopian—all three attempted to find some solution for the social and economic dislocations caused by the French and Industrial Revolutions. All three began to write around 1800, published major works a decade later, and attracted followers who created Owenite, Saint-Simonian, and Fourierist movements in the 1820s and 1830s.

"Socialism: Utopian and Scientific" offers a shrewd, well-informed, and sympathetic interpretation of the work of the utopian socialists. But this essay (originally part of a polemic against the German economist Eugen Dühring) was never intended to provide a comprehensive assessment of utopian socialism. Instead Engels emphasized aspects of utopian socialism that anticipated the Marxist critique of capitalism and dismissed much of the rest as "fantasy" unavoidable at a time when capitalist production was "still very incompletely developed." Engels praised Fourier as a brilliant satirist of bourgeois society, Owen as an articulate spokesman for the demands of the working class, and Saint-Simon as the inspired prophet of a postcapitalist industrial order. At the same time, however, Engels criticized the utopian socialists for ignoring the importance of class conflict and failing to think seriously about the problem of how the ideal society might be brought into being. What the utopian socialists had failed to grasp, in Engels's view, was that the development of capitalism and the growth of the factory system were themselves creating the material conditions both of proletarian revolution and of humanity's ultimate regeneration.

Despite its polemical origins, "Socialism: Utopian and Scientific" provided a paradigm within which historians worked for almost a century. In histories of socialism from G. D. H. Cole to George Lichtheim, the utopian socialists were seen as "precursors" whose theories were flawed by their faulty understanding of history and class conflict. The problem with this perspective is that it is both teleological and reductionist: teleological because it assumes that socialism reached its final "scientific" form in the writings of Karl Marx, and that the work of the utopians was valuable only insofar as it anticipated that of Marx; reductionist because it treats the development of socialism largely as a reflection of the rise of the working-class movement.

FEATURES OF UTOPIAN SOCIALISM

Since the late twentieth century, however, some historians have called for a reassessment of utopian socialism that would grasp its inner logic and place it in its historical context. Viewed in this perspective, utopian socialism would seem to have four main features.

First, it can be seen in economic terms as a reaction to the rise of commercial capitalism and as a rejection of the prevailing economic theory that the best and most natural economic system is one in which the individual is free to pursue private interests. Coming at an early point in the development of capitalism, the utopian socialists had a firsthand view of the results of unregulated economic growth. They shared a sense of outrage at the suffering and waste produced by early capitalism, and they all called for at least some measure of social control over the new productive forces unleashed by capitalism.

Second, the critique and the remedies proposed by the utopian socialists were not, however, merely economic. They were writing out of a broader sense of social and moral disintegration. Competition for them was as much a moral as an economic phenomenon, and its effects could be seen just as clearly in the home as in the marketplace. Thus the utopian socialist critique of bourgeois society resembled that of conservatives such as Thomas Carlyle and socially conscious novelists such as Honoré de Balzac and Charles Dickens. Utopian socialists believed that the French and Industrial Revolutions had produced a breakdown of traditional associations and group ties, that individuals were becoming increasingly detached from any kind of corporate structure, and that society as a whole was becoming increasingly fragmented and individualistic. Egoism was the great problem: the Saint-Simonians called it "the deepest wound of modern society." And the utopian socialists' vision of a better world was clearly the result of a search for some substitute for the old forms of community that egoism and individualism were destroying.

Third, the utopian socialists all disliked violence and believed in the possibility of the peaceful transformation of society. Fourier and Saint-Simon had lived through the French Revolution and had been imprisoned during the Terror; they had no desire to see their ideas imposed by force or violent revolution. In any case they believed that this would not be necessary. Like Owen, Fourier and Saint-Simon expected to receive support for their ideas from members of the privileged classes. In that sense they were social optimists, and their optimism was rooted in their belief in the existence of a common good. Like the Enlightenment philosophes, they were convinced that there was no fundamental or unbridgeable conflict of interests between the rich and the poor, the propertied and the propertyless.

Finally, there is an important point to be made about the form in which the utopian socialists presented their ideas. Each described himself as the founder of an exact science—a science of social organization—that would make it possible for humankind to turn away from sterile philosophical controversy and from the destructive arena of politics and to resolve, in scientific fashion, the problem of social harmony. But one of the striking features of the thought of the utopian socialists is that while they consistently presented their theories as rooted in the discovery of the true laws of human nature and society, they also spoke in the tones of religious prophets. For them the laws of nature were the laws of God, and the new science was the true religion. This blending of science and religion, and prophecy and sociology, was one of the hallmarks of the thinking of the utopian socialists and their followers in the period prior to 1848.

UTOPIAN SOCIALIST MOVEMENTS
The movements created by the followers of Saint-Simon, Owen, and Fourier flourished during the period 1830–1848. First on the scene were the Saint-Simonians, a group of brilliant young people, many of them graduates of the École Polytechnique, the most prestigious school of engineering and applied science in France. Gathering around Saint-Simon in his last years, they regarded him as the prophet of a new world in which science and love would work together to bring about the material and moral regeneration of humanity. After his death in 1825, they founded journals and organized lecture tours designed to elaborate and spread his ideas. By 1830 they had created what they themselves described as a "faith"—a new religion that aimed simultaneously at harnessing the productive forces of the emerging industrial society, at bettering the condition of "the poorest and most numerous class," and at filling what they perceived as the moral and religious vacuum of the age. Eventually the movement was torn apart by a series of painful schisms, in the course of which the charismatic Prosper Enfantin (1796–1864) made himself "supreme father," excommunicated various "heretics," and issued a call for the "rehabilitation of the flesh." After a brief period of communal living, a spectacular trial, and a general exodus to Egypt in search of the "female messiah," the Saint-Simonian movement broke up. But in their sober years of maturity many of the former Saint-Simonians went on to play important roles in French public life, promoting the colonization of North Africa, the development of railroads, and the industrialization of France during the Second Empire (1852–1870).

The Owenites and the Fourierists were less spectacularly eccentric than the Saint-Simonians. But each group attracted many followers during the 1830s and 1840s. For a time in the early 1830s the Owenites were deeply involved in labor organization and the effort to create a great national federation of trade unions. This effort peaked in 1833–1834, but for another decade the principal Owenite journal, *The New Moral World,* continued to attract a substantial working-class readership. Most of the energy of the Owenites, however, went into a series of attempts to create working-class communities in which property was held in common and social and economic activity was organized on a cooperative basis. Inspired to some degree by the successful model factory that Owen himself had created at New Lanark in

Scotland, seven such communities were created in Britain between 1825 and 1847 and another in America at New Harmony, Indiana. None of them lasted very long. But the cooperative trading stores created by working-class followers of Owen were more successful, and the history of the modern cooperative movement is generally traced back to the founding of an Owenite store in Rochdale, England, in 1844.

The followers of Fourier also attempted to create experimental communities or "phalanxes" based on his theory (or rather on a watered-down version of his theory). Their efforts focused particularly on America, where some twenty-five Fourierist phalanxes were established in the 1840s. In France the Fourierists turned away from community building in the late 1840s and drew closer to the democratic and republican critics of the July Monarchy of King Louis-Philippe (r. 1830–1848). Under the leadership of the social reformer Victor Considerant (1808–1893), Fourierism became a political movement for "peaceful democracy," which was to play a brief but significant role in 1848.

The 1840s in France were also marked by the rise of a new generation of utopian socialists who emerged to create sects and ideologies of their own. Étienne Cabet (1788–1856), a former conspiratorial revolutionary who had been influenced by Owen while an exile in England, attracted a substantial working-class following with the austere and authoritarian communist utopia described in his novel, *Voyage en Icarie* (1839). Pierre Leroux (1797–1871), a former Saint-Simonian, propounded a mystical humanitarian socialism, arguing that social reform should be guided by a new religion of humanity. The Christian socialist Philippe Buchez (1796–1865) helped found a working-class journal, *L'Atelier,* and inspired groups of artisans to form producers' cooperatives. There was also an important group of feminist socialists, many of whom had passed through Saint-Simonianism or Fourierism, who began to find a voice in the 1840s. Flora Tristan (1803–1844), Pauline Roland (1805–1852), and Désirée Véret (1810–1891?) all pursued and deepened Fourier's insight that the emancipation of women is the key to all social progress. And Tristan's proposal for a workers' union in *L'Union ouvrière*

(1843) can now be seen as a kind of early syndicalist utopia.

As they spread and multiplied, the ideologies of utopian socialism became part of a broad current of democratic and humanitarian thought in which the boundary lines between socialism and democratic republicanism became blurred. By 1848 utopian socialism had merged with other ideologies of the democratic Left to form a single movement that was broadly democratic and socialist. The shared foundation that held this movement together included a faith in the right to work and in universal (male) suffrage, a belief that the differences between classes and nations were not irreconcilable, and a program of "peaceful democracy" which assumed that if politicians would only appeal to the higher impulses of "the people," a new era of class harmony and social peace would begin.

In 1848 with the fall of the July Monarchy in France and of repressive police states in much of the rest of Europe, European radicals at last had their chance at power. But universal suffrage proved to be no panacea for the Left. In France the working-class insurrection of June 1848 shattered the dream of the utopian socialists that a "democratic and social republic" might usher in a new age of class harmony. Thereafter the program of "peaceful democracy" ceased to have any political meaning. The result of the failure of the 1848 revolutions, then, was to crush the idealistic and humanitarian aspirations of the second generation of utopian socialists and to destroy the vision of class collaboration that had been central to their thought.

See also **Fourier, Charles; Owen, Robert; Roland, Pauline; Saint-Simon, Henri de; Socialism; Tristan, Flora.**

BIBLIOGRAPHY

Beecher, Jonathan. *Charles Fourier: The Visionary and His World.* Berkeley and Los Angeles, 1986.

———. *Victor Considerant and the Rise and Fall of French Romantic Socialism.* Berkeley and Los Angeles, 2001.

Carlisle, Robert B. *The Proffered Crown: Saint-Simonianism and the Doctrine of Hope.* Baltimore, Md., 1987.

Claeys, Gregory. *Machinery, Money, and the Millennium: From Moral Economy to Socialism, 1815–1860.* Princeton, N.J., 1987. On the Owenites.

6

Engels, Friedrich. "Socialism: Utopian and Scientific." In *The Marx-Engels Reader,* edited by Robert C. Tucker, 683–717. 2nd ed. New York, 1978.

Harrison, J. F. C. *Quest for the New Moral World: Robert Owen and the Owenites in Britain and America.* New York, 1969.

Johnson, Christopher H. *Utopian Communism in France: Cabet and the Icarians, 1839–1851.* Ithaca, N.Y., 1974.

Lichtheim, George. *The Origins of Socialism.* New York, 1969.

Manuel, Frank E. *The Prophets of Paris.* Cambridge, Mass., 1962.

Stedman Jones, Gareth. Introduction to *The Communist Manifesto,* by Karl Marx and Friedrich Engels, 3–187. London, 2002.

JONATHAN BEECHER

VAN GOGH, VINCENT (1853–1890), Dutch painter.

Vincent Willem van Gogh is a classic example of the self-taught artist who, possessed of a unique talent and despite numerous setbacks, succeeded in securing a place in history. Although he drew passable landscapes and cityscapes in his youth, he did not become an artist until he was twenty-seven. It is remarkable, then, that in the ten years from 1880 to 1890 he was able to produce an impressive oeuvre, which by the time of his death included approximately nine hundred paintings and eleven hundred works on paper. In addition, he left some nine hundred letters filled with penetrating observations about his life and the role of art, artists, and literature. This correspondence is considered one of the most important of his era.

CHILDHOOD

Van Gogh had a carefree childhood. He was the eldest son of a close-knit minister's family in the rural village of Zundert, in the south of Holland. The rural surroundings gave him not only a lifelong love of nature but also an enduring nostalgia for the country of his youth. His Protestant upbringing was marked by an individualistic avowal of faith in which Christ's humanity was central. Even though Van Gogh would later execrate the church as an institution, a symbolic and personal appreciation of nature as revelation remained a feature of his work.

Until he opted for brush and pen in 1880, he was the proverbial jack-of-all-trades and master of none. After a fragmentary education, he was hired as the youngest shop assistant in The Hague's branch of the French art and print dealer Goupil and Company, in which his uncle Vincent Van Gogh (1820–1880) was a partner. He learned the trade and developed a respectable knowledge of the visual arts. He was especially drawn to the work of the Dutch seventeenth century, the Barbizon school, and the Hague school. In the evenings, he immersed himself in religiohistorical and theological questions, in the course of which he was deeply moved by the book *La vie de Jésus* by the French theologian Ernest Renan (1823–1892). He gradually linked every experience to biblical texts, becoming preoccupied above all with the possibility of bringing consolation to humanity. He lost interest in the art business and was finally dismissed in 1876.

Convinced that he had a social mission to fulfill, he successively tried to earn his keep as a teacher and assistant preacher in England's Ramsgate (1876) and as a bookseller in Holland's Dordrecht (1877). Having failed at both, he decided to follow in his father's footsteps. But despite unremitting application, an attempt to study theology in Amsterdam in 1877 and 1878 was also unsuccessful. His appointment as evangelist among miners in Belgium's Borinage district (1879) likewise ended badly. To his parents, who were close to despair, this signified the end of a conventional career. Van Gogh too was at his wits' end. He dismissed suggestions that he become a lithographer, bookkeeper, carpenter's apprentice, and even a baker.

Finally, his brother Theo (1857–1891), who had also been employed at Goupil's since 1873, suggested he become an artist.

DUTCH PERIOD

Doggedly, Van Gogh strove to master the fundamentals of drawing, relying on textbooks. For a long time, his guiding lights were the French theoretician Armand Cassagne (1823–1907) and the artist Charles Bargue (c.1825–1883). He taught himself perspective, proportion, and human anatomy by copying old master drawings. He applied himself to social-realistic subject matter, which led, among other things, to such striking results as *The Bearers of the Burden* (1881). After moving in with his parents in Brabant's Etten, in southern Holland, at the beginning of 1881, he took his themes from the rural setting and local peasant community. In this, he was inspired by the French rural realists Jules Dupré (1811–1889) and especially Jean-François Millet (1814–1875), who for many years became his artistic and spiritual mentor.

Mounting friction with his parents prompted Van Gogh's departure for The Hague, where he briefly took drawing and painting lessons from Anton Mauve (1838–1888), a well-known representative of the Hague school, and got to know Dutch painters such as George Hendrik Breitner (1857–1923), with whom he explored the city's environs. Van Gogh underwent further training in perspective and life drawing, resulting in an important series of cityscapes, something that would remain a fixed genre in his oeuvre, along with numerous figure studies, among them *Sorrow* (1882), and studies of heads for which he got the local population to pose. As a great admirer of prints with social-realist themes from such illustrated magazines as the *Graphic,* he attempted to imbue his figures with a robust, expressive force. In addition, he explored the possibilities of color, which resulted in drawings such as *The Poor and Money* (1882).

Following Millet, Van Gogh decided to abandon The Hague in order to further his skills as rural realist in unspoiled nature. The breakup of his difficult relationship with Sien Hoornik (1850–1904), a former prostitute with whom he had lived since 1882, hastened his decision, and at the end of 1883 he set out for the northern Dutch province of Drenthe, where landscape and peasant life moved to the foreground of his work. He stayed for three months, given over to profound loneliness.

Themes that paralleled those of Millet continued to preoccupy him during his stay in the still largely pristine Neunen in Brabant (1883–1885), although local weavers at work also appear. Painting became his principal activity, and although Van Gogh tested his ideas against those of his fellow artist and correspondent Anthon van Rappard (1858–1892), he was once again thrown back primarily on himself, relying for guidance on the color theories of the Romantic painter Eugène Delacroix (1798–1863), as formulated by, among others, the French art historian Charles Blanc (1814–1881). Employing a rich impasto stroke and dark palette—for which he was indebted to painters of the Hague school and the Barbizon school—he attempted to apply Delacroix's ideas on color in numerous studies without having seen any of Delacroix's paintings. Convinced of his progress and believing that before long he would be able to make marketable art, he attempted to complete fully developed paintings, of which *The Potato Eaters* (1885) was the first.

TO PARIS

The death of his father in 1885 and subsequent familial tensions obliged Van Gogh to leave Nuenen. He went to Antwerp with the goal of making saleable art and honed his skill in portraiture and cityscape; he also took lessons at the academy. Toward the end of February 1886, he rather suddenly departed for Paris, moving in with Theo, who had been supporting him since 1881. Two years of experimentation and artistic encounters followed. His style and repertoire underwent a radical transformation and expanded considerably. After a short period in the studio of the history painter Fernand Cormon (1845–1926), where he did a great deal of drawing from nude and plaster models, he fell under the influence of the impasto-rich and brightly colored work of the Provençal artist Adolphe Monticelli (1824–1886). He made a study of the color work of Delacroix and became fascinated by Japanese prints, which he collected passionately, and by the work of the contemporary French impressionists and young avant-garde of painters, including Émile Bernard (1861–1941) and Henri de Toulouse-Lautrec (1864–1901).

Self portrait by Van Gogh, 1887. Musée d'Orsay, Paris, France/Bridgeman Art Library

He experimented intensively with the impressionistic brush stroke technique, applied the post-impressionists' pointillist technique, began using a much lighter palette, and incorporated decorative elements in his work. This led to such noteworthy results as *Portrait of Père Tanguy, Park Voyer d'Argenson,* and series after series of cityscapes in watercolor.

THE STUDIO OF THE SOUTH

In the beginning of 1888, fatigued by city life and yearning for unspoiled regions, Van Gogh left for Arles, in the south of France, which reminded him of the bright colors of Japan as he had seen it in prints. In the meantime, he had developed into a complete artist with a spontaneous, vigorous style who increasingly applied such elements of form as color and line independently, without sacrificing the expressive power of his subject matter. The rural setting around Arles inspired a remarkable series of drawings and paintings filled with harmonious color effects: blooming orchards, *The Sunflowers,* and *The Harvest.* Convinced that he could make an artistic contribution, he urged Theo, to whom he sent his works in exchange for his support, to make sure he kept these works well secured.

His desire to form an artists' community in the south appeared to have become a reality with the arrival, in October 1888, of his mentor Paul Gauguin (1849–1903). The two artists worked closely, discussing all sorts of painterly issues, including whether or not it was possible to work from the imagination. But only nine weeks later, the collaboration was interrupted when the first signs of Van Gogh's mental illness manifested themselves and he cut off his left earlobe. From then until his death, he would know long periods of depression, anxiety attacks, self-mutilation, and profound despair.

In April 1889, Van Gogh voluntarily committed himself to a psychiatric clinic in nearby Saint Rémy. His former optimism had been replaced with a feeling of gloom about the future. Nevertheless, as he had before, he made a virtue of necessity. He discovered new subject matter, such as the irises in the overgrown and walled-in clinic garden, and translated several beloved black and white prints of Millet and Rembrandt into colorful canvasses. Whenever his health permitted, he would also work outside, where he added Provence's cypresses and olive trees to his repertoire.

RETURN TO THE NORTH

In May 1890, exhausted, he left the south of France and settled in the Auvers-sur-Oise, near Paris. Here he once again took up what he called "the study of landscape and peasant life," which had fascinated him throughout his painting life. He was enthusiastic about the village and the rustic setting and worked feverishly on a variety of landscapes—spacious fields, wheat stacks, and sunsets—in his characteristic, expressive language of form and brilliant color. He seemed to have recovered. The shock therefore was great when on 27 July he fatally wounded himself with a shot to the chest in a field near the village. Two days later he died in the arms of Theo, his anchor and support.

See also **Avant-Garde; Barbizon Painters; Delacroix, Eugène; Gauguin, Paul; Millet, Jean-François; Painting.**

BIBLIOGRAPHY

Druick, Douglas, and Peter Kort Zegers. *Van Gogh and Gauguin: The Studio of the South*. New York, 2001.

Faille, J.-B. de la. *The Works of Vincent Van Gogh: His Paintings and Drawings*. Amsterdam, 1970.

Hulsker, Jan. *Vincent and Theo Van Gogh: A Dual Biography*. Ann Arbor, Mich., 1990.

———. *The New Complete Van Gogh: Paintings, Drawings, Sketches*. Rev. ed. Amsterdam, 1996.

Ives, Colta, et al. *Vincent Van Gogh: The Drawings*. New York, 2005.

Stolwijk, Chris, et al. *Vincent's Choice: The Musée Imaginaire of Van Gogh*. Amsterdam, 2003.

Van Gogh, Vincent. *The Complete Letters of Vincent Van Gogh, with Reproductions of All the Drawings in the Correspondence*. 3 vols. New York, 1958.

Van Heugten, Sjraar et al. *Vincent Van Gogh: Drawings*. 3 vols. Amsterdam, 1996–2001.

CHRIS STOLWIJK

VENICE. On the eve of the French Revolution, as the capital of an independent Republic, Venice still ruled over an extensive territory stretching along the Adriatic coast into Dalmatia, and deep into Lombardy. Venice had long before lost its position as the Mediterranean's dominant commercial center, falling victim to the rise of the Atlantic economy, and due to an inability to compete with bigger states. Indeed, by the mid-eighteenth century, the Habsburg free port of Trieste had begun to emerge as a rival even within the Adriatic. Nevertheless, Venice—still ruled by a narrow patrician oligarchy—was by no means the decadent and marginalized state often portrayed by contemporaries and subsequent historians alike. It remained a significant trading center, could deploy a sizeable fleet, and, in cultural terms, could still produce figures of the caliber of the playwright Carlo Goldoni (1707–1793) and the sculptor Antonio Canova (1757–1822).

THE END OF THE VENETIAN REPUBLIC

The collapse of the Republic of Saint Mark in 1797 was not the consequence, as has frequently been suggested, of the cowardice and corruption of Venice's patrician class, but a direct result of changes in international relations brought about by the French Revolution. During the second half of the eighteenth century, the Venetian government had recognized that the only possible means of surviving in the face of expansionist neighbors was to adopt a policy of neutrality. When the Directory's Army of Italy invaded Italy in 1796 under the command of Napoleon Bonaparte (later Napoleon I, r. 1804–1814/15), the Venetian state had attempted to keep to this policy, but Austrian and French forces soon violated Venice's neutrality. In the spring of 1797, Napoleon invaded the Republic's mainland territories, establishing Jacobin satellite municipalities in many of the cities hitherto under its rule. Napoleon used a popular anti-French rising in Verona and resistance to French incursion into the lagoon as a pretext to occupy Venice itself. Faced with a French ultimatum, and anxious to avoid bloodshed or French reprisals, the last Doge, Ludovico Manin (r. 1789–1797), transferred power to the French authorities. Napoleon briefly set up a Jacobin municipal republic in the city, but almost immediately entered secret negotiations with the Austrians. In October 1797, these resulted in the Treaty of Campoformido. By this treaty, Venice and most of its former mainland territories to the east of the river Mincio were transferred to Habsburg rule in exchange for territorial concessions elsewhere.

AUSTRIAN AND NAPOLEONIC RULE

Austrian troops arrived in Venice in January 1798. The city remained under the relatively benign rule of the Habsburgs until January 1806, when, by the Treaty of Pressburg, Napoleon (now crowned Emperor) annexed the city and its remaining territory to his satellite Kingdom of Italy. Until its liberation by Austrian forces in the spring of 1814, Venice languished under Napoleonic rule. Reduced to the status of a provincial capital, and with its remnants of trade destroyed because of Anglo-French naval rivalry and economic warfare, the plight of the Venetians under Napoleon was further exacerbated by heavy conscription, rapacious taxation, and the systematic plundering of Venice's art.

The Vienna settlement acknowledged the Austrian Emperor, Francis I (r. 1804–1835), as ruler of Venetia. Although the newly created Kingdom of Lombardy-Venetia was technically separate from the rest of the empire, in practice most key decisions were made in Vienna. Such centralized rule was unpopular among Venetians. There was also disappointment that much of the machinery and personnel of the Napoleonic system was retained. Venice continued to suffer from a heavy tax burden and conscription, and many Venetians were angered by the large numbers of "foreigners" (both German-speakers and Lombards) who dominated the higher ranks of the civil service. Nevertheless, government expenditure rose massively under Austrian rule, and the reign of Francis I saw a gradual increase in the numbers of Venetians playing a role in the administration. A major source of resentment remained the apparently preferential treatment given to Trieste, although in 1830 Venice was granted the same free port status as its rival. Another fillip to the Venetian economy came in the form of causeway linking the city with the mainland, completed in 1846. Despite such measures, Venice was characterized by poverty and unemployment. Surprisingly, until the later 1840s there was very little active opposition to Habsburg rule. The one attempted rising—a naval mutiny led by the Bandiera brothers, Attilio (1810–1844) and Emilio (1819–1844)—failed spectacularly.

CULTURAL RESPONSES IN THE EARLY NINETEENTH CENTURY

In the Napoleonic and Restoration periods, Venice's greatest artist was the sculptor Canova, whose exquisite marbles were valued throughout Europe. In literary terms, the city was famous for the work of Ugo Foscolo (1778–1827), who flirted with the Napoleonic regime but went into exile in 1815.

In the aftermath of the Napoleonic Wars, Venice began again to attract steadily larger numbers of travelers, including such figures as the French Romantic François-René de Chateaubriand (1768–1848), the novelist Stendhal (Henri Beyle; 1783–1842), the Irish poet Thomas Moore (1779–1852), and Lord Byron (1788–1824). Literary reactions to Venice were far from consistent, but few writers engaged with its current political and economic state; they preferred instead to explore a mythologized version of its past, and used the modern city as a trope for decay. This was echoed in representations by painters such as Joseph Mallord William Turner (1775–1851) and Richard Parkes Bonington (1802–1828) whose sketches showed contemporary Venice, but whose finished works tended to populate it with figures from much earlier

periods. To the extent that foreign travelers did address the contemporary situation, they were generally critical of Austrian rule. One notable exception to this was John Ruskin (1819–1900), who loathed contemporary Venetians and bizarrely located the start of Venice's decline in 1418. However, the general trend was reflected in the description of the city offered by Charles Dickens (1812–1870) in his *Pictures from Italy* (1846): in contrast with the gritty realism of the rest of the book, his chapter on Venice is entitled "An Italian Dream."

THE 1848 REVOLUTION AND THE UNIFICATION OF ITALY

The passive nature of Venice completely changed in 1848. Grievances had been growing since the late 1830s, as Venetians became increasingly intolerant of the bureaucratic and unresponsive nature of Austrian rule, of high taxation used to service the imperial debt, and of heavy-handed censorship. Matters were aggravated by the rule of the mentally weak Ferdinand I (r. 1835–1848), whose inability to provide direction was highlighted by the economic crisis of the so-called hungry forties. During 1846 and 1847, the people of Venice and its mainland increasingly criticized Austrian rule. The most eloquent opponent of the regime was Daniele Manin (1804–1857), who had risen to prominence during debates over the construction of a railway line between Venice and Milan. His persistent—although initially far from radical—attacks on Habsburg misrule landed him briefly in prison; on his release he assumed the role of champion of Venetian interests against alleged Austrian oppression. Revolution in France, the fall of Prince Clemens von Metternich (1773–1859) in the face of popular demonstrations in Vienna, increasing agitation in Hungary, and unrest elsewhere in Italy—including insurrection in Milan, which led to the retreat of the Austrian commander Count Joseph Radetzky (1766–1858)—generated panic among the authorities in Venice, and the governor, Aloys Palffy, evacuated the city. A provisional regime was swiftly established under the direction of Manin, who declared the establishment of a Republic of Saint Mark. The threat from Austria encouraged the population of the mainland to seek closer links with Milan and Sardinia-Piedmont, tying Manin's policy more closely to that of Piedmontese King, Charles Albert (r. 1831–1849), than he would have wished. However, defeat of

Venice, 1840 Painting by J. M. W. Turner. Turner visited Venice three times between 1819 and 1840 and was much attracted by its luminous atmosphere. It became one of his favorite subjects for landscape. VICTORIA & ALBERT MUSEUM, LONDON/ART RESOURCE, NY

Charles Albert by Habsburg forces at Custoza (July 1848) forced the Venetians to rely on their own resources to safeguard their newly won independence. Although the rest of the peninsula experienced risings in 1848 and 1849, the Venetian revolution endured longer than any other, eventually succumbing to military blockade and cholera.

In the aftermath of revolution, Venice was subjected to the stern administration of the elderly Radetzky, before a milder regime was introduced under Archduke Maximilian of Habsburg (1832–1867) in 1857. Nevertheless, relations between Vienna and the local population had been badly damaged, and many Venetians increasingly looked toward Italian unity as a means to escape from Austrian rule. This stance was strengthened when Manin publicly renounced his former republican sympathies and called on Italians to support unification under the Piedmontese monarchy. Hopes that Venice might be annexed by the Piedmontese evaporated in 1859, when the French emperor

Napoleon III (r. 1852–1871) broke his promise to the prime minister Count Cavour (Camillo Benso; 1810–1861) that he would free all of northern Italy from Austria. The creation of the new Kingdom of Italy in 1860 led to intermittent calls for the seizure of Venetia. In 1865, the Austrians rebuffed an Italian offer to purchase the region. Acquisition of Venetia finally took place in 1866, when the Italians fought against Austria in alliance with Prussia. Despite defeats on land and sea by the Austrians, the Italians were still able to gain Venice and its mainland provinces, thanks to Prussian victory and the diplomatic involvement of Napoleon III. Legitimacy was given to the annexation by an overwhelmingly positive vote in a plebiscite, which was nevertheless marred by rigging and intimidation.

VENICE UNDER ITALIAN RULE

Neither Venice nor the Venetian mainland initially benefited from Italian unity. As a port Venice continued to decline in the face of competition from other maritime cities in the peninsula. The opening of the Suez Canal in 1869 and Venice's selection as chief port of the India Mail in 1872 did act as a slight stimulus to trade, which was increasingly located in the west of the city (near the railway) rather than around Saint Mark's Square. Venetians, however, remained generally indifferent or hostile to their new status as Italians, a fact reflected in their unwillingness to stand as parliamentary candidates in the 1870s.

Economic problems persisted in the late nineteenth century, and, until the 1890s, Venetia witnessed some of Italy's highest rates of emigration, albeit usually to European destinations rather than to the New World. Yet, despite the poverty of the region, Venice gradually reconciled itself to Italian rule in the decades before World War I. This in part reflected a gradually improving economy, helped by the growth of industry in the 1880s (including the establishment of the Stucky grain mill and pasta factory on the Giudecca and construction of warships in the Arsenale), and, more significantly, by the massive expansion of tourism. Venice now appealed not only because of its romantic past, but also because of the development of the Lido as a center for sea bathing.

VENICE AND CULTURE, 1866–1915

Despite the establishment of a biennial international art festival in 1895, the later nineteenth and early twentieth centuries were not an especially fertile period for Venetian art or literature. In general, however, the city was more interesting as a stimulus to foreign artists, writers, poets, and composers than to homegrown ones. The most famous resident Italian writer in the years before World War I was the nationalist firebrand Gabriele d'Annunzio (1863–1938), whose novel *The Flame of Life* (1900) played with the contrasts between Venice past and modern. In very different ways, Henry James (1843–1916) and Thomas Mann (1875–1955) loaded Venice with symbolic significance.

The tension between Venice past and present was evident in the city's treatment by other creative artists. Many remained obsessed with Venice's exotic past, as evidenced in Hans Markart's painting *Homage to Queen Caterina Cornaro* (1873), in the Johann Strauss (1825–1899) opera *A Night in Venice* (1883), and the Venetian plays of Hugo von Hofmannsthal (1874–1929), as well as in many of the canvases of the Venetian painter Giacomo Favretto (1898–1964). British views of the city continued to be heavily influenced by the backward-looking legacy of Ruskin. However, the city was also periodically home to a wide range of British, including the historians Rawdon Brown (1803–1883) and Horatio Brown (1854–1926), the poet and historian John Addington Symonds (1840–1893), and the novelist and fantasist Frederick Rolfe (1860–1913), who, while deeply interested in its past, engaged passionately with the modern city and its inhabitants. A similar preoccupation characterized the work of many American and British painters, such as Robert Frederick Blum (1857–1903), John Singer Sargent (1856–1925), Maurice Brazil Prendergast (1859–1924), and Sir Samuel Luke Fildes (1843–1927), who sought to portray a living city (albeit in a sometimes sentimentalized form). In so doing they echoed local painters, such as Ettore Tito (1867–1941), who was anxious to portray scenes of everyday Venetian life rather than turning the city into a symbol of past glory. The most radical response to the city in this period, however, came in 1910 when the leader of the Futurists, Filippo Tommaso Marinetti (1876–1944), declared rhetorical war against a Venice that he saw as no more than a ridiculous museum.

See also **Milan; Naples; Rome; Trieste; Vienna.**

BIBLIOGRAPHY

Laven, David. *Venice and Venetia Under the Habsburgs, 1815–1835.* Oxford, U.K., 2002.

Pemble, John. *Venice Rediscovered.* Oxford, U.K., 1995.

Plant, Margaret. *Venice: Fragile City 1797–1997.* New Haven, Conn., 2002.

Zorzi, Alvise. *Venezia austriaca, 1798–1866.* Rome, 1985.

DAVID LAVEN

VERDI, GIUSEPPE (1813–1901), Italian operatic composer.

Giuseppe Verdi was the most influential and popular composer of Italian opera during the second half of the nineteenth century. Born on 9 or 10 October 1813 to a family of small farmers and tavern keepers in the hamlet of Roncole, near Busseto, his musical talents were recognized early and cultivated by his parents, as well as by a local priest who instructed him in organ performance. Having spent his teenage years as church organist of San Michele in Roncole, he applied to the Milan Conservatory but was denied admission in part because, at eighteen, he exceeded the usual entering age. He relocated to Milan anyway, studying composition privately and working as a rehearsal pianist for the Milanese Società Filarmonica. Verdi received his first important break at the age of twenty-six when Bartolomeo Merelli, the impresario of Milan's Teatro alla Scala, agreed to produce his first opera, *Oberto, conte di San Bonifacio* (1839; Oberto, count of St. Boniface). The work was enormously successful for a composer of such youth and inexperience, and it served as the catalyst for a career that was to span six full decades. During these years, Verdi composed twenty-eight operas for cities throughout Italy, as well as for Paris, London, St. Petersburg, and Cairo, and he was celebrated throughout Europe as the greatest Italian musical dramatist of the century. In the early twenty-first century, Verdi retains a place of honor in the pantheon of the nineteenth century's great composers, and his operas remain among the most beloved in the repertory.

Verdi experienced one of his only true failures early in his career with his second work, the comic opera *Un giorno di regno* (Milan, 1840; King for a day), which was removed from La Scala's boards following its one and only disastrous performance. Embittered by this setback, and still reeling over the closely spaced deaths of his only two children (Virginia on 12 August 1838 and Icilio Romano on 22 October 1839) and his first wife (Margherita on 18 June 1840), Verdi allegedly resolved to quit composing (though he continued to participate in Milan's musical life, rewriting portions of *Oberto* and overseeing rehearsals of the work). His next opera, *Nabucco,* was produced less than two years later (also at La Scala), and was an unprecedented success, catapulting Verdi from a local hero into a national and international superstar. His career thereafter was characterized by a steady stream of commissions and triumphs, and it has become common to divide his output into three periods:

"early" (1839–1849), "middle" (1849–1862), and "late" (1863–1891). His early period was his busiest, yielding fourteen operas including *Ernani* (Venice, 1844), *Attila* (Venice, 1846), and *Macbeth* (Florence, 1847). During the middle period, Verdi completed ten works, seven of which remain in today's repertory: *Luisa Miller* (Naples, 1849), *Rigoletto* (Venice, 1851), *Il trovatore* (Rome, 1853; The troubadour), *La traviata* (Venice, 1853; The fallen woman), *Les Vêpres siciliennes* (Paris, 1855; The Sicilian vespers), *Simon Boccanegra* (Venice, 1857; revised, Milan, 1881), and *Un ballo in maschera* (Rome, 1859; A masked ball). Verdi's final period was his least productive, in large part because his firmly established reputation and finances permitted him the leisure to compose only when he desired. During this quarter century, he wrote the *Messa di Requiem* (Milan, 1874) and four operas: *Don Carlos* (Paris, 1867; revised, Milan, 1884), *Aïda* (Cairo, 1871), *Otello* (Milan, 1887), and *Falstaff* (Milan, 1893). Throughout most of his career, Verdi was accompanied by the soprano Giuseppina Strepponi (1815–1897), who created the leading female role in *Nabucco* and was one of Verdi's staunchest advocates. They lived together for over a decade before marrying in 1859. Verdi died in Milan on 27 January 1901.

The early decades of Verdi's career overlapped with the Risorgimento (the movement for Italian unification), and his role as patriot and politician formed an integral component of his reputation. Beginning in 1858, the acronym VERDI was used to promote the popular choice for king (*Vittorio Emmanuele, Re d'Italia*), and the slogan "Viva Verdi!" became a common rallying call among patriots. Following independence, Verdi was elected to the first Italian parliament and later honored as senator for life. His most important role in the Risorgimento, however, was as a composer whose operas, especially their choruses, served as anthems symbolizing a burgeoning national identity. Since the early 1990s, however, the political significance of this music has come under question. Some have suggested that the composer's preunification reputation has been misrepresented and that his choruses became political anthems only after Italian unification. This argument has encouraged a new round of research that has reconfirmed Verdi's position as the *vate* (bard) of the Risorgimento and has opened the discussion to inquiries about political messages woven into the works of Verdi's contemporaries as well as his own. That such debate still surrounds Verdi's operas is a clear sign of the immediacy with which this music still speaks to audiences of the early twenty-first century, and with which it will continue to move opera lovers for years to come.

See also **Music; Opera; Rossini, Gioachino.**

BIBLIOGRAPHY

Balthazar, Scott L., ed. *The Cambridge Companion to Verdi.* Cambridge, U.K., 2004.

Budden, Julian. *The Operas of Verdi.* 3 vols. London, 1973–1981. Rev. ed., Oxford, U.K., 1992.

Parker, Roger. *Leonora's Last Act: Essays in Verdian Discourse.* Princeton, N.J., 1997.

Phillips-Matz, Mary Jane. *Verdi: A Biography.* Oxford, U.K., 1993.

HILARY PORISS

VERGA, GIOVANNI (1840–1922), Italian novelist.

Giovanni Verga was the greatest Italian novelist of the second half of the nineteenth century and the most important exponent of *verismo* (nineteenth-century Italian realism). He was born in Catania into a family of wealthy landowners with noble ascendancy on the paternal side (the father had the right to bear the title of knight). An earnest supporter of the Italian national cause, he served in the National Guard from 1860 to 1864, when he left due to his increasing uneasiness with the way the Italian army was repressing "brigandage" in the southern regions following unification. His early literary training took place in Sicily, but in 1869 he moved to Florence, at the time the capital of Italy, where he developed a lasting friendship with Luigi Capuana (1839–1915), the theorist of *verismo.* He left Florence in 1872 to move to Milan, then the center of a thriving publishing industry and of a lively literary and society scene, in which he became an untiring participant. He resided in the Lombard city for twenty years before returning permanently to Sicily. In his later years, with the advent of mass politics and frequent social

and political turmoil in Italy, his political conservatism and nationalism became more vehement. Shortly before he died, he was appointed senator.

After a literary debut with novels that dealt with patriotic themes, including *I carbonari della montagna* (1861–1862; The Carbonari in the mountains) and *Sulle lagune* (1863; In the lagoons), he wrote stories featuring mostly society men and women and focusing on tragic love entanglements, at times based on the author's experiences, such as *Una peccatrice* (1866; A sinner), *Storia di una capinera* (1869; Story of a blackcap), *Eva* (1873), and *Eros* (1875). In 1874 he published his first short story on a different subject, the harsh life of a poor Sicilian woman ("Nedda"). In the following years, under the influence of French naturalism and of positivism (especially the emerging investigative literature on the Southern Question, the problem of governance of and the persistent poverty of the southern regions after unification of the country), he further devoted himself to the representation of Sicily and the Sicilians both in short story collections (*Vita dei campi,* [1880; Life in the fields], *Novelle rusticane* [1883; Little novels of Sicily]) and in novels that abandoned the conventions of the picturesque then dominating the literature on Sicily.

In his greatest realistic novel, *I Malavoglia* (1881; The house by the medlar tree), he describes the vicissitudes of the Toscano family, Sicilian fishermen whose traditional ways are disrupted by the demands of the Italian state (which "steals" the first son for service in the army) and by the economic difficulties that ensue from a bad business deal. The solidarity among the members of the old family clan becomes a casualty in the struggle for material well-being and in the new and harsher conditions of an increasingly competitive society. Stylistically and linguistically the novel is original and unconventional. In its attempt to tell the story from the point of view of the community in which the Malavoglia family's vicissitudes unfolded, it is replete with popular sayings that are supposed to express the wisdom of the community. And in order to render the language of ordinary Sicilians it is written in a "spoken" Italian that tries to reproduce the syntactical structures of the local dialect.

Verga intended *I Malavoglia* to be the first in a cycle of five novels describing the *vinti* (conquered), those vanquished by the crushing tide of progress in five different social strata. However, after writing *I Malavoglia*, Verga completed only the second novel in the series, entitled *Mastro-don Gesualdo* (1889). Powerfully imbued with Verga's pessimistic view of social life, this is the grim but vivid tale of a self-made Sicilian commoner, ruthlessly devoted to increasing his possessions, who tries to gain acceptance into the status-conscious local nobility by marrying an impoverished noblewoman. Having failed in this and other respects, he dies a lonely death in the house of the only daughter, who is ashamed of his low origins.

Italian *verismo* shared several features with French naturalism, from the desire to represent contemporary society in a manner "true to reality," to the focus on the determinants of life in different social strata, to the rhetoric of impersonality. In contrast to the urban focus of French naturalism, however, Italian *veristi* mainly represented a rural world under pressure from a changing political and economic order. Also in contrast to French naturalism, *verismo* never achieved fame abroad. Not even in Italy did *I Malavoglia* encounter the favor of the public and the critics and it was only after World War II and in the context of the rise of literary neo-realism that this masterpiece of Italian realism was fully appreciated and became enshrined in the literary canon. More positive was the reception of *Maestro-don Gesualdo*, but during Verga's lifetime fame came to him primarily with the theatrical and then operatic adaptation, by Pietro Mascagni, of one of his Sicilian short stories, "Cavalleria rusticana," (1884; Rustic chivalry) which premiered in Rome in 1890.

See also **Carducci, Giosuè; D'Annunzio, Gabriele; Realism and Naturalism; Zola, Émile.**

BIBLIOGRAPHY

Asor Rosa, Alberto, ed. *Il caso Verga*. Palermo, 1972.

Brand, Peter, and Lino Pertile, eds. *The Cambridge History of Italian Literature*. New York, 1996.

Merola, Nicola. *Giovanni Verga*. Florence, 1993.

Moe, Nelson. *The View from Vesuvius: Italian Culture and the Southern Question*. Berkely, Calif., 2002.

Verga, Giovanni. *Tutte le novelle*. Edited by Carla Riccardi. Milan, 1979.

———. *Tutti i romanzi*. Edited by Enrico Ghidetti. Florence, 1983.

SILVANA PATRIARCA

VERNE, JULES (1828–1905), French novelist.

For many years, Jules Verne was routinely paired with H. G. Wells as one of the founding fathers of modern science fiction. It is increasingly clear that the true picture is more complex. In his "Scientific Romances," Wells composed extrapolations; the main axis of his work—as in most science fiction—is Time. Verne, who published fifty-five *Voyages Extraordinaires* between 1863 and the year of his death, was less interested in the fate of the Western world than in the explosive growth of Europe over the years of his career; his main axis is Space. Verne is perhaps the ultimate prose poet of geography. His early work in particular can therefore be understood as a geography of the European explosion; these early novels celebrate a sense that to travel the world is to possess the world. The explorers, scientists, military adventurers, and daring entrepreneurs who populate most of his early fiction transform the darkness of the world. They are light-bringers. Tales that have been understand as manuals for young imperialists include *Cinq semaines en ballon* (*Five Weeks in a Balloon*, 1863); *Voyage au centre de la terre* (*Journey to the Center of the Earth*, 1864); *Vingt mille lieues sous les mers* (*Twenty Thousand Leagues Under the Sea*, 1870), and *Le Tour du monde en quatre-vingts jours* (*Around the World in Eighty Days*, 1874). Verne's novels have rarely been out of print.

Unfortunately for his reputation, however, Verne's work has persistently been misunderstood. Anglophone students have in general been reluctant, therefore, to examine his work for more comprehensive insights into that period (1860–1880) when the scientific and industrial progress of Europe seemed an entirely natural justification for imperialism. But even the most eager scholar would have found the texts themselves, as they have been known for a century or more, almost impenetrable, because the true complexity of Verne's imaginative take on the late nineteenth century has been deeply obscured by the notorious badness, until well into the twentieth century, of almost all translations of his work. It was normal for his early translators to cut up to 40 percent of the original texts and to bowdlerize what remained to render the result "suitable" for the juvenile audiences to which it was assumed Verne catered exclusively; moreover, the multiple ironies and ambivalences of these tales, which often sternly addressed political issues, were systematically expunged.

Furthermore, almost a century after his death, French scholars have begun to discover that even Verne's original French texts had suffered prior emasculations at the hands of his longtime publisher, Pierre-Jules Hetzel (1814–1886), who went so far as to reject an entire 1863 novel (*Paris au XXe Siècle* [*Paris in the Twentieth Century*]) because it took a mildly iconoclastic view of the "triumph" of Europe. As Verne's novels dealt directly with Europe's conquering of the world through applied science and technology, it is something of a tragedy that the full range of his understanding of these vital decades was so thoroughly obscured.

In later years, it became more difficult to conceal from readers Verne's examinations of the darker implications of the conquest of the planet—though even in the twenty-first century, Anglophone readers will have no access to the harsher implications of *L'île à hélice* (Propeller island, 1895)—as all political satire was stripped out of the English translation, *The Floating Island* (1896), though Verne's final, devastating image of the consequences of travel does remain. The two communities on this artificial island, unable to agree on where they should go next, rip their habitat apart. Verne's original French text has never been published; but the image of empires about to burst asunder did survive his censors.

There is, of course, much of Verne's work that combined didactism and a purer joy of storytelling. The dawn-like elation of discovering something new around the next corner of the world has never been so ringingly narrated. And the thousands of pages of his work as a whole constitute, in classic late nineteenth-century style, an exposition of the world, a glittering narrative of the world on display. In the end, Verne was his century's great romancer.

See also **Explorers; Wells, H. G.**

BIBLIOGRAPHY

Evans, Arthur B. *Jules Verne Rediscovered: Didacticism and the Scientific Novel.* New York, 1988.

Evans, Arthur B., ed. "A Jules Verne Centenary." Special issue of *Science Fiction Studies* 95, vol. 32, part 1 (March 2005).

Lottman, Herbert R. *Jules Verne: An Exploratory Biography.* New York, 1996.

Smyth, Edmund J., ed. *Jules Verne: Narratives of Modernity.* Liverpool, 2000.

JOHN CLUTE

VICTOR EMMANUEL II (1820–1878; ruled 1861–1878), first king of Italy.

Victor Emmanuel (born 14 March 1820) took the throne of the Kingdom of Piedmont-Sardinia at age twenty-eight. He succeeded his father, Charles Albert (r. 1831–1849), who abdicated after the Austrians defeated Piedmontese forces at the Battle of Novara in 1849. Twelve years later, 17 March 1861, with all but Venice, Rome, Trieste, and the Trentino united under the aegis of Piedmont, he accepted the title King of Italy.

When he took power in 1849, Victor Emmanuel II endorsed the constitution granted by his father the year before and reluctantly agreed to Austria's stiff terms for an armistice. Parliament rejected the armistice, and the new king dissolved it (29 March 1849) and called new elections only to see the voters reaffirm democratic control. The king dissolved the Chamber again and appealed to the people to return a more favorable majority with the Proclamation of Moncalieri, 20 November 1849. This time moderates took charge (9 December 1849), and they endorsed the peace treaty with Austria on 5 January 1850.

Victor Emmanuel's ability to stand up to the Austrians and to undercut the democrats without using force or violating the constitution won him the epithet "the gentleman king." In this early crisis, he insisted on the royal prerogative to make war and peace and used his power to dissolve

PUNCH, OR THE LONDON CHARIVARI—November 17, 1860.

RIGHT LEG IN THE BOOT AT LAST.

Garibaldi. "IF IT WON'T GO ON, SIRE, TRY A LITTLE MORE POWDER."

Right Leg in the Boot at Last. Cartoon from the English satirical journal *Punch*, 17 November 1860. Garibaldi's conquest of the Kingdom of the Two Sicilies and the subsequent unification of the peninsula under Victor Emmanuel II are lampooned. BIBLIOTHÈQUE NATIONALE, PARIS, FRANCE/BRIDGEMAN ART LIBRARY/GIRAUDON

parliament to bring it in line with his more moderate views. His constitutional authority and his interest in using it gave him political influence, especially as the Kingdom of Piedmont-Sardinia gained prominence in the movement to unify Italy.

While he agreed with moderates on constitutional rule and Piedmont-Sardinia's national mission, Victor Emmanuel remained conservative on religious matters. He resisted a bill to dissolve monastic orders, but at the urging of close advisors, he signed the law (29 May 1855). At odds over religious policy, the king and his prime minister Count Cavour (Camillo Benso, 1810–1861) found common ground on foreign affairs, agreeing to join France and England against Russia in the Crimean War (4 March 1855). Contributions to the war gave Piedmont-Sardinia a place at the Congress of Paris (opened 25 February 1856) and brought acknowledgment of the Italian

question. As Piedmont-Sardinia gained prominence, republicans and patriots elsewhere on the peninsula increasingly looked to Victor Emmanuel for leadership of the national movement.

The exact nature of Victor Emmanuel's role in the events leading to unification remains the subject of debate. Historians attribute the creation of Italy under Piedmontese rule to some combination of the diplomatic finesse of Cavour, the actions of the French emperor Napoleon III (1808–1873), the success of Giuseppe Garibaldi (1807–1882) and his Red Shirts, the popular drive for liberation, and the pressure of events. At the least, Victor Emmanuel did not obstruct unification, and according to most assessments, he assisted the process in key ways. In particular, he managed in volatile conditions to maintain contacts with the democratic movement while successfully presenting himself to moderates and frightened foreign governments as the only plausible guarantee against popular revolution.

The attempt of the Italian Felice Orsini (1819–1858) on Emperor Napoleon III's life (14 January 1858) opened a critical sequence of events. Napoleon III met with Cavour (July 20–21) and agreed to support Piedmont's effort to expel Austria from northern Italy. He accepted the creation of a northern Italian kingdom under Victor Emmanuel as part of an Italian confederation of states. Victor Emmanuel agreed in turn to cede Nice and Savoy to France and to marry his daughter Clotilde to the emperor's cousin, Prince Napoleon (alliance signed 24 January 1859). War broke out with Austria 27 April 1859, and French and Piedmontese troops forced an Austrian retreat. Under pressure from Napoleon III and over strong protests from Cavour, Victor Emmanuel accepted the truce of Villafranca (8 July 1859) and received control over Lombardy, causing Cavour to resign.

Meanwhile the duchies of central Italy (Tuscany, Modena, Parma, Bologna) collapsed, and moderate leaders moved rapidly to take control. They requested annexation to Piedmont-Sardinia, and with the encouragement of England and the sanction of plebiscites, Victor Emmanuel agreed. With the king's support and against the wishes of Cavour (who returned to power 21 January 1860), Garibaldi organized an army of volunteers and prepared to invade Sicily. The rapid liberation of Sicily from the Spanish Bourbons alarmed European powers, and

Victor Emmanuel publicly warned Garibaldi against crossing to the mainland, while privately urging him on. When Garibaldi landed in southern Italy (18 August), the Piedmontese army invaded the Papal States to stop him (10 September 1860). The forces met at Teano (26 October), and Garibaldi ceded Sicily and Naples to Victor Emmanuel.

As the first king of united Italy, Victor Emmanuel actively influenced foreign policy, working with his ministers to annex Venice (1866) and Rome (1870). Because parliamentary factionalism weakened cabinets, his authority to appoint ministers drew him into internal politics as well. Initially he favored the Right and then, with the "parliamentary revolution" of March 1876, he accepted the Left's arrival in power. His actions helped reduce the opposition of republicans to monarchy and of the South to unification under the North.

Victor Emmanuel died 9 January 1878 and was buried in the Pantheon in Rome.

See also **Crimean War; Italy; Risorgimento (Italian Unification); Umberto I.**

BIBLIOGRAPHY

Primary Sources

Victor Emmanuel II. *Le lettere di Vittorio Emanuele II, raccolte da Francesco Cognasso.* Turin, 1961. A collection of the king's letters.

Secondary Sources

Mack Smith, Denis. *Victor Emanuel, Cavour, and the Risorgimento.* London, 1971.

————. *Italy and Its Monarchy.* New Haven, Conn., 1989.

SUSAN A. ASHLEY

VICTORIA, QUEEN (1819–1901; ruled 1837–1901), queen of the United Kingdom.

The future Queen Victoria was born at Kensington Palace in the greater London area on 24 May 1819. She became queen of the United Kingdom of England, Scotland, and Ireland on 20 June 1837. After a reign of sixty-three-and-a-half years, the longest in British history, she died on 22 January 1901 at Osborne House, her winter home on the Isle of Wight. Her name became an adjective, "Victorian," because people increasingly associated her life and

her reign with such nineteenth-century ideals as a devoted family life, earnestness, public and private respectability, and obedience to the law. As the personal embodiment of her kingdom and her empire, she was ever eager to ensure that her land was held in high esteem by its European neighbors and throughout the world for its economic and military strength and as a model of modern civilization. During her lifetime, Great Britain was noted for its pioneering developments in science, industry, and finance; for its rapid growth of population; and for becoming the first large country in which the majority of the population lived in cities. Queen Victoria was the official head of state not only of the United Kingdom but also of the expanding worldwide British empire, which included Canada, Australia, New Zealand, India, and parts of Africa.

BACKGROUND AND CHILDHOOD

Although King George III, who reigned from 1760 to 1820, had fifteen children, his three eldest sons had no legitimate children who survived. In 1817 his fourth son, Edward Augustus, duke of Kent, married a German noblewoman, Victoire Marie Louise (the daughter of one duke and the widow of another), for the specific purposes of producing an heir to Britain's throne. He brought her to England just in time for little Victoria's birth. When the baby princess was just eight months old, her father died. Victoria's mother, the duchess of Kent, raised her in Kensington Palace with the help of German governesses, private English tutors, and the duchess's brother, Leopold. The last had been married briefly to an earlier heir to the British throne, Princess Charlotte, who had died in childbirth, and in 1831 he became king of the newly independent state of Belgium.

Victoria learned to speak and write German and French as readily as English. She was also taught literature, history, geography, and the Bible. She was given lessons in singing and in playing the piano, as well as in painting, a hobby that she enjoyed into her sixties. On the accession of her uncle, King William IV, in 1830, she became heir apparent to the throne and, at the behest of her mother, she took several lengthy summer tours through England and Wales that included both country estates and city centers. Had King William IV died any sooner, Victoria's mother would have become princess regent, but he lived just long enough—until 20 June 1837—to enable Victoria at age eighteen to inherit the throne in her own right.

EARLY REIGN

Immediately on becoming queen, Victoria began regular meetings with William Lamb, second viscount Melbourne, Britain's prime minister at the time. The two grew very close, and the grandfatherly Lord Melbourne (1779–1848) taught Victoria how the government of her country worked on a day-to-day basis. Britain in the nineteenth century was a constitutional monarchy, and the king or queen was the head of state who was expected to rule by means of a prime minister as the head of government, with the members of his cabinet serving as the heads of administrative departments. They were also members of, and required the support of, the United Kingdom Parliament, made up of an elected House of Commons and a (largely) hereditary House of Lords. When a general election left no single political party with an overall majority, the monarch initiated the process of government formation by inviting a particular parliamentarian to serve as prime minister and "form a government."

In practice, ultimate executive authority no longer lay with Queen Victoria, but a significant degree of influence remained to her—in matters of policy as well as in the appointment of cabinet members, ambassadors, and archbishops and bishops of the Church of England, an institution that the monarch served as "supreme governor." On a daily basis she perused boxes of cabinet papers and diplomatic correspondence, and she conferred regularly by letter and in person with all ten of her prime ministers. In private, Queen Victoria was ever prepared to speak her mind. Much of the queen's time was also devoted to ceremonial activities such as the award of honors and the official opening and (until the 1850s) closing of each year's session of Parliament.

Because Melbourne led the Whig Party (later known as the Liberal Party), Victoria became publicly identified with that party rather than with the opposition Tory (or Conservative) Party. The Whigs were known for their relative sympathy for freedom of speech and of the press and for greater religious liberty for those Britons who (as

independent Protestants or Roman Catholics or Jews) did not belong to the established Church of England. They were also becoming increasingly sympathetic to the promotion of international free trade. For the time being, the Tories were more concerned with maintaining the land's established institutions and with keeping the electorate within the limits—one adult male in five—set by the Reform Act of 1832.

The young queen hoped that the Whigs and their parliamentary allies would maintain their House of Commons majority and that Melbourne would remain prime minister. When it appeared in 1839 that he might have to give up the post, the queen successfully used her influence to keep him. In the so-called Bedchamber Crisis, she refused to allow the Tory leader, Sir Robert Peel (1788–1850), to change the aristocratic Whig ladies at her court. Peel then gave up the task of "forming a government," and Melbourne continued as prime minister for two more years. A new general election in 1841 resulted in a decisive Tory majority in the House of Commons, however, and Victoria was compelled to accept Peel in his place.

THE YEARS WITH ALBERT (1840–1861)

Victoria's early years as queen were filled not only with government papers but also with parties, dances, concerts, and with visits by eligible potential husbands. In 1839 Victoria fell in love with one of these, her first cousin, Prince Albert of the small German duchy of Saxe-Coburg-Gotha. They were married on 10 February 1840, and Albert soon came to take a keen interest in the government of his new country. He served as his wife's private secretary, and he persuaded her that, even as they both took an intense behind-the-scenes interest in the ministries that governed in Victoria's name, publicly she should stand above party. Albert was an exceptionally serious and studious young prince who was more interested in science, music, and scholarship than in traditional aristocratic sports and pastimes. He served as chancellor of Cambridge University and he became the prime inspirer of the Great Exhibition of the Works of All Nations, the first true World's Fair, which was held in London's Hyde Park during the summer of 1851.

Queen Victoria, Prince Albert and the Prince of Wales at Windsor Park with Their Herd of Llamas. Anonymous painting, nineteenth century. PRIVATE COLLECTION/BRIDGEMAN ART LIBRARY

Back in 1846 the royal couple had encouraged the efforts of Sir Robert Peel to abolish the Corn Laws and lead Britain toward international free trade, but in the process Peel's Conservative Party split in two. During the 1850s, with a two-party tradition in temporary disarray, the influence of the monarch on the formation of nineteenth-century ministries reached a nineteenth-century highpoint. In 1851, royal initiative led to the dismissal of the popular Henry John Temple, third viscount Palmerston, from his post. The foreign secretary appeared too sympathetic to liberal nationalist groups undermining their fellow European monarchs, and he had failed too often to consult the queen before sending dispatches to British diplomats abroad. Although initially unhappy with the manner in which their kingdom drifted into the Crimean War (1854–1856) against Russia, Queen Victoria became an enthusiastic supporter of the conflict once fighting had begun, and on 5 February 1855 she named

Palmerston as wartime prime minister. She personally instituted the Victoria Cross as Britain's highest award for wartime valor.

Although respected by most of his new countrymen, Albert was little loved; he was sometimes criticized as an interfering foreigner, and his heavy German accent did not help. For the emotional Victoria, the stalwart Albert resembled a knight in shining armor, however, and between 1840 and 1857 they became the parents of nine children, all of whom grew to adulthood: Victoria (b. 1840), Albert Edward (b. 1841), Alice (b. 1843), Alfred (b. 1844), Helena (b. 1846), Louise (b. 1848), Arthur (b. 1850), Leopold (b. 1853), and Beatrice (b. 1857). The royal family seemed to be a model family, a family that increasingly enjoyed a private domestic life either at Windsor or at Osborne House (on the English Channel coast) or at Balmoral Castle (in the Scottish Highlands), both of the latter rebuilt on the basis of Albert's designs. Victoria and

Albert took an intense personal interest in the upbringing of their children, which they did not leave solely to nannies and governesses.

THE YEARS OF WIDOWHOOD

Queen Victoria never recovered entirely from Albert's death on 14 December 1861 at the age of forty-two. For almost a decade she remained in strict mourning. She rarely set foot in London, and she avoided most public occasions (such as the state opening of Parliament). She made exceptions for the unveiling of statues dedicated to Prince Albert and, after a few years, for attendance at army reviews. During the later 1860s her absence from the public stage caused several respectable politicians as well as radical agitators to propose that the United Kingdom be transformed into a republic. Behind the scenes, the queen continued to peruse papers and to talk and write to her ministers. She also found comfort in a loyal domestic staff headed by her favorite attendant, a Scottish Highlander named John Brown. Her influence determined the appointments of several bishops and archbishops. It also led to the passage of statutes such as an act of 1876 that restricted the right of scientists to experiment on living animals and an act of the same year that proclaimed Victoria empress of India.

In her youth she had been known as "Queen of the Whigs," but in the course of the 1870s she privately came to prefer Benjamin Disraeli, the leader of the Conservative Party (1868–1881) to William Ewart Gladstone, the leader of the Liberal Party (1868–1875, 1880–1894). In Victoria's eyes, Disraeli seemed more concerned with upholding Britain's international prestige and consolidating its empire. She made little secret of her disappointment with the results of the general election of 1880, which left her no choice but to reappoint Gladstone as prime minister. He impressed her as too much the popular demagogue prepared to tamper with the kingdom's institutions. She interpreted Gladstone's unsuccessful proposals in 1886 and again in 1893 to grant "Home Rule" (domestic self-government) to Ireland as a step to break up the British Empire. She was more sympathetic to the Conservative ministries led by Robert Arthur Gascoyne-Cecil, third marquess of Salisbury, that

Caricature of Queen Victoria. From *Le Musée de Sires, feuille de caricatures,* by Auguste Roubille, 1901. PRIVATE COLLECTION/BRIDGEMAN ART LIBRARY/ THE STAPLETON COLLECTION

governed Britain during most of the final fifteen years of the nineteenth century.

THE GRANDMOTHER OF EUROPE

During the decades after Albert's death, Queen Victoria remained increasingly concerned with her ever-growing family. All nine of her children married, and eight of them had children of their own. Most of those children and grandchildren married into the nobility of Europe. Thus one granddaughter became the tsarina of Russia and others the queens of Spain, Romania, Greece, and Norway; the aging matriarch become known as the "Grandmother of Europe."

The most important of such dynastic marriages involved Victoria's eldest child, also known as Victoria, who in 1858 at age seventeen wed Crown Prince Frederick, the heir to the kingdom of Prussia and (after 1871) also the German Empire. Albert and Victoria hoped that the marriage would strengthen Anglo-German relations and help transform Prussia into a liberal constitutional monarchy journals published in 1868 and 1884 helped humanize her in the eyes of her subjects. Her Golden Jubilee (the fiftieth anniversary on the throne), which brought monarchs from all over Europe to London, was celebrated with great enthusiasm in 1887, and her Diamond Jubilee of 1897 evoked an even greater spirit of national and imperial pride. British political leaders and military regiments from five continents marched in London; the gathering provided the occasion for the very first meeting of colonial prime ministers—a precedent for the twentieth-century Commonwealth. After the Boer War (1899–1902) began, the aged queen became a single-minded champion of the British war effort, which included a state visit to Ireland in April 1900 (only the fourth of her reign) to thank Irish soldiers in the British army in Africa for their bravery. She both endured military defeats and celebrated victories before her own life ended on 22 January 1901 at Osborne House. A week-and-a-half later, after an elaborate military procession from Osborne to Windsor by ship, train, and horse-drawn gun carriage, her funeral was followed by a burial next to Albert in the Frogmore Mausoleum.

CONCLUSIONS

The very length of Queen Victoria's sixty-three-and-a-half-year reign gives a deceptive impression of continuity and stability to what proved a period of dynamic change within the British Isles and the world. The queen sympathized with many of these changes such as the railroad, the camera, and the use of anesthetics in childbirth. She was more doubtful about others, such as the rapid increase in the size of an electorate that by 1901 included most men and (in local government elections) some women. She preferred to see women preside over the home and to serve as matchmakers, hostesses, and volunteer social workers rather than as doctors or lawyers. A more disciplined political party system diminished her political influence only a little in the course of her reign, and by the time of her death she had become the world's best-known and most admired ruler and its most famous woman. She also remained a symbol of strict morality, good manners, and devotion to duty. She took great pride in her role as the formal head of the world's largest multiracial and multireligious empire, and (unlike some of her ministers) she believed in the civil rights of all her subjects. Thus

Queen Victoria with her granddaughter Alexandra (left, holding baby daughter Tatiana), her grandson-in-law, Tsar Nicholas II of Russia (standing, left), and her son Albert Edward (later King Edward VII). ©HULTON-DEUTSCH COLLECTION/CORBIS

like that of Britain. Such hopes were to be disappointed as the crown prince was to be limited by cancer to a reign of ninety-nine days in 1888. Frederick's son (Queen Victoria's eldest grandson), the German emperor William II, was to lead the Central Powers during World War I (1914–1918) against the Allied coalition formally headed by another grandson (King George V of Great Britain) and by the husband (Tsar Nicholas II of Russia) of a granddaughter. Queen Victoria was often disappointed in her own immediate heir, Albert Edward, a slow learner who generally preferred play to work. His marriage in 1863 to the beautiful Alexandra of Denmark was popular, however, and the prince and princess of Wales enjoyed their role as social arbiters.

The prince of Wales had to wait patiently to inherit the kingship, as during the 1880s his mother become more visible again and regained her earlier popularity. Excerpts from her private she became the first modern British monarch to confer a hereditary peerage on a Roman Catholic and the first ever to confer one on a professing Jew. In a world familiar with authoritarian rulers, she remained a symbol of the type of constitutional government in which change came by election and by parliamentary legislation rather than by revolution.

See also **Alexandra; Corn Laws, Repeal of; Crystal Palace; George IV; Imperialism; India; Nicholas I; Tories; William II; William IV.**

BIBLIOGRAPHY

Primary Sources

Hibbert, Christopher, ed. *Queen Victoria in Her Letters and Journals.* London, 1984. A chronological compilation of many of the queen's own writings that enables the reader to see the world through her eyes.

The Letters of Queen Victoria. First series edited by Arthur Christopher Benson and Viscount Reginald Baliol Brett Esher, London, 1908; second series edited by George Earl Buckle, London, 1926–1928; third series edited by George Earl Buckle, 1930–1932. The single largest series of letters, nine volumes in all, by and to the queen. Emphasizes her political roles rather than her family life.

Secondary Sources

Arnstein, Walter L. *Queen Victoria.* Basingstoke, U.K., and New York, 2003. Focuses on the monarch's political, military, and religious roles.

Hibbert, Christopher. *Queen Victoria: A Personal History.* London, 2000.

Longford, Elizabeth. *Victoria, R. I.* London and New York, 1964. The first biography to make full documented use of the unpublished Royal Archives at Windsor. A sympathetic yet balanced account.

Strachey, Lytton. *Queen Victoria.* London, 1921. The single most widely read life and a notable example of biography as a work of literary art.

Vallone, Lynne. *Becoming Victoria.* New Haven, Conn., 2001. The fullest account of the queen's early years.

Warner, Marina. *Queen Victoria's Sketchbook.* London and New York, 1979.

Weintraub, Stanley. *Victoria: An Intimate Biography.* New York, 1987.

Williams, Richard. *The Contentious Crown: Public Discussion of the British Monarchy in the Reign of Queen Victoria.* Aldershot, U.K., 1997.

Woodham-Smith, Cecil. *Queen Victoria from Her Birth to the Death of the Prince Consort.* London, 1972. The

most detailed fully documented account of the first half of Victoria's life.

WALTER L. ARNSTEIN

VIENNA. Traditionally the seat of the Habsburg dynasty and the capital of its central European territories, Vienna experienced both great development and relative decline in the nineteenth century. With a population in 1789 of roughly 200,000, Vienna was the third-largest city in Europe after London and Paris. It experienced, like most major cities, an extraordinary population boom in the period. By 1914 Vienna's population was over two million, but the city was now only fourth-largest in Europe, having been overtaken by Berlin. This was symbolic of the waning significance of Vienna as a political center, due to the checkered career of the Habsburg dynasty. It is indeed virtually impossible to disentangle Viennese history from Austrian history in general, and the name *Vienna* came to symbolize for the national communities of the Habsburg Monarchy not simply a city but rather the whole nexus of central power of the Habsburg state.

Vienna was not only a political and administrative but also a major economic and cultural center. It underwent dramatic modernization, especially after midcentury, even though the relative slowness of this development compared to Berlin's explosive growth gave rise to an image of Vienna as the conservative, even backward, *other* capital of central Europe. By 1900 it enjoyed a cultural reputation as a more old-fashioned, less avant-garde center than either Paris or Berlin, and it is only in retrospect that fin-de-siècle Vienna, the capital of a decadent multinational empire at the crossroads of so many of the positive and negative movements in the coming modern world, has come to be seen as a major center of innovation in its own right.

1789–1815: WAR AND PEACE

In 1789 Vienna was still a walled city, surrounded on three sides by steep banks (on the fourth by a short stretch of the Danube River), beyond which the city's suburbs spread. Architecturally the city was dominated by the baroque. The enlightened absolutism of Joseph II's rule had liberalized Viennese cultural and intellectual life, and the city had

The New Market, Vienna. Engraving, 1799. ©HISTORICAL PICTURE ARCHIVE/CORBIS

become the center of the German musical world. Combining both tendencies, Wolfgang Amadeus Mozart's hymn to (Masonic) reason, *Die Zauberflöte* (*The Magic Flute*) was premiered at Vienna's Theater auf der Wieden in September 1791. The outlook for enlightened reform was already darkening by 1789, however, and the consequences of the French Revolution, along with the deaths in quick succession of Joseph II and Leopold II, set Austria on a course by which Vienna, as seat of the Habsburgs, came to represent the ideological nemesis of the revolution.

Revolutionary opposition in Vienna itself was slight and was snuffed out ruthlessly, but Austria lost a series of wars to Revolutionary and Napoleonic France, and Vienna was occupied twice by French armies, in 1805 and 1809. On the second occasion a part of Vienna's fortifications, at the Hofburg, was razed. The cost of these lost wars had a devastating effect on Habsburg finances, leading to state bankruptcy in 1811, with long-term damage to the Austrian, and Viennese, economies.

Cultural life, however, carried on. During these bleak years Ludwig van Beethoven premiered most of his symphonies in Vienna, and the premiere of his opera *Fidelio* in November 1805 occurred during the French occupation, with many of the audience being French officers. Habsburg efforts after 1805 to encourage German nationalism even attracted a group of conservative German Romantic poets to the city as Germany's "capital," although the defeat of 1809 ended this project.

Count Metternich's astute diplomacy after 1809 and the defeat of the French in Russia in 1812–1813 brought about a radical reversal of Austria's, and Vienna's, fortunes by 1814. In September 1814 Vienna became the site of the congress that was to reconstruct pre-Napoleonic Europe. The Congress of Vienna was an opportunity for Austria and the Viennese to entertain the other European powers and to persuade them to see Europe Metternich's conservative way, which to a large extent they did. The congress also confirmed Vienna's reputation as a city of many amusements but not one at the vanguard of progress. The Prince de Ligne commented that: "Le congrès ne marche pas; il danse" (the congress does not walk [i.e., make progress]; it dances). The congress ended in June 1815 with a fairly durable settlement, but the comment was quite prescient about Vienna in the coming years.

1815–1848: BIEDERMEIER AND *VORMÄRZ*

By the 1820s Vienna's population, including the suburbs, had risen to roughly 300,000, with surplus labor from the countryside flooding into the city's proto-industrial outskirts. Economic growth, however, lagged, and population growth was not matched by modernization of the city's infrastructure. Gas lighting was introduced in 1817 but not systematically. The Danube flooded disastrously in 1830, and the lack of an adequate water supply resulted in a cholera epidemic in 1831 and 1832. A new water supply system, built after 1835, was ineffective. A new gate was punched through the walls at the Kärntnertor, but otherwise the old city remained walled in.

The city's political life was similarly stifled. Metternich and his master, Francis I, reacting to the upheavals of the French Revolution, were determined to stop all political change, and the public sense of relief after the revolutionary crisis soon turned to a sense of stagnation. Under Metternich's "system," Austria and Vienna became watchwords throughout Europe for oppression, and although this reputation was exaggerated, the secret police and censorship system was quite well developed. Viennese intellectual life suffered as a result, and even Austria's greatest writer of the era, Franz Grillparzer, a loyal bureaucrat, was seriously affected by the censor's interventions.

Yet musical life continued to flourish. Beethoven's Ninth Symphony was first performed in Vienna in 1824, and Franz Schubert produced all of his great work in the period, dying in 1828. The waltz, developed by Joseph Lanner and Johann Strauss the Elder, first became part of Viennese life. In drama, Vienna's Burgtheater under Joseph Schreyvogel became the premier German stage. Given the political and intellectual climate, the dominant style of the period was one of domestic, private, inward-looking simplicity, which came to be known as Biedermeier.

The revolutions in western Europe in 1830 and the death of Francis I in 1835 ushered in a new era of frustration with the "system" and a shift toward optimism about the possibilities of progress that came to be known in retrospect as *Vormärz* (Before March 1848). In popular theater the change could be seen in the succession from the fantasy plays of Ferdinand Raimund to the ribald satire of Johann Nestroy. The most obvious expression of the new approach was Eduard Bauernfeld's play *Grossjährig* (Of age), performed, remarkably, at the Burgtheater in 1847. This cultural shift paralleled and reflected economic and technological change in the city. In 1838 the Nordbahn, Austria's first steam railway, financed by the Rothschilds, reached Vienna, and by the 1840s Vienna was linked up to the Continental rail system; in the 1840s a proper gas distribution system was being installed. In 1847 the Austrian Academy of Sciences was founded. Vienna was, haphazardly, becoming a modern city.

1848–1861: REVOLUTION, REACTION, REFORM?

With the population of Vienna approaching 400,000 by 1848, such incoherent improvements were not keeping pace with the basic needs of the populace. The harvest failures of 1846 and 1847 led to economic depression and near-starvation in Vienna's ever-growing lower classes. Meanwhile the Habsburg machinery of government had effectively ground to a halt and was pressed on all sides, especially in Hungary, by calls for greater autonomy and freedoms. News of revolution in France in late February 1848 led to a demonstration in Vienna on 13 March. This turned to revolt when troops fired on the crowd and to revolution when a panicked Habsburg family sacked Metternich, acceding in the days following to many of the demands of the "revolutionaries."

The revolution of 13 March 1848 marked the high point of Vienna's involvement in Austrian politics in the nineteenth century. Over the next months Vienna remained at the center of the revolution in the Austrian Empire. An elected constituent assembly, the Reichstag, met there in July. However, national divisions in the monarchy and social and ideological divisions within Vienna severely compromised the revolution. Most decisive was the failure of the revolutionaries to wrest

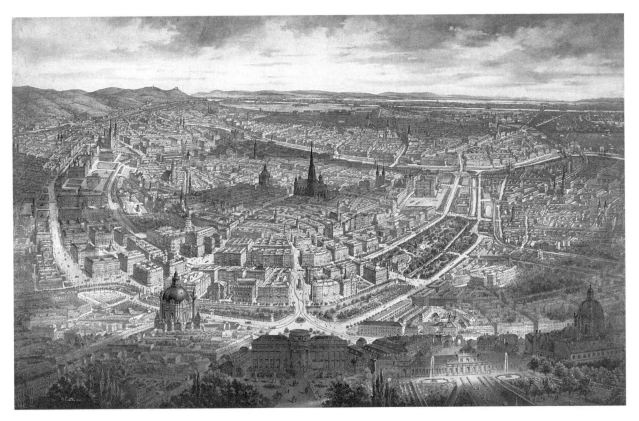

Bird's eye view of Vienna. Engraving by Gustav Veith, 1873. Erich Lessing/Art Resource, NY

control of the military from the Habsburgs. After another radical revolt in Vienna in October, a Habsburg army under Prince Alfred Windischgrätz bombarded and then conquered the city. Several revolutionary leaders were executed, and the city was put under martial law until 1853.

The revolution had a detrimental effect on the city's economy, but culturally and intellectually it produced a huge outpouring of pent-up creativity, reflected in the flood of publications in the period. It is telling, however, that one of the most memorable plays of the period was Nestroy's *Freiheit in Krähwinkel* (Freedom in Krähwinkel), a positive but skeptical account of the revolution's dynamics, and that the most famous musical piece was Johann Strauss the Elder's *Radetzkymarsch,* a loyalist celebration of Habsburg victory against the Italians (and the revolution).

Under the "decreed constitution" (1849–1852), Vienna was given a Provisional Communal Ordinance on 6 March 1850. This integrated the suburbs fully into the city administration, creating

a nine-district municipality that lasted until 1890. It allowed for an elected 120-man council (on a very narrow, tax-based, tri-curial franchise), which in turn elected a mayor. Theoretically, the law gave Vienna considerable autonomy, but the imposition of (neo-)absolutism in 1852 ended this. The centralist neoabsolutist regime wanted, however, to develop Vienna as a suitable capital for a modern absolutist Habsburg state. Hence it initiated in 1857 one of the most beneficial changes in Vienna's modern history: the demolition of the city walls and their replacement by a broad boulevard, the Ringstrasse (Ring Street). The collapse of the neoabsolutist regime in 1859 and 1860 led to the restitution of the 1850 ordinance in 1860, and the March 1861 municipal elections created a large liberal majority that set about modernizing Vienna in earnest.

1861–1890: RINGSTRASSE LIBERALISM
By 1859 Vienna had a population of over 500,000; in 1869 it reached 607,000; in 1890, 828,000. This population increase reflected Vienna's growth

as an economic center, but as a political center Vienna declined in importance. The catastrophic defeat by Prussia in 1866 meant that Austria, and hence Vienna, was shut out of Germany. The Ausgleich (compromise) with Hungary in the same year also greatly reduced the range of Vienna's administrative rule, which now only extended over Cisleithania, the Austrian half of Austria-Hungary. Vienna enjoyed a much larger degree of municipal autonomy after the *Reichsgemeindegesetz* (Imperial Communal Law) of 1862. From 1861 it hosted the new representative assembly, the Reichsrat; after 1867, however, this was only for Cisleithania. Vienna did remain the seat of the "common" ministries (foreign, defense, and financial) of Dualist Austria-Hungary and the main residence of the emperor and court.

In the economic sphere Vienna developed spectacularly in the early liberal era of 1860 to 1873. Known as the *Gründerjahre* (founders' years), this period saw massive gains for Austrian entrepreneurs (hence the name), who invested much of their profits in the imperial center, especially in the new developments around the Ringstrasse. Of particular note were the many "palaces" built by Jewish financiers such as Gustav Epstein and Friedrich Schey, who, with their families, became an important part of Vienna's "second society" (the "first" being the court and high nobility).

The new liberal administration modernized major parts of Vienna's infrastructure: new banks were built for the Danube (1862–1875), a new aqueduct providing water from the Alps was finished in 1873, a large number of schools and hospitals were built, and the Central Cemetery was opened in 1874. The Ringstrasse became the site for major civic and imperial—and heavily representational—buildings, among them the twin Natural and Art History Museums, the university, the new Burgtheater; the Greek classical parliament, and the Belgian-Gothic Rathaus (city hall) among them. By the 1880s Vienna had been transformed into an exemplary modern nineteenth-century capital.

Yet by then, the German liberal hegemony in Austria no longer existed. The economic boom came to a halt in the crash of 1873, brought on by a wave of speculation surrounding Vienna's hosting of the International Exhibition that year combined with another cholera outbreak. The Lib-

erals lost their majority in the Reichsrat in 1879 to the conservative and federalist "Iron Ring." Vienna remained a bastion of liberalism, but only because of its restrictive franchise. The emergence in the 1880s of anti-Semitic German nationalism in student and middle-class circles and the anti-Semitic Christian Social movement in the lower middle classes, together with the reconstitution of the Social Democrats in 1888 at nearby Hainburg, signaled by 1890 the approaching end of the liberal era in Viennese politics.

Culturally and intellectually this period is usually seen as relatively barren as Vienna became, in Hermann Broch's phrase, a "value vacuum." The 1860s had seen the emergence of Viennese operetta, inspired by Jacques Offenbach's works. Johann Strauss the Younger's *Die Fledermaus* was first performed in 1874. (His "Blue Danube" waltz appeared in 1867.) Vienna also became the home of Johannes Brahms in 1878 and remained a major center of the German musical world. In art the period was dominated by the sensual historicism of Hans Makart, whose orchestration of the Ringstrasse parade celebrating the Silver Wedding of Francis Joseph and Elisabeth in 1879 is seen by many as the epitome of the parvenu kitsch of the Ringstrasse style. At the same time, the university prospered, especially its renowned medical school, and a sophisticated press, most notably the *Neue Freie Presse* (founded 1864), developed to serve the emergent, sizable educated class. The results were soon evident.

1890–1914: VIENNA 1900

On 18 December 1890 the incorporation of Vienna's outlying suburbs was made law, effective January 1892. Vienna became a city of nineteen districts with a population of 1,365,000. Partly due to this expansion, the municipal elections of 1895 saw a shocking defeat for the Liberals by a Christian Social and German Nationalist coalition, whose platform was anti-Semitism. This was initially resisted by the Habsburg authorities, and the anti-Semites' leader, Karl Lueger, was only confirmed as mayor by the emperor Francis Joseph after much delay, in 1897. From that point on, however, the Christian Socials were able to manipulate the franchise to ensure their complete hegemony over Viennese politics. Lueger's rule was in

Head of a Woman. Sketch by Gustave Klimt. As founder of the Vienna Sezession group, which was instrumental in developing the art nouveau style in Austria, Klimt was one notable example of the rich cultural environment in Vienna in the late nineteenth and early twentieth centuries. NEUE GALERIE, LINZ, AUSTRIA/BRIDGEMAN ART LIBRARY

Yet this was also the period in which the cultural and educational investments of previous generations came to fruition in a series of great cultural and intellectual achievements, known collectively as fin-de-siècle Vienna or "Vienna 1900." These included Freud's development of psychoanalysis; the art of Gustav Klimt and the Secession as well as of the Austrian expressionists, including Egon Schiele and Oskar Kokoschka; the music of Gustav Mahler and the young Arnold Schoenberg; the beginnings of the philosophical Vienna Circle; Austromarxism; and major contributions in such fields as physics, physiology, economics, medicine, law, and sociology. Vienna had a flourishing literary world that comprised far more than mere "coffeehouse wits" and included major writers such as Hugo von Hofmannsthal, Arthur Schnitzler, and Karl Kraus. It also developed a thriving popular mass culture, especially in operetta.

Part of this was to be expected in a city that by 1910 had a population of more than 2,031,000 and had continued to expand as the major educational and economic hub of the Dual Monarchy. In retrospect, however, the achievement of Vienna 1900, especially its very early insights into the modern world's problems, requires explanation. Some see this as a result of the alienation of liberals from power and the retreat of the next generation into the refuge of art; others have, more narrowly perhaps, pointed to the very large presence, even predominance, of Jews as creators and supporters of this culture.

Jews were not the largest minority group in Vienna: estimates put those of Czech origin as about a quarter of Vienna's quite polyglot populace before 1914, whereas Jews were by then under 10 percent of the whole. Yet the Jews were the group that became the designated "outsiders"; they also were the group that invested by far the most proportionally in secondary and higher education. This, combined with their position within Vienna's social and economic structures (heavily overrepresented in commerce and the liberal professions), as well as the alienation caused by the success of political anti-Semitism in the city, helps account for the remarkable Jewish presence in the circles of the modern culture that has made Vienna 1900 so famous. In this view, it is precisely because Jews were threatened by the developments in late Habsburg Vienna that they recognized the problems with

practice much more moderate than his rhetoric suggested, and his municipalization of the city's utilities and expansion of amenities are seen by most as contributing to a golden era in Vienna's history. Nevertheless, his anti-Semitism, though seen as opportunistic, had practical effects on city policies and cast a pall over life for Vienna's Jews, as well as encouraging the prejudices of those who were not mere opportunists, such as Adolf Hitler.

Vienna was around 1900 the central stage for Cisleithanian mass politics. From 1890 there was an annual mass march by the Social Democrats on 1 May along the Ring; in 1897 and 1898 the Badeni affair, which touched on German-Czech relations, led to clashes in parliament and the streets; and from 1905 to 1907 there were mass demonstrations in favor of universal suffrage (passed in 1907). The national divisions of the last years of the monarchy tended, however, to see parliament stagnate and power pass from Vienna to the provincial, national centers.

modernity and progress that only appeared later to others and so were forced to come up with solutions that anticipated later developments elsewhere.

See also **Austria-Hungary; Cities and Towns.**

BIBLIOGRAPHY

Primary Sources

Musil, Robert. *The Man without Qualities.* 2 vols. Translated by Sophie Wilkins. New York, 1995. Translated from *Der Mann ohn Eigenschaften,* edited by Adolf Frisé. 2 vols. Reinbek, Germany, 1978.

Schnitzler, Arthur. *The Road to the Open.* Translated by Horace Samuel, with a foreword by William M. Johnston. Evanston, Ill., 1991. Translated from *Der Weg ins Freie.* Frankfurt-am-Main, 1961.

Secondary Sources

Barea, Ilsa. *Vienna.* New York, 1966.

Beller, Steven. *Vienna and the Jews, 1867–1938: A Cultural History.* Cambridge, U.K., and New York, 1989.

Beller, Steven, ed. *Rethinking Vienna 1900.* New York and Oxford, U.K., 2001.

Boyer, John W. *Political Radicalism in Late Imperial Vienna.* Chicago, 1981.

———. *Culture and Political Crisis in Vienna.* Chicago, 1995.

Broch, Hermann. *Hugo von Hofmannsthal and His Time.* Translated by Michael P. Steinberg. Chicago, 1984.

Csendes, Peter. *Geschichte Wiens.* Vienna, 1990.

Janik, Allan, and Stephen Toulmin. *Wittgenstein's Vienna.* Chicago, 1996.

Schorske, Carl E. *Fin-de-Siècle Vienna: Politics and Culture.* London, 1980.

Spiel, Hilde. *Vienna's Golden Autumn, 1866–1938.* New York, 1987.

STEVEN BELLER

VIOLLET-LE-DUC, EUGÈNE (1814–1879), French architect.

Considered by many to be one of the most important theoreticians of architecture in the modern era, Eugène Viollet-le-Duc is renowned for his restorations of Gothic architecture in France during the nineteenth century. He began his professional career at a very young age with the Commission des Monuments Historiques soon after its formation as a government bureau in 1837. The commission was responsible for the classification of buildings as historical monuments, which rendered them eligible to receive credits from the state for their restoration and upkeep. Viollet-le-Duc quickly became the public and intellectual face of the commission, working alongside the director Prosper Mérimée, who was his close friend and lifelong supporter.

Viollet-le-Duc's most famous restoration projects were carried out under the auspices of the commission: the abbey church at Vézelay, begun in December 1839; the cathedral of Notre-Dame in Paris with Jean-Baptiste-Antoine Lassus (from 1844); the abbey church of Saint-Denis (from 1846); the walled town of Carcassonne (from 1849); Amiens cathedral (from 1849); and the Château de Pierrefonds (from 1858, and funded by Napoleon III's personal treasury). In addition to actual restoration work, Viollet-le-Duc was a prolific writer, with numerous books and articles to his credit. His famous *Dictionnaire raisonné de l'architecture française du XIe au XVIe siècle* (Reasoned dictionary of French architecture from the eleventh to the sixteenth century), published in ten volumes (1854–1868), is his philosophy of gothic architecture in the form of a dictionary. These writings influenced modern architects, such as Le Corbusier and Frank Lloyd Wright. Beginning in 1858, Viollet-le-Duc published the first volume of his equally ambitious but lesser known *Dictionnaire raisonné du mobilier français de l'époque carlovingienne à la Rénaissance* (1858–1875; Reasoned dictionary of the French bank from the Carlovingians to the Renaissance). His more forthrightly personal and polemical two-volume *Entretiens sur l'architecture* (1863 and 1872; *Discourses on Architecture*, 1875) contrasts his architectural pedagogy and epistemology with the given course of education provided by the state-run École des Beaux-Arts. As a true polymath his other writings ranged from a book on Mont Blanc in the French Alps to a series of pedagogical books/novels for adolescents and articles on politics and military strategy.

Although Viollet-le-Duc's reputation as a theorist of architecture has fared well over the years, his restoration practice has undergone significant reevaluations in the last century. Until the 1960s, his restoration work was vilified, the responses ranging from mild criticism to vitriolic attack.

Notre Dame de Paris c. 1835, before Viollet-le-Duc's addition of the spire. Engraving by J. H. Le Keux after a drawing by Thomas Allom. MARY EVANS PICTURE LIBRARY

Whereas architects of the modern tradition valorized his emphasis on a "constructive" relationship to the past—which has been reduced in historiography to Viollet-le-Duc's supposed championing of "structural rationalism"—others, such as the architectural historian Achille Carlier, severely criticized Viollet-le-Duc's interventionist approach to restoration. With the "fantastic" restoration of Pierrefonds serving as the prime example of his supposedly overzealous imagination, his restorations were taken to be "monstrous" in the literal sense of that term: producing a new entity out of the previous remains of the given building. From this perspective, Viollet-le-Duc was judged rather harshly in comparison to the anti-interventionist philosophies of restoration personified by John Ruskin and Marcel Proust (often conveniently overlooking the fact that both had a profound admiration for Viollet-le-Duc's work). Beginning in 1980, a more even-handed approach to Viollet-le-Duc's restoration work became the norm with the spate of catalogs and collected essays published to mark the centennial of his death.

See also **Paris; Ruskin, John; Schinkel, Karl Friedrich.**

BIBLIOGRAPHY

Primary Sources

"Ouvrages de Viollet-le-Duc." In *Viollet-le-Duc: Catalogue d'exposition,* 397–404. Paris, 1980. This section contains a fairly comprehensive bibliography of Viollet-le-Duc's publications including books, articles, prefaces, and work done in collaboration with other scholars.

Viollet-le-Duc, Eugène. *The Foundations of Architecture: Selections from the "Dictionnaire raisonné."* Translated by Kenneth D. Whitehead. New York, 1990. Includes good translations of some key entries in the *Dictionnaire raisonné.*

Secondary Sources

Bergdoll, Barry. Introduction to *The Foundations of Architecture: Selections from the "Dictionnaire raisonné,"* by Eugène Viollet-le-Duc. New York, 1990.

Notre Dame de Paris c. 1870, after the addition of the spire. Color lithograph by Kronheim from the periodical *Sunday at Home.* MARY EVANS PICTURE LIBRARY

Boudon, Françoise. "Le réel et l'imaginaire chez Viollet-le-Duc: Les figures du *Dictionnaire de l'architecture*." *Revue de l'art* 58–59 (1983): 95–114.

Bressani, Martin. "Notes on Viollet-le-Duc's Philosophy of History: Dialectics and Technology." *Journal of the Society of Architectural Historians* 48, no. 4 (1989): 327–350.

Damisch, Hubert. "The Space Between: A Structuralist Approach to the *Dictionnaire*." *Architectural Design Profile* 17 (1980): 84–89.

Lee, Paula Young. "'The Rational Point of View': Eugène-Emmanuel Viollet-le-Duc and the *Camera Lucida*." In *Landscapes of Memory and Experience*, edited by Jan Birksted, 63–76. London, 2000.

Leniaud, Jean-Michel. *Viollet-le-Duc; ou, Les délires du systéme*. Paris, 1994.

Middleton, Robin. "The Rationalist Interpretations of Classicism of Léonce Reynaud and Viollet-le-Duc." *AA Files* 11 (1986): 29–48.

Murphy, Kevin D. *Memory and Modernity: Viollet-le-Duc at Vézelay.* University Park, Pa., 2000.

O'Connell, Lauren M. "Viollet-le-Duc on Drawing, Photography, and the 'Space outside the Frame.'" *History of Photography* 22, no. 2 (1998): 139–146.

Summerson, John. "Viollet-le-Duc and the Rational Point of View." In his *Heavenly Mansions and Other Essays on Architecture,* 135–158. London, 1949. Reprint, New York, 1963.

Vinegar, Aron. "Memory as Construction in Viollet-le-Duc's Architectural Imagination." *Paroles Gelées* 16, no. 2 (1998): 43–55.

———. "Viollet-le-Duc, Panoramic Photography, and the Restoration of the Château de Pierrefonds." In *International Viollet-le-Duc Colloquium,* edited by Werner Oechslin. Zürich, forthcoming.

ARON VINEGAR

VIRCHOW, RUDOLF (1821–1902), German pathologist and anthropologist.

Rudolf Virchow contributed to the transformation of medical knowledge in the nineteenth century and was a founding figure for the discipline of anthropology in Germany. He was born in Schivelbein, Pomerania (today Swidwin in northwest Poland), on 13 October 1821 and died in Berlin on 5 September 1902. After receiving his degree in 1843, Virchow practiced medicine in Berlin until he was suspended for his radical political views during the revolutions of 1848. He accepted a faculty position in Würzburg and returned to Berlin in 1856. He became the leading figure at Berlin's Pathological Institute, where he worked for forty-six years and trained generations of doctors and scientists.

As a coeditor and leading author of several medical handbooks, Virchow published the findings of contemporary clinical research. His pathbreaking *Die Cellularpathologie* (1858; *Cellular Pathology*) argued that cells are the building blocks of higher units of life and that they are mutually dependent. This attention to the vital nature of cells produced a series of new ideas about the formation and spread of disease. Before Virchow and his generation, doctors viewed disease primarily as a problem in the body's blood stream (the humors) or as an affliction of the nervous system. Virchow's microscopic study of cells challenged traditional views of illness by arguing that cells themselves were healthy or diseased. This discovery is central to modern medicine's understanding of tumors and cancer.

Virchow vigorously advocated applications of scientific knowledge beyond the laboratory. His reports on infectious diseases in central Europe from 1848 and 1852 urged doctors to lead the fight for better sanitation conditions and higher levels of literacy and prosperity among rural populations. After his return to Berlin in 1856, Virchow served on the city council as a public health expert. He campaigned for a modern sewer system in the city and promoted improvements in the heating and ventilation of public institutions, such as hospitals, schools, military barracks, and prisons. Following his research on parasitic worms as the cause of trichinosis, Virchow started a vigorous campaign for meat inspection in 1872. These reforms grew out of Virchow's belief that science would bring progress to society, and they were part of the broad program of nineteenth-century liberalism that championed rational thinking and positive state reforms.

Virchow also had a career on the national political stage. In the 1860s, he opposed Prime Minister Otto von Bismarck's plans for military spending in the Prussian Diet. After the unification of Germany in 1871, Virchow supported the national Kulturkampf (the "cultural struggle" to eliminate the influence of Catholicism in politics and education). He felt that science and rationality would flourish in a state free of clerical influence. Virchow served as a delegate to the German Empire's Reichstag from 1880 to 1893.

From the 1860s until his death, Virchow shaped the fields of prehistoric archaeology and anthropology in Germany. He championed an empirical approach to archaeology that eschewed patriotic or romantic conclusions and challenged the idea that prehistoric finds were directly related to contemporary national communities. Virchow was also active outside central Europe as a delegate to international conferences and as an archaeologist in Egypt, Turkey, and central Asia. Virchow was equally significant as the organizer of the German Anthropological Society and the Berlin Society for Anthropology, Ethnology, and Prehistory, the most important networks for anthropology and archaeology in Germany. Virchow's reputation as a leading scientist contributed to the status of these organizations, and his efforts helped to secure state support for Berlin's Museum for Ethnology, which opened in 1886.

Traditional scholarship has admired Virchow's achievements in medicine and anthropology and presented him as a champion of objective science and rational reforms. Recent work, however, has placed Virchow, German anthropology, and liberalism's faith in science in a broader intellectual context. In this rendering, Virchow's interest in studying human beings during an epoch of national strength and imperialism contributed to the rise of biological racism in Germany. This contrasts the idea of categorizing human differences, which underpinned nineteenth-century anthropological thought, with Virchow's liberal politics and his public rejection of anti-Semitism and ethnic definitions of nation-states. Beyond this debate about the place of anthropology within German history, Virchow stands as an extraordinary individual. By the 1890s, he knew nine languages and was recognized internationally as a tireless researcher and a master synthesizer of medical and anthropological knowledge. He was named to the Prussian Academy of Sciences in 1873 and chosen as rector of the University of Berlin in 1893. Virchow was a true polymath who was able to grasp and shape entire fields of study in a way that would be unimaginable in the twenty-first century's era of scientific specialization.

See also **Public Health.**

BIBLIOGRAPHY

Ackerknecht, Erwin. *Rudolf Virchow: Doctor, Statesman, Anthropologist.* Madison, Wisc., 1953. An admiring survey of Virchow's major ideas and publications.

McNeely, Ian. *"Medicine on a Grand Scale": Rudolf Virchow, Liberalism, and the Public Health.* London, 2002. Draws attention to the connection between political liberalism, science, and public health policies.

Zimmerman, Andrew. *Anthropology and Antihumanism in Imperial Germany.* Chicago, 2001. A recent study that connects Virchow and German anthropology to the history of imperialism and the rise of scientific worldviews.

BRENT MANER

VLADIVOSTOK. Founded in 1860, Vladivostok became the major commercial and naval port of the Russian Far East. Its history epitomizes the challenges faced by tsarist Russia as a multiethnic empire and as a military power in the north Pacific.

Count Nikolai Muraviev-Amursky, governorgeneral of Eastern Siberia, established the town on the site of a Chinese hamlet before the region was formally ceded by China to Russia. The name he gave it, which translated to "Ruler of the Orient," belied its precariousness in an area contested by the rival imperialist nations of Europe and Japan. Situated at the end of a peninsula jutting 32 kilometers (20 miles) into Peter the Great Bay off

the Sea of Japan, the Russian Navy had doubts about moving its Far Eastern squadron there from the more secure Nikolayevsk further north. The port freezes over during winter, and maritime access to the town can be controlled by hostile navies (as occurred during the Russo-Japanese War). Movement of settlers and transport of troops to Vladivostok from the central Russian provinces required travel along the slow and primitive overland routes across Siberia or over the high seas.

These communications deficiencies were among the factors behind the decision to build the Trans-Siberian Railroad. Groundbreaking for the railroad took place at Vladivostok in 1892, but construction along the Amur River, which connected the region with the rest of Siberia, was deemed too expensive. An alternative presented itself after 1896 when the Russian government received permission to build the Chinese Eastern Railroad through Manchuria. In 1897 the Russians arranged a leasehold over the Liaodong Peninsula, including the naval base at Port Arthur and commercial port at Dalian (Dalny), where a substantial amount of Vladivostok's commercial and naval traffic shifted. Tsarist defeat in the subsequent Russo-Japanese War (1904–1905) and withdrawal from southern Manchuria led to the revival of Vladivostok, but the strategic disadvantages remained.

By that time the town had grown from a collection of huts to the largest city of Siberia, with a population of nearly one hundred thousand. It was the capital of the Maritime Territory and had become a center of intellectual life with the founding of the Society for the Study of the Amur Region (1884) and the Oriental Institute (1899), dedicated to the study of Asian languages. Commercial activity also flourished in a modern district featuring ten banks and branches of European, Japanese, and Russian-owned firms. As a sign of the growing reputation of the city, twelve nations opened consulates there.

Russian policymakers were dissatisfied, however. The presence of ex-convicts, fugitives, and Chinese bandits (*hong huzi*), along with a sizable number of sailors and stevedores, made Vladivostok the murder capital of Siberia. Foreign visitors were struck by its cosmopolitanism, but also its filth and violence. Russians who lived there lamented its isolation from European Russia.

The demography of the city also alarmed the central government, ever concerned about its loose grip on a vast territory. In 1912 more than half the legal residents of the city were Russians, but their numbers were nearly balanced by 27,000 Chinese, 8,000 Koreans, and 3,000 Japanese. The city's Asian inhabitants dominated economic life, with Chinese and Koreans making up 90 percent of the unskilled labor force on the railroad and the docks and supplying virtually all of the city's produce, firewood, water, and animal feed. The Japanese competed in the service sector as barbers, servants, photographers, and, most commonly, prostitutes—in brothels that were often fronts for Japanese government espionage operations. Although occasional fighting broke out between Russians and Asians, intermarriage was a more common occurrence.

Russian officialdom's fear of the "Yellow Peril" and desire to modernize through governmental uniformity and Russification made the state of affairs in Vladivostok seem a threat rather than an opportunity. The Revolution of 1905 fueled these anxieties as enlisted men awaiting repatriation from the Russo-Japanese War rioted and Trans-Siberian Railroad workers went out on strike. No major socialist cells had been active in the city, and order was restored quickly, but St. Petersburg felt com-pelled to step up Russian migration to the town, whose population grew by more than thirty thousand before 1917. This ended up making the town less secure for the government because Russian workers were more politically conscious and open to revolutionary agitation than the Chinese coolies they displaced, although before World War I the secret police kept these tendencies in check. With an influx of refugees and prisoners of war from the German and Austrian armies and the rise of Bolshevik and Menshevik activism after February 1917, the stage was set for the upheavals experienced by the city in the coming revolutionary and civil war years.

See also **Russia; Russo-Japanese War; Siberia.**

BIBLIOGRAPHY

Kabuzan, V. M. *Dal'nevostochnyi krai v XVII–nachale XX vv., 1640–1917: Istoriko-demograficheskii ocherk.* Moscow, 1985.

Marks, Steven G. *Road to Power: The Trans-Siberian Railroad and the Colonization of Asian Russia, 1850–1917.* Ithaca, N.Y., 1991.

Stephan, John J. *The Russian Far East: A History.* Stanford, Calif., 1994.

STEVEN G. MARKS

WAGNER, RICHARD (1813–1883), German composer.

Richard Wagner was the most prominent German composer of the nineteenth century, but he was much more than a musician; he was a social movement in his own right, a focus of passionate adulation and equally passionate condemnation.

Wagner was born on 22 May 1813. He came into the world at a time of great political turmoil, which was only fitting considering the turmoil he would generate himself over the course of his life. Napoleon I was defeated at the "Battle of the Nations" near Leipzig in October 1813, a defeat constituting the beginning of the end for the French emperor but by no means the end of the cascading changes brought on by the French Revolution. Those changes helped define the political and social context in which Wagner—a true Napoleon of the arts—lived and worked.

EARLY YEARS

One of the victims of the typhus epidemic that swept over Leipzig in the wake of the Battle of the Nations was Friedrich Wagner, a police registrar and father of nine children, the youngest being six-month-old Richard. But in fact, Friedrich Wagner may not have been Richard's father at all, because Wagner's mother, Johanna, was intimate with a local painter and poet named Ludwig Geyer, whom she then married nine months after Friedrich's death. Although Geyer became the only father Richard actually knew, the composer could never be sure about the identity of his biological father. More vexing still, at least in his eyes, was the suggestion (since proven to be baseless) that Geyer was Jewish. The thought that he might himself carry the "taint" of Jewish blood undoubtedly fueled Wagner's growing anti-Semitic phobia. The composer's enduring anxieties about his origins also found expression in his operas, which, among other idiosyncrasies, betray an obsession with fatherless children.

The first years of Wagner's childhood were happy and secure enough, for Geyer obtained a position in the court theater in Dresden and dutifully cared for the large family he had inherited. Geyer died, however, when Richard was only eight, leaving an emotional hole in the boy's life. Before departing the scene, Geyer passed on to his youngest son a budding passion for things theatrical. In introducing the boy to the Romantic composer Carl Maria von Weber, Geyer also kindled in him an enthusiasm for music. As a schoolboy, however, Wagner did not demonstrate any great skill in music—certainly he was no child prodigy like Wolfgang Amadeus Mozart. His primary interest was in drama, especially William Shakespeare, who appealed to his sense for the fantastic and grotesque. He also cultivated a passion for the ancient Greek tragedians, whose influence, like that of Shakespeare's, later appeared prominently in his operas.

Wagner began his study of musical composition in his late teens, when he fell under the electrifying influence of Ludwig van Beethoven. His first significant musical undertaking was a piano

Richard Wagner. Chalk portrait by Franz von Lenbach. SNARK/ART RESOURCE, NY

transcription of Beethoven's Choral Symphony. At Leipzig's Thomasschule he took violin lessons from a member of the Gewandhaus Orchestra, and he studied counterpoint and harmony with the cantor of the Thomaskirche, where Johann Sebastian Bach had worked a century earlier. Yet musical study was by no means Wagner's sole preoccupation. Upon entering Leipzig University he became caught up in the rowdiness of student life, and in 1830, when the revolutionary spirit emanating from France spread to Leipzig, Wagner enthusiastically joined a mob of students in sacking a brothel and laying siege to a prison.

FIRST OPERAS

Wagner's initial forays into operatic composition did not give much evidence of the innovative mold breaker he was to become as a mature artist. His first three operas, *Die Feen* (1833–1834; The fairies), *Das Liebesverbot* (1834–1836; The ban on love), and *Rienzi* (1837–1840), followed in the traditions of German and Italian Romantic opera, employing

the conventional recitative, aria, duet, and choral forms. While writing these pieces, and for some time thereafter, Wagner was forced to make his living conducting other men's works in provincial theaters. Meagerly compensated for these duties, but determined not to live like a church mouse, Wagner began to run up large debts. Money problems and creditor-evasion would remain fixtures in his life.

The need to escape creditors lay partly behind Wagner's move to Paris in 1839. As an impoverished and unknown provincial from Germany, Wagner was in no position to make an impact in Louis-Philippe's Paris, where charismatic virtuosi such as Franz Liszt and Frédéric Chopin ruled the day. While in Paris Wagner received invaluable assistance from the German-Jewish composer Giacomo Meyerbeer, whom Wagner later came to despise and to blame for all the tribulations that attended his sojourn in Paris. In his essay *Das Judentum in der Musik* (1850; Judaism in music), Wagner held up Meyerbeer as an example of alleged creative sterility among Jews.

DER FLIEGENDE HOLLÄNDER AND LATER WORKS

Wagner's opera *Der fliegende Holländer* (The flying Dutchman) premiered (with Meyerbeer's assistance) in Dresden in 1843. Although this work still contained many trappings of conventional opera, it anticipated the composer's later "music-dramas" in its use of leitmotivs. *Holländer* was not a critical or popular success, and Wagner began increasingly to clash with the musical establishment. The clashes continued during his tenure as Kapellmeister (a conducting post) at the Royal Court of Saxony in Dresden, where he served from 1843 to 1849. Although he was able to get his next opera, *Tannhäuser*, mounted in Dresden in 1845, he fought with the orchestra and court officials over its staging. When the revolutionary turmoil of 1848 swept into Saxony the following year he joined in the fighting, motivated both by political idealism and the hope that a new social-political order might be more receptive to his work.

As a result of his participation in the abortive Saxon revolution, Wagner was obliged to flee to Switzerland, beginning an exile in that land that would span, with various interruptions, some twenty-three years. Here he composed *Der Ring des Nibelungen* (1851–1874), *Tristan und Isolde* (1857–1859), and *Die Meistersinger von Nürnberg* (1862–1867), as well as his seminal prose essays *Die Kunst und die Revolution* (1849; Art and revolution) and *Das Kunstwerk der Zukunft* (1849; The artwork of the future). In the prose works he called for an artistic revolution through which traditional operatic forms would give way to a "total work of art" uniting poetry, music, drama, and dance in a profound exploration of the human condition. His music-dramas, above all *Der Ring, Tristan,* and *Parsifal* (1877–1882), put this ambitious conception into practice.

BAYREUTH FESTIVAL

In order to translate his aesthetic ideals to the stage Wagner felt he needed a new kind of opera house, which in turn demanded a generous patron. The composer believed he had found his "angel" in young King Louis II of Bavaria, who upon coming to the throne in 1864 called Wagner to Munich and promised to build him a new theater there. However, Wagner's luxurious living at state expense, his meddling in royal politics, and his notorious affair with Cosima von Bülow, the wife of the pianist and conductor Hans von Bülow and illegitimate daughter of Liszt, so soured the people of Munich that Louis was forced to send Wagner away in late 1865. (Wagner married Cosima in 1870, following her divorce from Bülow.) He returned to exile in Switzerland until 1872, when, following the establishment of the new German empire, he moved to Bayreuth, in northern Bavaria, in hopes of finally realizing his dream of building a special theater for the production of his work. The choice of Bayreuth was motivated partly by Wagner's desire once again to exploit the largesse of Louis, but also by his hope of casting his envisaged annual music festival as an "artistic sister" of German unification, thereby securing financial support from the imperial government. In the end Wagner proved unable to win significant backing from Berlin, but with help from Louis and an innovative subscription system he was able to launch his "Richard Wagner Festival" with the first complete *Ring* production in 1876.

The inaugural Bayreuth festival was not a success financially, and Wagner was unable to put on another festival until 1882, when he premiered *Parsifal.* As conductor for this performance Wagner employed Hermann Levi, a Jew, whose services he was obliged to accept under an agreement with Louis.

Among the harshest critics of *Parsifal,* and indeed of the entire Bayreuth enterprise, was the philosopher Friedrich Nietzsche. Earlier on Nietzsche had been a fervent admirer of Wagner, whose concept of the "total work of art" helped inspire Nietzsche's first book, *The Birth of Tragedy* (1872). But Nietzsche was disgusted by what he saw as Wagner's surrender to Christianity in *Parsifal,* and by the composer's toadying to the imperial government in his efforts to fund Bayreuth. Wagner, who had been flattered by Nietzsche's adulation, was deeply wounded by the criticism. The two former friends remained estranged on Wagner's death in 1883.

WAGNER AND NAZISM

In addition to launching the Bayreuth music festival, which Cosima Wagner carried on after his death, Wagner brought together in Bayreuth a coterie of disciples who dedicated themselves to perpetuating his musical and philosophical legacy. Known as the Bayreuth Circle, this group interpreted the composer's contradictory ideas one-sidedly as an endorsement of the authoritarian, racist, and chauvinistic views they themselves championed. Their influence, along with Adolf Hitler's personal infatuation with Wagner's operas, later turned Bayreuth into a kind of "court theater" for the Third Reich. Ever since, some commentators have seen Wagner as an intellectual "forefather" of Nazism.

The question of Wagner's connection to Nazism continues to inspire impassioned debate among historians and cultural critics, as does the relationship between his political ideas and his music. Is Wagner's art indelibly "corrupted" by his sociopolitical views? Can one enjoy his music with a clear conscience? These questions will probably persist as long as Wagner's operas are performed.

See also **Beethoven, Ludwig van; Liszt, Franz; Louis II; Nietzsche, Friedrich; Revolutions of 1848.**

BIBLIOGRAPHY

Gray, Howard. *Wagner.* London, 1990.

Gregor-Dellin, Martin. *Richard Wagner: His Life, His Work, His Century.* Translated by J. Maxwell Brownjohn. San Diego, Calif., 1983.

Gutman, Robert W. *Richard Wagner: The Man, His Mind, and His Music.* New York, 1968.

Large, David Clay, and William Weber, eds. *Wagnerism in European Culture and Politics.* Ithaca, N.Y., 1984.

Millington, Barry, ed. *The Wagner Compendium: A Guide to Wagner's Life and Music.* London, 1992.

DAVID CLAY LARGE

WALDECK-ROUSSEAU, RENÉ (1846–1904), prime minister of France (1899–1902) and a central figure in the campaign to separate church and state.

Pierre-Marie-René Waldeck-Rousseau was born in western France, the son of a lawyer from Nantes who served in the Constituent Assembly of 1848 that established the Second Republic. He followed his father's career, but had only moderate success in his practice at Rennes (Brittany). Waldeck-Rousseau was educated in Catholic schools, but had left the church and supported the anticlerical republicanism of Léon Gambetta (1838–1882). He joined the Gambettist republican party at Rennes and was elected at age thirty-two to the Chamber of Deputies in the republican landslide of 1879.

Waldeck-Rousseau joined Gambetta's opportunist faction in the Chamber, and was rewarded with the Ministry of the Interior in Gambetta's only cabinet (1881–1882). In these years he developed a liberal republicanism, supporting individual liberty and championing the Press Law of 1881 that created broad freedom of the press. When he stood for reelection in 1881, his program stressed the freedom of labor. As minister, Waldeck-Rousseau drafted a law of associations granting workers full rights of unionization. Gambetta died before this law could be adopted, and Waldeck-Rousseau joined many Gambettists in supporting Jules Ferry (1832–1893). He received the Ministry of the Interior in Ferry's government of 1884–1885, in which post he won adoption of the Law of Associations in 1884, a law often referred to as the Waldeck-Rousseau Law.

When Ferry was driven from office in 1885, and the climate of opinion shifted against liberal reforms, Waldeck-Rousseau lost interest in parliamentary life. He chose not to stand for reelection in 1889 and devoted himself to his Parisian legal practice. Waldeck-Rousseau's mastery of the civil code, attention to detail, and skill at untangling complexity earned him considerable wealth in commercial law.

CHURCH AND STATE
After a decade in retirement from politics, Waldeck-Rousseau was persuaded to run for a vacant senate seat from the Loire in 1894 and was elected by such an overwhelming margin that friends persuaded him to run for the presidency in 1895, although he lost to Félix Faure (1841–1899). He returned to the senate for a full term in 1897, again by a huge margin. Rather than champion legislative causes, Waldeck-Rousseau used his political popularity to work behind the scenes to construct a "great republican circle" linking all elements of French republicanism. This put Waldeck-Rousseau in a respected, centrist republican position during the most tumultuous phase of the Dreyfus affair, with the result that he was asked to form a cabinet in June 1899, following the republican electoral victory.

Waldeck-Rousseau served as prime minister for one of the longest terms of the Third Republic (1899–1902) and did so at a time of great national crisis. He tried to create a cabinet with broad appeal, taking the Ministry of the Interior and Religion for himself, retaining Theophile Delcassé (1852–1923) at the Quai d'Orsay, and including such diverse figures as General Gaston-Alexandre-Auguste de Galliffet (1830–1909, who had led the suppression of the Paris Commune of 1871 and was detested on the left) at the Ministry of War and Alexandre Millerand (1859–1943, the first socialist to sit in a government) at the Ministry of Commerce and Industry.

Waldeck-Rousseau steered France through a period of labor unrest, critical court cases associated with the Dreyfus affair, and the beginning phases of the radical anticlericalism of the early twentieth century. He strove to maintain a moderate course on questions concerning the church, and he opposed the separation of church and state, although he merely postponed it for a few years.

The debate on religion under Waldeck-Rousseau focused on revising the Law of Associations. In November 1899, he drafted a bill to apply this law to religious congregations. The debate on this bill, and the application of the resulting Law of Associations of 1901, accelerated the demand for the separation of church and state, and this ultimately led to Waldeck-Rousseau's resignation. He had wanted government control over the Catholic religious orders, allowing them some freedom to act (analogous to his law for workers in 1884). Instead, the Law of Associations of 1901 became the instrument by which most religious orders were disbanded.

Although his republican coalition won a major electoral victory in June 1902, the discouraged prime minister chose to retire, citing his health. His successor, Emile Combes (1835–1921), then carried out the anticlerical agenda of separation; Waldeck-Rousseau died following an operation for cancer of the pancreas in 1904.

See also **Caillaux, Joseph; Clemenceau, Georges; Gambetta, Léon-Michel; Separation of Church and State (France, 1905).**

BIBLIOGRAPHY

Primary Sources

Waldeck-Rousseau, René. *La Défense républicaine.* Paris, 1902.

———. *Action républicaine et sociale.* Paris, 1903.

———. *Politique française et étrangère.* Paris, 1903.

Secondary Sources

Partin, Martin O. *Waldeck-Rousseau, Combes, and the Church: The Politics of Anti-Clericalism, 1899–1905.* Durham, N.C., 1969.

Sorlin, Pierre. *Waldeck-Rousseau.* Paris, 1966.

STEVEN C. HAUSE

WALES. In 1845 Frederick Engels commented that the Welsh "retain pertinaciously" their separate nationality. This sense of nationality was often retained against the condescension of the English. The position of Wales in the United Kingdom differed from that of Scotland or Ireland because Wales had been "incorporated" in the English realm in the sixteenth century rather than joined by parliamentary union as Scotland had been in 1707 or as Ireland would be in 1800. Consequently, Wales had few institutional expressions of its identity, and the nineteenth century would see the creation of many of its modern national institutions. Initially, however, this lack of distinctively Welsh institutions created a cultural space for religion, especially Protestant Nonconformity, to thrive and become a powerful marker of national identity. During the nineteenth century the national movement would be primarily concerned with achieving parity with the other nations of Britain, a brief attempt in the 1880s and 1890s to achieve self-government within the United Kingdom notwithstanding. With the expansion of the franchise during the century, most Welsh people developed a sense of citizenship rooted in a dual identity based on their linguistic and religious particularity on the one hand and loyalty to the British state on the other.

At the end of the eighteenth century Wales was a thinly peopled country on the verge of momentous new changes. The majority of the people worked the land on poor upland farms dominated by a tiny aristocratic elite, while towns were small-scale and functioned as hubs of regional markets and cultural life. The impact of industrialization in the late eighteenth and early nineteenth centuries was profound. This first phase consisted of mining and the manufacture of metals like copper and iron in some of the biggest industrial concerns in the world. These developments were mainly financed by English capitalists. In the south of the country, small villages like Merthyr Tydfil were transformed into thriving, if socially unstable, urban centers, whereas ports like Swansea experienced more measured growth. The country was affected by the political ferment of the late eighteenth century, with Welshmen like Richard Price and David Williams becoming philosophers of the American and French Revolutions.

In a country with a sparse population, demographic change was striking. Population growth comfortably exceeded 10 percent in every decade during the first half of the nineteenth century, rising to nearly 18 percent in the decade from 1811 to 1821. Much of this growth was experienced in the countryside, where agriculture was unable to absorb the excess and migration to the towns acted as a safety valve. Even so, major agrarian disturbances

TABLE 1

Population of Wales, 1801–1911		
Year	Population	% Change
1801	601,767	—
1811	688,774	14.5
1821	811,381	17.8
1831	924,329	13.9
1841	1,068,547	15.6
1851	1,188,914	11.3
1861	1,312,834	10.6
1871	1,421,670	9.7
1881	1,577,559	11.1
1891	1,776,405	12.6
1901	2,015,012	13.5
1911	2,442,041	18.6

SOURCE: Data from *Census of England and Wales*, 1801–1911.

erupted in southwest Wales in the form of the Rebecca riots (1839–1844). Whereas some historians see this episode as an expression of anger by the small farmers, others interpret it as community revolt with much wider social appeal. At the same time, the Chartist movement took root in other parts of the country. By mid-1839 about one-fifth of the population of south Wales were Chartists. Thousands of armed rebels marched on Newport on 4 November 1839 in what was intended to be the first step in a British rising. At least twenty-two were shot by the waiting soldiers and the rising failed. The movement revived in 1842 and 1848 but never regained the same momentum as in its early days.

STABILITY AND PROGRESS

The transition from the agrarian and industrial revolt of the 1830s and 1840s to the period of mid-Victorian stability and political quiescence is one of the most striking developments of nineteenth-century Wales. It was a result of the stabilizing effect of the growth of railways, an increasing attachment to political reformism following the failure of Chartism, and the growing influence of the Nonconformist chapels. Public debate in these decades was shaped by religious allegiances. In 1851 a little more than half the population attended a place of worship, over three-quarters of whom did so in a Nonconformist chapel. Religious revivalism—like the trans-Atlantic revival of 1859—swelled the ranks of the denominations in both rural and industrial areas. Together with a popular culture rooted in the ideals of respectability and sobriety, the country was provided with the components for a new sense of national identity. Central to this was an episode known as "the Treachery of the Blue Books." In 1847 government education commissioners published a report that denigrated the morals of the Welsh people as a whole, and more particularly those of women. This inaugurated a campaign to restore the reputation of the Welsh people, conducted from the pulpit, in public meetings and especially in the newspaper and periodical press in both Welsh and English languages. As well as the respectable public face of Wales, however, social tensions occasionally produced conflict, such as with the frequent anti-Irish riots in the towns and the widespread conflicts over poaching in rural areas.

This period of cultural change is epitomized by the re-establishment, from 1858, of the annual National Eisteddfod, a popular cultural festival based on literary and musical competition, which was held in a different part of the country each year. Although drawing heavily on "traditional" culture, it ensured mass appeal because of a combination of the rise in literacy and the expansion of the press in both languages. Such cultural innovations were underpinned by economic change. The coal industry grew rapidly in south Wales in mid-century, as did slate quarrying in the northeast. Whereas in 1851 less than 20 percent of the population lived in settlements of more than five thousand inhabitants, just under 50 percent did so by 1891, and the trend was inexorably in this direction. Between 1850 and 1870 some 2,300 kilometers of railway were built to connect these towns. The creation of a dense railway network linked the different parts of the country in ways previously unthought of and went some way toward unifying the country.

LIBERALISM AND THE NATION

A striking feature of politics after the Reform Act of 1867 was the overwhelming dominance of the Liberal Party, which won a clear majority of Welsh parliamentary seats in every election until 1922. As a result, some historians see this one-party domination as the creation of a national movement, while others portray the Liberal hegemony in terms of the rise of middle-class leadership. The party provided a voice for those outside the estab-

Portrait of a Welsh market woman, Carmarthen, Wales, c. 1900. ©HULTON-DEUTSCH COLLECTION/CORBIS

Some major issues remained unresolved. Although not as serious as the Irish land question, rural grievances remained intractable. Between 1886 and 1891 a tithe war broke out throughout rural Wales, partly as a consequence of the international agricultural depression. In 1887 only 10.2 percent of the land was owned by the men and women who farmed it, and landlordism remained a powerful force. But between 1910 and 1914 all the major landowners began to sell land, and it was bought overwhelmingly by their tenants; thus on the eve of war, power relations in rural society were changing dramatically. This was a harbinger of a more fundamental social revolution in the countryside after 1918. The cornerstone of Welsh Liberal demands, disestablishment of the Church of England in Wales, remained unresolved until 1919.

A concern with establishing national institutions permeated popular culture, as witnessed by the creation of the Football Association of Wales (1876) and the Welsh Rugby Union (1881), both of which facilitated competition on the international stage; the competition of nonstate nationalities in international sporting competitions is a peculiar feature of British life that originated at this time. Rugby, in particular, came to be regarded as a popular embodiment of Welsh identity. Other sports, like boxing, also flourished, with boxers such as Jim Driscoll and Freddie Welsh winning international acclaim.

PEOPLE, LANGUAGE, AND GENDER

Population growth quickened once again from the 1880s and in-migration was mainly responsible for an increase of more than 18 percent during the first decade of the twentieth century. Regional disparities became acute from this decade, with 46 percent of the country's population residing in the single county of Glamorgan by 1911. The export-oriented coal industry drew in large numbers of migrants from rural Wales and from England and transformed the industrial valleys of south Wales into frontier towns, while at the same time fueling the dramatic growth of ports like Cardiff and Barry.

These far-reaching changes produced two long-term social trends: first, regarding language, and second, regarding the balance between the sexes in industrial society. By 1901 only a little over half the

lishment, including industrialists, professionals, farmers, and other members of the middle class. In an attempt to mobilize the people against an Anglicized aristocracy and the established church, the Liberal MP Henry Richard asserted that "the Nonconformists of Wales are the people of Wales." In the 1880s and 1890s the party was a vehicle for ambitious young men like Tom Ellis and David Lloyd George, who combined a radical social agenda with nationalism. Their aim was parity with the other nations of the United Kingdom, rather than separatism, and parliament passed distinctive legislation for Wales for the first time in the 1880s on matters such as temperance and education. In 1893 a federal University of Wales was established, and it rapidly became an influential cultural institution.

Young miners wash coal in Bargoed, Wales, 1910. ©HULTON-DEUTSCH COLLECTION/CORBIS

population spoke the Welsh language, a proportion that dropped below half during the following decade for the first time in history. By 1891 nearly 17 percent of the population was English-born. Industrial society was skewed numerically in favor of males, and the quintessential symbols of this culture were masculine: the coalminer, slate quarryman, rugby player, and male chorister. By contrast, the only significant female symbol in this period was the Welsh "mam" (mother), a figure associated with home and hearth. Such gendered conceptions of class and national identity were influential for much of the following century.

Liberalism still dominated the political landscape, with not a single Conservative MP being elected from Wales in the landslide election of 1906. The first socialist MP, Keir Hardie, was elected at Merthyr Tydfil in 1900. Mass trade unions gained increasing importance; the South Wales Miners'

Federation, which became the most important institution in Welsh life during the first half of the twentieth century, was founded in 1898. The years after 1909, usually termed the Great Unrest, mark something of a watershed in industrial society. Industrial disputes were numerous during these years and serious riots erupted, including anti-Semitic and anti-Chinese disturbances. Syndicalist ideas found a receptive audience in some quarters. The consensual politics of the older trade union leaders were brusquely swept aside. At the same time, the women's suffrage movement became more militant, contributing to an atmosphere of general social malaise. These events stand in stark contrast to the extravagant royal pageantry associated with the Investiture of the Prince of Wales at Caernarfon Castle in north Wales in 1911.

By the eve of World War I, Wales had been transformed by economic, demographic, cultural, and political developments. It was overwhelmingly an industrial and urban country and had one of the densest railway networks in the world. It remained one of Engels's submerged "unhistoric nations," but a national revival had taken place, and new national cultural institutions had been created.

See also **Great Britain; Ireland; Scotland.**

BIBLIOGRAPHY

Davies, John. *A History of Wales.* London, 1993.

Jenkins, Geraint H., ed. *The Welsh Language and Social Domains in the Nineteenth Century, 1801–1911.* Cardiff, 2000.

Jenkins, Philip. *A History of Modern Wales, 1536–1990.* London, 1992.

John, Angela V., ed. *Our Mothers' Land: Chapters in Welsh Women's History, 1800–1939.* Cardiff, 1991.

Jones, David J. V. *Rebecca's Children: A Study of Rural Society, Crime and Protest.* Oxford, U.K., and New York, 1989.

Jones, Gareth Elwyn, and Dai Smith, eds. *The Peoples of Wales.* Llandysul, Wales, 1999.

Jones, Ieuan Gwynedd. *Mid-Victorian Wales: The Observers and the Observed.* Cardiff, 1992.

Morgan, Kenneth O. *Wales in British Politics, 1868–1922.* 3rd ed. Cardiff, 1980.

O'Leary, Paul. *Immigration and Integration: The Irish in Wales, 1798–1922.* Cardiff, 2000.

Williams, Gwyn A. *When Was Wales? A History of the Welsh.* Harmondsworth, U.K., 1985.

PAUL O'LEARY

WALLACE, ALFRED RUSSEL (1823–1913), British naturalist, geographer, humanist, and social critic.

Discoverer and champion of the theory of evolution by natural selection, Wallace was one of nineteenth-century Britain's most outspoken intellectuals. His insights into evolution are his most enduring legacy, and much has been written about his relationship with his famous friend and colleague, Charles Darwin (1809–1882). Wallace's interests and publications ranged beyond evolutionary biology into political and spiritual arenas, much to the disappointment of Darwin and many of his scientific colleagues. The disagreements between the two founders of modern evolutionary theory remain unresolved, both within and beyond the scientific community. In his later years Wallace believed in a unity that underlay all physical, biological, social, and spiritual phenomena. Some of his later books, such as *Darwinism* (1889) and *Studies Scientific and Social* (1900), exemplify the evolutionary theism that surrounded his scientific analyses of the whole of nature.

He was the eighth of nine children born to Mary Anne Greenell and Thomas Vere Wallace, but only Alfred and two of his siblings survived past early adulthood. His family could barely afford the six years of formal education he received at the one-room Hertford Grammar School. Wallace, like his father, never held a permanent job and suffered from financial difficulties throughout his life. He married in 1866 and two of his three children survived to adulthood.

In his youth, Wallace was exposed to secular and reformist political ideas as well as to phrenology and mesmerism. He became self-educated in various branches of science and natural history while working as a surveyor, and for a short time as a teacher. Well-read in the natural history literature of the day, Wallace shared his reactions with his new friend Henry Walter Bates, who introduced him to entomology. Deeply intrigued by the question of the origin of species, Wallace proposed to Bates that they travel to South America as self-employed specimen collectors for the then-growing natural history trade. The traveled together to Brazil in 1848 and parted ways shortly thereafter. Wallace learned the rugged ropes of tropical fieldwork during four years of collecting in the Amazon basin. Although he amassed thousands of birds and insects, his specimens and most of his notes were destroyed in a fire at sea. Nevertheless, Wallace published several scientific articles and two books, and made enough of a name for himself in London's scientific circles to embark on a journey to the Malay Archipelago (Malaysia, Indonesia, and part of New Guinea) as a fellow of the Royal Geographical Society.

Wallace traveled widely among the islands from 1854 to 1862, collecting biological specimens for his own research and for sale, and writing scores of scientific articles. He would be well known to naturalists for his collections alone, amassing more than 125,000 specimens, hundreds of which were new to science. Here he penned the essay for which he is now best known, in which he proposed that new species arise by the progression and continued divergence of varieties.

Wallace returned to England at the age of thirty-nine and continued to make significant contributions to natural history, especially *The Geographical Distribution of Animals* in 1876, but his views on spiritualism and human evolution fell outside of the scientific naturalism that dominated scientific thought.

He died at the age of ninety, having published twenty-one books, including a two-volume autobiography in 1905, and over seven hundred articles, essays, and letters. Wallace has been variously characterized as the nineteenth century's greatest explorer-naturalist, the quintessential outsider, a spur to Darwin, and a crank. In the early twenty-first century scholars have begun to expand on the limited biographies of Wallace that prevailed in the twentieth century. These works (especially those by Fichman and Slotten) present a more complex figure, a fiercely intellectual but no less spiritual man, a brave and original thinker, who while shaping the history of modern Western science was also shaped by progressivism and by a rising tide of socialist and spiritualist beliefs. He believed that his most important contribution was the extension of natural selection into the social realm. For Wallace, improvement of the human race depended on natural selection acting on well-educated, economically free men and women in an egalitarian social system.

See also **Darwin, Charles; Evolution; Huxley, Thomas Henry.**

BIBLIOGRAPHY

Camerini, Jane R., ed. *The Alfred Russel Wallace Reader: A Selection of Writings from the Field.* Baltimore, Md., 2002.

Fichman, Martin. *An Elusive Victorian: The Evolution of Alfred Russel Wallace.* Chicago, 2003.

Moore, James. "Wallace's Malthusian Moment: The Common Context Revisited." In *Victorian Science in Context,* edited by Bernard Lightman, 290–311. Chicago, 1997.

Raby, Peter. *Alfred Russel Wallace: A Life.* London, 2001.

Slotten, Ross A. *The Heretic in Darwin's Court.* New York, 2004.

JANE R. CAMERINI

WARFARE. *See* **Armies; Military Tactics.**

WAR OF 1812. The war that began in 1812 between the United States and Great Britain resulted from the French Revolutionary and Napoleonic Wars of the 1790s and early 1800s. Both France and Britain violated American neutral rights, and the United States objected to these transgressions. Ultimately, America exhausted both its diplomacy and its patience, declaring war on Britain on 18 June 1812. Preoccupied by its fight with Napoleon, Great Britain tried at the last minute to avoid war with the United States, and efforts were under way from its outset to conclude it. Nonetheless, the war lasted for two and a half years and would be instrumental in transforming Anglo-American relations from suspicious enmity to grudging respect and eventually firm partnership.

CAUSES

During the early years of the Franco-British conflict, the United States prospered because European powers used neutral shippers to supply their colonies. Yet the breakdown of the Peace of Amiens (1802) in 1803 abruptly changed that situation as France renewed its war against Britain. When Admiral Horatio Nelson decisively defeated the French fleet off Trafalgar (21 October 1805) and Napoleon crushed Britain's continental allies at Austerlitz (2 December 1805), a stalemate resulted with Britain's Royal Navy supreme on the seas and Napoleon's Grande Armée apparently invincible in Europe. Unable to fight each other by force of arms, the two powers resorted to commercial warfare, a move that unavoidably targeted the United States, which was claiming the right as a neutral to trade with both countries. Although both Britain's Orders in Council and France's Berlin and Milan decrees restricted American trade, most Americans found British behavior more offensive because of the Royal Navy's use of impressment—the abduction of sailors from American merchant vessels—to man British warships.

In 1807, impressment nearly provoked war when HMS *Leopard* waylaid the U.S. Navy frigate *Chesapeake* and seized four of her sailors. Rather than resorting to war, however, President Thomas Jefferson persuaded Congress to pass the Embargo Act in December 1807. The plan was to deprive warring Europeans of U.S. trade until they respected American neutral rights, but commercial restriction failed as Americans openly flouted the embargo and seethed under government efforts to enforce it. Congress repealed the unsuccessful embargo in 1809 but continued commercial restriction with the temporary Non-Intercourse Act (1809) and Macon's Bill No. 2 (1810). Both were failures, but Macon's Bill No. 2 was an embarrassing one: the United States resumed trade with the entire world, including Britain and France, but pledged to sustain it with the country that ended trade restrictions and stop it with the other. Napoleon, a master of deceit, hinted he would drop his restrictions, an obvious lie that President James Madison chose to treat as truth. The United States stopped trade with Britain.

As Anglo-American tensions mounted in 1811, other issues drove the countries toward war. Indian unrest on America's western frontier was actually the result of indigenous native resistance led by the Shawnee Tecumseh and his brother Tenskwatawa ("the Prophet"), but many Americans believed it to be the product of British agitation. When Indiana territorial governor William Henry Harrison destroyed Tecumseh and the Prophet's town at the Battle of Tippecanoe (7 November 1811), it drove the Indians into a British alliance.

In late 1811, Madison called Congress into special session, and a prominent faction, the War Hawks, urged a resolute defense of American honor and security. The most popular War Hawk, Kentuckian Henry Clay, was elected Speaker of the House and steered a course that finally compelled Madison to send a war message to Congress on 1 June 1812. Congress responded with a formal declaration of war on 18 June 1812, but the divisive congressional debates and close votes on the declaration were a portent of American disunity in the coming conflict.

The minority Federalist Party doubted the stated reasons for going to war with Great Britain. Federalists accused Republicans of wanting to expand American territory with the conquest of Canada, not reclaim American honor and preserve neutral rights. The war's proponents were primarily western and southern farmers, they noted, who were improbable champions of free trade and sailors' rights. New Englanders, who had the greater material interest in protecting trade, were the war's most adamant opponents. Most scholars have concluded, however, that these appearances are deceptive. Farmers had a stake in preserving access to foreign markets for their produce and yearned to protect American honor. Aside from any expansionist schemes, the plan to invade Canada was dictated by the fact that Canada was where the British were. The United States declared war in 1812 to avenge the insult of impressment and stop injuries caused by the Royal Navy's interference with America's overseas trade. Britain finally did realize the danger of alienating the United States and was in the process of repealing the Orders in Council while Congress was voting for war, but the delay in receiving this news from London made it irrelevant. Fighting had already begun, and Britain, in any case, was unwilling to abandon impressment.

THE WAR

Although Americans regarded Canada as a realistic military objective, repeated attempts to invade and occupy it proved fruitless. Occasionally they were disastrous, as when Michigan territorial governor William Hull's 1812 campaign ended with his surrendering Detroit, a catastrophe that exposed the entire Northwest to British occupation and Indian depredations. Hull's replacement, William Henry Harrison, barely kept an army together under the British onslaught. Elsewhere along the Canadian border in 1812 American plans proved equally ineffective, if not quite as ruinous. Brigadier General Henry Dearborn's political clashes with unwilling New England state militias prevented a campaign against Montreal, and the Niagara frontier proved invulnerable to American invasion attempts.

This dismal chronicle might have sunk American hopes altogether had it not been for the small U.S.

Navy's unexpected success during the war's opening months. Because the Royal Navy was blockading Napoleonic Europe, it was short of ships for the American conflict, and aggressive American captains commanded skilled crews aboard powerful frigates that were more than a match for their British counterparts. Victories by celebrated ships such as the USS *United States* and USS *Constitution* (dubbed "Old Ironsides" by her crew) thrilled Americans and dismayed Britain. In 1813, however, the consequences of Napoleon's ill-advised invasion of Russia signaled a dramatic decline in his fortunes, and more British ships could prosecute the American conflict. The Royal Navy asserted its dominance in 1813, bottling up the dangerous American frigates and mounting damaging raids along the coast, especially in Chesapeake Bay where Admiral Sir George Cockburn was particularly destructive.

American attempts in 1813 to invade Canada at first appeared to be just as futile as the previous year's had been. Dearborn crossed the Niagara River but had limited success and lost all gains as he tried to move into Upper Canada. The northeastern Canadian border remained impervious as well. Although the ineffectual Dearborn resigned, his replacements, Major Generals James Wilkinson and Wade Hampton, could not overcome personal differences to stage a march on Montreal. On 10 September 1813, however, American commodore Oliver Hazard Perry's stunning victory over Sir Robert Barclay's squadron secured American control of Lake Erie. Perry's soon famous message of "we have met the enemy and he is ours" marked the war's turning point in the Northwest. William Henry Harrison retook Detroit and hounded its fleeing defenders under Brigadier General Henry Procter, defeating them at the Battle of the Thames (5 October 1813). Tecumseh's death in the battle ended Anglo-Indian cooperation in the region.

The contest's decisive year would be 1814, for Napoleon's defeat and abdication (April 1814) allowed Britain to shift veteran soldiers from Europe to North America; meanwhile competent, aggressive officers were given command of American armies. In the spring, Major General Andrew Jackson defeated Red Stick Creeks in the Mississippi Territory, and Major General Jacob Brown crossed the Niagara River, took Fort Erie, and marched north to rendezvous with Commodore Isaac Chauncey's Lake Ontario squadron. Chauncey's squadron failed to appear, and Brown retreated, but not before fighting the war's bloodiest battle, a stalemate at Lundy's Lane (25 July 1814). Meanwhile, the British launched offensive operations in upstate New York and Chesapeake Bay. Major General Robert Ross scattered green American militia at Bladensburg, Maryland, and occupied Washington, D.C. (24 August 1814), burning its public buildings, including the Capitol and Executive Mansion. Following this symbolic but strategically irrelevant success, the British attacked Baltimore (12–13 September 1814), but Fort McHenry, which protected Baltimore's Inner Harbor, withstood a relentless naval bombardment. When an American sharpshooter's bullet mortally wounded General Ross, the British called off the attack. The British invasion along Lake Champlain ended when an American naval squadron under Commodore Thomas Macdonough crippled Captain George Downie's ships on Plattsburgh Bay (11 September 1814), and at Plattsburgh, New York, Alexander Macomb's Americans repulsed veterans under Canada's governor-general Sir George Prevost.

PEACE

Despite these victories, New England dissidents met at Hartford, Connecticut, in late 1814 to voice grievances and protest the war. Occurring in the shadow of recent American successes, the Hartford Convention caused the rest of the country to question New England's loyalty and the Federalist Party's patriotism. In addition, New England dissent that insisted the war could only end badly coincided with the war's relatively acceptable conclusion. American and British peace commissioners who had been meeting in Ghent since late summer finally signed a peace treaty on Christmas Eve, 1814. Although the Treaty of Ghent did not address impressment or neutral rights, both parties regarded it as a satisfactory termination of the conflict. Britain had endured a quarter century of war in Europe and was eager to rid itself of the distraction of one in North America. The United States was relieved to escape the grave consequences of serious military defeat. The treaty thus restored all territory to the status quo antebellum, literally the situation as it existed before the war.

The United States emerged from the contest more energized and united than it had been before or during it. Andrew Jackson's crushing defeat of Lieutenant General Sir Edward Pakenham's forces outside New Orleans on 8 January 1815 had occurred after the signing at Ghent but before the treaty's ratification. The nearly simultaneous occurrence of Jackson's victory and the news of the peace convinced many Americans that they had won the war. Britain, on the other hand, was ready to pursue diplomatic efforts to conciliate Americans and rehabilitate relations with them. In the coming years, important agreements both fixed and demilitarized the U.S.-Canada border, and other disputes were frequently submitted to arbitration. Anglo-American relations would occasionally be strained, but they would never again break, marking an evolving partnership that was to have a continuing and profound impact on Europe and the rest of the world.

See also **French Revolutionary Wars and Napoleonic Wars; Great Britain; Imperialism.**

BIBLIOGRAPHY

Coles, Harry L. *The War of 1812.* Chicago, 1965.

Heidler, David S., and Jeanne T. Heidler, eds. *Encyclopedia of the War of 1812.* Annapolis, Md., 2004.

———. *The War of 1812.* Westport, Conn., 2002.

Hickey, Donald R. *The War of 1812: A Forgotten Conflict.* Urbana, Ill., 1989.

Horsman, Reginald. *The War of 1812.* New York, 1969.

Mahon, John K. *The War of 1812.* Gainesville, Fla., 1972.

DAVID S. HEIDLER, JEANNE T. HEIDLER

WARSAW. Warsaw first rose to prominence in the sixteenth century, when Poland and Lithuania joined to form a united republic. Because the city is located conveniently between the two capitals of Cracow (Kraków) and Vilnius, and along the Vistula River leading to the major port city of Gdańsk, it was used for meetings of the Sejm (parliament) from 1569, and as a royal residence from 1596. During the next two centuries Warsaw was repeatedly damaged by warfare and political turmoil, and the city's economy was severely crippled. When Poland was conquered and partitioned in 1795,

Warsaw was relegated to the status of a provincial town within the Kingdom of Prussia. The population of the city fell in a few short years from a pre-partition size of 150,000 to a mere 60,000 inhabitants.

Napoleon fashioned a puppet state called the Duchy of Warsaw in 1807, thus returning a bit of the city's former importance. Although the duchy fell with its founder, Warsaw remained a capital after 1815 when the Congress of Vienna sponsored the creation of the "Kingdom of Poland" as a semiautonomous state linked to the Russian Empire by a common hereditary ruler. The tsars steadily eroded the self-rule of the kingdom, but Warsaw retained its role as an administrative center. Above all, though, it was the focal point of the Polish national movement: Warsaw was the primary site for political agitation and public demonstrations, and it was the launching point for major uprisings in 1830 and 1863. Because of Warsaw's symbolic importance, national independence is traditionally dated from the moment the city came under Polish authority on 11 November 1918.

After Warsaw was linked to the major regional capitals by rail lines (Vienna from 1848, St. Petersburg from 1862), it developed rapidly into a major industrial and commercial center. Already in 1880 Warsaw had nearly 400,000 people, and by 1910 it had 750,000, making it the third-largest city in the Russian Empire and one of the fastest-growing cities in Europe. It continued to expand after the restoration of Polish independence, exceeding one million people by 1925. Warsaw's urban infrastructure and architecture grew apace with this population growth: a modern sewage system was installed in 1872, gas lines were laid in 1856, the first tram line (horse-drawn) began service in 1866, a telephone system was in place from 1881, and electric power was available from 1903.

Most of Warsaw's inhabitants in the nineteenth century were Polish-speaking Roman Catholics, but Jews made up more than one-third of the population. Assimilation was limited, but certainly more common in Warsaw than in the countryside (the city's main synagogue featured sermons in Polish from the 1850s onward). An influx of rural Jews at the end of the century increased the dominance of the Yiddish-speaking population. There were also about forty thousand Russian soldiers stationed in and around Warsaw at the start of the twentieth century.

Even during the era of the partitions, Warsaw continued to be a focal point for Polish cultural, intellectual, and artistic life. The city's vibrant theatrical scene featured the National Theater Company, which was founded in 1765 and housed from 1833 in a magnificent opera house known as the Wielki Teatr (Great Theater). Warsaw's first major public art museum was created in 1862 and renamed the National Museum in 1916. The University of Warsaw was founded in 1816, but it had a troubled history: between 1831 and 1862 it was closed because the tsarist authorities feared student unrest, and between 1869 and 1915 Russian was the exclusive language of instruction. Nonetheless, the university produced many of the greatest intellectual and cultural figures of the era, including most of the so-callled Warsaw positivists (a late-nineteenth-century political and literary movement defined by a liberal worldview and a naturalistic style). Though unable to serve as a center of political authority in the nineteenth century, Warsaw remained the symbolic capital of the country for many cultural and intellectual purposes.

See also **Austria-Hungary; Cities and Towns; Lithuania; Nationalism; Poland; Prague; Russia.**

Corrsin, Stephen D. *Warsaw before the First World War: Poles and Jews in the Third City of the Russian Empire, 1880–1914.* Boulder, Colo., 1989.

Drozdowski, Marian M., and Andrzej Zahorski. *Historia Warszawy.* 4th ed. Warsaw, 1997.

Kieniewicz, Stefan. *Warszawa w latach, 1795–1914.* Warsaw, 1976.

BRIAN PORTER

WATERLOO. After eleven months of exile on the Mediterranean island of Elba, Napoleon Bonaparte returned to France in March 1815 and restored his empire. Meeting in Vienna to discuss the postwar reorganization of Europe, the Allies who had vanquished Napoleon one year earlier wasted no time. Renewing their alliance to form the Seventh Coalition, Great Britain, Prussia, Russia, and Austria planned to have armies totaling almost 1 million men invade France by July. After Napoleon failed to convince the allies of his peaceful intentions, he devised a strategy of knocking one or more of the belligerents out of the war before they could combine their forces and overwhelm him.

Napoleon's return did not catch the allies wholly unprepared. Allied observation corps in Belgium steadily received reinforcements during the spring of 1815 to create an Anglo-Dutch army of 90,000 men under the command of Arthur Wellesley, the Duke of Wellington, and the Royal Prussian Army of the Lower Rhine: 120,000 Prussians under Field Marshal Gebhard Leberecht von Blücher. Napoleon decided to strike these allied forces with his own 125,000-man Army of the North. After smashing through the Prussian forward posts on 14 and 15 June, the emperor inflicted a bruising defeat on Blücher at Ligny on the 16th with the right wing of the French army. On the same day, the left wing, under the command of Marshal Michel Ney, encountered Wellington's army at Quatre Bras. The resulting stalemate allowed Wellington to withdraw to Waterloo. The confusion of the French I Corps, which marched back and forth between Ligny and Quatre Bras without participating in either battle, also allowed the Prussian army to retreat unhindered north to Wavre, fifteen miles east of Waterloo. A series of blunders on the rainy day of 17 June placed the French at a decided disadvantage. Napoleon incorrectly assumed that the Prussians had retreated eastward along their line of communications, and assigned 33,000 men under the command of Marshal Emmanuel de Grouchy to drive Blücher out of Belgium. He did not release the pursuit until 11:00 A.M. Then Grouchy took the wrong direction and failed to close the road between Waterloo and Wavre.

After receiving Blücher's promise of support, Wellington took up a defensive position south of Waterloo with 68,000 men and awaited Napoleon and his 72,000 men on 18 June. While mud prevented Napoleon from launching his attack until 11:30 A.M., the Prussian IV Corps commenced its march to Waterloo at 4:30 A.M. followed by II and I Corps—a total of 70,000 men. Blücher's III Corps

2442   EUROPE 1789 TO 1914 remained at Wavre as rear guard and was eventually attacked by Grouchy, but the combat had no influence on the monumental events at Waterloo.

Napoleon opened the attack with a spirited assault by his II Corps on the entrenched farm of Hougoumont on Wellington's right wing. The garrison held, and two hours later, at 1:30 P.M., the French I Corps tested Wellington's left and eventually had to fall back. The British then countered with a cavalry charge that ground to a halt before massed French artillery. Shortly thereafter Napoleon noticed troops moving on his extreme right; by 2:00 P.M. reports confirmed the approach of Blücher's Prussians. While Napoleon shifted his reserves to meet the new threat on his right, Ney squandered the French cavalry in massed, unsupported charges between 3:45 and 5:00 P.M. that failed to break the British infantry squares in Wellington's center. Just as the survivors of Ney's charges limped back to the French line, Blücher's IV Corps attacked the French right. As more Prussian units arrived, Blücher extended his front to threaten Napoleon's line of retreat. While Napoleon oversaw the struggle against the Prussians around the village of Plancenoit, Ney managed to capture the fortified farm of La Haie Sainte around 6:00 P.M. With Wellington's center almost bled dry, Ney called for reinforcements, but all available units had to be committed against the Prussians. Napoleon eventually managed to shift his Imperial Guard from Plancenoit to his center, but the opportunity to destroy Wellington had passed. At 7:30 P.M., Napoleon ordered eight battalions of the guard to spearhead one final assault against Wellington's center. Wellington brought up his last reserves, which repulsed the attacking guard. Seeing the elite guardsmen routed and realizing that Grouchy would not arrive in time, the French army began fleeing the battlefield around 8:30 P.M. Only two battalions of the Old Guard maintained order to cover Napoleon's exit from the battlefield. French losses amounted to 33,000 men and 220 guns, while the Allied armies sustained 22,000 casualties.

The battle of Waterloo represents the climax of Napoleon's way of war. During the latter years of his reign, he had experienced the consequences of failing to develop an adequate general staff system to direct the operations of multiple armies in theaters as far apart as Portugal and Russia. His reluctance to nurture his subordinates in the art of strategy and to create advanced military schools for the training of officers inhibited the French army's ability to produce commanders who could conduct independent operations. Just as Napoleon exited the stage of history following the battle of Waterloo, so too ended the age when operations and battle could be directed solely by the genius of one man.

See also French Revolutionary Wars and Napoleonic Wars; Hundred Days; Napoleon; Wellington, Duke of (Arthur Wellesley).

BIBLIOGRAPHY

Primary Sources
Siborne, William. *History of the War in France and Belgium in 1815.* London, 1844.

Secondary Sources
Bowden, Scott. *Armies at Waterloo.* Arlington, Tex., 1983.

Chandler, David. *Waterloo: The Hundred Days.* London, 1980.

MICHAEL V. LEGGIERE

WEBB, BEATRICE POTTER (1858–1943), British socialist.

Best known as a leader of the British Fabian Society in the late nineteenth and early twentieth centuries, Beatrice Potter Webb was also an early empirical sociologist, the author of important works of social and political history, and a brilliant diarist and autobiographer. The daughter of Richard Potter (1817–1892), a railway magnate and lumber merchant, and Lawrencina Heyworth Potter (1821–1882), a bluestocking and would-be novelist, she was raised with her eight sisters by nannies and governesses on a Gloucestershire estate and in a London flat during the Season. Her grandfathers, businessmen who made their fortunes in cotton and trade in the north of England, were Radicals and Nonconformists. In rebellion against the privileged and yet constraining social ethos of her immediate family, she invoked the political and religious dissent of her Lancashire ancestry as her true heritage. As a young woman she chafed at the idea that an advantageous marriage

Why this demand for State intervention from a generation reared amidst rapidly rising riches and disciplined in the school of philosophic radicalism and orthodox political economy?... The origin of the ferment is to be discovered in a new consciousness of sin among men of intellect and men of property; a consciousness at first philanthropic and practical...; then literary and artistic...; and finally, analytic, historical and explanatory.... The consciousness of sin was a collective or class consciousness; a growing uneasiness, amounting to conviction, that the industrial organization, which had yielded rent, interest and profits on a stupendous scale, had failed to provide a decent livelihood and tolerable living conditions for a majority of the inhabitants of Great Britain.

Beatrice Webb, *My Apprenticeship* (pp. 178–180).

was the only imaginable vocation for a woman of her class and sought refuge in the intellectual tutelage of her mother's friend Herbert Spencer (1820–1903), the Potter family's "philosopher on the hearth." She surprised both Spencer and her family when she married the socialist Sidney James Webb (1859–1947), the son of a milliner and hairdresser, in 1892. Together, along with colleagues George Bernard Shaw (1856–1950), Sydney Olivier (1859–1943), Graham Wallas (1858–1932), Edward Reynolds Pease (1857–1955), and William Clarke (1852-1901), they led the Fabian Society in its early years.

Webb's autobiography, *My Apprenticeship* (1926), tells a story that is in many ways paradigmatic of the spiritual struggles, political transformations, and personal conflicts of many members of her generation. She describes the first half of her life as a search for "creed" and "craft" carried out within the context of what she called the "mid-Victorian Time-Spirit," an ethos in which, as she put it, "the impulse of self-subordinating service was transferred, consciously and overtly, from God to man" (*My Apprenticeship*, pp. 142–143). As a protégée of Spencer, the individualist philosopher, and daughter of laissez-faire capitalists, she questioned the principles of self-interest

that left vast numbers of citizens in poverty and was drawn to a collectivist approach to economic and social organization. As a religious spirit, she moved away from Christian orthodoxies and gravitated to the "religion of humanity" of Auguste Comte (1798–1857) and the beliefs of English positivists like Frederic Harrison (1831–1923). As a woman, she railed against the marriage market of the London Season, rejected the idea of a husband who would completely eclipse her and her own aspirations, and sought a vocation outside of wedlock. During the 1880s, Webb considered the possibility of marriage to Joseph Chamberlain (1836–1914), then a leader in the Radical Party. Webb resisted Chamberlain's political ideas, then more radical than her own, and his imperious personality, even as she felt deeply drawn to him. In the end, she wrote in her diary, marriage to someone like him might be disastrous: "I shall be absorbed into the life of a man whose aims are not my aims; who will refuse me all freedom of thought in my intercourse with him; to whose career I shall have to subordinate all my life, mental and physical" (*Diary*, vol. 1, p. 111).

Webb was saved from the depressing aftermath of her failed relationship with Chamberlain and her stultifying life as dutiful, unmarried daughter by an invitation from her cousin Charles Booth (1840–1916) to assist him in his mammoth survey of poverty in London. Booth, himself influenced by positivism and moved by current debates about the extent of poverty in England, left his work as a Liverpool shipowner and devoted himself to a project that lasted over fourteen years. If Comte and Spencer led Webb to an interest in the study of society, Booth gave her the opportunity to practice— and partly to invent—the craft of social investigation. Her contributions to Booth's *Life and Labour of the People in London* (1889–1903) consisted of empirical studies of three metropolitan groups: dock laborers, sweatshop workers, and Jewish immigrants. At times using disguise and the technique of what would come to be known as participatory observation, Webb was able to produce both vivid accounts of East End life and analyses of the structure of labor.

Now embarked on a craft, Webb began to move toward the creed of socialism. She was drawn to Fabianism because of her experiences with research, interest in the cooperative movement,

Beatrice Webb. Undated photograph taken by George Bernard Shaw. NATIONAL TRUST, SHAW CORNER, HERTFORDSHIRE, UK/ BRIDGEMAN ART LIBRARY. THE SOCIETY OF AUTHORS, ON BEHALF OF THE BERNARD SHAW ESTATE.

and growing belief in the need for state regulation of labor, as well as by reading *Fabian Essays,* edited by Shaw and published in 1889. Although the origins of the Fabian Society were utopian and quasi religious, its leading members had, by this time, become gradualists committed to a scientific understanding of the historical evolution of society and to the propagation of state socialism, beginning with municipal collectivism. Sidney Webb's own contribution to the *Essays,* on the "historic basis" of socialism, relied on theorists like Spencer and Comte, as well as John Stuart Mill (1806–1873). When Beatrice married Sidney Webb, she embraced a political and intellectual way of life that combined belief, work, and what she called a "loving partnership."

As co-authors, husband and wife produced many tomes of political and economic history, among them *The History of Trade Unionism* (1894), *Industrial Democracy* (1897), and the nine-volume *English Local Government* (1903–1929). They also founded the London School of

Economics and launched *The New Statesman.* In 1905, Webb was appointed by Arthur James Balfour (1848–1930) to the Royal Commission on the Poor Law that investigated the state and efficacy of relief in Britain. Ultimately she and Sidney crafted and then campaigned for a minority report. The report dissented from the majority view that destitution could be alleviated through reform rather than, as the Webbs believed, wholly abolished. Sidney Webb joined the Labour governments of 1924 and 1929, while Beatrice engaged in campaigning and Labour Party politics and embarked on the writing of her autobiography. After the defeat of the second Labour government the Webbs turned their investigative attentions to the Soviet Union, which seemed to them to represent a "new civilization" that could enact the social, economic, and political principles for which they had long worked. Of all the aspects of the Webbs' long careers, this idealization of Soviet communism was the most controversial and the most criticized.

The Webbs have often been caricatured as Gradgrinds and ultra-rationalists. H. G. Wells (1866–1946), their colleague in the Fabian Society, satirized them in *The New Machiavelli* (1911). Virginia Woolf (1882–1941) wrote with bemusement of the Webbs' visits to her home to discuss politics with her husband, Leonard, also a Fabian, and famously recorded in her diary that Beatrice declared marriage to be "necessary as a waste pipe for emotion" (Woolf, p. 196). Since the mid-1990s or so the Fabians—and the Webbs in particular—have warranted a second look from theorists in search of non-communist strains of socialism. Reevaluations of Webb have regarded her as a figure in her own right and have often focused on the literary dimensions of her work, her contribution to sociology, and her exemplary struggles with the constraints of Victorian femininity.

See also **Fabians; Shaw, George Bernard; Socialism; Spencer, Herbert.**

BIBLIOGRAPHY

Primary Sources

Webb, Beatrice. *Our Partnership.* Edited by Barbara Drake and Margaret I. Cole. London, 1948.

———. *My Apprenticeship*. Cambridge, U.K., 1979.

———. *The Diary of Beatrice Webb.* Edited by Norman and Jeanne MacKenzie. 4 vols. Cambridge, Mass., 1982–1985.

Webb, Sidney, and Beatrice Webb. *The Letters of Sidney and Beatrice Webb.* Edited by Norman MacKenzie. 3 vols. Cambridge, U.K., 1978.

Woolf, Virginia. *The Diary of Virginia Woolf.* Edited by Anne Olivier Bell. Vol. 1. London, 1977.

Secondary Sources

Adam, Ruth, and Kitty Muggeridge. *Beatrice Webb: A Life, 1858–1943.* London, 1967.

Caine, Barbara. "Beatrice Webb and the 'Woman Question.'" *History Workshop Journal* 14 (Autumn 1982): 23–43.

Hynes, Samuel. "The Art of Beatrice Webb." In *Edwardian Occasions*, 153–173. New York, 1972.

Lewis, Jane. *Women and Social Action in Victorian and Edwardian England.* Stanford, Calif., 1991.

Nord, Deborah Epstein. *The Apprenticeship of Beatrice Webb.* London, 1985.

DEBORAH EPSTEIN NORD

WEBER, MAX (1864–1920), German social scientist.

While posterity views Max Weber primarily as a sociologist, his contemporaries knew him as an economist. He also made seminal contributions to economic history, political science, the history of law, and the philosophy of social science. Weber, in brief, is one of the giants of social science and his knowledge was truly encyclopedic.

Weber was born into a wealthy and well-connected upper-middle-class family in Erfurt. His father was a magistrate and later a member of the Reichstag, and his mother a deeply religious person of Huguenot ancestry. As a child Weber already showed a strong interest in reading and taking notes, especially in historical topics. As a student he focused on law, especially the history of law, but he also studied history, philosophy, and economics.

Though he wrote his dissertation as well as his *Habilitation* thesis in the field of law, Weber was soon offered a professorship in economics; the reason for this was his impressive writings in this field as a member of the Verein für Sozialpolitik (Association for Social Policy). His academic career continued to be spectacularly successful until the end of the 1890s, when he had a nervous breakdown that stopped him from further academic work.

Though he never fully recovered, Weber soon began to write again and lived most of his remaining years as a private scholar. In 1904–1905 he published *The Protestant Ethic and the Spirit of Capitalism*, which made him famous inside as well as outside of Germany. A few years later he started to work on what was to become another landmark study, *Economy and Society* (1910–1914). He also completed several volumes in a project called *The Economic Ethics of the World Religions* (1920–1921).

Weber was a friend of major intellectuals of his time such as Georg Simmel (1858–1918), Ernst Troeltsch (1865–1923), and Georg Jellinek (1851–1911). In 1893 he married a distant relative, Marianne Schnitger (1870–1954), who became active in the women's movement and a scholar in her own right. After her husband's death, Marianne Weber organized his work for publication and in other ways nurtured his reputation.

Weber was intensely interested in politics and repeatedly tried to get a foothold in professional politics. This failed, and he was probably also temperamentally unsuited for routine political activity, which he famously described in "Politics as a Vocation" (1921) as the slow drilling through hard boards. Weber was, in contrast, quite influential through his many newspaper articles on political topics, especially during World War I. He also helped to write the constitution of the Weimar Republic.

Weber wrote in several different social science disciplines. Besides his two dissertations in the history of law, he also wrote voluminously on the legal aspects of the stock exchange. In economic history, there is his famous economic and social history of antiquity, as well as his early study of rural workers in imperial Germany. A volume on general economic history also exists, reconstructed from students' notes. Weber's most important articles in the philosophy of social science have been collected in a separate volume, and so have his writings on politics. Finally, there are Weber's works in sociology: *The Protestant Ethic and the*

Spirit of Capitalism, Economy and Society, and *The Economic Ethics of the World Religions.*

The Protestant Ethic is without doubt Weber's most famous as well as his most controversial work. Its main thesis is that a certain type of Protestantism ("ascetic Protestantism") helped to create the spirit of modern, rational capitalism. In doing so, it also helped to put an end to traditional capitalism and usher in a new period in the history of the West that Weber describes as an "iron cage." What had started out as an attempt by Martin Luther (1483–1546), John Calvin (1509–1564), and other Protestant reformers to improve the relationship of the believer to God, had paradoxically ended up as a more efficient way to make money.

Exactly how this whole development came about constitutes the most controversial part of the so-called Weber thesis. According to what may be termed Weber's hypothetical reconstruction, the typical Calvinist tried to counter religious anxiety by looking for signs that he or she was doing well in the eyes of an inscrutable God. One of these signs was material wealth, which made the Calvinists invest their business activities with religious energy and methodical intent. Soon the economic mentality of the Calvinists and other ascetic Protestants became the norm in economic life—and Western capitalism had acquired a new mentality. This mentality eventually translated into a set of new capitalist institutions, such as the modern factory, the joint-stock corporation, and so on.

The Weber thesis had hardly been published before it was attacked. Much of the criticism in Weber's time and into the twenty-first century, however, is based on a misreading of his argument. It is often claimed, for example, that Weber regarded "Protestantism" as "the cause" of "capitalism," while what he argues is that *ascetic* Protestantism was *one* of the causes of a new capitalist *mentality.* Nonetheless, Weber's work contains little empirical support of his thesis, perhaps because he primarily tried to show how modern rational capitalism *could* have emerged, drawing on the type of cultural analysis in which Weber at this point of his life was deeply interested. One way of summing up a century of debate about *The Protestant Ethic* is to say that while most social scientists reject Weber's argument, it still has a number of defenders.

The Protestant Ethic was part of a larger research project that Weber spent much of World War I working on. This project, which Weber called "The Economic Ethics of the World Religions," had two major goals. First, Weber wanted to explore the role of religions other than Protestantism in promoting or blocking the birth of modern rational capitalism. And second, Weber wanted to explore what role rational forms of behavior and culture played in making the West into the leader of the modern world.

Weber never completed this project, but the work that he did produce gives a clear indication of his findings. As to the first question, he established that most of the major religions in the world have in one way or another blocked the emergence of modern, rational capitalism. Hinduism, as Weber explains in *The Religion of India* (1958), legitimated the caste system. Buddhism, in contrast, set a high priority on withdrawing from the concerns of life in this world, something that led to a disinterest in material wealth. Taoism helped to prevent rational capitalism from emerging in Southeast Asia by exalting magic, according to *The Religion of China* (1951); Confucianism had a similar affect through its ethical justification of traditionalism.

The rise of the West, according to Weber, is intimately connected to the central role that rationalism came to play in a number of areas of social life. Besides the economy, there is also art, architecture, music, and the state. In all of these areas, and more can be added, the West developed a certain mentality that made it possible for Europe to take the lead in the world and impose its leadership on other civilizations.

While some see *The Protestant Ethic* and the volumes that make up *The Economic Ethics of the World Religions* as Weber's most important achievement, others point to *Economy and Society.* Again, this was a work that he never completed. When he died he had finished the first four chapters and various drafts for the rest of the work, leaving it to posterity to figure out what he had intended to include.

While controversy still rages over whether the content of the existing editions adequately captures Weber's intentions, the scholarly quality of his work has never been questioned. In chapter 1 of *Economy and Society,* Weber presents a very ambitious program for what he terms an *interpretive sociology:* that is, a sociology that is concerned with social action and the meaning with which actors invest their behavior. Chapter 1 also contains a famous typology of sociological concepts.

In addition, *Economy and Society* contains important chapters on economic sociology, sociology of law, and sociology of religion. Other chapters contain Weber's famous theory of bureaucracy, the concept of status, and the typology of domination (rational, traditional, and charismatic). To this may be added a wealth of historical material as well as a superb account (in the current English edition) of the political situation in imperial Germany.

While *Economy and Society* contains a highly sophisticated analysis of various social mechanisms that operate throughout society, it also gives voice to Weber's view of the modern world. According to Weber, the modern world is becoming increasingly rationalized, a process that is taking place in all of society's different spheres. Religion and the economy, for example, are becoming more methodical and rational. In several spheres, bureaucracy—defined by Weber as efficient and dutiful administration—is also becoming ever more present.

There exist good reasons to regard Weber as one of the most important social scientists of all times, and of the same stature as scholars like Montesquieu (1689–1755), Alexis de Tocqueville (1805–1859), and Karl Marx (1818–1883). While an enormous secondary literature has been devoted to Weber's writings, many parts of his work are still relatively unexplored or little understood. His consistent focus on the most central and difficult problems in social science—such as causality, culture, and social structure—makes his work ever modern.

See also **Capitalism; Protestantism; Sociology.**

BIBLIOGRAPHY

Primary Sources

Weber, Max. *The Protestant Ethic and the Spirit of Capitalism.* Translated by Talcott Parsons. London, 1930.

————. *Max Weber on the Methodology of the Social Sciences.* Translated and edited by Edward A. Shils and Henry A. Finch. New York, 1949.

————. *The Religion of China.* Translated and edited by Hans H. Gerth. New York, 1951.

————. *The Religion of India.* Translated and edited by Hans H. Gerth and Don Martindale. New York, 1958.

————. *Economy and Society: An Outline of Interpretive Sociology.* Edited by Guenther Roth and Claus Wittich. Translated by Ephraim Fischoff. New York, 1978.

————. *General Economic History.* New Brunswick, N.J., 1981.

————. *Gesamtausgabe.* Frankfurt, 1984.

————. *Weber: Political Writings.* Edited by Peter Lassman and Ronald Speirs. Cambridge, U.K., 1994.

Secondary Sources

Bendix, Reinhard. *Max Weber: An Intellectual Portrait.* Garden City, N.Y., 1960. An important introduction to Weber's work, minus his methodology.

Käsler, Dirk. *Max Weber: An Introduction to His Life and Work.* Chicago, 1988. This is the best overall introduction to Weber's work and life.

Marshall, Gordon. *In Search of the Spirit of Capitalism: An Essay on Max Weber's Protestant Ethic Thesis.* London, 1982. An excellent introduction to the debate surrounding *The Protestant Ethic and the Spirit of Capitalism.*

Mommsen, Wolfgang. *Max Weber and German Politics 1890–1920.* Translated by Michael S. Steinberg. Chicago, 1984. The major study of Weber's political ideas.

Sica, Alan. *Max Weber: A Comprehensive Bibliography.* New Brunswick, N.J., 2004. A major bibliography of the secondary material on Weber as well as existing translations of his work.

Swedberg, Richard. *The Max Weber Dictionary.* Stanford, Calif., 2005. A helpful guide to key words and central concepts in Weber's work.

Weber, Marianne. *Max Weber: A Biography.* Edited and translated by Harry Zohn. New York, 1975. The only existing biography of Weber's life, written by his wife.

RICHARD SWEDBERG

WEININGER, OTTO (1880–1903), Austrian writer.

Otto Weininger is a notorious figure in modern European history, largely because of his one book, *Geschlecht und Charakter: Eine prinzipielle Untersuchung* (1903; Sex and character: An investigation of principles), a voluminous treatise that "proved" that women and Jews did not possess rational and moral selves and, therefore, neither deserved nor needed equality with Aryan men or even simple liberty. Writers and thinkers as different as Franz Kafka (1883–1924), Ludwig Wittgenstein (1889–1951), Karl Kraus (1874–1936), James Joyce (1882–1941), Robert von Musil (1880–1942), Elias Canetti (1905–1994), Günter Grass (b. 1927), and Germaine Greer (b. 1939) were struck, although not necessarily persuaded, by Weininger's racist and misogynist vision of the world.

Otto Weininger was born on 3 April 1880 to a Jewish family of Vienna, the second child and oldest son of Adelheid Frey (1857–1912) and Leopold Weininger (1854–1922). After graduating from high school in 1898, he enrolled in the philosophical faculty of the University of Vienna, where he attended lectures on logic, experimental psychology, pedagogy, the history of philosophy, and a wide range of scientific and medical topics. His friends remembered him as a somber and serious youth who scorned the alcoholic and lubricious pursuits of average university students and spent his free hours discussing "the most difficult philosophical subjects."

In 1900 Weininger's friend Hermann Swoboda embarked on psychoanalysis with Sigmund Freud (1856–1939), who told him that all human beings were partly male and partly female, or "bisexual." Swoboda reported Freud's observation to Weininger, who, galvanized by this idea, immediately decided to write a monograph on sexuality entitled *Eros und Psyche: Eine biologisch-psychologische Studie* (Eros and Psyche: A biopsychological study). He eventually developed this tract, which argued that human beings were androgynous in their bodies as well as minds, into a Ph.D. dissertation under the supervision of the noted philosopher Friedrich Jodl. It was completed in 1902 and published the next year by the renowned firm of Wilhelm Braumüller as *Geschlecht und Charakter: Eine prinzipielle Untersuchung.*

Long before the completion of the dissertation, however, Weininger had become increasingly preoccupied with Kantian philosophy, "Jewishness," "the woman question," and the shortcomings of modern experimental psychology. A project that had begun by arguing the ambiguity of sexual difference thus became a somewhat heterogeneous text that was still organized around the notion of sexual difference but now included long and dense discussions of woman's place in the universe, the masculine character of genius, the nature of the Jew, and the contamination of modern reason, thought, and art by effeminacy. This was not as eccentric as it might seem: the meanings of femininity (and indeed, of gender itself) were at the very heart of turn-of-the-twentieth-century debates about the nature and future of civilization—to deal with the former *was* to deal with the latter and vice versa. Woman, Weininger concluded, was amoral, soulless and utterly and pervasively sexual; the Jew was largely similar. Man, on the other hand, was microcosmic and protean—genius, morality, and creativity were always exclusively and necessarily male. Many of these arguments were linked with (or framed in response to) contemporary scientific and medical theories of sexuality and psychology, and documented in an enormous critical apparatus.

The book attracted little notice after publication but then its author, returning deeply depressed from a holiday, killed himself in the house where Beethoven had died. This dramatic suicide boosted sales of *Geschlecht und Charakter,* and some of Weininger's drafts and aphorisms were hastily collected by his friends and published as *Über die letzten Dinge* (On last things). Reviews of *Geschlecht und Charakter* appeared in profusion, Weininger's life was pored over by psychiatrists, and his work was championed by Vienna's most pugnacious cultural critic, Karl Kraus. Although not a straightforward misogynist, Kraus strongly endorsed Weininger's views about the pervasive sexuality of Woman and shared his anxieties about the degeneracy of Western civilization. After World War II, however, scholars have tended to approach *Geschlecht und Charakter* as an encyclopedic repository of fin-de-siècle racist and misogynist thought. While some continue to focus on Weininger's own prejudices in relative isolation, most now use *Geschlecht und Charakter* to explore the racial and sexual anxieties that pervaded the world in which the book was written and which it sought to influence.

See also **Anti-Semitism; Feminism; Freud, Sigmund; Vienna.**

BIBLIOGRAPHY

Primary Sources

Weininger, Otto. *Sex and Character: An Investigation of Fundamental Principles,* translated by Ladislaus Löb, edited by Daniel Steuer and Laura Marcus, Bloomington, Ind., 2005. New and complete translation of *Geschlect und Charakter* (1903), superseding the incomplete English version of 1906.

Secondary Sources

Harrowitz, Nancy A., and Barbara Hyams, eds. *Jews and Gender: Responses to Otto Weininger.* Philadelphia, 1995. Collection of informative articles on Weininger, his work, and his milieu.

Janik, Allan. *Essays on Wittgenstein and Weininger.* Amsterdam, 1985. Pioneering essays on the importance of contextualizing Weininger.

Sengoopta, Chandak. *Otto Weininger: Sex, Science, and Self in Imperial Vienna.* Chicago, 2000. Emphasizes the importance of biological and medical themes in Weininger's work.

CHANDAK SENGOOPTA

WELFARE. The European public welfare state began in the late nineteenth century, supplementing and sometimes supplanting private charity. Private charity, usually religious, had long dispensed alms, but increasingly public, generally secular state-welfare programs developed, especially beginning in the 1870s. Although some scholars had argued that the welfare state began in Germany during the time of Otto von Bismarck (chancellor, 1871–1890), when modern historians use the lens of gender, they understand that welfare began in many countries of western Europe at approximately the same time, but took different forms.

WELFARE AND THE "DESERVING POOR," 1815–1870

Moral and religious convictions about poverty shaped charity and welfare policies. Religious charities believed that the poor would always form the bottom of the social and economic hierarchy, but sought to help those whom they thought deserved aid. Definitions of the "deserving poor" differed little by region or religion. They were the honest poor whose misfortunes were unpreventable, or those who *could not* care for themselves: abandoned or orphaned children, the insane, men and women too old or sick to work, and morally upstanding people who faced a sudden disaster. The able-bodied poor, customarily adult men, who *would not* work were labeled "undeserving" of poor relief.

In Britain, as well as on the Continent, poor relief was locally based. Municipalities in England, France, and the German states required recipients to have lived in the community for a number of years to become eligible. Married women belonged to the domicile of their husbands, which denied them a right to poor relief as individuals. In the 1820s settlement and domicile requirements began to break down in Europe, as people increasingly moved around to get better jobs in response to labor demand. Legal settlement in new parishes was harder to acquire, and many poor barely subsisted on the margins of their new residences.

New ideologies and conditions gave rise to the New Poor Laws of 1834 in Britain. This reform sought to restore the middle-class work ethic and moral values by tightening the criteria for aid and fostering self-support. It held poor families, specifically the men, responsible for their own survival. The New Poor Law developed prison-like workhouses as a punishment for those, especially men, who committed the "crime" of being a pauper. Indigent mothers of ex-nuptial children could also be taken into the workhouse and separated from their children as a disciplinary measure. Poor Law guardians incarcerated nonproviding fathers or indigent mothers in separate workhouse wards from each other and from their children. There was no clear separation between charity and public poor relief, with close cooperation between local Poor Law authorities and charitable organizations.

Across Europe, religious charities and secular welfare attempted to buttress the family as the bulwark of the social order. On the Continent almost every major European city enlarged the parameters of welfare to include policies for maternal assistance to prevent infant mortality. Moscow, St. Petersburg, and Hamburg, as well as most of the major cities of the Habsburg Empire, France, Italy, Spain, and Portugal inaugurated free maternity hospitals where poor pregnant women could deliver their babies in secret. These same cities and countries often established foundling homes to permit abandonment as an alternative to abortion and infanticide, and to save the honor of the woman and her family. In predominantly Catholic countries such as France, Portugal, and Spain, and in cities such as Brussels and those on the Italian peninsula, foundling hospitals became the most important form of public welfare until late in the nineteenth century.

PUBLIC WELFARE, 1870–1914

Between 1870 and 1914 traditional local poor relief coexisted with modern centralized state intervention, as welfare greatly expanded. State bureaucracies and legislators established new criteria for welfare, pertaining more to the needs of the state and less to the older moral strictures. Many local private charities that developed earlier in the century expanded and flourished. But they diminished in importance on a national level vis-à-vis a new interest in state insurance programs and the developing rationalized welfare state. For a welfare state to develop, local politicians had to accept the notion that poor relief was less a gift from the rich and more the right of the poor, which they did by the end of the century.

Poverty became a social disease rather than a moral disorder under the powerful discourse of medical professionals, their allies in government, and the positivist philosophy of the era. Needs of state in terms of the health of the population, educational reform, industrial and military expansion, urban unrest, and agricultural development came to outweigh the religious and moral imperatives so powerful in earlier decades and affected welfare programs accordingly. Furthermore, the difficult conditions of industry and the growing militancy of male laborers led to debates about the need for the state to protect workers. As a result, after 1870 public welfare institutions increased. Welfare did not so much take over from declining charity as it added additional layers of assistance. In Germany, the country that reputedly began the national welfare state in the 1870s and developed an interventionist state in the 1890s, there was little opposition between private charity and public welfare. Rather, the two worked in tandem.

The valorization of maternity during the later nineteenth century translated into legislation, as social reformers enacted family welfare reforms centered on mothers and children. Social welfare programs designed to keep mothers and babies together started throughout Europe in the early 1870s and took similar forms in France, England, Germany, and Russia. Politicians and reformers in many western countries became increasingly willing to intervene directly in the family in order to protect children. At the same time, they glorified, dignified, and sought to protect motherhood. Public welfare authorities in England, France, and Germany perceived that underprivileged families were in a state of crisis contributing to high infant mortality, and thought the problem could be partially resolved by providing some subsidies to needy mothers who were breastfeeding their infants, establishing well-baby clinics and free milk dispensaries, teaching women how to be better mothers, and by providing school meals.

Child protection was inseparable from the protection of motherhood, and it included legislation regulating children's and women's labor in Britain, Germany, and France. Authorities in western Europe regarded women as mothers, and motherhood became a social function. Politicians consequently enacted aid programs to support maternity. In Germany, this led to the protection of working mothers through maternity insurance and pregnancy leave. Generally, German infant welfare organizations fell under private auspices, such as the League for Protection of Mothers. In Russia, day nurseries and boarding institutions for infants of widowed, deserted, or working mothers developed as part of an effort to reduce infant mortality. Russian efforts were in keeping with their philosophy that the state could raise children better than poor, uneducated, working mothers. The major difference between child protection reforms in Russia and in countries of western Europe revolved around concepts of women's roles as workers. Western European authorities viewed women primarily as mothers; Russians viewed women primarily as workers.

To defend children from abusive parents, the French, British, and German governments enacted almost identical legislation enabling state welfare authorities to decide which parents were placing their children in moral danger and then deprive those parents of authority over their children. Police and welfare agents would subsequently remove the children from their parental homes and place the children with relatives, in foster care, or in institutions. In these instances, as in many other aspects of welfare, public authorities entered the private spaces of the underprivileged. The French Parliament enacted a law protecting these "morally abandoned" children in 1889, the same year that the British Parliament enacted the law for the Prevention of Cruelty and Protection of Children that allowed state authorities to remove children from their families when circumstances warranted it. Scottish Poor Law authorities, who had been separating children from abusive or dangerous family situations for decades and boarding them out, continued this process in the interest of protecting the children and imbuing them with sober work habits. Comparable German legislation came about a decade later.

The significance of motherhood is evident in legislation in Britain, Germany, and France that treated childbirth as an illness entitled to medical assistance. The French law of 1893 on free medical assistance assimilated childbirth with other illnesses and allowed women in labor free admission to the public hospitals. Britain's National Health Insurance Act of 1911 allotted a pittance to women who had enrolled in the insurance program, either on their own or through their husbands. The 1883 German law on health insurance entitled insured women factory workers to minimal benefits for three weeks of maternity leave after childbirth, but coverage was optional and rarely paid. Even Russia had a workers' insurance law in 1912 that provided for maternity benefits.

In France, the creation of mothers' pensions, or aid to mothers (including the unwed) to encourage breast-feeding and prevent child abandonment provided another building block to the welfare state. Despite the opposition of church authorities who regarded payments to unwed mothers as a "subsidy to debauchery," mothers' pensions began in France in the 1870s and 1880s with programs of aid to single and married mothers. Portugal developed an equivalent system called a "subsidy of lactation" to aid indigent parents and widows or widowers, as well as unwed mothers. Despite opposition from church authorities, regions of Italy almost immediately followed France with similar programs of subsidies to single mothers who nursed their babies. In Italy, however, the motive

was not a perceived depopulation but rather the desire to moralize poor, unwed mothers. Although much of the British, German, and Russian legislation for the protection of children and mothers resembled French programs, the differences between France and the other countries are two-fold. One is a question of timing. France's various programs for the protection of motherhood began in Paris and other cities in the 1870s, developed through the 1880s, and became nationally legislated in 1893, 1904, and 1913. Second, France was among the first to offer programs of aid to non-married mothers to prevent infant mortality on a national scale in 1904. Except for Russia, Italy, and Portugal, other nations' laws restricted mothers' pensions to widows or married mothers.

Welfare in the form of maternity leaves varied in their comprehensiveness and remuneration. The Swiss were pioneers in this area; their 1877 law provided for eight weeks of leave, before and after delivery, and prohibited women from returning to factory work until six weeks after childbirth. One year later, in 1878, Germany enacted a three-week leave after childbirth, but neither the Swiss nor the German leaves included benefits or pay. By 1883 both Germany and Austria-Hungary had paid maternity leaves of three weeks after delivery for insured women, but the amount varied with each insurance program. Sweden put family policies into law in 1900 when it gave mothers a four-week maternity leave after the birth of a child. Mothers received no money, just time off from work to breast-feed. By 1900, Great Britain, Portugal, Norway, Sweden, Holland, and Belgium provided unpaid maternity leaves after delivery. France, along with Spain, Italy, Denmark, and Russia, lagged behind these other countries in instituting any kind of maternity leave, even without pay. In 1911 Sweden instituted a program to protect and care for women and their babies through maternity and convalescent homes as well as by giving women a subsidy to breastfeed their babies. In 1913 when France legislated paid maternity leaves before and after childbirth, Luxembourg, Germany, Switzerland, Sweden, and Austria-Hungary had paid leaves, and only Switzerland had a maternity leave *before* delivery. Maternity leaves and child welfare were just some examples of welfare at the turn of the century designed to keep families together.

The revolving table at the foundling home, Paris. Lithograph, 1862. The use of a revolving table to allow people to preserve their anonymity while relinquishing infants to the care of foundling homes was mandated in France in 1811, when responsibility for the care of such infants was transferred from the central government to the departments. The number of children brought to the homes subsequently increased dramatically, leading to the abolition of the practice. BIBLIOTHÈQUE NATIONALE, PARIS, FRANCE/ THE BRIDGEMAN ART LIBRARY

Politicians in all countries sought to use welfare to form a moral citizenry and create a stable working class. The German town of Elberfeld provides one example of how cities used poor relief to further their agenda of social discipline of the poor through inspections. The central goal of the Elberfeld system was to find work for the poor with a fixed domicile. Many German cities followed the Elberfeld model, but increased industrialization and migration after German unification made the Elberfeld system unworkable; reformers replaced it with a new, centralized, national system. The Bismarckian social insurance provisions of the 1880s and family welfare schemes of the 1890s aimed to integrate the working class into established society. To win support from male workers, in the 1880s the German government provided a welfare plan that included health insurance and old-age pensions for many of them.

The impetus for welfare reforms at the end of the century may have come as a result of the general depression and fears of mass unemployment that struck most of Europe from the mid-1880s to mid-1890s. During these years the poor became more visible, and thus more of a perceived threat to an orderly society. The rise of industrial capitalism transformed poverty from a social into a political problem, as welfare state capitalism developed in response to crises in classical capitalism. Politicians redefined poverty to justify the state's intervention in support of the patriarchal ideal and the *raison* d'état. Specifically, the decline in agriculture and the migration of young to the cities in the late 1880s added to a large pool of urban labor (with many unemployed) and an elderly population remaining in the rural areas.

Public welfare began to try to address some of the problems of workers and the elderly, beginning with national insurance programs for sickness, disability, and old age. In Germany, social reformers eventually recognized that deserving workers had a right to experience old age without financial hardships, and that it would be unjust to let them live out their lives under conditions worse than while they were still working. When old age came to be recognized as a separate stage of life in the late nineteenth century, old-age pensions became a subject of legislation. In England and France the debate continued over the divisions in how much families bore responsibility for the elderly and how much that responsibility devolved on welfare institutions. At the end of the century, public assistance made pensions available to proportionally fewer of the aged than it had before 1870, and the amount was reduced. In the absence of sufficient welfare, elder care devolved on families.

State welfare was insufficient to deal with the problems of poverty and unemployment. In many countries, charitable organizations and mutual aid societies existed alongside public poor relief. Stable breadwinner working men in almost all countries established voluntary mutual aid societies designed to protect their members, and women formed cooperative guilds for self-help. Private charities remained important everywhere, although many became more secular.

By the end of the nineteenth century neither charities nor welfare had enough money or facilities to meet the demand. Layers of institutions and of jurisdictions—municipal, local, regional, and national—provided private charity and public welfare. They combined their recognition of economic need, however, with a moral commitment to promote and reward working-class women's domesticity and men's steady work habits. Welfare measures in the last decades of the century involved a change in cultural concepts. Reformers recast the relationship between the sexual and social order, between the family and the state, and between what they thought of as the public and private spheres.

The family remained the linchpin of the social order, but public welfare permitted a greater variety in acceptable family structures. With the change in attitudes came increased programs to provide medical, old-age, and accident insurance to workers.

USING WELFARE, 1815–1914

The poor became knowledgeable consumers in the welfare market as they negotiated their way within the available programs. Unlike the middle classes who blamed the poor for their own plight, the poor themselves blamed the wider world over which they had no control. Therefore they regarded poor relief as a "right" during a crisis: an unexpected death (especially of the male breadwinner), illness or accident to the male breadwinner, childbirth, old age, unemployment, or having many young children at home. By the end of the century, some reformers also asserted that welfare was a right.

Welfare allowed men and women a form of "disciplinary individualism" in which a person voluntarily conformed to requirements and tried to use the laws and institutions to their own ends. They used institutions as a safety net. In England, Ireland, Belgium, and Holland families used the workhouses as institutions of last resort. Entering one meant loss of respectability, and the elderly felt this sense of shame quite keenly. Others, perhaps those less needy, decided not to request poor relief to avoid the disgrace of pauperism. Outdoor relief (assistance in the poor's own homes and outside of institutions) was preferable to the detested workhouses, although it was an income subsidy insufficient to provide food, fuel, and shelter for its recipients. In England, between 60 and 80 percent of the recipients of poor relief, both in the workhouse and outdoors, were adult women and children, equally divided. More than half of the women were single parents. Changes in the British Poor Laws (1834 and 1871) making outdoor relief more restrictive led to adaptive family strategies. If neighbors and relatives possibly could feed another mouth, they stood ready to help by taking in young children so the child might avoid the parish workhouses.

In France, Italy, and Russia, in acts of desperation, women abandoned hundreds of thousands of children at institutions each year. At the height

Destitute Men Applying for Admittance to a London Night Refuge. Engraving by Gustave Doré c. 1869–1871. IMAGE SELECT/ART RESOURCE, NY

of child abandonment around midcentury, approximately twenty-six thousand children per year were abandoned in Moscow and St. Petersburg. In Paris during the peak decade of the 1830s, around five thousand per year were abandoned, and more than forty-four thousand abandoned children under twelve were alive in all of France in a given year of that decade. Spain and Portugal saw fifteen thousand per year abandoned; a fifth of all babies were abandoned in Warsaw; half of all babies in Vienna and two-fifths in Prague; a third of all babies in Milan and Florence.

Mothers, especially the unwed, may have been driven to abandon their babies because of their impoverishment and their working conditions that precluded work and care for their infant. The higher rates of illegitimacy and rural-to-urban migration also contributed to a greater proportion of abandoned ex-nuptial children. The baby's gender did not matter to single mothers, but married women abandoned more girls than boys. Welfare policies also affected mothers' decisions to aban-

don. When government policy permitted, families used institutions to their own advantage, allowing the state to raise the children until they could reclaim them. When public authorities imposed restrictions on child abandonment, the desperate continued to abandon their babies. However, other welfare resources for mothers, such as aid for maternal breast-feeding or day-care centers, often accompanied restrictions on infant abandonment, especially in France. Few questioned the entitlement of children to food and sustenance through welfare when their mothers could not provide. Dealing with the elderly was a different matter.

Family support of the elderly was critical. Widowhood amplified problems of economic insecurity and possible destitution for women more than men. The aged in Britain relied on complex systems of support from their own wages and pensions, and from their children and Poor Law relief. At the turn of the twentieth century, the establishment of widows' pensions in England enabled fortunate men and women to benefit from that insurance, and in 1908 all deserving poor were eligible for old-age pensions. The Dutch government established regulated and regimented old-folks' homes for widows and unmarried elderly women. In Paris, poor widows were approximately half of those on the welfare roles of public assistance. In Germany old age was not used as a category to determine the distribution of poor relief, which was geared for the sick and disabled.

Until after World War I, state insurance schemes were geared to help the individual, including the aged, whereas poor relief was understood as a subsidiary measure that kicked in when all family support had failed. Europe was not a monolithic entity and a multiplicity of regional and national patterns prevailed. In England, a strong desire to imbue the poor with the donors' concepts of morality and respectability influenced welfare and poor relief. Authorities in England and Germany channeled welfare through the male breadwinner. France, however, tried to reconcile women's productive and reproductive roles, and welfare went directly to the mothers, with guidelines and supervision from the state. In Russia, quite unlike Great Britain, poverty was not considered a sin, and authorities did not noticeably distinguish between the deserving and undeserving poor. Russia also did not develop a national welfare system. By 1914, British paupers had a right to public assistance in the parish of their birth or settlement. In Germany, national insurance plans developed for workers, all towns provided some poor relief, and rural areas were required to establish relief commissions for the poor. The French enacted comparable legislation, and approximately three-fourths of French men and woman had access to assistance for hospital care or other forms of temporary relief on the eve of World War I. A welfare system is a product of an urban society. It developed more completely during the nineteenth century in more urban countries with an ideology that understood that a welfare system benefited the entire nation.

See also **Bismarck, Otto von; Class and Social Relations; Poor Law; Poverty; Trade and Economic Growth; Working Class.**

BIBLIOGRAPHY

Accampo, Elinor, Rachel G. Fuchs, and Mary Lynn Stewart. *Gender and the Politics of Social Reform in France, 1870–1914.* Baltimore, Md., 1995.

Baldwin, Peter. *The Politics of Social Solidarity: Class Bases of the European Welfare State, 1875–1975.* New York, 1990.

Barry, Jonathan, and Colin Jones, eds. *Medicine and Charity before the Welfare State.* London and New York, 1991.

Behlmer, George K. *Friends of the Family: The English Home and Its Guardians, 1850–1940.* Stanford, Calif., 1998.

Bock, Gisela, and Pat Thane, eds. *Maternity and Gender Policies: Women and the Rise of the European Welfare States, 1880s–1950s.* London and New York, 1991.

Boyer, George R. *An Economic History of the English Poor Law, 1750–1850.* Cambridge, U.K., 1990.

Cunningham, Hugh, and Joanna Innes, eds. *Charity, Philanthropy, and Reform from the 1690s to 1850.* New York, 1998.

Daunton, Martin, ed. *Charity, Self-Interest, and Welfare in the English Past.* London, 1996.

Dickinson, Edward Ross. *The Politics of German Child Welfare from the Empire to the Federal Republic.* Cambridge, Mass., 1996.

Finalyson, Geoffrey. *Citizen, State, and Social Welfare in Britain, 1830–1990.* Oxford, U.K., 1994.

Fuchs, Rachel G. *Abandoned Children: Foundlings and Child Welfare in Nineteenth-Century France.* Albany, N.Y., 1984.

_____. *Poor and Pregnant in Paris: Strategies for Survival in the Nineteenth Century.* New Brunswick, N.J., 1992.

Gouda, Frances. *Poverty and Political Culture: The Rhetoric of Social Welfare in the Netherlands and France, 1815–1854.* Lanham, Md., 1995.

Horn, Pamela. *Children's Work and Welfare, 1780–1890.* Cambridge, U.K., 1995.

Humphreys, Robert. *Sin, Organized Charity, and the Poor Law in Victorian England.* New York, 1995.

Katz, Michael B., and Christoph Sachße, eds. *The Mixed Economy of Social Welfare: Public/Private Relations in England, Germany, and the United States, the 1870s to the 1930s.* Baden-Baden, 1996.

Kertzer, David I. *Sacrificed for Honor: Italian Infant Abandonment and the Politics of Reproductive Control.* Boston, 1993.

Kidd, Alan J. *State, Society, and the Poor in Nineteenth-Century England.* New York, 1999.

Lees, Lynn Hollen. *The Solidarities of Strangers: The English Poor Laws and the People, 1700–1948.* Cambridge, U.K., 1998.

Lewis, Jane. *The Voluntary Sector, the State, and Social Work in Britain: The Charity Organisation Society/Family Welfare Association since 1869.* Aldershot, U.K., 1995.

Lindemann, Mary. *Patriots and Paupers: Hamburg, 1712–1830.* New York, 1990.

Lindenmeyr, Adele. *Poverty Is Not a Vice: Charity, Society, and the State in Imperial Russia.* Princeton, N.J., 1996.

Mandler, Peter. ed. *The Uses of Charity: The Poor on Relief in the Nineteenth-Century Metropolis.* Philadelphia, 1990.

Prochaska, Frank. *Women and Philanthropy in Nineteenth-Century England.* Oxford, U.K., 1980.

Ransel, David L. *Mothers of Misery: Child Abandonment in Russia.* Princeton, N.J., 1988.

Steinmetz, George. *Regulating the Social: The Welfare State and Local Politics in Imperial Germany.* Princeton, N.J., 1993.

Thane, Pat. *Foundations of the Welfare State.* London, 1982.

Van Leeuwen, Marco H. D. *The Logic of Charity, Amsterdam, 1800–50.* Houndmills Basingstoke, U.K., 2000.

RACHEL G. FUCHS

WELLINGTON, DUKE OF (ARTHUR WELLESLEY) (1769–1852), British army general and politician.

The Duke of Wellington has been admired far more for his command of the British army than for his contribution to parliamentary politics. He was Britain's most revered and respected army general during the nineteenth century, but also a very unpopular prime minister. Born in Ireland into the Anglo-Irish aristocracy, Arthur Wesley (later Wellesley) was the third surviving son of Garret Wesley, the first Earl of Mornington, and Lady Anne. His family's difficult financial circumstances after the early death of his father in 1781, in addition to his poor performance at Eton and a French military academy, dampened his prospects. His ambitious but less talented eldest brother, Richard, launched Wellington's military career in 1787 by obtaining for him a commission in the 73rd regiment.

Wellington started at the bottom of the officer ranks but quickly worked his way up by transferring from regiment to regiment and by serving as aide-de-camp to the lord lieutenant of Ireland beginning in 1787. With the outbreak of war between Britain and revolutionary France in 1793 came Wellington's first serious battlefield test. In 1794 he sailed for the Netherlands with the 33rd regiment, and while it was a disastrous campaign, he later claimed to have learned from his commanders' mistakes. Success in the field would have to wait for India, where he served from 1797 to 1805. He gained notable victories in Mysore (1799), where he was appointed governor, and at Assaye (1803). At the same time, he obtained valuable experience in administration and diplomacy.

Though recognized for his military success in India with a knighthood, Wellington's greatest renown came during the Napoleonic Wars, especially in the Iberian Peninsula, where Napoleon's military occupation caused deep anger and resentment. Wellington arrived in 1808 to assist the rebelling Spanish and Portuguese. He drove off the French at Rolica and repulsed a French attack at Vimeiro, but was ordered by a newly arrived senior officer to sign an armistice. The unpopularity at home of the Convention of Cintra resulted in an official inquiry, but Wellington suffered no serious harm. In 1809 he was in command in Portugal and

by 1814 had pushed the French out of Spain and back across the French border. A series of major victories, for example at Talavera (1809), Salamanca (1812), and Vitoria (1813), catapulted him to war-hero status and earned him the titles of duke and field marshal. Wellington's military success can be attributed to his stunning grasp of defensive tactics, his attention to supply lines, and his ability to act decisively under pressure. When the Napoleonic Wars ended, he was appointed ambassador to the restored Bourbon court and served as a delegate to the Congress of Vienna, but was recalled to the army when Napoleon escaped from Elba. Wellington and Napoleon faced each other for the first and last time at the battle of Waterloo on 18 June 1815. Napoleon suffered a terrible defeat after the Prussians, commanded by Gebhard von Blücher, joined Wellington's battered but unyielding troops.

In command of the army of occupation in France until 1818, Wellington never fought another military battle, just political ones. His political career began early. He represented Trim in the Irish Parliament (1790–1797) and served as member of Parliament (MP) for Rye (elected 1806) and chief secretary to Ireland (1807–1809). When he returned from France, he joined the cabinet of Lord Liverpool (Robert Banks Jenkinson; 1770–1828) as master-general of the ordnance (1818–1827). While positioning himself above party politics, he was firmly aligned with the Tories. He distrusted the liberal wing of the party but was more pragmatic and less reactionary than the ultra-Tories. He thus opposed the expansion of democracy but retreated from entrenched positions in the interest of political order. This pragmatism helps to explain why during his term as prime minister (1828–1830) progressive reforms were enacted, including the repeal of the Test and Corporation Acts (1828) and the passage of Catholic Emancipation (1829), which together opened political office to Protestant dissenters and Roman Catholics.

Wellington's most costly political blunder was refusing to compromise over parliamentary reform and the expansion of the electorate, which brought the opposition Whigs into power. Wellington continued to be politically active, serving in Robert Peel's cabinet as foreign secretary (1834–1835) and minister without portfolio (1841–1846). Though his opposition to parliamentary reform tarnished his public standing, by the time of his death he had recovered his status as a selfless elder statesman, which a state funeral, burial in Saint Paul's Cathedral, and numerous public statues make abundantly clear.

See also **French Revolutionary Wars and Napoleonic Wars; Great Britain; Tories.**

BIBLIOGRAPHY

Primary Sources

Gurwood, John, ed. *The Dispatches of ... the Duke of Wellington.* 13 vols. London, 1834–1839.

Wellington, Arthur Wellesley. *Supplementary Despatches, Correspondence, and Memoranda of ... the Duke of Wellington ... Edited by His Son, the Duke of Wellington.* 15 vols. London, 1858–1872.

Secondary Sources

Gash, Norman, ed. *Wellington: Studies in the Military and Political Career of the First Duke of Wellington.* Manchester, U.K., 1990.

Longford, Elizabeth. *Wellington.* 2 vols. London and New York, 1969–1972. Remains the classic account.

Thompson, Neville. *Wellington after Waterloo.* London, 1986.

ELISA R. MILKES

WELLS, H. G. (1866–1946), British novelist, journalist, historian, sociologist, and futurologist.

Herbert George Wells was born into an impoverished lower-middle-class family and was apprenticed to a draper at age fourteen. He won a scholarship to the Normal School of Science (now part of Imperial College, London), where he studied biology under Thomas Henry Huxley (1825–1895). Subsequently, he worked as a teacher and then as a journalist, producing a series of scientific speculations for a number of leading periodicals including the *Fortnightly Review* and *Nature*.

Wells began his varied and prolific literary career with a succession of "scientific romances," which are generally acknowledged as the pioneers of science fiction. *The Time Machine* (1895) is a fable set in the year 802701 and portrays the split of the human race into two species—the dainty Eloi and the monstrous, subterranean Morlocks—

along class lines. This was followed by *The Island of Doctor Moreau* (1896), *The Invisible Man* (1897), *The First Men in the Moon* (1901), and other works. These works were inspired by the reassessment of humanity's place in nature initiated by the theory of natural selection described by Charles Darwin (1809–1882). They display Wells's lifelong preoccupation with evolutionary time and contain, to varying degrees, social allegory, foreboding about the future (often arising out of the laws of thermodynamics), and an assessment of the impact of scientific advancement upon the social order. Wells's output as a scientific romancer was paralleled by a series of fantastic novels, notably *The Wonderful Visit* (1895) and *The Sea Lady* (1902). In the 1890s, he also embarked upon a career as the author of such unforgettable short stories as "The Stolen Bacillus" (1893), "The Red Room" (1896), and "The Door in the Wall" (1906).

After 1900, Wells diversified his energies into a number of fields. His determination to establish himself as a mainstream novelist began with *Love and Mr. Lewisham* (1900) and culminated in *Tono-Bungay* (1909). In *Kipps* (1905) and *The History of Mr. Polly* (1910), Wells displayed considerable sympathy for the "little man." *Ann Veronica* (1909), which considers sexual equality and the issue of women's rights, caused considerable controversy. He famously feuded with Henry James (1843–1916), whom he ruthlessly caricatured in *Boon* (1915). Wells's insistence that novelists should fulfill a didactic purpose, rather than indulge in art for art's sake, also caused his estrangement from Joseph Conrad (1857–1924). *Anticipations* (1902), his first major work of futurology, examined the scientific and social trends that might shape the twentieth century. Wells joined the Fabian Society in 1903, but severed relations after a polemical exchange with leading members George Bernard Shaw (1856–1950), Beatrice Potter Webb (1858–1943), and Sidney James Webb (1859–1947); he depicted the Fabians in *The New Machiavelli* (1911). During his Fabian period, Wells wrote *A Modern Utopia* (1905), which established the popular conception of him as one of the twentieth century's few unequivocally utopian writers. Wells foresaw many of the advancements in modern warfare, including the use of poison gas in

2458

EUROPE 1789 TO 1914

World War I (In *The War of the Worlds* [1898]) and the development of the tank (in the short story "The Land Ironclads" [1904]). In *The World Set Free* (1913), he predicted the atomic bomb.

Wells was an outspoken critic of the League of Nations but campaigned tirelessly towards global unification, which he saw as the only alternative to annihilating conflict. He was pivotal to the Sankey Declaration on the Rights of Man, a precursor of the United Nations Charter. Wells's readership as a novelist declined in the 1920s, as attention turned to younger novelists such as Virginia Woolf (1882–1941) and James Joyce (1882–1941). However, he continued to reach a vast audience, particularly with *The Outline of History* (1920, abridged as *A Short History of the World*, 1922). Wells saw human history as a "race between education and catastrophe," and increasingly endeavored to facilitate the synthesis of existing nations into a "World State." Wells famously debated with world leaders, including U.S. presidents Theodore Roosevelt (1858–1919) and Franklin Delano Roosevelt (1882–1945). He met with Vladimir Lenin (1870–1924) in 1920 and with Lenin's successor, Joseph Stalin (1879–1953), in 1934. Wells's *The Shape of Things to Come* (1933, with its cinematic version, *Things to Come,* appearing in 1936), confirmed his status as a great popularizer of scientific and political ideas. Wells's last book, *Mind at the End of Its Tether* (1945), is a deeply pessimistic vision of humanity, which should be understood as a despairing response to the outcome of World War II. His *Experiment in Autobiography* (1934) is a lively account of Wells's involvement in the controversies of his own age.

See also **Fabians; Science and Technology; Verne, Jules.**

BIBLIOGRAPHY

Haynes, Roslynn D. *H. G. Wells: Discoverer of the Future.* New York, 1980.

MacKenzie, Norman, and Jeanne MacKenzie. *The Time Traveller: The Life of H. G. Wells.* London, 1973.

Parrinder, Patrick. *Shadows of the Future: H. G. Wells, Science Fiction, and Prophecy.* Syracuse, N.Y., 1995.

Partington, John S. *Building Cosmopolis: The Political Thought of H. G. Wells.* Aldershot, U.K., 2003.

STEVEN MCLEAN

WESTERNIZERS. The Westernizers (*zapadniki*) were a loosely organized group of Russian intellectuals, who from the late 1830s to the mid-1850s engaged the Slavophiles (*slavianofily*) in a bitter debate about Russia's past, its national identity, and its probable future. The trigger for this debate was Petr Chaadayev's "First Philosophical Letter" (written 1828, published 1836), which charged that Russians, cut off from the Roman Catholic Church and therefore from the living source of European civilization, were "orphans with one foot in the air" who had contributed nothing to the world. Stung to the quick, the Slavophiles defended the Orthodox Church and Old Russian social forms and folk traditions as superior to the religious, social, and political institutions of the "rotten," "barbarous" West. In response, the Westernizers claimed either that Russia had always been a member of the European community of nations or that Russia, in spite of its peculiar origins, was gradually becoming Europeanized and would eventually join the West as an equal partner in the civilized community of nations. Aside from their role in this pivotal debate, the Westernizers were significant in another regard: they contributed to the birth of a distinctively Russian agrarian socialism—the genesis of Russian anarchism and liberalism. Their tiny group was the intellectual seedbed of progressive politics in mid-nineteenth-century Russia.

It is customary to divide the Westernizers into two smaller groups. The moderate Westernizers included the historians Timofei Granovsky (1813–1855) and Sergei Soloviev (1820–1879), the legal expert Konstantin Kavelin (1818–1885), and the jurist Boris Chicherin (1828–1904). Sometimes the literary critic Pavel Annenkov (1813–1887) and the novelist Ivan Turgenev (1818–1883) are also added to the list of moderates. The radical Westernizers included the literary critic Vissarion Belinsky (1811–1848), the great memoirist Alexander Herzen (1812–1870), and the future anarchist Mikhail Bakunin (1814–1876).

As a historian of medieval and early modern Europe, Granovsky traced the development of centralized states, representative governments, and educated civil societies in the West. His university lectures strongly implied that Russian history had belatedly followed the Western pattern of social evolution, so that contemporary Russians could see their future in Europe's immediate past. Soloviev's classical *History of Russia from Ancient Times* (published in twenty-eight volumes from 1851 to 1879) argued that Russia, like the West, had gradually moved from an association of tribes to a modern state, based on common religious and political values and ruled by an enlightened government. Although he thought that Peter the Great (r. 1682–1725) had contributed much to this development, Soloviev saw Peter and other Europeanizers as organic products of a Russian past that from time immemorial had begun slowly converging with the West. Kavelin emphasized the slow development in Russia of abstract ideas (such as duty to the state, citizenship, and the rule of law) crucial to the appearance of a modern Europeanized polity. In his 1847 essay "An Analysis of Juridical Life in Ancient Russia," he pointed to the complete development of the free individual (*lichnost*) as the final goal of Russian history. Chicherin, younger by a generation than other moderates, used their insights into Russian history and law as the basis of a liberal political program. In his essay "Contemporary Tasks of Russian Life" (1855), he made the case for the abolition of serfdom, freedom of conscience and the press, and an independent court system. Annenkov and Turgenev wrote memoirs chronicling the Westernizer–Slavophile debate from perspectives agreeable to the Westernizers. Turgenev's early fiction, especially *A Sportsman's Sketches* (1852), contributed to the abolition of serfdom by showing Russian serfs as sympathetic human beings. Russian contemporaries and subsequent scholars (including Isaiah Berlin and Leonard Schapiro) regarded Turgenev as a Westernizer and moderate liberal.

Among the radical Westernizers the leader was Belinsky, who contended in the article "Russia before Peter the Great" (1842) that only Peter's forceful intervention in backward, semibarbarous Russia had made it possible for Russia to join the community of civilized nations. According to Belinsky, Peter was "a god who breathed a living soul into the colossal, sleeping body of ancient Russia." Belinsky's "Letter to Gogol" (1847) lamented Russian religious oppression and the existence of serfdom, and pointed to Russian writers' moral responsibility to expose injustice. Belinsky had no

patience with the Slavophiles' apologies for pre-Petrine Russia or for their religious "obscurantism." Bakunin's polemic against conservatism, "The Reaction in Germany" (1842), was a thinly veiled call for social revolution in the name of a "new religion of humanity." By the late 1840s both Bakunin and Herzen had come to believe that Russia might actually precede the West in inaugurating social justice, if only the peasant commune could be emancipated, peacefully or forcefully, from governmental interference. Herzen's "The Russian People and Socialism" (1851) made the case for the Russian commune as socialist ideal. Subsequently, Bakunin achieved fame as a revolutionary Pan-Slav and as the apostle of Russian anarchism in Europe. Herzen achieved renown as the "father of Russian socialism."

See also **Bakunin, Mikhail; Belinsky, Vissarion; Chaadayev, Peter; Herzen, Alexander; Intelligentsia; Russia; Slavophiles; Soloviev, Vladimir; Turgenev, Ivan.**

BIBLIOGRAPHY

Berlin, Isaiah. *Russian Thinkers.* New York, 1978.

Copleston, Frederick C. *Philosophy in Russia: From Herzen to Lenin and Berdyaev.* Tunbridge Wells, U.K., 1986.

Edie, James M., James P. Scanlan, and Mary-Barbara Zeldin, eds. *Russian Philosophy.* Vol. 1: *The Beginnings of Russian Philosophy: The Slavophiles; The Westernizers.* Chicago, 1965.

Hamburg, G. M. *Boris Chicherin and Early Russian Liberalism, 1828–1866.* Stanford, Calif., 1992.

Walicki, Andrzej. *A History of Russian Thought from the Enlightenment to Marxism.* Translated by Hilda Andrews-Rusiecka. Stanford, Calif., 1979.

G. M. HAMBURG

WHIGS. The Whigs were one of the two main opposing political parties in Great Britain in the eighteenth and early nineteenth centuries. The term originally referred to the opposition to James II in the decade before the Glorious Revolution of 1688. The Whigs led Parliament from 1715 to 1760 before losing the confidence of the Crown and electorate. In December 1783 King George III selected William Pitt the Younger to lead a new

Tory government. The Whigs would remain out of power until 1830, save for Charles James Fox's participation in 1806 in the "ministry of all the talents" under the conservative Lord Grenville.

PARTY IDENTITY

During the reign of George III (1760–1820) the Whigs constituted less of a party per se than a network of aristocratic families operating in Parliament through patronage and influence. Unity relied on personal loyalty, shared ideology, or the simple desire for power. Modern party alignments emerged after 1784, when new political crises, including the controversy over the American Revolution, roused public opinion. The most prominent Whig faction, headed by the second Marquis of Rockingham, advocated freedom for the American colonists and counted the Irish-born philosopher and parliamentarian Edmund Burke among its ranks.

The Whigs cherished fundamentally aristocratic attitudes and regarded themselves as the natural protectors of English liberties and civil institutions against the influences of the Crown. They looked upon society as a hierarchical set of interdependent relationships and looked down upon the authoritarian uses of state coercion. Their vision was of a consensual and cooperative civil society bound together by deferential citizens with reciprocal rights and responsibilities, led by a socially responsible and benevolent governing class. Government powers were to be bounded by law, custom, and humane principles. Whigs stood firmly against monopolies in commerce, religion, and politics.

THE POLITICS OF OPPOSITION

Fox led the Whig opposition for many of these years, representing the interests of religious dissenters, provincial industrialists, and a rising middle class. His support for the French Revolution of 1789 and his opposition to the war against France pushed some moderate Whigs to support Pitt and isolated Foxites from growing conservative sentiment. Between 1803 and 1806 the party rebuilt itself, as Fox and Lord Grenville drew in Whigs who had left over the French Revolution. A Foxite core, the more conservative Grenvillites, and Samuel Whitbread's radical "Mountain" (named in ironic reference to Maximilien Robespierre's allies in the National Convention) comprised the spectrum of Whig

opposition until the defeat of Napoleon in 1815. Though diverse in their principles, all factions supported Catholic emancipation and the general expansion of civil liberties.

Between 1808 and 1830 the Whigs established themselves as an effective opposition. Henry Brougham, a Scottish barrister and leading Whig parliamentarian, advanced his party's fortunes by extending party activity beyond Westminster to the nation as a whole, appealing to provincial merchants and manufacturers frustrated at their exclusion from influence. He opened up county and borough politics through contested parliamentary elections and played to public opinion and the press to keep Tory governments on the defensive.

The Whigs benefited from Tory Prime Minister Liverpool's stroke in 1827 and the government's split over Catholic Emancipation in 1829. In 1830 William IV (r. 1830–1837) turned to the Whigs under the leadership of Earl Grey to form a government. Grey and his successor, Lord Melbourne, pursued a general program of measured reform over the next decade.

POWER, REFORM, AND DISSOLUTION

The government's bold Reform Act of 1832 replaced notoriously "rotten" boroughs, which had few voters, with representatives for the previously unrepresented manufacturing districts and cities. It also increased the size of the electorate in England and Wales by over two hundred thousand persons, or almost 50 percent. The basis of voting, however, remained a property qualification. Some working-class voters lost the right to vote as a result of the abolition of old franchise rights.

The 1832 Reform Act initiated a political realignment that favored the Whigs and would fuel the emerging Liberal Party well into the 1880s. The Whig leadership had connected high politics with middle-class provincial interests and public opinion, forming the bedrock of Victorian liberalism.

Returned with a huge majority at the general election of December 1832, the Whigs carried out a number of other important reforms. A statute in 1833 ended slavery in the British colonies, while another charter reduced the East India Company from a monopolistic trading power to a purely administrative organ.

In 1834 the new Poor Law was passed. The law grouped parishes into unions and placed them under the control of elected boards of guardians, with a national Poor Law Board in London. Its basic principle—that outdoor poor relief should cease and that conditions in workhouses should be "less eligible" than the worst conditions in the labor market outside—was bitterly resented by workers and many writers throughout the country and led to outbreaks of violence. As the Whigs provoked working-class hostility, they saw the spread of Chartist campaigns, which attacked the Reform Act as a sellout to the upper classes and opposed the new Poor Law.

Lord Grey's successor, Lord Melbourne, successfully passed the Municipal Corporations Act of 1835, which replaced old oligarchies in local government with elected councils. Many unincorporated industrial communities received their first governmental powers. Melbourne failed, however, to find effective answers to the pressing financial, economic, and social questions of the day. These questions grew after 1836, when a financial crisis unleashed an economic depression accompanied by a series of bad harvests.

Once the Whigs began to live with the reforms they had enacted in the early 1830s, they lost their radical vitality and fell into decline. By 1840, they had alienated many of the groups that had originally cooperated with their reforming legislation, such as the Dissenters, Evangelicals, and Benthamites. The Whigs also lost radical members disillusioned with the limited nature of factory reform and the failure to end squalor in the towns, and they acquired a reputation for the occasional endorsement of repressive measures, as in the case of the Tolpuddle Martyrs of 1834.

The Tories under Robert Peel won the 1841 election. During the 1840s the Whig label lost its political meaning as reformers gathered under the Liberal banner.

See also **Fox, Charles James; Liberalism; Poor Law; Tories.**

BIBLIOGRAPHY

Hay, William Anthony. *The Whig Revival, 1808–1830.* New York, 2005.

Jenkins, T. A. *Gladstone, Whiggery, and the Liberal Party, 1874–1886.* Oxford, U.K., 1988.

Mitchell, Leslie. *The Whig World.* London, 2005.

Parry, Jonathan. *The Rise and Fall of Liberal Government in Victorian Britain.* New Haven, Conn., 1993.

Smith, E. A. *Whig Principles and Party Politics: Earl Fitzwilliam and the Whig Party, 1748–1833.* Manchester, U.K., 1975.

Wasson, Ellis Archer. *Whig Renaissance: Lord Althorp and the Whig Party, 1782–1845.* New York, 1987.

STEPHEN VELLA

WHITE TERROR. *See* Counterrevolution.

WILBERFORCE, WILLIAM (1759–1833), British statesman, philanthropist, and religious leader.

William Wilberforce led the campaign in the British Parliament against slavery and was an influential philanthropist and religious leader. He was born in Hull, Yorkshire, the son and grandson of merchants who had grown rich through the town's trade with the Baltic. Wilberforce was educated at Hull Grammar School, Pocklington School, and St John's College, Cambridge. Due to the early deaths of his father and uncle, he inherited considerable wealth while still a teenager. In 1797 he married Barbara Spooner and had two daughters and four sons, including Samuel Wilberforce (1805–1873), later Bishop of Oxford.

In 1780 Wilberforce became member of Parliament (MP) for Hull, and in 1784 was elected for Yorkshire, the largest constituency in England, which gave him an important political power base. He was also very well connected at Westminster, being a close friend of the prime minister, William Pitt the Younger (1759–1806), and of other leading figures. In 1785–1786, Wilberforce experienced a period of spiritual crisis, which resulted in his conversion to evangelical Christianity and his subsequent conviction that "God Almighty has set before me two great objects, the suppression of the slave trade and the reformation of manners" (Wilberforce and Wilberforce, vol. 1, p. 149). Wilberforce commenced his parliamentary campaign against the slave trade in May 1789. In January 1790 he secured a Select Committee to examine the evidence, and in April 1791 moved for leave to bring in an abolition bill. Insecurity arising from the context of the French Revolution made Parliament fear such a measure could have subversive consequences, and Wilberforce was initially decisively defeated. An extensive campaign of popular agitation and petitioning ensued, causing the House of Commons to vote in 1792 for gradual abolition, but this measure was blocked by the House of Lords. Wilberforce's efforts had to be maintained for a further sixteen years, until eventual victory was secured in 1807.

Meanwhile, Wilberforce was also pursuing his agenda for moral and spiritual reform. In 1787 he had helped to secure a Proclamation for the Encouragement of Piety and Virtue and worked hard to disseminate and implement it. In 1797 he published *A Practical View of the Prevailing Religious System of Professed Christians in the Higher and Middle Classes of this Country Contrasted with Real Christianity*. This was a critique of nominal Christianity and a call to widespread conversion to evangelicalism, as a means of both personal and national salvation. The book was widely read and very influential in contributing to an ongoing process of religious revival. During the 1790s and 1800s, Wilberforce was a central figure in the so-called Clapham Sect of wealthy lay evangelicals that supported parliamentary campaigns on the slave trade and other matters and was instrumental in the formation of numerous religious societies.

After the abolition of the slave trade in 1807, Wilberforce continued to have a prominent independent role in Parliament, particularly as a kind of national moral arbiter. In 1813 he played a significant part in securing the admission of missionaries to India, and from 1814 campaigned for the abolition of the slave trade by other nations. He enjoyed only limited immediate success, but ensured that the matter would remain firmly on the diplomatic agenda.

In 1823 a parliamentary campaign for the abolition of slavery itself was initiated. Wilberforce gave it strong moral support, but he was aging fast and unable to take a significant active part. He retired from Parliament in 1825 and died in 1833, just three days after hearing that the abolition bill had passed its third and final reading in the House of Commons.

Wilberforce's career has given rise to controversy on two specific issues. First, there is debate regarding the real importance of his personal role in the campaign against the slave trade. It is generally agreed, however, that he provided crucial parliamentary leadership, although the wider extraparliamentary campaign was primarily the work of others. Second, there is an acknowledged tension between his advocacy of the abolition of slavery and other reforming causes, and his willingness to countenance repression of political radicalism, both in the 1790s and in the disturbed years following the restoration of peace in 1815. It was also alleged that his preoccupation with slaves in the West Indies blinded him to the sufferings of the poor at home.

Nevertheless, Wilberforce's achievements were undeniably substantial. In addition to specific legislation, he was important in demonstrating how an independent political campaign pursued with great consistency and integrity could eventually bring striking results, and in providing a moral and spiritual example that stimulated significant changes in cultural attitudes.

See also **Great Britain; Slavery.**

BIBLIOGRAPHY

Primary Sources

Wilberforce, Robert Isaac, and Samuel Wilberforce. *The Life of William Wilberforce.* 5 vols. London, 1838. A detailed account by two of Wilberforce's sons, containing much rich material, but stronger on religious than political aspects.

Secondary Sources

Oldfield, J. R. *Popular Politics and British Anti-Slavery: The Mobilisation of Public Opinion against the Slave Trade 1787–1807.* London, 1998.

Pollock, John. *Wilberforce.* London, 1977. A scholarly biography.

JOHN WOLFFE

WILDE, OSCAR (1854–1900), Irish playwright.

Oscar Fingal O'Flahertie Wills Wilde was, as he said of himself, a "man who stood in symbolic relation to his times" (*De Profundis*). He was born on 16 October 1854, at 21 Westland Row in Dublin. His father, Sir William Wilde, a leading ear and eye surgeon, devoted himself to caring for the city's poor. His charitable dispensary later developed into the Dublin Eye and Ear Hospital. He also was the author of several noteworthy books on archaeology and Irish folklore.

Wilde's mother, Jane, was also a writer, as well as an activist for Irish nationalism, an early suffragist, and a socialist. Under the pen name Francesca Esperanza Wilde, she drew note in Dublin's political circles by publishing a series of defenses of Irish nationalism. After the family moved to more fashionable quarters on Merrion Square in June of 1855, Lady Wilde convened a regular Saturday afternoon salon with guests such as the writer Sheridan le Fanu, Samuel Lever, the lawyer and nationalist leader Isaac Butt, and the antiquarian and poet Samuel Ferguson.

EDUCATION AND CAREER

This circle was Wilde's milieu until the age of nine, when he was enrolled at Portora Royal School in Enniskillen, Fermanaugh. He graduated in 1871, gained entrance to Trinity College, Dublin, and studied classics there from 1871 to 1874. He won the Berkeley Medal, the highest honor in classics granted at Trinity, which helped him gain a scholarship to Magdalen College, Oxford. At the age of twenty Wilde moved from Ireland to England and continued to excel in his studies. He graduated from Oxford in 1878 with a double first, and won the 1878 Oxford Newdigate prize for his poems *Ravenna*.

Wilde returned to Dublin after Oxford and fell in love with Florence Balcome. She, however, spurned Wilde and became engaged to Bram Stoker. Wilde announced his intention to leave Ireland permanently because of the romantic misfortune. He took up quarters in London in 1878, and spent the next six years living off a lucrative lecturing career that took him to France and on a Continental tour of the United States.

Wilde's celebrity as a lecturer derived from his involvement at Oxford in the aesthetics movement, a new cult of decorative arts and aesthetic theory originated by William Morris (1834–1896) and his circle. Wilde captivated the media, who made him spokesperson for the movement. By 1881 the cult of the "Aesthetes" was important enough that Gilbert and Sullivan lampooned it in the popular operetta, *Patience*, which popularized Wilde as an effete poet who "strolled down Picadilly with a medieval lily in his hand." The show was a hit, and Wilde was a celebrity, though none of his major writings had yet appeared.

The success of the operetta's premiere in New York prompted its producer, Richard D'Oyly Carte (1844–1901), to arrange Wilde's 1882 American lecture tour. Newspapers in the larger cities attacked Wilde, describing at length his pasty white skin, and his odd, lyrical intonation. The mining towns of the West, ironically, applauded Wilde; one of the most favorable press notices about him appeared in the Leadville, Colorado, *Gazette* in 1881.

Wilde returned to Dublin only twice during this period of lecturing. On one of those visits in 1884 he met Constance Lloyd, the daughter of a wealthy London family, and proposed almost instantaneously. They wed on 29 May 1884. Lloyd's allowance of 250 pounds yearly was a considerable asset, and the couple cultivated a life of luxury at 16 Tite Street in London. In the next two years they had two sons, Cyril (1885) and Vyvyan (1886).

Wilde commenced a series of journalistic appointments. He reviewed for the *Pall Mall Gazette* from 1887 to 1889, and then became editor of *Woman's World*, which he fashioned into a laboratory for exploring the decorative arts and a mouthpiece for socialist reformation. The period immediately after taking the editorship was one of extreme creative productivity for Wilde. In 1891 his most important prose writings appeared in the collection *Intentions*, which included "The Decay of Lying" and "The Critic as Artist," and his only novel, *The Picture of Dorian Gray*, was serialized in *Lipincott's Magazine*. Mainstream reviewers praised Wilde's prose but condemned his morality. Max Nordau, whose influential book *Degeneration* (1895) attacked aestheticism, used the novel as an

Oscar Wilde. ©Bettmann/Corbis

wright George Bernard Shaw (1856–1950) to call him "our only serious playwright." Wilde's next—and last—play, *The Importance of Being Earnest,* opened at the Haymarket only a month after *An Ideal Husband,* putting Wilde in the enviable position of having two simultaneous West End hits.

TRIALS

The notes for works left by Wilde suggest he intended to have a long career as a playwright. However, 1891 also saw the beginning of Wilde's intimacies with Lord Alfred Bruce Douglas (1870–1945), the son of John Sholto Douglas, 8th Marquess of Queensberry. Douglas, a devotee of the cult of aestheticism, became Wilde's constant companion in the London social world.

Douglas had not yet come of age and had no allowance, and Wilde's flagrant displays of spending and support, as well as the attention paid by the public to the men's extravagance, snubbed the father's position as financial authority. To retaliate, the marquess made a plan to interrupt the opening night of *The Importance of Being Earnest* with an insulting delivery of vegetables made to the playwright while his play was in progress. Warned of the plot, Wilde had the marquess barred from the theater. The next day, 18 February 1895, the marquess left a calling card for Wilde at the Albemarle club. On the back he had written, "For Oscar Wilde posing as a Somdomite [*sic*]."

Goaded by Douglas, Wilde pressed charges of criminal libel against the marquess. The ensuing events ended any hopes Wilde had of sustaining his career and left him financially and emotionally destitute. In April the crown took over prosecution, and the solicitor Edward Clarke based his case against the marquess almost entirely on Wilde's own assertions that the accusation of being a sodomite had no basis. To challenge that claim, Edward Henry Carson, barrister for the defense, located several lower-class boys who claimed to have had intimacies with Wilde. The revelation laid waste to the prosecution, humiliated Wilde, and prompted the dismissal of the case.

Carson's witnesses, however, provided the ground for the crown to arrest Wilde on 6 April 1895, on charges of "committing acts of gross indecency with other male persons: under section 11 of the 1885 Criminal Law Amendment Act." Wilde,

example of how degenerate artists hasten the "moral laxity and decay" of a nation.

In 1891 Wilde also wrote *Lady Windermere's Fan,* the first of four stage hits that elevated Wilde into a West End legend. It opened as an immediate hit at St. James' Theatre in London in February 1882, and earned Wilde an astonishing seven thousand pounds. He followed it with *A Woman of No Importance* at the Haymarket Theatre in London on 19 April 1893, which was hailed as the best "comedy of manners" since Richard Brinsley Sheridan (1751–1816). In his third West End hit, *An Ideal Husband,* Wilde crafted his epigrams and wit around a political melodrama, prompting the socialist play-along with Alfred Taylor, who had allegedly solicited the services of young men for Wilde, faced twenty-five counts. The jury deadlocked on all charges except one, of which they acquitted Wilde.

Despite entreaties from luminaries such as Bernard Shaw and even from the marquess's own attorney, Edward Carson, the crown stood adamant in its desire to secure a conviction, and pursued a second trial under the prosecution of the solicitor-general himself, Frank Lockwood. The crown's motives are a matter for speculation. Ambiguous letters between Queensberry and Prime Minister Rosebery (Archibald Philip Primrose), who was widely suspected of having had a homosexual affair earlier in his career with another of Queensberry's sons, suggest that Rosebery might have been blackmailed into pursuing prosecution. More generally, the British government had become uncomfortably associated with prurience by several well-publicized scandals that called into question the moral ethics of certain government officials. The prosecution of Wilde might have seemed a way to redeem the government against its own transgressions.

Wilde himself, however, was the leading contributing factor. In 1892 the lord chamberlain refused to license the performance of Wilde's newest play, *Salome,* because it contained biblical characters. Wilde reacted publicly and his anger resounded across London society. In 1893 he published the play in a French edition, as if to snub the parochial taboos of the English system, and in 1894 he published an English fine art edition with pornographic illustrations by Aubrey Beardsley (1872–1898). Such actions showed little respect for authority. Also, Wilde's Irish origins and his flaunting of new, commercially derived money caused further contempt. In many ways, this was a prosecution about nationality and class as much as it was about sexual behavior.

The third trial resulted in the verdict of guilty on all charges save one, and Wilde served two years at hard labor in prison, the last eighteen months of it at Reading Gaol. He was released on 19 May 1897. Penniless and abandoned by his wife and sons (as well as by Douglas), he adopted the name Sebastian Melmoth, after the title character of *Melmoth the Wanderer,* and lived in self-imposed exile from society and the aesthetic movement.

Only two pieces of any significance issued from Wilde after release. *The Ballad of Reading Gaol* (1898), a poem seeking to elicit compassion for prisoners, and *De Profundis* (1905), a long letter written to Douglas from prison that provides Wilde's most personal statement of his philosophies of art, life, and himself.

Wilde died of cerebral meningitis on 30 November 1900, only three years after his release. He was buried in the Cimitière de Bagneux on the outskirts of Paris, but was later relocated by generous friends to the more prestigious Père Lachaise Cemetery, where his grave is marked by a commissioned monument from sculptor Sir Jacob Epstein (1880–1959).

See also **Avant-Garde; Carpenter, Edward; Homosexuality and Lesbianism; Morris, William; Symonds, John Addington.**

BIBLIOGRAPHY

Cohen, Ed. *Talk on the Wilde Side: Toward a Genealogy of Discourse on Male Sexualities.* New York, 1993.

Cohen, Philip K. *The Moral Vision of Oscar Wilde.* Rutherford, N.J., 1978.

Ellmann, Richard. *Oscar Wilde.* New York: Viking, 1987.

Ellmann, Richard, ed. *Oscar Wilde: A Collection of Critical Essays.* Englewood Cliffs, N.J., 1969.

Foldy, Michael S. *The Trials of Oscar Wilde: Deviance, Morality, and Late-Victorian Society.* New Haven, Conn., 1997.

Gagnier, Regenia A. *Idylls of the Marketplace: Oscar Wilde and the Victorian Public.* Stanford, Calif., 1986.

Hyde, H. Montgomery. *Oscar Wilde: A Biography.* London, 1975.

Nassaar, Christopher S. *Into the Demon Universe: A Literary Exploration of Oscar Wilde.* New Haven, Conn., 1974.

Nunokawa, Jeff. *Oscar Wilde.* New York, 1995.

Shewan, Rodney. *Oscar Wilde: Art and Egotism.* London, 1977.

Sinfield, Alan. *The Wilde Century: Effeminacy, Oscar Wilde, and the Queer Movement.* London, 1994.

Summers, Claude J. *Gay Fictions: Wilde to Stonewall: Studies in a Male Homosexual Literary Tradition.* New York, 1990.

Woodcock, George. *The Paradox of Oscar Wilde.* New York, 1950.

GREGORY BREDBECK

WILLIAM I

WILLIAM I (in German, Wilhelm I; 1797–1888), emperor of Germany (1871–1888) and king of Prussia (1861–1888).

William I was the second son of the future King Frederick William III of Prussia and Louise of Mecklenburg. As the younger brother of the heir, William was expected to make a career in the military, and this was a role that he relished. He served in the wars against Napoleon I and was devoted to the army.

In 1829 William married Princess Augusta of Saxe-Weimar-Eisenach. The union produced two children: Frederick, who later reigned as Frederick III, and Louise, who married the grand duke of Baden. William's marriage was one of convenience; he had abandoned his love affair with a Polish countess, Elise Radziwill, who was not deemed to be a suitable consort for a Prussian prince. William and his wife were ill-suited temperamentally and politically; he particularly had no use for his wife's more liberal political views.

William's conservatism and advocacy of the use of force against the forces of change earned him the enmity of revolutionaries during the revolutions of 1848, and he was forced to flee to England incognito. When the tide of the revolution turned, William returned to Prussia and commanded the troops that put down a republican insurrection in Baden.

As the result of the revolution, Prussia became a constitutional monarchy. Although William was no advocate of constitutionalism, he believed that the monarch had the obligation to uphold the constitution. His beliefs on this score were tested in 1858 when he became regent of Prussia after his brother, King Frederick William IV, was declared unfit to rule. As regent, William gave hope for progressive change when he appointed moderate liberals to his cabinet. But after he became king in 1861, he introduced military reform bills that ran afoul of liberals in parliament who believed that it would create an army that would be used to suppress reforms. Liberals in the Prussian parliament repeatedly rejected his army reform bills, as government operations ground to a halt. For weeks, relations between crown and parliament stood at an impasse, and William threatened to abdicate. Liberals advocated the accession of William's son Frederick, who was more liberal than his father, whereas conservatives flocked to William's nephew Frederick Charles, who threatened to do away with the constitution altogether.

In September 1862, at the height of the crisis, William accepted his advisors' suggestion to appoint Otto von Bismarck as prime minister. Bismarck found a convenient loophole in the constitution that allowed him to push through the king's military reforms. Bismarck then proceeded to assuage liberals' anger over his manipulation of the constitution by achieving their long-held desire for a united Germany under Prussia, which became a reality after Prussia's victories over Austria in 1866 and France in 1871. William I commanded troops during the Franco-Prussian War of 1870–1871, received the surrender of Napoleon III at Sedan, France, and was proclaimed German emperor in the Hall of Mirrors at Versailles.

William reigned as emperor for the next seventeen years, despite advanced age and two attempts on his life. Although Bismarck told his biographers he was a mere servant of his emperor, historians usually refer to the period of William's rule as the Age of Bismarck, because the chancellor dominated both domestic and foreign policy. Yet William was no mere cipher of his chancellor; he often disagreed with his policies. William did not favor Bismarck's struggle against the Roman Catholic Church during the 1870s, and gave it only his tacit consent. In the end, William was a modest, hard-working, and conscientious ruler. His letters and memoranda show that he carefully thought through issues affecting his realm. Though his militarism and conservative views often put him at odds with radical elements in the German Empire, he was a popular monarch.

As William lay dying at the age of ninety-one, his wife permitted a cameo of Elise Radziwill to be placed in his hand. After clutching it briefly, the old emperor passed away. He was succeeded by his son Frederick, who was ill with cancer and reigned for only three months. Frederick in turn was succeeded by his son, who became Emperor William II. Although the young emperor worshiped his late grandfather, it was Germany's misfortune that he lacked the elder man's conscientiousness and sense of restraint.

See also Austro-Prussian War; Bismarck, Otto von; Danish-German War; Franco-Prussian War; Frederick William IV; Germany; Prussia; Revolutions of 1848.

BIBLIOGRAPHY

Aronson, Theo. *The Kaisers.* London, 1971.

Börner, Karl Heinz. *Kaiser Wilhelm I, 1797 bis 1888: Deutscher Kaiser und König von Preussen.* Cologne, Germany, 1984.

Marcks, Erich. *Kaiser Wilhelm I.* Leipzig, Germany, 1897.

Schultze, Johannes, ed. *Kaiser Wilhelms I: Weimarer Briefe.* Berlin, 1924.

PATRICIA KOLLANDER

WILLIAM II (in German, Wilhelm II, 1859–1941, ruled 1888–1918), German kaiser and king of Prussia.

William II, the last king of Prussia and German emperor, possessed a royal lineage that might well have been the envy of many another European sovereign. He was the eldest grandson of both the first German emperor, William I (r. 1871–1888), and Queen Victoria (r. 1837–1901), and was a descendant of Russian tsars as well. From the moment of his birth in 1859 he was destined for a great future but also beset by handicap, for as a result of his protracted delivery his left arm was paralyzed for life. Although the child learned to accept this misfortune and became remarkably adept at sports, his mother, Victoria, was mortified that her son was less than physically perfect. She made her disappointment evident, and thus began the pronounced estrangement between mother and son that endured until her death when William was forty-two.

William's education from the time that he was seven until he reached eighteen and was ready for a university was in the hands of the stern, unappeasable and relentless Georg Hinzpeter. No wonder that in 1877, when William finally escaped his grasp, he found great pleasure in his new life at the University of Bonn, where, however, he was an indifferent student. After two years he had had enough and took up a military career that was infinitely more to his liking. In the army, he would declare, he found not only his true vocation but also the warm family atmosphere that his mother had deliberately withheld. William's fellow officers greeted him cordially, but very few could detect any real military talent in their future ruler. Government officials, who periodically attempted to introduce William to diplomatic or domestic affairs, similarly found him unimpressive.

By the time William was in his mid-twenties he was an object of some concern. Willful, conceited, lazy, and unjustifiably self-impressed, he was to his father, the genuinely heroic Crown Prince, a bogus "compleat lieutenant" and to Otto von Bismarck (1815–1898), the imperial chancellor, a loquacious nullity. The thought of such a stripling on the throne was disquieting, but William II would follow old William I, born in 1797, and the Crown Prince, born in 1831. Young William's succession, it seemed, would be postponed for at least a decade or two, during which time he might somehow manage to become more mature. That optimistic hope fell to pieces in the fall of 1887, when the Crown Prince was diagnosed as suffering from a fatal carcinoma of the larynx. Whether he would live to succeed his ninety-year-old father seemed in doubt. William I died in March 1888, and ninety-nine days later the Crown Prince, who had succeeded him as Emperor Frederick III, expired from his malady. William II, at twenty-nine, was now the German kaiser and king of Prussia.

As ruler, the new kaiser was persuaded that he was endowed by God Almighty with powers and responsibilities and that his authority, thoroughly upheld by both the Prussian and imperial constitutions, was to be personally exercised however he wished. William was avidly supported in this estimation by his entourage, men frequently military by profession, almost entirely sycophantic in behavior, and whose principal qualification for appointment to the entourage was their unquestioning allegiance to the young ruler. This inflation of William II's ego was also served by his wife, the Empress Augusta Victoria (1858–1921), a lackluster, prosaic woman who lived entirely in her consort's shadow. The first casualty of William's personalized monarchy was Bismarck, a man of titanic self-assurance and Caesarian mien, who was sent packing early in 1890. The new chancellor, General Leo von Caprivi (1831–1899), found that the emperor and his entourage could not effectively be resisted, an experi-

The Car of the German Empire Driven by Wilhelm II.
Cover illustration by Thomas Heine for the German satirical journal *Simplicissimus*, 1907. PRIVATE COLLECTION/BRIDGEMAN ART LIBRARY. © 2005 ARTISTS RIGHTS SOCIETY (ARS), NEW YORK/ VG BILD-KUNST, BONN.

ence that his successor in 1894, Prince Chlodwig von Hohenlohe-Schillingsfürst (1819–1901), also found to be true. Hohenlohe would last until 1900, when he yielded to Bernhard von Bülow (1849–1929), who was known as "the eel" for his oleaginous manner and suave handling of his imperial master. Although insistent on making full use of his prerogative, William was so inconstant and dilatory, so prone to sudden changes of opinion and to new enthusiasms, he in fact was not the supreme autocrat he believed himself to be. The so-called *persönliches Regiment* (personal regime) was actually exercised by his aristocratic minions in the military and civil bureaucracy.

The work that William's dutiful servants had to perform was complicated because of the kaiser's incessant, bombastic intrusions. The last kaiser believed himself to be a genius, especially at warfare and diplomacy, two areas he preferred to domestic affairs. Resolutely moral, anti-Catholic, and Francophobe, he wrote France off as racially inferior and eternally inimical to the German Empire.

Toward Great Britain, the land of his disliked mother's birth, William was ambivalent. He envied its wealth but loathed what he considered its moral laxity and lust for power. The Slavs, like the French, were a lesser breed, but the Russian tsars, being like himself—autocrats of limitless power—could be useful allies. Since the Italians were beneath notice as Latins and degenerates and the minuscule kings from the house of Savoy little more than hairy dwarfs, only Austria-Hungary was a truly suitable ally for imperial Germany. William greatly admired Emperor Francis Joseph I (r. 1848–1916), and one of the very few consistent strands in his life was his devotion to the Habsburg sovereign. In diplomacy, William fostered the alliance of 1879 with Austria-Hungary, hoped in vain to rope Russia in as an ally, and alienated the British by his offensive behavior and by the construction beginning in 1898 of a vast battleship-based navy. By 1914, Germany had no allies other than Austria-Hungary, and that was perhaps more a liability than an asset.

Within Germany, William aspired to make himself popular, and to achieve this aim he began his reign trying to pose as the friend of the working class. This did not capture the multitudes and William eventually grew resentful of the ever increasing rise of the doctrinarily Marxist Social Democratic party, which following the elections of 1912 became the largest faction in the imperial legislature. Meanwhile, William had alienated the second most numerous party, the Catholic Center, by his resolute prejudice against Catholicism, nor did he have many admirers among the middle parties representing the interests of business and commerce. As a result, William's governments staggered through a series of parliamentary crises and the regime was increasingly discredited. William's own stature sank in popularity as a result of these difficulties and also because of a variety of scandals, some of them surrounding accusations of homosexuality involving a number of his closest associates in the entourage. The reign of the last kaiser was not only full of unresolved crises, it was also messy and unedifying.

Finally, William's regime was dreary. The kaiser's court, though splendid and run like clockwork, was a bore. The throne was adamantly opposed to any innovations in the arts and patronized only those who praised the sovereign and delivered traditional works of second- or third-rate quality. There was no place in William's artistic galaxy for Richard Georg Strauss (1864–1949) or Max Liebermann (1847–1935) or Gerhart Hauptmann (1862–1946).

Germany's antediluvian political system was paradoxically coexistent with one of the most remarkable economic upsurges any nation in Europe enjoyed in the nineteenth and early twentieth centuries. Industry prospered and commerce spread around the world. William II is not entitled to any credit on this score, for he was snobbish toward the middle class although he envied their wealth. An occasional entrepreneur, notably the Krupps of Essen or Albert Ballin (1857–1918), the Hamburg shipping magnate, might fraternize with the kaiser, but none was ever part of the inner circle, and William remained as ignorant of economics as he was of almost everything else.

In 1913, William celebrated the twenty-fifth anniversary of his ascension to the Prussian and imperial throne. The occasion was appropriately pompous but also rather contrived, for the sovereign being honored was neither popular nor notably respected. Throughout his reign there were suspicions that he was mentally unbalanced, and many who knew him well believed this to be the case, citing as evidence William's irrepressible loquacity, incessant traveling, astounding tactlessness, and nervous prostration at moments of crisis. William in fact may have been the victim of porphyria, a genetic disorder that has mental as well as physical symptoms. The kaiser's Germany was rich, it was powerfully armed, but it had few friends, a number of notable enemies, and a marked lack of internal political stability. Just a year after the observance of the anniversary, Germany found itself at war, blockaded at sea and outnumbered on land. The fate of Germany, in that ominous moment in its history, rested on a man utterly unequal to the challenge, an emperor who, for all his splendor, was a vacuous, blundering epigone who reduced his splendid inheritance to inglorious ruin.

See also **Bismarck, Otto von; Frederick III; Germany; Nicholas II; William I.**

BIBLIOGRAPHY

Primary Sources

Röhl, John C. G., ed. *Philipp Eulenburgs Politische Korrespondenz.* 3 vols. Boppard am Rhein, 1976–1983.

Secondary Sources

Cecil, Lamar. *Wilhelm II: Prince and Emperor, 1859–1900.* Chapel Hill, N.C., 1989.

———. *Wilhelm II: Emperor and Exile, 1900–1941.* Chapel Hill, N.C., 1996.

Hull, Isabel V. *The Entourage of Kaiser Wilhelm II, 1888–1918.* Cambridge, U.K., 1982.

Röhl, John C. G. *Young Wilhelm: The Kaiser's Early Life, 1859–1888.* Translated by Jeremy Gaines and Rebecca Wallach. Cambridge, U.K., 1998.

———. *The Kaiser's Personal Monarchy, 1888–1900.* Cambridge, U.K., 2004.

Röhl, John C. G., and Nicolaus Sombart, eds. *Kaiser Wilhelm II. New Interpretations: The Corfu Papers.* Cambridge, U.K., 1982.

LAMAR CECIL

WILLIAM IV (1765–1837), king of Great Britain and Ireland (1830–1837) and king of Hanover (1830–1837).

William Henry was the third son of George III and Charlotte of Mecklenburg-Strelitz. In 1779 he was sent to sea as a midshipman in the hope that the Royal Navy would instill disciplined habits and offer him a career of public service. He saw action against the Spaniards off Cape St. Vincent, and subsequently his competence as a naval officer won the approval of his superiors who included Horatio Nelson. From 1783 to 1785 he resided in Hanover. In 1789 he became duke of Clarence and St. Andrews and earl of Munster. He played no part in the French Wars that commenced in 1793, and his promotion to admiral in 1798 was a formality. He resumed an active connection with the Navy in 1827 when he was appointed lord high admiral, but he clashed with members of his advisory council and resigned.

From 1791 William cohabited with Dorothy Jordan, an actress. A caring father, he fostered the marital and career prospects of their ten children (surnamed FitzClarence). William terminated his relationship with Jordan in 1811, and in 1818 he married Adelaide of Saxe-Meiningen. Although their children died in early infancy, the marriage was a happy one. William had no cultural or intellectual interests. His undignified appearance and eccentric mannerisms, together with behavior and language that smacked of the quarterdeck, attracted ridicule in polite society, but his bluff geniality contributed to the popularity he enjoyed at various times during his reign.

William became king in 1830 on the death of his brother, George IV. He played a major part in two episodes that altered the British constitution. The first of these was the struggle for the Reform Act by which Earl Grey's Whig government enlarged the parliamentary electorate in 1832 and removed some anomalies from the representative system. Wishing to restrict the extent of the change and abate controversy, William would have preferred to see the legislation carried by a coalition of Whigs and Tories or by a Tory government, but at two crucial junctures he supported his Whig ministers in the face of strenuous Tory opposition. He deferred to their insistence on a general election in 1831 at which they won a majority in the House of Commons, and, when the Tories blocked the legislation in the House of Lords, he agreed to create enough Whig peers to pass the Reform Act if the Tory lords persisted in their opposition. The threat was enough to carry the day, setting a precedent for the subordination of the House of Lords to the wishes of the House of Commons. William's popularity during the controversy was indicated by an illustration in *The Extraordinary Black Book*, a radical tract that contained an illustration showing a people's king surrounded by ministers who were "Friends of Reform, Foes of Revolution."

The second episode counteracted this favorable impression. Alarmed by the liberalism of his ministers and encouraged by Tory sympathizers, who included his wife and some of his children, William dismissed the Whigs in 1834 and installed a Tory government led by Sir Robert Peel. He was emboldened by a precedent from the years 1783 and 1784 when his father had ousted a Whig-dominated coalition and appointed a more congenial government that was confirmed in office by a general election. William miscalculated; at the ensuing general election, the voters rejected the Tories. William had to endure the humiliation of reinstating the Whigs, who not only pursued policies that were repugnant to him but also took the opportunity to restrict the hostile activities of his court circle. It was the last time that a British monarch dismissed a government with a House of Commons majority.

William's enthusiasm for reform was always limited. Before coming to the throne he had supported Catholic emancipation but defended the institution of slavery. During the crisis that attended the passing of the Reform Act he was reluctant to depart from the eighteenth-century constitutional theory that envisaged a balance of power between the monarchy, the House of Lords, and the House of Commons. After 1832 he attempted to protect the privileges of the Protestant church establishment in Ireland, and he regarded the activities of the Irish nationalist leader Daniel O'Connell as little better than treasonous. William also disagreed with his ministers' policy of supporting liberals in Portugal, Spain, and other parts of continental Europe.

The last years of his reign were uneventful. William died in 1837 and was buried in Windsor Castle. He was succeeded in the United Kingdom by his niece, Victoria, and in Hanover, where the Salic law of succession excluded women from the throne, by his brother, Ernest Augustus.

See also **George IV; Great Britain; Wellington, Duke of (Arthur Wellesley); Whigs.**

BIBLIOGRAPHY

Brock, Michael G. *The Great Reform Act*. London, 1973. The standard work on the 1832 Reform Act.

Newbould, Ian. *Whiggery and Reform, 1830–1841*. London, 1990. A modern study of the Whig reformers of the 1830s.

Ziegler, Philip. *King William IV*. London, 1971. A biography that draws on the royal archives and other major primary sources.

ALEX TYRRELL

WINDTHORST, LUDWIG (1812–1891), German politician.

Germany's greatest parliamentarian, Ludwig Josef Ferdinand Gustav Windthorst, served simultaneously in the Prussian and the German national parliament (Reichstag), where as leader of the Center Party he took the floor more than any other speaker. His wit, sang-froid, and tactical genius were the marvel of all. When political upheavals in 1878 made the Center and its associate members the Reichstag's largest grouping, a position it would keep until 1912, Windthorst held the parliamentary balance of power.

EARLY CAREER

Windthorst's politics were colored by an early Anglophilia (born in Hanover, he was a subject of the English crown until he was twenty-five) and a libertarianism nourished by his experience as member of a religious and political minority: as a Catholic in Protestant Hanover, and after its annexation in 1866, as a Hanoverian loyalist in a Germany first truncated and then dominated by Prussia. After education at the Universities of Göttingen (1830–1831) and Heidelberg (1832–1833), Windthorst quickly became the leading lawyer in his native Osnabrück, although he was functionally blind by his thirtieth year. Appointed to several prestigious offices, he was serving on the Hanoverian Supreme Court when in 1848 revolution opened the possibility of a political career. In 1849 he was elected to the diet's lower chamber, and in 1851, its president.

Windthorst was twice appointed Justice Minister (1851–1853 and 1862–1865), the only Catholic to hold cabinet rank in the history of the kingdom. In spite of Hanover's chronic constitutional crisis, he succeeded in putting the reforms of 1848 into effect: public judicial proceedings, jury trials, reorganization of the courts, separation of justice from administration. Although distrusted by George V (r. 1851–1866) as a "jesuit," Windthorst's support for the German Confederation and his opposition to Prussian-led nationalism made him well known in particularist and pro-Austrian circles throughout Germany. After Prussia's annexation of Hanover in 1866, he represented his deposed monarch in negotiations with Otto von Bismarck (r. 1871–1890) over Hanoverian royal property (*Welfenfonds*), beginning an adversarial relationship that would last a lifetime. Contrary to agreement, Bismarck impounded the *Welfenfonds* in 1868, feeding Windthorst's pessimism about the future of rule of law in a Prussian-dominated Germany.

Elected to the Prussian lower house as deputy for Meppen, Windthorst could find no party to his liking, yet isolation did not intimidate a man that wags soon dubbed "the Meppen Party." In the Reichstag of the North German Confederation, he attracted allies from other recently annexed or marginalized states, forming a short-lived Federal-Constitutional Union. Elections to the all-German Customs Parliament in 1867, by returning like-minded deputies from the predominantly Catholic south, opened his eyes to the advantages of a democratic franchise. Working behind the scenes to unite particularists of all stripes, Windthorst succeeded in thwarting German nationalist hopes of turning the Customs Parliament into a forum for coaxing the southern states voluntarily into Bismarck's Confederation, foreshadowing his later reputation as "father of all hindrances." Windthorst voted against the constitution of the North German Confederation and later, of the German Empire, for failing to provide a house of lords, a supreme court, a cabinet collectively responsible to the Reichstag, and safeguards for the rights of member states. Cool to nationalism himself, Windthorst offered irritating reminders of his countrymen's double standard in applying the nationality principle. Thus he protested against annexing Alsace-Lorraine without consulting its population, demanded parliamentary representation for its citizens, and excoriated the suspension of civil law under the guise of military emergency.

AFTER 1870

In the Reichstag, Windthorst brought together in the Center Party a diverse collection of outsiders in the new empire—Prussian and southern Catholics, Poles and Alsace-Lorrainers, and Lutheran legitimists from Hanover (the latter as affiliated members). Even as they instilled the concept of a loyal opposition among their constituents, they were branded as *Reichsfeinde* ("enemies of the Reich") by the Bismarckian press. Although his hopes that the Center might attract Protestants beyond Hanover were disappointed, Windthorst insisted that his party champion the same rights for Protestants and Jews that it demanded for Catholics. In November 1880 he repeatedly threatened to resign his seat if the Center supported the anti-Semitic side in a debate on the Jewish Question in the Prussian House of Deputies. In January 1886 he sponsored a successful Reichstag motion censuring the Prussian government for expelling, almost overnight, more than thirty thousand undocumented Poles and Jews in the East.

Windthorst's distrust of state power had intensified during the Kulturkampf ("battle for civilization," 1872–1887), when Bismarck, with broad support in parliament and the public, sponsored legislation to subordinate the Catholic Church to the state. Windthorst joined the bishops in calling for civil disobedience to laws that conflicted with conscience.

Windthorst amazed contemporaries by his skill not only in holding his extremely heterogeneous party together, but in shifting it rapidly right and left, as opportunities appeared. In 1873, hoping to split the National Liberals or at least to force them to choose between angering Bismarck or their own voters, he persuaded his instinctively conservative colleagues to sponsor a series of democratic motions: to replace the plutocratic franchise and open voting in Prussian state elections with the Reichstag's manhood suffrage and secret ballot; to end the newspaper tax and other press restrictions; and to institute salaries for Reichstag deputies. Liberal leaders, warning that association with Windthorst was a political "kiss of death," succeeded in tabling the motions. Although the defense of the Reichstag's rights and its democratic franchise became central to the Center Party's program, Windthorst's residual monarchism, and fears of the tyranny of the majority, kept him from advocating parliamentary sovereignty.

Not alarmed by the rise of Social Democracy, Windthorst worked to integrate socialism's adherents into parliamentary life, supporting motions to release socialist deputies from prison and, when they were too few to sponsor motions of their own, lending them Center signatures to enable their motions to come to the floor. Opposing all laws designed against specific groups ("exceptional legislation") as contrary to the principle of equality before the law, Windthorst led his party to reject Bismarck's Anti-Socialist Law in 1878 and, with some defections, its biannual renewals thereafter.

Votes such as these incurred the displeasure of Pope Leo XIII (r. 1878–1903), as did Windthorst's electoral alliances with Left Liberals in the 1880s. Already suspect for having voiced opposition in 1869, both privately and with other Catholic deputies in a hastily assembled "Berlin Laymen's Council," to the prospective declaration of papal infallibility, Windthorst was increasingly seen by the pontiff as an obstacle to his own plans to negotiate a solution to the Kulturkampf. Aiming also to enlist Bismarck's help in recovering Rome for the Holy See (a cause Windthorst considered not only lost, but no longer even desirable), Leo kept Windthorst ignorant of the course of negotiations and stymied Center Party initiatives in parliament, hoping to offer the chancellor the party's votes on political matters as an inducement for ecclesiastical concessions. Windthorst declined to oblige, suggesting that separation of church and state on the North American model was preferable to compromising constitutional principles.

In 1887, when the Center, in accord with its platform's demand for parliamentary control of the purse, defeated Bismarck's seven-year military budget (*Septennat*), the chancellor dissolved the Reichstag and waged an uproarious election campaign against the Reichsfeinde. Leo gave Bismarck permission to leak a papal note that had instructed Windthorst to support the *Septennat* as quid pro quo for a prospective settlement of the Kulturkampf. The Bismarckian press, which had previously scoffed at the Center's professed independence of church authority on political questions, now expressed itself scandalized at Windthorst's "disobedience," gloating at the pope's apparent disavowal of the overwhelmingly Catholic party. The Center was returned unscathed, but Windthorst was forced to acquiesce in Leo's ecclesiastical "Peace Settlement" that same year, although it left many Catholic demands unsatisfied.

Windthorst shared little of the passion of Catholic thinkers for social reform, although he gave tepid support to the Center's sponsorship of factory legislation in 1877. His experience in Osnabrück, whose Protestant patriciate controlled access to guilds, made him sympathetic to free enterprise and free trade. He resisted Bismarck's plans for a tobacco monopoly and for the nationalization of railways, fearing abuses if vast numbers of workers became dependent on an employer-state. The Center supported compulsory health insurance for workers in 1883 and workman's compensation in 1884, financed by contributions from workers and employers, or, in the latter case, by employers alone. But in 1889, when substantial numbers of older and conservative colleagues broke ranks to support Bismarck's old age and disability insurance, partially funded by the state, Windthorst felt betrayed.

Yet he was rarely dogmatic on economic questions. The demands of its constituency led the Center to precede Bismarck in advocating tariffs in 1879 and to support increases in grain duties in 1885 and 1889. Even so, Windthorst succeeded in passing a provision to distribute much of the income generated by the tariff to Germany's member states, thus frustrating Bismarck's hopes for an imperial revenue-producing mechanism beyond the control of representative bodies.

After years of Bismarck's vilification ("Two things sustain my life and make it sweet: my wife and Windthorst. One is for love, the other for hate" [Tiedemann, vol. 2, p. 3]), it was to Windthorst that the chancellor turned in March 1890, when national elections deprived him of a reliable majority. Bismarck agreed to a number of ecclesiastical concessions, but his approach to Windthorst was itself a sign that the chancellor's power was waning. When word of the interview leaked out, the ensuing scandal gave William II (r. 1888–1918), furious at being left in the dark about so signal a change of course, the excuse he needed for Bismarck's dismissal.

Though Windthorst insisted that the Center was a political, not a religious party, the Catholic clergy provided its electoral machinery and Germany's bishops, a power base that he employed against both Leo XIII and the occasional obstreperous clerical colleague. His own influence within the church in Germany was unequaled, extending to episcopal appointments and other ostensibly ecclesiastical matters. Within the Center delegation, priests were his most reliable allies. Although by the 1880s some aristocratic rivals, dismayed by their party's continued oppositional course, chaffed under one-man rule, they commanded no comparable support. Windthorst discouraged the formation of other mass organizations of Catholics, whose moves outside parliament might limit his own tactical flexibility. When in summer of 1890 Catholic aristocrats met to establish an organization to respond in kind to the religious polemics of the recently founded Protestant League, Wind-

thorst reacted with horror. Marshalling allies in party, clergy, and press, he transformed the nascent Catholic League into the very different Volksverein für das Katholische Deutschland (People's Association for Catholic Germany), which combined the functions of adult education, information bureau, and training program for the Center's party workers. With 805,000 members by 1914, it became one of the largest voluntary organizations in Germany.

More than any figure of his generation, Windthorst embodied the transition from notable to mass politics. Even in old age, he was a tireless presence at rallies throughout the country, drawing crowds of thousands, who burst into song ("The Little Excellency," composed in his honor) at his entrance. He turned disadvantages into assets: his lack of the noble title customary among his peers fostered the rumor (which he never denied) that he was the son of peasants. Conspicuous ugliness and a stature that did not reach five feet made him the darling of cartoonists, especially during debating duals with the giant Bismarck. The elfin, bespectacled, eminently civilian parliamentarian ("the Civilian Moltke"; "General *Schlauberger*" [sly dog]) offered a counter-symbol to the authoritarian values exemplified by Germany's field marshals, elite officials, and aristocratic chancellors. At his death he was given all the honors of a state funeral, critics complained, and the Social Democratic press proclaimed him "the most popular man in Germany." Yet anti-parliamentary and anti-Catholic sentiment continued to color his image among nationalists of both liberal and conservative persuasions, and the currents that Windthorst embodied—Catholic, federalist, and constitutionalist—became fully acceptable to the majority only after the founding of the Federal Republic of Germany in 1949.

See also **Catholicism, Political; Center Party; Germany; Kulturkampf; Prussia.**

BIBLIOGRAPHY

Primary Sources

Tiedemann, Christoph von. *Aus sieben Jahrzehnten. Erinnerungen.* 2 vols. Leipzig, 1905–1909.

Windthorst, Ludwig Josef Ferdinand Gustav. *Ausgewählte Reden gehalten in der Zeit von 1861–1891.* 1903. 3 vols. Reprint, Hildesheim, Zurich, and New York, 2003.

———. *Briefe 1834–1880.* Edited by Hans-Georg Aschoff with Heinz-Jörg Heinrich. Paderborn, Germany, 1995.

Briefe 1881–1891: um einen Nachtrag mit Briefen von 1834 bis 1880 ergänzt. Edited by Hans-Georg Aschoff with Heinz-Jörg Heinrich. Paderborn, Germany, 2002.

———. *Ludwig Windthorst, 1812–1891.* Edited by Hans-Georg Aschoff. Paderborn, Germany, 1991. Brief edition of Windthorst's most important speeches, annotated and put in context.

Secondary Sources

Anderson, Margaret Lavinia. *Windthorst: A Political Biography.* Oxford, U.K., and New York, 1981. Translated into German as *Windthorst: Zentrumspolitiker und Gegenspieler Bismarcks*, with an expanded bibliography, 1988. First critical scholarly biography, notable for uncovering Windthorst's close relations to the clergy and conflicts with Leo XIII.

Bachem, Karl. *Vorgeschichte, Geschichte und Politik der Deutschen Zentrumspartei: Zugleich ein Beitrag zur Geschichte der katholischen Bewegung, sowie zur allgemeinen Geschichte des neueren und neuesten Deutschland 1815–1914.* Vols. 3–5. Cologne, 1927–1932. Invaluable resource by knowledgeable Center politician, personally close to Windthorst in his later years, based on a rich collection of contemporary materials.

Colonge, Paul. *Ludwig Windthorst (1812–1891): (Sa pensée et son action politiques jusqu'en 1875).* 2 vols. Lille and Paris, 1983. Exhaustive coverage.

Goldberg, Hans-Peter. *Bismarck und seine Gegner: die politische Rhetorik im kaiserlichen Reichstag.* Düsseldorf, 1998. Analyzes Bismarck's rhetoric and that of his principal parliamentary antagonists: Windthorst; the Social Democrat August Bebel; and the Progressive Eugen Richter.

Hüsgen, Eduard. *Ludwig Windthorst.* Cologne, 1907. Classic, if uncritical, biography by editor of a Center Party newspaper in Düsseldorf who was eyewitness to some of the events described. Enriched with contemporary caricatures, campaign doggerel, and long quotations.

Meemken, Hermann, ed. *Ludwig Windthorst, 1812–1891: christlicher Parlamentarier und Gegenspieler Bismarcks: Begleitbuch zur Gedenkausstellung aus Anlass des 100. Todestages.* Meppen, Germany, 1991. Revealing photographs, caricatures, and other contemporary graphics along with articles that are valuable for illuminating Windthorst's connections with his Emsland constituency in northwestern Germany.

MARGARET LAVINIA ANDERSON

WINE.

Wine was one of the principal alcoholic beverages consumed in Europe during the long nineteenth century. Beer and wine had already been staple elements in the daily diet throughout Europe for centuries because they were safer to drink than the available water, which was often contaminated by human, animal, and industrial waste.

Several themes bear on the history of wine between 1789 and 1914. They include changes in production and consumption patterns, the effects of the temperance movements and phylloxera, and shifts in the cultural status of wine.

WINE IN 1789

At the end of the eighteenth century, wine was consumed by common people in areas where viticulture flourished, and where wine was inexpensive because it did not have to be transported to market or could be produced on a local or domestic scale. Thus, wine consumption was widespread in Spain, Portugal, France, Italy, and Greece, and those regions of central and eastern Europe where grapes were cultivated.

Elsewhere, beer, ale, and distilled spirits were more commonly consumed, but because wine had a social cachet, it was imported for consumption by those who could afford it. The middle and upper classes in northern Europe also consumed beer and spirits, but wine was a socially valued beverage and wine merchants did brisk business in England, the Netherlands and Belgium, Scandinavia, and Russia.

The English market, for example, soaked up huge volumes of wine from Bordeaux and Port (wine fortified with brandy) from Portugal. A 1793 guide to St. Petersburg noted that wealthy people there drank wines from Bordeaux, Burgundy, and Champagne, and also Hungarian wines that were also popular because they are "strong, very alcoholic, and warm the blood" (Phillips, p. 202). Even where wine was available locally, as in northern Italy, wine was imported from France because it was reputed to be of higher quality.

It is impossible to provide useful figures on per capita consumption because total production is often unknown and drinking patterns are unclear. Enough wine was brought into Paris in the 1780s to enable each inhabitant—women, children, and men—to consume between three and six liters of wine a week. But adult men clearly drank more than women and children, and some tavern records suggest that men might have downed two liters of wine a day.

Although contemporary commentators condemned drunkenness, they accepted wine as a basic part of the daily diet. The political scientist Jean-Baptiste Moheau wrote in the 1780s that wine is "an excellent beverage for the poor, not only because it is a food but also because it is very good protection against physical decay" (Phillips, p. 203).

The popularity of wine in eighteenth-century France led to complaints that high taxes on it led to clandestine wine-shops and smuggling. Wine was regularly smuggled into Paris—sometimes through channels bored through the city walls—and taverns selling less expensive wine outside the walls (where the city tax was not levied) did a roaring trade on holidays.

In response to complaints about sales taxes, the Revolutionary government abolished the tax on wine in 1791 and, at midnight on 1 May, a convoy of hundreds of carts brought an estimated 2 million liters of wine into Paris for sale at the new, tax-free price. Even when a tax was re-imposed in 1798, wine was still cheaper than it had been before the Revolution.

THE NINETEENTH CENTURY

The Revolutionary and Napoleonic periods promoted the wine industry in France, and annual production rose by a third between the late 1780s and the period from 1805 to 1812. The area under viticulture increased, especially in southern France, and governments subsidized the wine industry by purchasing vast volumes of wine for military rations and hospitals during the Revolutionary and Napoleonic Wars (1792–1815).

During the nineteenth century, several developments favored the spread of wine consumption throughout Europe. One was an improvement in transportation brought about by railroads from the 1850s onward. Until then, the cheapest means of moving wine was by water (river or coastal shipping), but trains could carry bulk wine inexpensively, and the railroad extended the market reach of wine regions. From the 1860s, the wines of southern France (especially Languedoc) began to penetrate the large working-class markets in Paris and France's northern industrial cities.

There were also developments in elite wines, and regions like Bordeaux consolidated their reputations for producing premium wines. In 1855, at the request of Napoleon III, the seventy-nine most expensive wines from some of Bordeaux's most prestigious districts were classified into five categories (known as *Crus* or "Growths"). In the same period, in the Italian region of Tuscany, Baron Ricasoli set out the approved grape varieties for modern Chianti.

During the nineteenth century, too, modern Champagne was born. In the 1820s Veuve Clicquot introduced new techniques of production that were widely adopted and became known as the "Champagne Method," while in mid-century Champagne began to move from the sweet sparkling wine it had been, to the drier styles now most common.

TEMPERANCE

While the European wine industry was growing, expanding its markets and developing expensive, premium wines, two threats emerged. The first was an unprecedented movement against the consumption of any more alcohol than was needed for basic dietary purposes. This temperance movement was a coordinated expression of the concern that had been articulated sporadically for centuries, as civic and church commentators warned against the social and personal consequences of excessive drinking. By the end of the nineteenth century, some temperance movements began to call for total abstinence and a ban on the production of beverage alcohol.

Anti-alcohol movements like these attracted less support in Europe, especially Continental Europe, than in North America and Australasia. In Europe, wine and beer were entrenched in diet and culture. And to the extent that sources of potable water needed to be available before alcohol could be removed from the diet, much of Europe lagged behind other parts of the Western world.

Although the anti-alcohol campaigns made some inroads in England, they were largely ineffective in continental Europe. In France, a number of temperance organizations focused their campaigns solely on spirits and went so far as to encourage wine-drinking on the ground that wine was healthy and an antidote to alcoholism.

A side effect of the anti-alcohol campaigns was a decline in the reputation of wine as having therapeutic qualities. For centuries wine had been prescribed for digestive and other problems, and it was believed to have general tonic effects. In 1870–1871, one hospital in Darmstadt, Germany, went through 4,633 bottles of white and 6,332 bottles of red wine from the Rhine region, sixty bottles of Champagne, a few dozen bottles of superior white and red Bordeaux, and about thirty dozen bottles of Port.

Yet in the late nineteenth and early twentieth centuries, new drugs and painkillers (like aspirin), sedatives, and tranquilizers came onto the market. They were clinically tested and promised specific results, unlike wine, which was promoted as merely beneficial in a general sense.

PHYLLOXERA

The decline of wine as medicine had a long-term effect. A more serious and immediate threat to wine in nineteenth-century Europe was phylloxera, a vine-disease imported from North America that took hold in southern France in the 1860s and, during the following decades, devastated vineyards throughout almost the whole of Europe. For years—the timing varied from region to region—wine production fell and many consumers shifted to other beverages.

The phylloxera epidemic was a short-term blow to Europe's wine industry (a solution was put in place from the 1870s), but it had far-reaching effects. For one thing, it changed the map of European viticulture. In France, many marginal vineyards in the north were not replanted and the center of gravity shifted south, as the vineyards of Languedoc-Roussillon (now with rail access to northern markets) expanded dramatically.

All Europe's wine industries were affected by phylloxera. Spanish wine benefited at first, as an influx of French winemakers left their dying vines in regions like Bordeaux and began to work in Spanish regions such as Rioja. But then, Spain's vines died in turn. Italy's wine-producers experi-

enced a short sales boom as the French imported wine to make up their own shortfall. But phylloxera soon spread to Italy's vineyards, too.

When phylloxera reduced the wine supply, counterfeit and substitute wines (some made from raisins, others adulterated with all kinds of additives) flooded the European market. They damaged the reputation of established regions and led wine consumers to shift to beer and spirits, such as Scotch whisky in England and absinthe in France.

RECOVERY AFTER PHYLLOXERA

In an effort to recover its markets, the French wine industry enacted rules that became a model for wine laws in many countries in the twentieth century. The rules restricted the ingredients in wine and specified (for the first time) that it had to be made from fresh grapes. At the turn of the century, the French parliament declared wine to be a safe and healthy beverage.

France also adopted Appellation d'Origine Contrôlée laws to regulate the use of geographical names on wines. From 1908, wines could not be labeled "Champagne" unless they were made from grapes grown there. These laws were extended to other regions in the twentieth century and became the basis for wine laws throughout Europe.

Developments in France through much of the nineteenth century are so important not only because French wine was reputed to be the best in the world (winemakers came to France from across Europe and around the world to learn techniques), but also because France made more wine than any other country. In 1828, French wine production accounted for 40 percent of world output and France's 2 million hectares of land under vines was far greater than Italy's 400,000 hectares, Austria's 625,000, and Hungary's 550,000.

France was also the site of many of the technical advances in winemaking in the nineteenth century. The great French scientist Louis Pasteur devoted much of his time to research on wine, especially to understanding the process of fermentation. Ironically, the process of heating liquids to kill off bacteria (pasteurization) was used to produce unfermented grape juice that many temperance campaigners argued should replace wine in the Christian communion.

EUROPE 1789 TO 1914   2477

Despite the phylloxera episode and the efforts of anti-alcohol movements, wine retained its popularity among Europeans whether they drank cheap, ordinary wine or could afford the prestigious brands. Even when regular supplies of reliable fresh water became available, and even when the medical properties of wine were called into question, consumption rates remained high in many parts of Europe, especially Italy, Spain, and France.

Nonetheless, by 1900, production outpaced demand in some regions, prices fell, and some industries faced a crisis. In several French regions, producers and workers in wine-related jobs demonstrated in large numbers. Protests attracted 300,000 in Nîmes and 600,000 in Montpellier in 1907. In 1911, workers in Champagne destroyed hundreds of thousands of liters of Champagne during disturbances.

The outbreak of war in 1914 came to the aid of the French wine industry. Although the call-up of troops in August left wineries short-handed for what would prove a bumper harvest, the grapes were picked by older men, women, and children. The wineries of Languedoc donated 20 million liters to military hospitals, and soon the government was buying vast amounts of wine for soldiers' rations. The military wine ration was increased steadily as the war dragged on, and in 1917 French troops at the front consumed 1.2 billion liters of wine.

The long nineteenth century was bracketed by political upheavals that, in the short term at least, were good for the wine industry. In the one hundred years between, the industry and the status of wine in material, cultural, and medical terms went through a series of transformations that set the stage for wine's playing a different role in twentieth-century European society and culture.

See also **Alcohol and Temperance; Diet and Nutrition; Phylloxera.**

BIBLIOGRAPHY

Guy, Kolleen M. *When Champagne became French: Wine and the Making of a National Identity.* Baltimore, 2003.

Haine, W. Scott *The World of the Paris Café: Sociability among the French Working Class, 1789–1914.* Baltimore, 1996.

Loubère, Leo. *The Red and the White: The History of Wine in France and Italy in the Nineteenth Century.* Albany, N.Y., 1978.

Phillips, Rod. *A Short History of Wine.* New York, 2001.

Prestwich, Patricia E. *Drink and the Politics of Social Reform: Antialcoholism in France since 1870.* Palo Alto, Calif., 1988.

ROD PHILLIPS

WITTE, SERGEI (1849–1915), Russian politician.

Sergei Yulyevich Witte was born in Tiflis, Georgia, in 1849. His father was a Baltic German who moved up Peter the Great's Table of Ranks to become a hereditary noble. His mother was related to the ancient Dolgoruky princes; to Helena Blavatsky, a founder of theosophy; and to Rostislav Fadeyev, a leader of the Pan-Slavs. Witte shared the Pan-Slav view that the Russian autocracy united the empire's disparate nationalities. Married twice, Witte had two adopted daughters.

Following his degree in mathematics from the University of Novorossiisk, Witte entered the new field of railroading in Ukraine. He always considered railways key economic levers. His expert management of the southwestern railways and ideas on financing railways and strengthening the economy of the empire catapulted him to St. Petersburg to head the new Department of Railroad Affairs in the Ministry of Finance and then to the position of minister of finance.

As minister of finance (1892–1903), Witte supervised construction of the Trans-Siberian Railroad, put Russia on the gold standard, forged tariffs with Germany that included fairly favorable conditions for Russia, encouraged foreign investment, and stimulated industrialization through government purchase of domestically produced rails and equipment at above-market prices. During his administration technical and commercial schools increased seventeenfold. Small-scale businesses continued to proliferate. Witte published on economic subjects and to supplement the ministry of finance newspaper established a commercial-trade newspaper and a scholarly economic journal. He transmuted information received from chairing the Special Conference on the Needs of Agricultural Industry or Rural Industry into measures for agrarian improvement.

Although he used a loan from France in 1895 to finance the Chinese Eastern Railway through Manchuria, Witte opposed the Russian adventurism in Korea and Port Arthur that precipitated the Russo-Japanese War of 1904–1905. Palace intrigue resulted in Witte's dismissal as finance minister in 1903. As chair of the Committee of Ministers (1903–1905), however, Witte supervised significant laws and proposals. One implemented an imperial decree adding corporately elected members to the State Council, a legislative body dating from the early nineteenth century, composed of appointed officials. Other proposals concerned replacing peasant communes with private farmsteads, improving the position of ethnic and religious minorities, and expanding self-government—proposals that Peter Stolypin fleshed out and strove to implement between 1906 and 1911. In September 1905 Witte participated in the peace conference in Portsmouth, New Hampshire, ending the Russo-Japanese War and achieved favorable terms for Russia. He had reservations about local, popularly elected assemblies (zemstvos) and the establishment of a parliament, but to quell the general strike that erupted in the fall of 1905, Witte urged Tsar Nicholas II to institute a popularly elected, legislative Duma to complement the State Council. As chair of the Council of Ministers (October 1905–April 1906), a quasi–prime ministerial position, Witte tried to co-opt moderate liberal opposition leaders into the government. He worked out electoral regulations for the Duma, which represented all categories of adult males, though not fully and equally. Witte was awarded the title count for arranging a 2.25 billion franc loan from French, British, Dutch, Austrian, and Russian bankers, finalized in April 1906. He simultaneously resigned as head of the government because hostile political groups dominated the First Duma and because of tension with Tsar Nicholas.

Appointed to the State Council, Witte served in that upper parliamentary chamber until his death, on 13 March (28 February, old style) 1915. He opposed extension of zemstvos to the western provinces of the empire, on which Stolypin staked his career in 1911. Witte also opposed war with Germany, which broke out in 1914. Though not entirely due to Witte, the Russian economy was the fifth strongest in the world in the early twentieth century, with high growth rates that plunged during the 1904–1905 revolution but rebounded through 1913.

See also **Austria-Hungary; Nicholas II; Russia; Stolypin, Peter.**

BIBLIOGRAPHY

Primary Sources

Witte, Sergei. *The Memoirs of Count Witte.* Translated and edited by Sidney Harcave. Armonk, N.Y., 1990.

Secondary Sources

Gregory, Paul R. *Before Command: An Economic History of Russia from Emancipation to the First Five-Year Plan.* Princeton, N.J., 1994.

Harcave, Sidney. *Count Sergei Witte and the Twilight of Imperial Russia: A Biography.* Armonk, N.Y., 2004.

Mehlinger, Howard D., and John M. Thompson. *Count Witte and the Tsarist Government in the 1905 Revolution.* Bloomington, Ind., 1972.

Von Laue, Theodore H. *Sergei Witte and the Industrialization of Russia.* New York, 1963.

MARY SCHAEFFER CONROY

WOLLSTONECRAFT, MARY (1759–1797), radical thinker, polemicist, translator, and writer of fiction and educational and historical works.

Mary Wollstonecraft was the eldest of three daughters and the second of six children born to Edward John Wollstonecraft, a silk weaver of Spitalfields, London, and Elizabeth Dixon, from Ballyshannon, Ireland. Her father's subsequent failure as a gentleman farmer had the consequence that she spent her adult life constantly seeking independence by earning enough to support herself, her sisters, and later, her child. Her early educational works, *Thoughts on the Education of Daughters* (1786), *Original Stories from Real Life* (1788), and the anthology *The Female Reader* (1788) are fruits of her experiences as lady's companion, mistress of a school set up

Mary Wollstonecraft. Engraving after the portrait by John Opie. PRIVATE COLLECTION/BRIDGEMAN ART LIBRARY

with her sisters Eliza and Everina, and as governess to the Kingsborough family at Mitchelstown near Corke in Ireland; while her first novel *Mary, a Fiction* (1787) is based on an intense friendship with Fanny Blood. Her London publisher Joseph Johnson also employed her to review and abstract for his *Analytical Review*, founded in 1788, and to translate contemporary works.

Wollstonecraft's two best known works, *A Vindication of the Rights of Men* (1790), published anonymously in reply to Edmund Burke's *Reflections on the Revolution in France* (1790), and *Vindication of the Rights of Woman* (1792), published under her own name, owe their genesis to a London group of Dissenter friends in Newington Green, including Dr. Richard Price (1723–1791), whom Wollstonecraft met when running the school in the area, and to Joseph Johnson's circle—including the artist Henry Fuseli (1741–1825) and the radical thinker Thomas Paine (1737–1809). In these two works, stimulated by discussions on the French Revolution, Wollstonecraft argued for enfranchising those who had no

political rights because franchise was then based on ownership of property. She advocated representation and citizenship for both men and women, including the right to useful employment for both sexes.

In 1792, Wollstonecraft went to France to report on the French Revolution for Johnson, which enabled her to recover from an unhappy love for Fuseli. Her observations became *An Historical and Moral View of the Origin and Progress of the French Revolution and the Effect It Has Produced in Europe* (1794). In 1793, the year of the execution of the king of France, Louis XVI (r. 1774–1792), she began a relationship with Gilbert Imlay (c. 1754–1828), an American writer and trader, who, on the passing of the Law of Suspects (17 September 1793), registered her as his wife at the American Embassy. Wollstonecraft bore his child, Fanny, named after her friend who died in Portugal in 1785. After attempting suicide in 1795, she agreed to act as Imlay's business associate in an attempt to gain redress for the loss of a cargo of silver reputedly lost in Scandinavia. Her *Letters Written During a Short Residence in Norway, Denmark, and Sweden* (1796) was the literary spin-off from intricate and difficult negotiations on Imlay's behalf while traveling in Scandinavia with her baby daughter and maid. On her return to London, her reaction to Imlay's repeated unfaithfulness was a second suicide attempt. Miraculously saved from drowning in the River Thames in October 1795, she lived to marry the philosopher William Godwin (1756–1836) in 1797. Wollstonecraft wrote the never-finished "Lessons" for her daughter Fanny and worked on a further development of her feminist ideas in the novel *Maria; or, The Wrongs of Woman* (published posthumously in 1798), in which she presented an acute analysis of the intricate interrelation of class, gender, and love. Wollstonecraft died of puerperal fever on 10 September 1797, eleven days after the birth of her second daughter, Mary, the future Mary Shelley (1797–1851).

The publication by Godwin of *Memoirs of the Author of the Rights of Woman* (1798) continued the trend of turning Wollstonecraft the celebrity into an object of censure on account of her unconventional personal life, by revealing details of her sexual history. Less than a century later, however, the suffragist movement found in Wollstonecraft a champion for their cause. As antidote to the appropriation of Wollstonecraft by a variety of feminist persuasions, scholarship of the late twentieth and early twenty-first centuries has tended to concentrate on two areas: situating Wollstonecraft within the intellectual and social parameters of the late eighteenth century and making known further details of her eventful life. Mary Poovey (1984) discusses Wollstonecraft in relation to concepts of appropriate behavior of her time, and Barbara Taylor (2003) stresses the theistic framework of her thought. Lyndall Gordon's research on Mary Wollstonecraft's travels in Scandinavia (2005) reveals hitherto unknown details of that hazardous and demanding journey.

See also **Burke, Edmund; Feminism; French Revolution; Godwin, William; Shelley, Mary.**

BIBLIOGRAPHY

Primary Sources

Todd, Janet, and Marilyn Butler, eds. *The Works of Mary Wollstonecraft.* 7 volumes. London, 1989.

Secondary Sources

Gordon, Lyndall. *Mary Wollstonecraft: A New Genus.* London, 2005.

Poovey, Mary. *The Proper Lady and the Woman Writer: Ideology as Style in the Works of Mary Wollstonecraft, Mary Shelley, and Jane Austen.* Chicago, 1984.

Taylor, Barbara. *Mary Wollstonecraft and the Feminist Imagination.* Cambridge, U.K., 2003.

JENNIFER LORCH

WORDSWORTH, WILLIAM (1770–1850), British Romantic poet.

William Wordsworth is so synonymous with "Romanticism" that the period used to be called "The Age of Wordsworth." Born 7 April 1770, Wordsworth lived into the middle of the next century, when Victoria (r. 1837–1901) was Queen and Alfred Tennyson (1809–1892) and Robert Browning (1812–1889) the celebrated new poets. It is often said that Wordsworth "the poet" died in 1807, survived by stodgy didactic work, minor new

verse, repackaged older work, and a belated Poet Laureateship in 1843, yet his influence was considerable. Amid the encroachments of modern life, Wordsworth provided an enduring image of the poet as disciple of "Nature" and representative voice of feeling, whether of quiet sentiment, troubled passion, or moral severity. No less in life than in verse, he embodied "plain living and high thinking," at home in the Lake District in Northwest England, a region marked by natural beauty that he made famous. He was happy in his family life, yet often withdrew into meditation and depths of emotion.

Born in the Lake District, Wordsworth was one of five children. His father was a steward for a powerful local landlord, and the poet's boyhood was enjoyed in the market town of Cockermouth, with adventures in the nearby outdoors. The death of his mother when he was eight changed everything: his father, frequently away on business, sent William's sister Dorothy off to relatives and the brothers to school in distant Hawkshead. Five years later, his father died, and legal wrangling prevented the estate from being settled until 1802. In 1787 Wordsworth entered St John's College, Cambridge, to prepare for a living in the Church but Cambridge seemed an alien world to this native of the Lakelands. Vacationing in Europe in the summer of 1790, one year after the French Revolution, he caught the enchantment of millenarian hopes. He took his degree in 1791; that summer he toured Wales (climbing Mount Snowdon) and then returned to France in November 1791. Wordsworth was at once excited and troubled by the new politics of France. He found love with Annette Vallon, who bore their daughter, Caroline, in December 1792. But by then, depleted funds and a looming Terror had forced Wordsworth home, and, because of the ensuing war between England and France, it was not until 1802 (the Peace of Amiens) that he would see Annette and Caroline, just once more, prior to marrying a childhood sweetheart, Mary Hutchinson.

Across the turmoil of the 1790s Wordsworth grew "Sick, wearied out with contrarieties," and relinquished "moral questions in despair" (*Prelude* 10.900–01). The record of Wordsworth's activities from 1792 to 1795 is obscure. He may have become involved with radical politics at home and may have ventured to France. In 1795 a legacy of £900 enabled him to devote himself to poetry and reunite with his sister Dorothy (1771–1855), who was always to be his encourager, companion, scribe, and housekeeper. A new friend, the poet and journalist Samuel Taylor Coleridge (1772–1834), inspired Wordsworth with a fresh sense of mission and power. In 1797, he and Dorothy moved to Somerset to be near Coleridge, and the poets were soon collaborating on *Lyrical Ballads*. Regarded today as a landmark of Romanticism, this volume was published anonymously in 1798 to mixed reviews. When local political anxieties put the group under suspicion, the Wordsworths' lease was not renewed, and the trio decided to go to Germany for winter, to soak up the language, culture, and philosophy.

With more financial resources, Coleridge enjoyed the university towns, while the Wordsworths spent a miserable winter in the remote village of Goslar. It was here that Wordsworth drafted new poems for *Lyrical Ballads* and his first fragments of autobiography. Coleridge was urging him to write a major philosophical epic, and could abide the autobiographical turn only as preparatory, but for Wordsworth "the story of my life" (1.668) would become compelling epic in its own right. Returning to the Lake District in late 1799, the Wordsworths settled in Grasmere, their home for the rest of their lives. In 1800 a two-volume *Lyrical Ballads,* now signed as Wordsworth's, appeared with a controversial Preface declaring such principles as inspiration from "emotion recollected in tranquillity," the equation of "all good poetry" with "the spontaneous overflow of powerful feelings," and the tuning of poetic language to ordinary conversation, rooted in "nature" and "rural society." This manifesto was in part an exercise in mythmaking; but it also marked, said the critic William Hazlitt (1778–1830) in retrospect, "a new style and a new spirit." It set the terms of Wordsworth's fame, even as it focused the charges of his critics for decades on.

The steadily expanding household finally settled at Rydal Mount in 1813, when Wordsworth received a patronage position from the Tory government. The decade prior had been pained by several losses: his brother John, a sea captain, perished in a shipwreck in 1805; two of his and Mary's five children died in 1812; and by 1810 Coleridge's opium addiction and truancy from his own family led to strains in his relationship with Wordsworth. This resulted in a bitter alienation that was not mended until the late 1820s. Leading reviewers ridiculed *Poems in Two Volumes* (1807), and would be no kinder to *The Excursion* (1814), a nine-book epic "On Man, On Nature, and On Human Life." Yet the attention, and the advent of a collected *Poems* (in which the poems were arranged by conceptual category rather than by date) in 1815, confirmed Wordsworth's fame and importance, and he continued to write and publish in every decade of his long life.

During this life, *The Excursion* was regarded as his major work. The story of a ruined cottage in its first book was widely admired, and overall Wordsworth was prized for poems filled with pathos, such as "Michael" and "The Brothers" (in which, as he said in his Preface to *Lyrical Ballads*, the feeling gives importance to the action and situation); odes of crisis and troubled consolation, such as "Tintern Abbey" and "Intimations of Immortality from Recollections of Early Childhood"; and a wealth of exquisite sonnets, songs, and lyrics ("The Solitary Reaper" was among the most famous). Victorians revered the poet whose love of "Nature" could heal their "iron age," whose images of childhood and youth evoked simple joys, whose mature poetry gave unembarrassed voice to feeling. The poet John Keats (1795–1821) preferred the "dark passages" and "the burden of the mystery"—the poetry also of most interest to twentieth-century readers, for whom *The Prelude* (that preparatory autobiography) is the recognized major work. Just weeks after Wordsworth's death, this fourteen-book epic, composed across fifty years, appeared in print. Prelude it was: another version completed in 1805 was published in 1926, and then, further into the twentieth century, a two-book version from 1798–1799, and a five-book version from 1804. In this array of narrative forms and ceaseless revisions, of multiple selves, of writing reflexively as a poet about becoming a poet, *The Prelude* seems a venture of prescient modernism, but it also endures as a vivid imaginative reckoning with a life animated by the contradictory currents of its age.

See also **Coleridge, Samuel Taylor; Great Britain; Romanticism; Shelley, Percy Bysshe.**

BIBLIOGRAPHY

Primary Sources

The Poetical Works of William Wordsworth, ed. Ernest de Selincourt, revised by Helen Darbishire. Oxford, U.K., 1949–1959.

Wordsworth, William. *Poems.* Edited by John O. Hayden. Harmondsworth, U.K., 1977.

———. *The Prelude, 1798, 1805, 1850: Authoritative Texts, Context and Reception; Recent critical essays.* Edited by Jonathan Wordsworth, M. H. Abrams, and Stephen Gill. New York, 1979.

———. *The Prose Works of William Wordsworth.* Edited by W. J. B. Owen and Jane Worthington Smyser. Oxford, U.K., 1974.

Wordsworth, William, and Dorothy Wordsworth. *The Letters of William and Dorothy Wordsworth.* Edited and arranged by Ernest de Selincourt and revised by Chester L. Shaver, Mary Moorman, and Alan G. Hill. Oxford, U.K., 1967–1993.

Secondary Sources

Chandler, James K. *Wordsworth's Second Nature: A Study of the Poetry and Politics.* Chicago, 1981.

Ferguson, Frances. *Wordsworth: Language as Counter-Spirit.* New Haven, Conn., 1977.

Ferry, David. *The Limits of Mortality: An Essay on Wordsworth's Major Poems.* Middletown, Conn., 1959.

Gill, Stephen. *William Wordsworth: A Life.* Oxford, U.K. and New York, 1989.

Johnston, Kenneth R.. *The Hidden Wordsworth: Poet, Lover, Spy.* New York, 1998.

Jones, John. *The Egotistical Sublime: A History of Wordsworth's Imagination.* London, 1954.

Mahoney, John L. *William Wordsworth: A Poetic Life.* New York, 1997.

Onorato, Richard J. *The Character of the Poet: Wordsworth in "The Prelude."* Princeton, N.J., 1971.

Wolfson, Susan J. *The Questioning Presence: Wordsworth, Keats, and the Interrogative Mode in Romantic Poetry.* Ithaca, N.Y., 1987.

Wordsworth, Jonathan. *William Wordsworth: The Borders of Vision.* Oxford, U.K., 1982.

SUSAN J. WOLFSON

———

WORKING CLASS. The concept of class became a central organizing myth of nineteenth-century Europe. A narrative was constructed telling of the rise of the bourgeoisie and the working class's challenges to its hegemony. The invention of this terminology in approximately 1830 cannot be explained simply by the structural social changes generated by industrialization. Eighteenth-century Britain already had wage laborers in artisanal trades, protoindustry, agriculture, and new factories. They engaged in strikes, grain and anti-enclosure riots, and machine breaking—struggles underpinned by craft and community solidarity and justified as defense of a moral economy against emerging free-market practices. But the participants in these class conflicts before the emergence of a working class were called, variously, the crowd, the mob, or the people. Crucial changes in vocabulary emerged from the French Revolution. The bourgeoisie denounced "idle, parasitic" aristocrats and proclaimed its own virtues: industry, productivity, rationality, and moderation. British advocates of parliamentary reform eulogized the disenfranchised middle class of expanding industrial towns, claiming for them similar qualities. The rhetoric of liberty, equality, and fraternity and the rights of man was sufficiently inclusive to arouse popular support. However, both the Revolution of 1830 in France and the Reform Act of 1832 in Britain excluded workers from enlarged franchises. Outraged by this betrayal, politicized workers appropriated aspects of bourgeois discourse. They asked whether workers were not the truly productive class. A new terminology was born, generating mobilizing myths that were capable of providing a sense of identity for disparate groups and constructing a sociopolitical constituency. Soon contributions from Lyon silk weavers to a Saint Etienne miners' strike funds included messages of solidarity to "fellow members of the working class (*la classe ouvrière*)."

THE CONSTRUCTION OF A CLASS IDENTITY
Older usages persisted, however. In England, Chartist rhetoric still used the tropes of eighteenth-century radicals' denunciation of aristocratic "Old Corruption." Workers responded to narratives of "the people" promulgated by English Gladstonian liberals or French republicans. Yet workers proved adept at appropriating bourgeois discourses on property, domesticity, and family values for their own (class) purposes. Spitalfields silk weavers defended their threatened jobs by citing their rights to "property in labour" and insisted on male workers' need for a "family wage"

to support their wives and children. Hence the concept of the working class emerged as a result of changing self-awareness, marked by a sharp linguistic shift.

Stories told by individuals and groups about themselves nurtured class consciousness. Most of the hundreds of nineteenth-century worker autobiographers used class as the central category for their interpreting life experiences, viewing the world through the prism of class differences. These were not typical workers. Most workers with the literacy and inclination to write were male and skilled and they valued education not because it would bring them social promotion but for the self-emancipation it offered, and for its use in the emancipation of what they considered their class. Their fascination with ideas led some of them to be dismissed as eccentrics by their workmates. Some were scathing about the fecklessness, lack of intellectual curiosity, and brutality of some fellow workers. Although some made contacts with bourgeois liberals, most rejected liberalism. Marginal to their own class, they were acutely aware of nuances of class distinctions. Some were what Antonio Gramsci later called organic intellectuals—still close to their own class yet aware of broad issues and active in constructing a plebeian public sphere. Crucially, the stories they told about themselves shaped a working-class identity by imposing coherent narratives on the flux of complex social realities. These—secular versions of Christian conversion stories—emphasized how early poverty, exploitation, and humiliations were transformed once reading opened their eyes to the system of capitalist exploitation. They metamorphosed from victims into agents. Their duty was to educate their fellow workers who, once aware of their situation, could build a better society. Whereas the United States constructed narratives of individual upward mobility that might be possible for ambitious immigrants, Europe produced narratives of class salvation via collective struggle. These autobiographers also reminded readers of both the history and myths of workers' struggles. One prerequisite for a critical, counterhegemonic view of the world, critical of dominant bourgeois identity, was consciousness of who one was, rooted in a sense of where one had come from.

CLASS AND SOLIDARITY

By 1914 the working class had become a sociopolitical actor. Karl Marx's goal, "the constitution of the working class into a political party," appeared achievable. Germany's Social Democratic Party (SPD), with one million members, secured 34 percent of the vote. Trade unions, once confined to craft elites, were becoming centralized, industrial, mass organizations. Britain and Germany each had four million union members by 1914. France regularly experienced over a thousand strikes per year, five times the 1880s average. Strike rituals—street demonstrations, appeals for worker solidarity—became part of everyday experience in industrial Europe. Whereas elites once feared disorder and disease from what they considered to be criminal and dangerous classes, now they devised strategies to counter challenges from organized labor, including electoral concessions, welfare and municipal reforms, and social imperialism.

Widespread structural proletarianization underlay these developments. But one cannot simply assume levels of working-class consciousness or mobilization from the processes of industrialization. Marx had explained the defeat of the revolutions of 1848 by arguing that, outside of Britain and parts of France and Germany, Europe's proletariat remained small and immature. The success of future revolutions required industrialization. Subsequent trends partly confirmed Marx's predictions of a polarization between capital and labor. Some homogenization of labor occurred. Artisanal trades declined and casual and migrant workers were recruited into semiskilled jobs in large mechanized factories, mines, steel works, and on railways. However, no monolithic trend emerged, rather development was combined and uneven. Everywhere, the heavy industry of the Second Industrial Revolution coexisted in symbiotic relationship with dispersed, archaic sectors, and relied on pools of migrant or protoindustrial labor. Despite Germany's spectacular industrial development—coal and heavy engineering, chemicals and railways—28 percent of its labor force remained agricultural in 1900; substantial artisanal and protoindustrial sectors remained (Solingen cutlery; Saxon textiles). France remained 60 percent rural, with peasant proprietors and sharecroppers outnumbering agricultural laborers. Northern coalfields, Lorraine steel, and heavy engineering in Parisian and Lyonnais *banlieues* (suburbs) coexisted with small, high-quality artisanal production. Two-thirds of Italy's industrial workers were in the Milan/Turin/Genoa triangle. Spain's industries (Asturias coal; Bilbao steel and shipyards; Catalan textiles and engineering) were islands in a rural sea. After the emancipation of the serfs in the 1860s, tsarist Russia's state-sponsored industrialization quintupled the industrial workforce, to three million, between 1890 and 1914. But alongside St. Petersburg's large engineering plants, Moscow textile factories, and Donbas coal mines, a huge peasantry remained. The proletariat exceeded 50 percent of the population only in Britain. Yet there, as in France and Germany, many new workers were white-collar employees (bank clerks, shop assistants) whose identification with blue-collar proletarians was problematic.

Such structural developments engendered changes in family patterns and communities. Artisans' children, who once married largely within their craft communities, now chose marriage partners from a wider working-class background. Wage differentials between British skilled and unskilled occupations narrowed steadily. Upward mobility remained rare: 90 percent of British manual workers' sons themselves did manual jobs. Hereditary working-class communities emerged—later idealized for their neighborly values, which contrasted with bourgeois individualism and the crass commercialism of an emerging mass consumer culture. The Paris Commune of 1871 was underpinned by community solidarities of popular *faubourgs* (suburbs) after Georges-Eugène Haussmann's large-scale urban renewal projects threw together displaced inner-city artisans and recent migrants. But no single, model working-class community existed. Metallurgical workers might live in single-industry company towns, such as the Schneider family's Le Creusot, run by one paternalist employer, or in industrial cities such as Düsseldorf. Large cities provided workers with a range of potential industries and employers, and wider possibilities of relations with other social groups. Yet there was often little contact between the older Parisian *faubourgs* and the industrial *banlieues* that emerged around the city's periphery. Lifestyles, cultures, and experiences inevitably differed widely between these and other types of community. Marx assumed that industrial concentration, by drawing

workers together and creating shared experiences and grievances, would nurture class consciousness and organization. "Class-in-itself" would emerge naturally from "class-for-itself." However no simple correlation existed between levels of industrialization and worker militancy. Some workers in dispersed sectors proved more militant than others in what Marx considered more advanced sectors. Agricultural laborers, who were widely assumed to be deferential, supported anarchosyndicalist strikes in Apulia and the Po Valley in Italy, Andalusia in Spain, or the lower Languedoc vineyards in France. Half of unionized Italian workers in 1914 were in the Agricultural Workers' Federation (Federterra). The proletarianized peasants of southwest Russia were prominent in the Revolution of 1905. The Captain Swing revolt of rural workers in southern England in the early 1830s suggested that even "Hodge"—the stereotypical deferential, cowed English laborer—might resort to machine breaking and cattle maiming. Protoindustrial textile workers—favored by capitalists as a cheap, dispersed, and quiescent labor force—organized strikes in Dauphiné, France, and northern Italy in the 1890s. Marxists were suspicious of what they considered to be backward rural migrants to the city, whom they stereotyped as prone to drink and violence. Yet in late tsarist Russia, many such immigrants were radicalized by ongoing social conflict in their native villages, where some owned plots of land, and by their capacity to recreate the solidarities of the village commune (*mir*) in their urban neighborhoods.

Cross-national comparisons bring into question any rigid occupational determinism. Skilled engineering workers provided the backbone of the Marxist Social Democratic Party in Germany as well as key Bolshevik cadres in St. Petersburg, Russia. In Paris in 1900s, they supported syndicalist strikes against "scientific management," which threatened their shop-floor autonomy. Yet the Victorian labor movement's reformism has been ascribed to the moderation of a relatively privileged labor aristocracy—including engineers, whose union proved keen to exclude the unskilled and avoid strikes by bargaining with employers.

Yet occupational groups were strongly marked by the nature of their jobs. Dockers were low-skilled,

Working men's bar, Paris. Illustration by Steinlen from the French satirical journal *Gil Blas,* 11 August 1895. The illustrator emphasizes the grim faces of the patrons. MARY EVANS PICTURE LIBRARY

low-status workers operating in casual labor markets within tough waterfront cultures (Barcelona, Marseille, Hamburg). Their levels of unionization were erratic, and their strikes marked by violence against strikebreakers. By contrast, printers were natural labor aristocrats—literate, self-taught worker-intellectuals, and among the first to unionize. Even Russian printers were moderates—requesting respect from employers and the state; they were pushed reluctantly toward menshevism only by tsarist brutality. Miners' politics varied widely with location and with the national political culture but the shared dangers of mining created intense workplace solidarity, reinforced by the strong community identities of isolated pit villages.

RADICAL ARTISANS AND INDUSTRIAL WORKERS

Radical artisans dominated the early labor movements. Paris was Europe's revolutionary capital. The thousands killed or arrested during the Paris Commune of 1871, which Marx called the first

example of the working class in power, were tailors, shoemakers, building craftsmen, and furniture makers—an occupational profile strikingly similar to that of the sans-culotte activists of 1793. In Britain the factory system came earlier than in France. Northern mill workers were active in Chartist agitation and strikes in the 1830s. But skilled workers—handloom weavers, London craftsmen, and Sheffield cutlers—were central to early labor protest. Militancy among France's emerging industrial proletariat was sporadic and unorganized. Many miners and forge workers lived in tightly controlled, isolated, paternalist company towns such as Decazeville. Textile mill workers were often women and children—unskilled, new to industrial work, lacking organizational traditions. The notorious slums of Lille engendered more drunken despair than they did organized protest. France relied on artisanal skills for high-quality goods—silks, porcelain, fashions, and furniture—for niche markets. But the skilled trades faced varied threats. Less skilled, sometimes rural, labor was employed to do simpler, subdivided tasks. Apprenticeship training deteriorated. The chances of journeymen becoming small masters declined. Trades came to be dominated by merchants, who put out raw materials and orders and controlled credit. Nevertheless, artisans possessed the resources to resist. Their skills were still required in up-market sectors. High literacy sustained a radical artisan press. Craft-dominated neighborhoods (the silk weavers' Croix-Rousse in Lyon; Faubourg Saint Antoine in Paris) had community solidarity, mutual aid, and cooperative schemes. Journeymen and small masters, united by their hatred of big merchants, often drank and sang together in cafés or *goguettes* (popular singing societies). They drew on traditions of artisanal organization, such as that of the *compagnonnages,* associations that aided "tramping" journeymen, which had roots in the seventeenth and eighteenth centuries. Where once artisans dreamed of a republic of small, independent producers, the inexorable advance of capitalism pushed them toward collective solutions. In 1848 French artisans hoped that an associationist republic—one sympathetic to their cooperative aspirations—would establish banks offering cheap credit and put out orders to producer cooperatives, which had fifty thousand members in Paris alone.

However, before one accepts that labor movements originated in the work-based culture and grievances of artisans, question need to be raised. Were French artisans militant less because of occupational grievances—which were present in other industrializing societies—than because their political aspirations were raised in the decades after the revolution by contact with neo-Jacobin republicans? Was the craft-proud radical artisan a myth constructed by radical journalists, some of them former artisans—an image designed to counter bourgeois stereotypes about the drunken, brutal dangerous classes? Artisans in relatively secure trades (for example, carpenters) proved less militant than shoemakers and tailors, many of whom wished to escape from trades degraded by the practice of sweating, which forced them to work ever-longer hours performing increasingly subdivided tasks for inexorably declining wages. Were artisans less precursors of later proletarian activists than reactionary radicals, their desperate rearguard actions fueled by awareness that the industrial juggernaut would overwhelm their culture and communities? Factory proletarians, by contrast, could envisage no alternative to the new industrial system on which their jobs depended. They took time to develop the solidarity required for effective class mobilization. Hence the gap in popular protest—in Britain after 1850, in France after 1870—as artisan radicalism faded and before new proletarian militancy surfaced.

Multiple frictions existed within the artisanal world. Pressures on specific trades could lead to conflicts between journeymen and masters, as happened in Germany, where masters' guilds persisted. Generational tensions also existed. In Paris in 1848, older journeymen fought on the barricades but younger workers were recruited into the Garde Mobile (Mobile Guard) to fight for order. Journeymen's *compagnonnages* had a heritage of internecine, ritualized violence and job competition that could obstruct trade union solidarity. But the major myopia of artisan culture was the issue of gender.

GENDER

The construction of the working class was always gendered. Although some utopian socialists did support women's rights and employment opportunities, Chartism championed male suffrage. Misogynistic artisanal spokesmen portrayed "cheap and docile" female workers as the primary threat to their jobs and skills. Textile mills, which destroyed the handloom weavers' livelihoods, employed mainly female and child labor. Seamstresses replaced male tailors. Friedrich Engels depicted the "unsexing" of Manchester workers, whose patriarchal power ebbed away when their wives and daughters worked in the mills while the men performed domestic chores. Their status was bound up with the independence derived from what they considered honorable labor and property in skill. British trade unionists campaigned for votes for "heads of families" and for a family wage. Capitalist exploitation of female labor was considered an evil, exposing women to physical degradation and sexual harassment, depriving workers' homes of women's domestic skills. Trade unionists welcomed protective legislation, hoping that restrictions on the hours women could work would disqualify them from key jobs.

Labor movement iconography depicting brawny steelworkers and miners reflected the male domination of key Second Industrial Revolution industries. Yet the ideal of the wife remaining at home was attainable only for skilled workers. Women constituted a high proportion of the labor force—over 35 percent in France, where many married as well as single women worked. Yet women's work was imagined as marginal and supplementary, even for single women. With rare exceptions, as for example in tobacco factories, women's jobs were viewed as unskilled. Many worked in deplorable conditions in the sweated domestic trades, beyond the reach of factory inspectors or unions. Unsurprisingly, women rarely expressed a strong sense of identity with their jobs.

By 1900 the SPD was arguing in principle for women's equality as workers and citizens while denouncing "bourgeois feminism" and insisting that female oppression was a product of capitalism and could be abolished only after the revolution. Marxist textile unions in Germany and northern France recruited female workers, but their male leaders marginalized women's specific demands to focus on men, who were able to vote. Women's proportion of French union membership doubled to 10 percent between 1900 and 1914, but the printers' craft union fought rearguard actions

Wigan colliery workers, Lancashire, England. Postcard photograph c. 1890. The young women pictured here were employed as surface workers, whose job was to move and sort the coal. The growing need for coal throughout Europe in the nineteenth century created many jobs, but the work was extremely hazardous and accidents claiming hundreds of lives were common. MARY EVANS PICTURE LIBRARY

their municipal socialism aroused women's interest, since it offered the possibility of child care, health clinics, and similar services. Despite this, when women were enfranchised in parts of Europe after 1918 many proved reluctant to vote for workers' parties, which they perceived as male dominated and insensitive to women's concerns.

THE LEFT AND THE RIGHT

Labor movements sought to construct a cohesive working class that would act as a class by shaping disorderly social realities into a coherent narrative. But prioritizing the story of certain types of workers risked ignoring or alienating others. Workers—as postmodernists emphasize—had a variety of potential identities. Class, which was constructed in the workplace, was but one. The European right wing's strength in the era of mass politics lay both in its appeal to popular strata—peasants, the petty-bourgeoisie, white-collar workers—who were alienated by the proletarian discourse of socialism and in its appeal to elements of a working class fragmented along lines of religion, nationality, and ethnicity.

There was no necessary incompatibility between being a devout Christian and a class-conscious worker. The Christian socialism of Britain's Independent Labour Party was rooted, like popular liberalism, in the nonconformist chapels of northern England. Images of Christ the carpenter adorned the walls of French producer cooperatives in 1848. However, Catholicism's ties to the right wing meant that the French labor movement was stronger where workers were recruited from anticlerical rural regions—the Limousin, the Centre—than from clerical bastions such as Brittany. Catholic workers were alienated by the Left's militant anticlericalism. In 1871 the Paris Commune executed clerical hostages. Churches were burned during Barcelona's *semana trágica,* the "tragic week" in 1909 during which a popular insurrection took over the city. Spanish anarchism tapped the fury of a religious people outraged by the clergy's alliance with the rich. *Obreros conscientes* (self-educated "conscious workers"), spreading the anarchist gospel to wretched landless laborers of Andalusian latifundia, preached of a millennium of social justice once the countryside was purged of taxmen, landowners, the Civil Guard, and priests. Catholic workers in devout

against admitting them. Yet working-class women were active in protests outside the sphere of organized labor. They had long participated in food riots. Miners' wives policed pit villages during strikes, harassing and shaming strikebreakers. In Italy and southern French vineyards, women on picket lines dared troops to shoot the "weaker sex." Women's networks underpinned neighborhood solidarity, organizing tenant protests against landlords and providing abortion advice. As left-wing parties began to win control of some town councils in Britain, France, and Italy by the 1890s, regions such as Galicia and New Castile supported the right wing. The gulf between anticlerical male workers and their devout womenfolk was a feature of Latin Europe, fueling the men's suspicions that women's irrational superstition made them unfit for socialism. German socialism recruited among lapsed Protestants. Catholic workers in the Rhineland and Ruhr often supported the Center Party and Catholic unions.

Religious and ethnic tensions overlapped. Flemish migrants in northeastern French textile towns were criticized by French workers for their clericalism as well as for being strikebreakers. The Catholicism of Liverpool's Irish immigrants provoked a Tory vote among native Protestant workers. Ruhr trade union leaders oscillated between criticizing Polish miners for their docility and clericalism and lamenting their propensity for ill-disciplined wildcat strikes. French steel magnates in Lorraine exploited the cheap labor of Italian immigrants—who lacked the vote—while simultaneously playing on the xenophobia of French workers, who monopolized the skilled jobs, received company housing and voted for the radical Right in the 1890s. Jewish artisans in Paris's Marais district or London's East End were the targets of populist anti-Semitism.

In a Europe of economic rivalries and social Darwinism, workers were not immune to the lure of social imperialism. Elites had long exhibited what might be called class racism, viewing workers as a dark, inferior species—criminal and dangerous classes, who were diagnosed in quasi-biological terms and categorized by emerging criminology as pathologically degenerate. Eugenicists debated restricting the breeding of the poor in the East End slums of outcast London. But welfare legislation was introduced to improve the imperial "racial stock" and workers were re-classified as white. Birmingham workers voted for Tory municipal reformer Joseph Chamberlain, who argued that imperial protection guaranteed the export markets on which jobs depended. On the eve of 1914, mass demonstrations denounced South African mine owners for opening skilled jobs to black workers.

REFORMIST AND REVOLUTIONARY LABOR MOVEMENTS

However, socialist parties were built, and they countered the power of organized capitalism, including cartels and employers' associations. The German model—a mass party affiliated to industrial unions—set the pattern for northern and central Europe, achieving 40 percent electoral support in Finland and 25 percent in Austria, despite growing tensions between German and nationally conscious Czech workers. However, no two societies had identical experiences of class formation and mobilization. The peculiarities of each labor movement reflected historical experiences, culture, the nature of the particular state, employer strategies, and the ideologies available to workers. A plausible—if banal—generalization is that liberal states engendered reformist labor movements and authoritarian regimes engendered radical or revolutionary labor movements.

This latter was clearly true of tsarist autocracy. Unions were illegal in Russia, political protest was clandestine, and troop massacres of workers' demonstrations (Bloody Sunday in 1905; the Lena goldfields shootings in 1912) eroded residual popular loyalty to the tsar. Pragmatic reformism was impossible. While populists placed their hopes in the huge, discontented peasantry, Marxists targeted the small but rapidly growing urban proletariat, particularly St. Petersburg's skilled metalworkers. Yet it is difficult to locate Russian protest in any specific section of the working class, for it involved broad strata of the people. The urban population's ties to village Russia made it difficult to disentangle worker and peasant grievances. Workers' attitudes toward the revolutionary intelligentsia were ambivalent; gratitude was tinged with resentment at their claims that only intellectuals could bring full class consciousness to the workers and channel spontaneous protest into coherent strategies.

The liberal British model was very different. The first industrial nation eliminated its peasantry before 1800. By 1900, it was 80 percent urban. It had a parliamentary tradition. The franchise was gradually extended to broad strata of the working class. The early Industrial Revolution had been a bleak age, marked by appalling slum and factory conditions, periodic mass unemployment, and stagnant real wages. But during the mid-Victorian economic boom, wages rose and employers accepted negotiation with unions, which had been legal since the 1820s. Many trade unionists supported the Liberal Party of Prime Minister William Gladstone, perceived as sympathetic to workers' democratic interests. Popular politics and labor relations became harsher in the Great Depression of 1873–1896. Rising unemployment and employer intransigence challenged illusions of ongoing progress under capitalism. Eventually the Labour Party (1900) emerged because of worker alarm at legal threats to union rights. But the party, which was designed for the pragmatic defense of trade union interests, not to build socialism, attracted only 7 percent of the vote. The British paradox is, thus, that the world's first and largest proletariat produced a small, nonsocialist, workers' party. A dense working-class culture did exist, a distinctive lifestyle identifiable by the 1870s that persisted into the 1950s. This was a world of flat caps, fish and chips, Saturday afternoon soccer, seaside rail excursions, hobbies, and allotment gardens. Its communal and collective values were incarnated in friendly societies (consumer cooperatives with millions of members) and unions. Yet it was an introverted culture, more fatalistic and consolatory than radical, exhibiting little aspiration to challenge bourgeois hegemony. Valuing the liberties guaranteed by the state, including the freedom to bargain collectively, it otherwise wished to be left alone. Monarchy was widely accepted as symbolic of British fair play and a regime that rarely used troops against strikers. Socialism revived after 1880 but found difficulty in penetrating this culture.

In Germany, certain factors encouraged a similar integration of labor into the national political scene. Universal male suffrage came relatively early (1870), as did welfare legislation (the 1880s), which was introduced to woo workers from socialism. Real wages rose gradually. Workers could take patriotic pride in Germany's burgeoning industrial strength, and many were employed in defense industries. However if the labor movement's daily practice was pragmatic, the SPD's official ideology was Marxist. Its revolutionary stance was a response to the more authoritarian face of the Reich. Real power lay with the Junkers, army, and bureaucracy, not with a largely impotent Reichstag. The regime treated labor as enemies of the Reich. Three-tier local suffrage systems kept the left from municipal power. Anti-union laws (1878–1890) and intransigent heavy industrialists hindered the development of collective

Caney the Clown. Photograph from *Street Life in London,* 1878, by John Thomson and Adolphe Smith. Like other photographic surveys of the period, Thomson and Smith's work was intended to draw attention to the problems encountered by the poor and working classes. The text accompanying this photograph describes the difficult life of "Caney," who had been a successful comedic performer until injury forced his retirement. He subsequently supported himself by performing minor repairs for households in the neighborhood of Drury Lane. MARY EVANS PICTURE LIBRARY

bargaining and reformist unionism. Heavy indirect taxation penalized working-class consumers and funded armaments programs. By 1914 labor reformists and radicals were evenly balanced, the latter insisting that hopes of gradual democratization of the Reich were illusory.

Socialism in Germany emerged in the 1870s alongside an emerging working-class culture and before unions were free to organize. It sought to mold working-class life, nurturing an unparalleled alternative culture of libraries, choral and theater groups, and sports clubs. Ninety-five socialist papers sold 1.5 million copies daily. The ideological impact of this remains unclear. Perhaps workers borrowed escapist novels from party libraries rather than Marxist tracts. An emphasis on the classic

German musical and literary repertoire may have encouraged bourgeoisification of the tastes of respectable elements of the working class. Fears of jeopardizing this associational infrastructure may have made party officials reluctant to undertake open resistance to the Reich. Meanwhile, millions of workers outside this subculture, including rough elements of the working class, remained vulnerable to the lure of official patriotic propaganda and of an emerging mass commercial culture.

Reformist strands in French working-class culture were encouraged by the democratic Third Republic. Since the Revolution, labor activists had collaborated with radical republican lawyers and doctors who had flirted with associationist socialist rhetoric. Trade unions were belatedly legalized (1884). The republic sought to normalize industrial relations through arbitration procedures, encouraging reformist trends in the miners' unions through state enforcement of pit safety. Republican secular education appealed to working-class anticlericalism and fed their republican patriotism. Workers' autobiographies spoke affectionately of dedicated republican schoolteachers. Yet the republican/revolutionary tradition was deeply ambiguous. Workers felt betrayed by failures to implement the revolution's egalitarian promises by establishing a social republic. It was republicans who suppressed the Paris Commune in 1871 and still used troops to shoot strikers in major incidents (1891, 1900, 1908). Intransigent employers, reluctant to accept collective bargaining, used company paternalism or scientific management to deny unions shop-floor influence. Welfare was introduced later in France than in Germany and was less extensive. A revolutionary legacy of popular direct action inspired syndicalists, who dominated the Confédération Générale du Travail (CGT) union confederation in the 1900s. Syndicalism's emphasis on worker control appealed to craftsmen and skilled workers, who had once supported producer cooperatives. But it attracted unskilled laborers, dock workers, vineyard laborers, and dissident miners and rail workers critical of their unions' reformism. *Bourses du Travail,* where workers from various occupations met, coordinated regional strike strategies. The French labor movement was notoriously fragmented. Despite the foundation of a single Socialist Party in 1906, squabbling between reformist, Marxist, and quasi-syndicalist factions persisted. French socialist voting (16 percent) and union membership (10 percent) were below the levels in much of Europe. Yet levels of strike militancy and direct action were high.

After 1900, under Giovanni Giolitti, oligarchic Italian liberalism sought to integrate an emerging working class and woo reformist socialists by extending the franchise (1912) and introducing modest welfare measures and industrial relations reforms. But popular national identity remained weak in a peninsula fragmented by linguistic and regional diversities. Po Valley and Apulian landowners, suspicious of Giolitti's conciliatory strategy, hired gunmen to break strikes. Troops were also used against strikers, although fewer proletarian massacres took place than had happened in the 1890s. Maximalist socialists, who indulged in revolutionary rhetoric, and syndicalists were influential, particularly outside the northern industrial towns, whose workers were the principal beneficiaries of Giolitti's policies. *Camera del lavoro,* drawing together both skilled and unskilled workers from a variety of occupations, sustained a radical subversive culture (*souversismo*) that was at odds with the cautious reformism of the Socialist Party and the union confederation leaderships.

DIVERSITY AND CHANGE

The European working class was too diverse to embrace any single strategy or ideology. Many patriotic, religious, deferential, or female workers were beyond the reach of organized labor, although some joined Catholic, company, or other unions. Much worker protest was unorganized. Despite integrationist governmental strategies and rising real wages in western, northern, and central Europe, the scale of labor unrest in the decade before 1914 suggests widespread—although diverse and uncoordinated—frustration and anger. Even Britain experienced quasi-syndicalist strike waves from 1911 through 1914, with miners, rail workers, and dock workers expressing dissatisfaction with union bureaucracies and Labour Party reformism. Syndicalist aspirations for job control, dismissed as archaic by centralized industrial unions, still resonated with craft workers such as the Solingen cutlers in Germany. From Paris to St. Petersburg, skilled workers, faced with the tough work discipline imposed by scientific management, which eroded shop-floor autonomy, responded with small-scale acts of everyday protest—mocking foremen, slowing down their work, sabotaging, and pilfering. In the rapidly expanding Ruhr mining towns of Germany, with low levels of union organization, workers clashed violently with management and police. Labor organizers struggled to contain what they considered the less respectable forms of worker protest. SPD leaders were delighted by a massive Hamburg suffrage reform demonstration in 1905 but blamed lumpen, criminal elements from the docks for subsequent looting and clashes with the police.

The disintegration of labor movement and of working-class communities in late-twentieth- and early-twenty-first-century Europe has prompted skepticism about working-class agency in earlier periods. Postmodernism's emphasis on multiple, flexible identities questions the primacy of work-based identities. It has become difficult to envisage a world where millions of people proclaimed themselves working class and proud of it and saw themselves as the salt, not the scum, of the earth. It is true that many workers' allegiance to labor movements was conditional, pragmatic, and instrumental. No working class is ever definitively made. Capitalism endlessly undermines communities, establishing new industries in fresh locations where workers struggle to establish new solidarities. Doubtless, workers' grasp of socialist theories was sketchy. Yet many workers did believe that history was on their side. The reports of police spies who listened to Hamburg workers' conversations in bars suggested that many ordinary workers had internalized the SPD's vision of the world.

Outside of the repressive regimes of eastern and southern Europe, labor movements had benefited from the liberal constitutional systems established after the 1860s. But, as European liberalism proved reluctant to adapt to mass politics, it was workers' movements that carried progressive hopes for a future world of social justice. Perhaps the march to war in August 1914 suggests that in the last resort patriotism trumped class identity and internationalist class solidarity. Yet many French workers imagined that they were defending their republican homeland against reactionary Kaiserism, just as German workers believed they were defending their hard-won gains against repressive tsarism.

Many such workers, and their counterparts across Europe, participated in the massive labor unrest of 1917 through 1921, which swept away three empires.

See also **Chartism; Class and Social Relations; Cooperative Movements; Engels, Friedrich; Industrial Revolution, Second; Labor Movements; Marx, Karl; Peasants; Socialism; Syndicalism; Utopian Socialism.**

BIBLIOGRAPHY

Bell, Donald H. *Sesto San Giovanni: Workers, Culture, and Politics in an Italian Town, 1880–1922.* New Brunswick, N.J., 1986.

Berger, Stefan, and Angel Smith, eds. *Nationalism, Labour, and Ethnicity: 1870–1939.* Manchester, U.K., 1999.

Berlanstein, Lenard, ed. *Re-Thinking Labor History: Essays on Discourse and Class Analysis.* Urbana, Ill., 1993.

Bonnell, Victoria. *Roots of Rebellion: Workers, Politics, and Organizations in St. Petersburg and Moscow: 1900–1914.* Berkeley, Calif., 1983.

Calhoun, Craig. *The Question of Class Struggle: Social Foundations of Popular Radicalism during the Industrial Revolution.* Chicago, 1982.

Canning, Kathleen. *Gender and Changing Meanings of Work: Structure and Rhetoric in the Making of the Textile Factory Labor Force in Germany: 1850–1914.* Ithaca, N.Y., 1995.

Clark, Anna. *The Struggle for the Breeches: Gender and the Making of the British Working Class.* Berkeley, Calif., 1995.

Evans, Richard. *Proletarians and Politics: Socialism, Protest, and the Working Class in Germany before 1914.* New York, 1990.

Geary, Dick, ed. *Labour and Socialist Movements in Europe before 1914.* New York, 1989.

———. *European Labour Protest: 1848–1945.* London, 1981.

Hogan, Heather. *Forging Revolution: Metalworkers, Managers, and the State in St. Petersburg, 1900–1914.* Bloomington, Ind., 1993.

Kaplan, Temma. *The Anarchists of Andalusia: 1868–1903.* Princeton, N.J., 1977.

Katznelson, Ira, and Aristide Zolberg, eds. *Working-Class Formations: Nineteenth-Century Patterns in Western Europe and the United States.* Princeton, N.J., 1986.

Lidtke, Vernon. *The Alternative Culture: Socialist Labor in Imperial Germany.* New York, 1985.

Maines, Mary Jo. *Taking the Hard Road: Life Course in French and German Workers' Autobiographies in the Era of Industrialization.* Chapel Hill, N.C., 1995.

Merriman, John. *The Margins of City Life: Explorations on the French Urban Frontier, 1815–1851.* New York, 1991.

Miles, Andrew, and Mike Savage. *The Re-making of the British Working Class: 1840–1940.* London, 1994.

Perrot, M. *Strikes in France: 1870–1890.* Leamington Spa, U.K., 1987.

Prothero, I. J. *Radical Artisans in Britain and France: 1830–1870.* Cambridge, U.K., 1997.

Steinberg, Marc. *Fighting Words: Working-Class Formation, Collective Action, and Discourse in Early Nineteenth-Century England.* Ithaca, N.Y., 1999.

Thompson, E. P. *The Making of the English Working Class.* London, 1963.

ROGER MAGRAW

WORLD'S FAIRS. The origins of the world's fair (also known as international exposition, *exposition universelle, esposizione internazionale,* and *Weltausstellung*) lie in the Industrial Revolution, which vastly expanded manufacturing, trade, and transportation in the first half of the nineteenth century. Beginning with London's Great Exhibition in 1851, a series of world's fairs were held in Europe to showcase advances in manufacturing, science, and technology and gradually spread to other parts of the world, including the United States and Australia. The nineteenth-century world's fairs did not exhibit only machines and the products they manufactured. They attempted to summarize, categorize, and evaluate the whole of human experience. Displays of natural products, handmade goods, the fine arts, models, and ethnographic artifacts were also an important part of the exhibitions. Although the world's fairs sought to educate visitors about scientific and technological advances, entertainments and amusements gradually became a central feature of the events and sometimes even overshadowed their industrial component. The world's fairs celebrated international cooperation and peaceful competition among nations, but they were also sites of national rivalry, where countries celebrated their national identities and strove for prestige by exhibiting their manufactures, cultural achievements, and imperial possessions.

World's fairs grew out of the manufacturing exhibitions of the late eighteenth century. Unlike the great medieval fairs, the chief aim of the manufacturing exhibitions and later world's fairs was not buying and selling but exhibiting the latest machines and products in order to stimulate competition and economic progress. In Britain, the Royal Society of Arts held an exhibition of machinery and mechanical inventions in 1761, and small exhibitions of industrial products were held in Geneva in 1789, Hamburg in 1790, and Prague in 1791. The first national exhibition of industrial products, however, took place in France under the Directorate. In 1797 the Marquis d'Avèze, commissioner of the former Royal Manufactories, organized an exhibition of goods with the goal of promoting French industry and stimulating the purchase of the unsold porcelain, tapestries, and carpets that had accumulated since the Revolution and the British naval blockade. The exhibition was so successful that the interior minister, François Neufchâteau, announced plans to hold a series of national exhibitions in temporary buildings specially constructed for this purpose on the Champ-de-Mars. The first was held for three days in 1798 and featured a published catalog of exhibits as well as an official report, which underlined the French ability to compete with British industry. International economic competition was at the core of the industrial exhibition movement from the start.

France continued to hold national manufacturing exhibitions periodically throughout the first half of the nineteenth century, culminating in the 1849 exhibition, which lasted for six months and drew over 4,500 exhibitors. A number of European countries followed the French example, and between 1818 and 1851 national exhibitions were held in Bavaria, Belgium, Ireland, the Netherlands, Prussia, Russia, Spain, and Sweden to promote industrial development. In 1844 Berlin hosted an "All-German Exhibition," which foreshadowed the political unification of the German states. Although the British state showed no interest in organizing national exhibitions, mechanics institutes began organizing educational exhibitions of mechanical inventions and scientific discoveries throughout the country starting in 1837. During the debate on abolishing the protectionist Corn Laws, free-trade advocates organized a "Free-Trade Bazaar" in London's Covent Garden, and after 1847 the Royal Society of Arts sponsored annual national industrial exhibitions in London. The idea of holding an international industrial exhibition to educate domestic producers by exposing them to foreign manufactures was first raised in France, in 1834 and again in 1849, but protectionist arguments warning of foreign competition and industrial espionage proved persuasive and the idea was dropped, only to be picked up by Henry Cole, a member of the Royal Society of Arts, during his visit to the 1849 Paris exhibition. On his return to Britain, Cole discussed the possibility of hosting an international exhibition in London with the president of the Royal Society, Prince Albert, who threw his support behind the project. It was decided to establish a Royal Commission to raise funds and prepare for the exhibition, which was to be self-financing. While Prince Albert is sometimes given credit as the originator of the idea of holding an international exhibition in 1851, Henry Cole and the other members of the Royal Commission were the main organizing force behind the event. The commission was dominated by industrial and financial leaders who were liberal advocates of the economic doctrine of free trade. They saw the exhibition as an opportunity both to demonstrate to the world the virtues of commercial and political liberalism and to promote the export of British manufactures.

LONDON 1851

The Great Exhibition of the Works of Industry of All Nations, as it was called, has often been seen as a self-congratulatory celebration of Britain's confidence in its industrial might. One of the primary motivations for holding an international exhibition, however, was widespread anxiety about the quality of British industrial design. By exposing British manufacturers to the products of their Continental rivals, the exhibition's organizers hoped to stimulate them to improve the quality of their design in order to better compete in world markets. Nor was the nation united behind the Great Exhibition. Although the Corn Laws had been abolished in 1846, Britain was still deeply divided over the issue of free trade, and protectionists claimed that foreign manufacturers would steal British ideas. The memories of the Chartist

demonstrations and the European revolutions of 1848 aroused fears that the exhibition would attract large numbers of workers and foreign revolutionaries to London and lead to public disorder. The biggest controversy was over the permanent exhibition building proposed for Hyde Park, which opponents claimed would spoil the park and necessitate the removal of cherished trees. Hyde Park was saved from disfigurement by the adoption of Robert Paxton's innovative design for a glass-and-iron structure in the form of a basilica that would be high enough to contain trees and that could be disassembled and removed after the exhibition. Paxton's Crystal Palace, as it was dubbed, was the chief wonder of the Great Exhibition. Of immense proportions, it was inspired by the structure of conservatories and constructed using prefabricated components that were quickly assembled on the site in only seventeen weeks. The glass walls and roof permitted natural light to illuminate the Crystal Palace's five naves, the tallest of which soared to the height of Paris's Notre-Dame cathedral. It was sold after the exhibition and moved to south London.

The exhibition was opened by Queen Victoria and Prince Albert on 1 May 1851 in the presence of the ambassadors of the participating nations. It was an immediate success and earned a substantial profit by the time it closed in October. Contrary to the dire predictions of riot and disorder, the crowds attending the exhibition were well behaved, although as a precaution the Duke of Wellington discreetly stationed mounted troops around London before the opening. After a few weeks ticket prices were lowered to one shilling from Monday through Thursday in order to attract all classes of society. Over six million people visited the Great Exhibition, most of whom came to London by railway, some on cheap excursions organized by Thomas Cook. The Crystal Palace contained over 100,000 different exhibits from some fourteen thousand exhibitors. The exhibits were classified in four categories—raw materials, machinery, manufactures, and the fine arts—and thirty subcategories. The classification system reflected the exhibition's emphasis on the manufacturing process but did not exclude the arts or machines not used for industrial production. Exhibits were displayed according to their national origin, however, and only the British section was organized according to the official classification scheme. Foreign countries were free to organize their space as they saw fit. British exhibits, including those of the colonies, occupied half of the space in the Crystal Palace, while the other half held the displays of the thirty-eight other countries that participated in the exhibition. The physical arrangement of the exhibits was often random and confusing to the visitors who beheld the vast assortment of machines, models, agricultural produce, and art. Although the intention of the exposition was to educate the public about the processes and products of industry, it was also a great spectacle. The so-called lions of the exhibition included the Koh-i-noor diamond, the queen of Spain's jewels, the Gothic medieval court, the collection of stuffed animals from Württemburg, and a crystal fountain in which flowed eau de cologne. Among the other exhibits that received the most attention were the steam-powered working machines and electric telegraph in the British section, photography in the French section, the Colt revolvers and McCormick harvester in the American section, and the cornucopia of imperial treasures presented by the East India Company. Full-scale examples of improved houses for workers, designed by Prince Albert, were displayed outside the Crystal Palace.

The Great Exhibition was more than a mere display of goods; it was also an international competition that measured and compared the technological, economic, and artistic development of each nation. Adopting the practice of the French national exhibitions, the organizers appointed juries to evaluate the exhibits and gave prizes to those deemed best; 170 Council medals were awarded for innovation and 2,918 Prize medals for excellence in workmanship. Britain, with over half of the exhibitors, received the most awards, but France came in a close second even though it was represented by many fewer exhibitors. Most of Britain's Council medals were awarded for machinery, while France's were more evenly distributed among the various categories of classification. The Great Exhibition, while it confirmed Britain's leadership in manufacturing, was also a victory for French design. The German states won few Council medals but received numerous Prize medals, while the United States obtained few medals of either type, though the exhibition did raise awareness of its growing industrial power. After the exhibition ended the Royal Commission

Interior of the Crystal Palace, Great Exhibition, London, 1851. Designed by architect Joseph Paxton for the first of the major European exhibitions, the Crystal Palace was a vast glass and steel enclosure that provided an impressive showcase for the industrial and aesthetic treasures displayed within. ©HISTORICAL PICTURE ARCHIVE/CORBIS

published a voluminous official catalog containing detailed descriptions of every nation's exhibits together with discussions of the historical and scientific background. Other nations and some American states also published official reports and catalogs in which they evaluated the exhibition and its exhibits.

PARIS 1855

The Great Exhibition and its Crystal Palace quickly spawned imitations, eventually leading to a succession of international expositions throughout Europe and the world. Dublin and New York each held international exhibitions in 1853, but the next truly international world's fair took place in Paris in 1855. The French were determined to respond to the Great Exhibition and outdo their British economic rivals, and planning for the 1855 Exposition Universelle began in 1851. Like the Great

Exhibition, the first French world's fair celebrated international peace and cooperation, despite the ongoing conflict with Russia in the Crimea. Napoleon III intended the exhibition to showcase the achievements of his new Second Empire, to demonstrate that Paris was the artistic center of the world, and to encourage French industry to become more competitive. The exhibition was also used to strengthen relations with Britain, France's ally in the Crimean War, and Victoria and Albert visited Paris at Napoleon's invitation.

A permanent exhibition building, the Palace of Industry, was erected on the Champs-Elysées, where it remained in use until 1897. Although constructed of iron and glass like Paxton's Crystal Palace, it was more traditional in appearance, for its iron frame was hidden by a classical facade. It turned out that the Palace of Industry could not hold all the exhibits, and the machinery and fine arts had to be placed in secondary structures erected nearby. The 1855 exhibition was in many respects similar to that of 1851, but larger in size and with more exhibitors, about half of them French. Attendance was lower, at just over five million visitors, and the exhibition lost money. French and British industry again dominated the exhibition and took the majority of the awards. There were few innovations to be found in 1855, but among the novelties on display were new materials such as cement and aluminum and the new technique for electroplating silver. The British and French empires were prominently displayed, with large sections devoted to India and Algeria. The exhibition also contained a thematic section devoted to improvements in the lives of the working classes, which contained examples of inexpensive consumer goods and models of improvements in housing. The French placed much greater emphasis on the fine arts, in which France excelled, than the British had in 1851. About five thousand works of art from twenty-nine countries were exhibited in 1855, among them paintings by Jean-Auguste-Dominique Ingres, Eugène Delacroix, and the Pre-Raphaelites. Two of Gustave Courbet's canvases were not accepted for exhibition, so the young artist held his own exhibition outside the fine arts pavilion, the first of a number of alternative art exhibitions held by disgruntled artists at world's fairs.

Machinery on display, London International Exhibition, 1862. ©HULTON-DEUTSCH COLLECTION/CORBIS

LONDON 1862

Britain attempted to follow up on the success of the Great Exhibition with the International Exhibition of 1862. Yet the sequel failed to arouse the anticipated interest despite its larger size and the inclusion of many more works of art. The enormous brick building that was chosen to house the exhibition, whose size was its only outstanding feature, never gained the popularity of the Crystal Palace, which was still standing in its new location in south London. Prince Albert's death in late 1861 cast a shadow over the exhibition, while the United States, in the midst of a civil war, sent only a few items to display. The shortage of cotton caused by the war had crippled Britain's textile industry and reduced its exhibits. A number of technical innovations where on show, however, such as a calculating machine and Henry Bessemer's newly developed process for making steel. The exhibition attracted only slightly more visitors than in 1851, despite improvements in transport and communication, and closed with a substantial deficit. The 1862 exhibition's poor showing suggests that ever-bigger copies of the Great Exhibition had limited public appeal and that simply displaying a multitude of machines and objects was not enough to draw the crowds.

PARIS 1867

Although Dublin hosted a small international exhibition in 1865, the next important world's fair was held in Paris in 1867. The Exposition Universelle of 1867 established Paris as the center of the world's fair movement and significantly changed the look of subsequent world's fairs. Organized by the Saint-Simonian Frédéric Le Play, this was the first world's fair to expand outside of the main exhibition building, which was surrounded by international restaurants, an amusement park, and separate national pavilions constructed by the participating nations. Among the structures dotting the exhibition grounds and giving them a festive atmosphere were a picturesque Swiss chalet, an Indian temple, a Tunisian palace, a Gothic cathedral, and an English lighthouse. It was also the first world's fair to remain open in the evening and to include non-European peoples as part of the exhibits, in North African *tableaux vivants,* for example, and an Egyptian bazaar with native craftsmen and camel attendants. These innovations became standard in subsequent world's fairs. The Parisian excursion boats, or *bateaux mouches,* made their first appearance at the exhibition to take fairgoers sightseeing on the river Seine.

The elliptical main exhibition hall, an enormous iron-and-glass structure a mile in circumference, was designed to facilitate the classification and comparison of the displays by grouping them together by both product and nation. Breaking with the tradition established at the Crystal Palace of organizing the displays along national lines, Le Play attempted to combine two organizing systems: products and the nations that produced them. Concentric halls, each devoted to a particular category of objects, ringed a central garden in the interior of the exhibition hall. Each nation's products were arranged along lines radiating from the center and intersecting the concentric bands. This two-part classification system, much more ambitious than the schemes used in previous world's fairs, aimed to present a complete picture of human activity throughout the world from prehistoric times to 1867. Another concept introduced was the use of thematic displays of the "History of Work" and the "History of the Earth," which sought to put the entire exhibition in historical perspective. In seeking to organize, classify, and exhibit all of human history, the exhibition con-structed an epic of material progress in which European civilization played the leading role and created the illusion that scientific knowledge could order and control the world. The outer concentric hall contained the Gallery of Machines, a raised area affording views across the interior of the exhibition. A hydraulic elevator carried visitors to an observation platform on the roof. Among the novel exhibits in 1867 were petroleum, an American rocking chair, artificial limbs, the telegraph, and a working model of France's latest engineering feat, the Suez Canal. Demonstrations of new diving equipment were held each day, where the public could see men remain underwater for several hours in an iron tank. Among the spectators was Jules Verne, who incorporated the inventions he saw at the 1867 exposition in his novel *Twenty-Thousand Leagues under the Sea* (*Vingt mille lieues sous les mers,* 1870).

Like the 1855 exposition, that of 1867 celebrated the progress and prosperity ostensibly brought to France by the Napoleon III's Second Empire. France's colonies were prominently displayed, with separate sections devoted to Algeria, Tunis, and Morocco. The empire's proclaimed social ideals were manifested in an entire section of the exposition devoted to social welfare. It included exhibits of model sanitary housing for the poor and social projects to improve the lives of workers. Napoleon himself contributed a design for a workers' housing project, which unsurprisingly won a grand prize. The exposition, while a great success that attracted nearly seven million visitors and made a respectable profit, turned out to be the swan song of the Second Empire. The festivities were marred by the June execution of Napoleon's protégé Maximilian in Mexico and the return of his widow to Paris. King Victor Emmanuel II demonstrated his anger at Napoleon's meddling in Italian affairs by avoiding the exposition, while during his visit to Paris the tsar of Russia was nearly assassinated by a Polish patriot. Discontent with Napoleon's policies was growing at home, and the emperor's critics voiced their opinions more and more loudly. In addition, Prussia's rapid defeat of Austria the preceding year called into question whether France would long remain the leading power on the Continent. One of the sensations of the exposition was a fifty-ton steel cannon made by the German firm Krupp. Three years later the same cannon would be used to bombard Paris during the Franco-Prussian War.

LONDON 1871–1874

The four London International Exhibitions held from 1871 to 1874 represented an attempt to limit the size of world's fairs by focusing each year on specific categories of exhibits, together with scientific discoveries and the fine arts. They also took steps to avoid the international rivalry that had characterized previous world's fairs by organizing the displays according to class rather than nationality and by opting not to award prizes. Ten exhibitions were planned to be held over ten years in an assortment of temporary buildings erected near London's Albert Hall, which hosted a series of concerts. The first exhibition was relatively successful, but declining interest led to the decision to end the exhibitions after the 1874 season.

VIENNA 1873

The nineteenth century's only Germanic world's fair was held in Austria in 1873. The Vienna Weltausstellung marked the twenty-fifth anniversary of the coronation of Emperor Francis Joseph I and was intended to celebrate the country's recovery from its political and economic setbacks in the 1850s and 1860s, which included the separation of Hungary, as well as to publicize the ambitious program of urban planning and reconstruction that had made Vienna one of the grandest cities in Europe. The exhibition was held in Vienna's wooded Prater park on the banks of the Danube and was the first world's fair to have separate buildings devoted to industry, machinery, agriculture, and art, an innovation borrowed from Moscow's Polytechnic Exhibition of 1872. The main exhibition building was the Palace of Industry, an ornate structure in the Italian Renaissance style that was designed to be used as a permanent home for the Corn Exchange after the fair ended. Its vast nave was a half-mile in length, with sixteen galleries branching off to the sides. At the center was a rotunda under the world's largest dome. Within the Palace of Industry the exhibits were organized geographically, with the participating countries arranged from east to west and Austria at the center. In the park surrounding the Palace of Industry stood the buildings devoted to machinery, agricul-

ture, and art as well as numerous international pavilions and entertainment venues. While housing exhibitions at earlier world's fairs had focused on the needs of urban workers, at Vienna there was an extensive exhibit of rural homes from around the world. Visitors were entertained by open-air concerts at the Strauss pavilion, military bands, and gypsy musicians.

The Vienna exhibition devised the most complex system of display categories used at any nineteenth-century world's fair, comprising some twenty-six different categories, including new ones such as transportation, forestry management, the ownership of ideas, the education of women and children, the healing arts, and the living conditions of the common people. It focused more extensively than earlier fairs on social and educational issues and even had a category devoted to the cultivation of good taste among the population. Germany participated in the Vienna exhibition for the first time as a united nation and, after Austria, contributed the largest number of industrial exhibits, while France managed to mount a credible display despite the devastating defeat it had recently endured in the Franco-Prussian War. It was Japan, however, that made the biggest splash in its first large-scale effort at a world's fair. Japan's exhibits introduced Europeans to its art, culture, and industry, while the Japanese delegation to the Vienna exhibition carefully studied Western technology and industrial organization and published their observations in ninety-six volumes after returning home.

The 1873 exhibition was beset by a series of unfortunate events. The Vienna stock exchange was hit by a worldwide financial crisis and collapsed less than a week after Emperor Francis Joseph opened the exhibition, resulting in an economic depression and soaring unemployment. Fears of a repetition of the cholera outbreak of 1872 kept many visitors away from the city, while heavy rains damaged the exhibition buildings in late June. The exhibition suffered a huge financial loss, even though by the time it closed it succeeded in attracting more than seven million visitors.

PARIS 1878

In 1878 France's newborn Third Republic held a world's fair in Paris to demonstrate to the world that the nation had recovered from the Franco-Prussian War of 1870–1871. The Exposition Universelle of 1878 was a celebration of the republic and of French civilization, and it contributed to healing the divisions caused by the *seize mai* political crisis of the preceding year. As Victor Hugo enthused, "The world is our witness that France makes good use of defeat." However, some critics argued that France could not afford such a lavish expenditure when it had only recently paid off its indemnity to Germany, while French churchmen objected to the secular tone of the fair, for the republic forbade religious remarks in the opening ceremonies. French artists who specialized in battle scenes were enraged that the fair also forbade the exhibition of paintings whose subject was the Franco-Prussian War. The memory of France's defeat was still fresh, and the German government was pointedly not invited, although German artists participated unofficially. Sixteen million people attended the fair, but it closed with a sizable deficit.

The fair was organized similarly to its predecessor in 1867. The centerpiece of the exhibition was the Palace of Industry on the Champ-de-Mars, a rectangular building that housed most of the displays, which were again ordered by their class in one direction and by nationality in another. Visitors could choose to examine a single class of manufactures from around the world or all the manufactures of a particular country. A striking innovation was the Street of Nations in the central court of the Palace of Industry, where foreign nations built separate entrances to their exhibits, resulting in an eclectic assortment of national architectural styles. Some nations also built pavilions across the Seine in the Trocadéro Park, which was dotted with curiosities such as a Japanese farm, an Algerian café, and the head of Auguste Bartholdi's Statue of Liberty, the hand and torch of which had been exhibited two years earlier at the 1876 Centennial International Exhibition in Philadelphia. Exhibits by large manufacturers, such as the Singer Company's sewing machines and Schneider-Creusot's enormous pile driver, were very prominent at the fair and a sign of the coming domination of world's fairs by corporate displays and pavilions. A more exotic venue at the 1878 world's fair was the Street of Cairo, a collection of shops and a bazaar where North Africans were employed to serve visitors. The Cairo street proved so popular that it

became a staple fixture of world's fairs, increasing in size with each fair until it constituted an entertainment zone unto itself, with restaurants, cafés, and belly dancers in addition to dozens of shops.

The 1878 world's fair was the first to employ technology to control the temperature, through a system of pipes that carried water from the Seine under the raised floor of the Palace of Industry. Water was also harnessed to power hydraulic elevators that speeded visitors to the top of Trocadéro Hill, where a permanent palace was erected for concerts, art exhibits, and international congresses that were held as part of the world's fair. Some of the congresses had long-lasting consequences, such as the establishment of the International Postal Union, the introduction of international copyright laws, and the adoption of Braille as the recognized international system of touch reading. One of the most sensational events during the fair was the illumination of the Avenue and Place de l'Opera with Thomas Edison's new electric lighting. Edison's phonograph, first displayed to the public at the Philadelphia Centennial Exhibition in 1876, was introduced to Europeans at the 1878 Paris fair to great acclaim. Edison himself, self-taught and of modest origins, was lionized by much of the French press as an example of what the human mind could achieve in the absence of social barriers.

AMSTERDAM 1883
The 1880s and 1890s witnessed an explosion in the number of world's fairs and smaller international exhibitions, as the exhibition phenomenon spread far beyond Europe. The United States had hosted its first major world's fair in Philadelphia to celebrate the centennial of the American Revolution in 1876, and Australia held world's fairs in Sydney in 1879–1880, Melbourne in 1880–1881 and 1888–1889, and Adelaide in 1887–1888. Other international exhibitions took place in Atlanta (1881 and 1895), Boston (1883–1884), Calcutta (1883–1884), New Orleans (1884–1885), Antwerp (1885 and 1894), Edinburgh (1886), Glasgow (1888), Barcelona (1888), Chicago (1893), San Francisco (1894), Brussels (1897), Guatemala City (1897), Nashville (1897), and Stockholm (1897).

The first and only Dutch world's fair, the International Colonial and Trade Exposition of 1883, was the first to place empire at center stage.

While every world's fair since London's Great Exhibition had included numerous displays of the products of Europe's overseas empires, their main focus had been industry. The Amsterdam world's fair presented empire as spectacle. Unlike French world's fairs, the Dutch fair was organized by businessmen without government financial assistance, although the government did give its approval to the project. The facade of the main building, designed by a French architect, was an exotic pastiche of Indian motifs that curiously had no relation to the architecture of the Netherlands' own colonial possessions in the East and West Indies. Separate pavilions were devoted to colonial exhibits, the city of Amsterdam, and the monarchy, while arts and ethnographic displays were presented in the newly built Rijksmuseum. Only the Netherlands and Belgium mounted full-scale exhibits, but most European nations were represented as well as the United States, Haiti, Brazil, Uruguay, Venezuela, Japan, China, Turkey, Persia, and Siam. About one million people visited the fair, but its significance was much greater than attendance figures indicate. For the first time, a world's fair displayed villages inhabited by colonial peoples, who entertained visitors in displays of their native customs. Exhibits of exotic non-Western peoples by itinerant showmen dated back at least to the sixteenth century and were commonplace throughout Europe by the second half of the nineteenth century. Starting with the Amsterdam fair, however, the "native village" was a regular feature of European and American world's fairs. A mixture of commercial sensationalism, pseudoscientific anthropology, and imperial power, it served as a vivid contrast to the ultramodern technologies on display and seemed to confirm assumptions about the superiority of European civilization. In the era of the "new imperialism," colonial exhibits became an increasingly ostentatious component of the world's fairs, which celebrated colonialism as a force for human progress.

PARIS 1889
Held to commemorate the centennial of the French Revolution, the Paris Exposition Universelle of 1889 produced one of the modern world's great iconic images: the Eiffel Tower, a cast-iron tower that at 300 meters high was the tallest structure ever erected. Cherished today as the symbol of Paris, the naked iron skeleton of Gustave Eiffel's tower was initially seen by many Parisians as a hideous defilement of the city's skyline, by others as an expression of the primitive, barbaric power of industrial society. The tower was a hit with the public, however, and almost two million people ascended it by elevator during the exposition, including the Prince of Wales, W. F. "Buffalo Bill" Cody, Sarah Bernhardt, and Thomas Edison. The central axis of the fair on the Champ-de-Mars ran under the Eiffel Tower to the entrance of the main exhibition building, at the rear of which stood the Gallery of Machines, another feat of modern construction technology whose glass roof enclosed fifteen acres of exhibition space without support from internal columns. Among the mechanical wonders on display were a steam-powered tricycle, a German gasoline-powered motorcar, and a huge exhibit of Thomas Edison's multitude of inventions, including an electric phonograph that charmed the crowds by alternately playing the French and American national anthems. From electrically powered moving platforms suspended over the gallery visitors could look out onto the humming machinery in motion below. Like the Eiffel Tower, the Gallery of Machines offered the public spectacular views and constituted an attraction in itself, apart from the technology it exhibited, which had become part of the entertainment.

Some eighty other buildings filled the Champ-de-Mars and the banks of the Seine, containing displays of foreign industrial manufactures, the fine arts, horticulture, and agricultural products and machinery, as well as thematic displays such as one devoted to "Social Economy," an attempt by the French government to respond to growing labor unrest by displaying the gains made by the working class under the Third Republic. More successful was Charles Garnier's history of human habitation, comprising forty-nine structures depicting the evolution of housing through the ages. Another historical display used stationary tableaux to illustrate the development of human labor from prehistory to the present. The Trocadéro Palace contained ethnographic exhibits that included works of African, Oceanic, and pre-Columbian art. Many countries erected national pavilions, among which Mexico's contribution was an Aztec palace. A large section of the exposition was devoted to the French colonial empire, with palaces and pagodas designed by French architects to

The Exposition Universelle, Paris, 1889. This view of the fairgrounds shows the position and prominence of the Eiffel Tower.
©Corbis

house exhibits from colonies in Indochina, India, and Africa, where visitors could ride in rickshaws powered by Indochinese. As in 1878, colonial peoples were brought to Paris to populate villages representing Senegal, Tonkin, Tahiti, and other French imperial possessions. Paul Gauguin was inspired to go to Tahiti by the impression made on him by the living examples of "noble savages" he saw at the fair's Tahitian village.

Pleasure and entertainment eclipsed the industrial exhibits at the 1889 world's fair, which marked an important shift from the original focus of world's fairs on educating the public about advances in science and technology. In addition to the exotic spectacles offered by native villages,

concerts, balls, and theater performances were regularly held in the exposition's park, which contained a variety of international restaurants and cafés providing refreshments to fairgoers. At the Pavilion of Military Aeronautics, visitors could make an ascent in a tethered balloon, while in the Palace of Liberal Arts they could closely inspect a giant globe of the earth by riding to the top in an elevator and descending along an inclined walkway. Electricity was widely used to enhance the festive atmosphere, illuminating the fairgrounds by night to prolong visitors' enjoyment of the attractions in the park, which included a fountain display with colored lights. Each evening a tricolor searchlight atop the Eiffel Tower cast its beam across the darkened skies over Paris. A more serious attitude prevailed at the dozens of official international congresses that took place during the exposition and were devoted to topics ranging from alcohol abuse to women's role in the labor force. There were also some unofficial congresses, one of which, held by Marxist socialists, founded the Second International and adopted May First as the international holiday of labor.

Although some European monarchies refused the invitation to a world's fair celebrating the French Revolution, most countries were represented, if unofficially, by their firms, who refused to sacrifice publicity and profit for political considerations. Even members of the royal families of Britain and Russia, both of whom had vocally refused to take part in a celebration that paid tribute to the French Revolution, visited the exposition nevertheless. One of the most successful world's fairs of the nineteenth century, the 1889 Paris exposition attracted over thirty million visitors and even made a modest profit. It almost certainly boosted France's self-esteem, drew attention to France's colonial empire, and helped to draw a line over the divisive Boulanger affair of the preceding winter.

PARIS 1900

Less than three years after the close of the 1889 exposition the French government announced plans for another one in 1900, partly in order to seize the initiative from Germany, which had been considering holding its first world's fair. In France the 1890s were marked by political scandals, economic and demographic stagnation, and a growing sense of the nation's declining influence in the world. The disunity of the Third Republic had been only temporarily obscured by the triumphant success of the 1889 fair, and the exposition of 1900 aroused enormous controversy while still in the planning stages. Critics claimed that it would benefit only Paris to the detriment of the provincial economy, that it would morally corrupt the French, and that it would do nothing to further the interests of French businesses. Not since the preparations for London's Great Exhibition of 1851 had a world's fair aroused such concerted opposition. Supporters countered with arguments that emphasized the stimulus it would give to exports and the jobs it would create and contended that the honor and international prestige of France

were at stake. Although domestic opposition was overcome, diplomatic crises also threatened the exposition. The Fashoda crisis of 1898, when France backed down before British forces in East Africa, strained relations between the two countries, and French support for the Boers in their war with Britain did nothing to improve matters. The United States was insulted by the location its pavilion was allotted and had to be mollified with a more prominent position. More importantly, the drawn-out Dreyfus affair tarnished France's reputation and led some nations to consider a boycott of the exposition, a prospect averted only when Dreyfus finally received a presidential pardon in September 1899.

The world's fair of 1900 was the largest ever held in Paris. It attracted more than fifty million visitors, short of the official projection of sixty million but still a record that was only surpassed in 1967 at Montreal's Expo 67. Spread out on the Champ-de-Mars, Trocadéro Hill, along the banks of the Seine, and in the Bois de Vincennes (connected to the rest of the exposition by the city's new Métro line), it comprised over 80,000 exhibits divided into 18 classes and 121 subclasses. It was the last European world's fair to attempt to summarize the achievements of Western civilization, although its vast size and the chaotic arrangement of the multitude of exhibits made it almost impossible for visitors to take it all in. As at previous world's fairs, many worthy international congresses on various subjects took place, included two organized by French feminists. An event that heralded a new form of national competition for prestige was the second meeting of the modern Olympic Games, held in the Bois de Vincennes.

There was little in the way of architectural innovation at the 1900 exposition. The official buildings, such as the Grand Palais, the Petit Palais, and the Palace of Electricity, had their iron internal structures hidden by facades decorated in the ornate neoclassical style favored by the academics of the École des Beaux-Arts. On the left bank of the Seine the Street of Nations, inspired by the one in the 1878 exposition, was lined by foreign pavilions in historical national styles, such as Germany's sixteenth-century Rathaus. France's ally Russia occupied an enormous amount of space on Trocadéro Hill, where in addition to a Kremlinesque national pavilion it also contributed a pavilion of Asiatic Russia, in which visitors could make a simulated journey along the Trans-Siberian Railway. Finland, although part of the Russian Empire, asserted its separate identity with one of the most original buildings of the exposition, a superb national pavilion designed by Eliel Saarinen using native woods and decorative motifs inspired by Scandinavian nature. Another noteworthy structure was the theater of the American expatriate dancer Loie Fuller, designed in the art nouveau style by Henri Sauvage. Although the exposition was not the triumph of art nouveau that it is sometimes made out to be but rather an eclectic hodgepodge of extravagant and colorful buildings, elements of art nouveau were present in a number of structures, including the main staircase of the Grand Palais, René Binet's Monumental Gateway to the exposition grounds on the Place de la Concorde, and the fashionable Pavillon Bleu restaurant. The best examples, however, were to be found in the rooms of the German, Austrian, and Hungarian pavilions and in the entrances to Hector Guimard's Métro stations.

Among the new technologies on display were X-rays, wireless telegraphy, bicycles, automobiles, turbines, and cinema, but the exposition's massive use of electric lighting was the biggest marvel. Paul Morand, a contemporary chronicler of the exposition, dubbed electricity "the religion of 1900." In the Palace of Electricity visitors could watch the dynamos at work supplying electricity to power machinery and illuminate the exposition grounds at night to create a fairy-tale landscape. The Monumental Gateway, the bridges over the Seine, and the Eiffel Tower sparkled with thousands of incandescent lights, giving Paris a glimpse of the luminous future. Loie Fuller's dance performances, in which she employed colored lights and electric arc lamps together with her trademark flowing scarves, were a sensation. Another hit, the Cinéorama, used phonograph music, colored filmstrips, and ten synchronized projectors on a 360-degree screen to simulate a balloon ride in a vivid demonstration of the possibilities afforded by new technologies of entertainment.

The 1900 world's fair had an unprecedented number of commercial venues operated by private firms and businessmen. All the major French department stores had their own separate pavilions, as did the American McCormick Harvesting Machine Company and France's Schneider metallurgical firm. There were 207 restaurants and 58 different attractions with separate entrance fees, giving the exposition the character of a vast amusement park. Visitors could travel back in time in Vieux Paris or Andalusia in the Time of the Moors, take in the sights of faraway places in the Tour du Monde, make a sea voyage to Constantinople at the Maréorama, and view the moon through the world's largest telescope. An electric-powered moving sidewalk, modeled on the one that had made its debut at Chicago's World's Columbian Exposition in 1893, offered a novel terrestrial experience to those not daring enough to ride the giant Ferris wheel, another Chicago import. In addition to the extensive official colonial displays of France, Britain, Belgium, the Netherlands, and Portugal, there were commercial exhibits of native villages inhabited by African and Asian people as well as the ever-popular Street of Cairo and its belly dancers. The 1900 exposition was noteworthy, however, for one attempt to challenge the prevailing imperial and racist images of "primitive," non-European peoples in W. E. B. Du Bois's Exhibit of American Negroes, located in the Social Economy section of the exposition alongside other American exhibits of tenement houses and libraries. It contained materials on African American history, contemporary social and economic conditions, educational institutions, and literature.

Contemporary assessments of the 1900 world's fair were mixed. To be sure, the exposition had attracted an unprecedented number of visitors and probably infused money into the French economy, although a number of contemporary critics claimed that it was a financial catastrophe. Paris got new buildings and a new bridge over the Seine, the Pont d'Alexandre III. Most of the businessmen who had paid dearly for concessions lost money, however, and eventually got a partial refund of their fees. To some observers the exposition had revealed France's industrial weakness. The German technical and artistic exhibits outshone those of France, adding to French anxieties about their nation's decline. Others were struck by the contrast between the vast material riches on display and the inability of the exposition to adequately classify them in the interests of

The Grand Palais, Exposition Universelle, Paris, 1900. The opulent Beaux-Arts-style Grand Palais, designed under the supervision of lead architect Charles-Louis Girault, displayed fine art from around the world during the exposition. ©MICHAEL MASLAN HISTORIC PHOTOGRAPHS/CORBIS

scientific progress. Although some scholars have linked such pessimistic assessments of the 1900 world's fair to a fin-de-siècle loss of faith in science, reason, and progress among intellectuals, it is doubtful that their disillusionment was shared by the millions of ordinary visitors.

The 1900 Exposition Universelle was the climax of the series of world's fairs held between 1851 and World War I. Although world's fairs were held between 1900 and 1914 in Glasgow (1901), St. Louis (1904), Liège (1905), Christchurch, New Zealand (1906–1907), Dublin (1907), Brussels (1910), and Ghent (1913), none of them approached the size or scope of the one in Paris in 1900. By 1900 world's fairs were increasingly seen in Europe as a financial burden on their host countries and the participants, a phenomenon known as "exposition fatigue." Established firms were sometimes reluctant to interrupt their production by

shifting resources and labor into preparations for a world's fair, although new firms welcomed the opportunity to attract publicity and perhaps win prize medals for their products. In 1907 an international federation of exhibitors was set up in Paris to deal with issues relating to world's fairs, and in 1912 seventeen nations signed a convention to regulate international expositions. Although the convention was never ratified due to the outbreak of World War I, efforts to bring world's fairs under international supervision resumed after the war, eventually resulting in the formation of the Bureau of International Expositions, formed in Paris in 1931, which today is the regulatory body that supervises the conduct of world's fairs.

CONCLUSION

The great nineteenth-century world's fairs or universal expositions were regarded by contemporaries as historic events that had an enormous international impact. They spread ideas, created a universal exhibition language, and marked the stages of the rapid developments in applied science and technology in Europe and the world during the second half of the nineteenth century. One of the most important contributions of the world's fairs was to facilitate technology transfer, acquainting people from different countries with the latest improvements in technology and industrial design. Some manufacturers, such as Colt, McCormick, Edison, Bessemer, and Krupp, were very successful in using the world's fairs to find new markets for their products. The international exhibitions promoted the idea of social progress, too, through exhibits devoted to model housing, education, and public health issues. Exhibition techniques and novelties were also transferred from one world's fair to the next and between Europe and the rest of the world. Chicago's Ferris wheel of 1893 was a response to Paris's Eiffel Tower of 1889, and its success led the 1900 Paris world's fair to acquire its own Ferris wheel. The world's fairs influenced and were influenced by commercial entertainments and museum displays, from which they borrowed native villages and other ethnographic exhibits.

For Karl Marx, the nineteenth-century world's fairs were evidence of how capitalism had overcome national boundaries, but they were also important expressions of national rivalry and of national identities. France in particular consistently used international expositions to assert its superiority in the arts and its universal civilizing mission, which is why art exhibitions and displays of colonies and their inhabitants were such a key component of French exhibits. The world's fairs also offered opportunities to smaller or peripheral countries to assert or construct national identities in an international setting. Japan was remarkably successful in promoting its culture and industry at world's fairs, while Mexico forged a distinctive image of itself as a non-European but modern and progressive nation. Finland used world's fairs in the late nineteenth century to project a unique national identity in the face of St. Petersburg's campaign of Russification. Imperialism was a constant presence at the world's fairs from the Great Exhibition until well into the twentieth century. The ever more lavish colonial displays of the European empires raised their national prestige, reinforced existing cultural

and racial stereotypes, and proclaimed the progressive influence of European colonialism.

World's fairs have been interpreted as expressions of nationalism, imperialism, racism, consumerism, and capitalism, which they were. Yet they were also social rituals, and as such it is not surprising that they reflected the dominant ideologies of their historical settings. The world's fairs reveal much about the outlooks and intentions of their organizers, but their impact on the public is difficult to assess. Their size meant that it was impossible for most ordinary visitors to study the multitude of displays more than superficially. People went to the world's fairs not only to be educated but also to be entertained and have a good time, and throughout the nineteenth century the entertainments on offer grew more and more spectacular until the world's fairs resembled giant amusement parks.

The world's fairs' emphasis on the latest developments in human endeavor meant that they were a fleeting presence in the cities that hosted them, but they left behind a considerable material legacy. London's network of cultural institutions in south Kensington was founded with the profits from the Great Exhibition, while the Crystal Palace served as an exhibition hall and cultural center in south London until it was destroyed by fire in 1936. The profits from the Glasgow International Exhibition of 1888 funded the construction of the City Museum and Art Gallery on the exhibition grounds in Kelvingrove Park. In Paris, structures erected for its *expositions universelles* were often reused for years before being demolished to make way for new buildings for other expositions. The Trocadéro Palace stood until 1936 when it was replaced by the Chaillot Palace for the 1937 Exposition Universelle, while the Eiffel Tower, the Grand Palais, and the Petit Palais are today visible reminders of the impact of world's fairs on the appearance of Paris.

Their impact on art and architecture was mixed. By opening the 1855 and 1867 expositions to non-academic painters, Napoleon III undermined the power of the Académie des Beaux-Arts to determine taste, yet conservatives dominated the committees that selected works for display at the world's fairs until World War I. Only the Centennale exhibition in 1900 included representatives of modern trends in painting such as impressionism and postimpressionism. The Crystal Palace was an architectural sensation and spawned replicas in New York, Dublin, Munich, and other cities, but neoclassical, baroque, and Renaissance influences predominated in most of the main exhibition buildings constructed for world's fairs before World War I. Although art nouveau was very much in evidence at the 1900 world's fair, the Glasgow international exhibition of 1901 was dominated by Spanish Renaissance architecture and bore no trace of Glasgow's own modernist style, developed by Charles Rennie Mackintosh and his followers. National architectural styles incorporating folk elements and themes were developed for their world's fair pavilions by some countries, while European architects designed pavilions for colonies in "indigenous" styles that sometimes served after independence as the basis of new national styles. These national and indigenous styles are perhaps the most lasting architectural legacy of the world's fairs, for they influenced the development of the entertainment environment of the twentieth-century theme park.

See also **Civilization, Concept of; Consumerism; Crystal Palace; Imperialism; Industrial Revolution, Second; Popular and Elite Culture; Second International; Tourism.**

BIBLIOGRAPHY

Allwood, John. *The Great Exhibitions.* London, 1977.

Auerbach, Jeffrey A. *The Great Exhibition of 1851: A Nation on Display.* New Haven, Conn., 1999.

Celik, Zeynep, and Leila Kinney. "Ethnography and Exhibitionism at the Expositions Universelles." *Assemblages* 13 (1990): 34–59.

Chandler, Arthur. "Revolution: The Paris Exposition Universelle of 1889." *World's Fair* 7, no. 1 (1987): 1–9.

Curti, Merle. "America at the World's Fairs, 1851–1893." *American Historical Review* 55, no. 3 (1950): 833–856.

Davis, John R. *The Great Exhibition.* Stroud, U.K., 1999.

Fauser, Annegret. *Musical Encounters at the 1889 Paris World's Fair.* Rochester, N.Y., 2005.

Findling, John, and Kimberley D. Pelle, eds. *Historical Dictionary of World's Fairs and Expositions, 1851–1988.* Westport, Conn., 1990.

Greenhalgh, Paul. *Ephemeral Vistas: The Expositions Universelles, Great Exhibitions, and World's Fairs, 1851–1939.* Manchester, U.K., 1988.

Harris, Neil. "Expository Expositions: Preparing for the Theme Parks." In *Designing Disney's Theme Parks,* edited by Karal Ann Marling, 19–28. Paris, 1997.

Jeremy, David J. "The Great Exhibition, Exhibitions and Technical Transfer." In *The Great Exhibition and Its Legacy,* edited by Franz Bosboch and John R. Davis, 129–139. Munich, 2002.

Kaiser, Wolfram. "Vive la France! Vive République? The Cultural Construction of French Identity at the World Exhibitions in Paris 1855–1900." *National Identities* 1, no. 3 (1999): 227–244.

Kusamitsu, Toshio. "Great Exhibitions before 1851." *History Workshop* no. 9 (1980): 70–89.

Mainardi, Patricia. *Art and Politics of the Second Empire: The Universal Expositions of 1855 and 1867.* New Haven, Conn., 1987.

Mandell, Robert D. *Paris 1900: The Great World's Fair.* Toronto, 1967.

Mattie, Eric. *World's Fairs.* Princeton, N.J., 1998.

Mitchell, Timothy. "The World as Exhibition." *Comparative Studies in Society and History* 31, no. 2 (1989): 217–236.

Rancière, Jacques, and Patrick Vauday, "Going to the Expo: The Worker, His Wife and Machines." In *Voices of the People: The Social Life of "La Sociale" at the End of the Empire,* edited by Adrian Rifkin and Roger Thomas, 23–44. London, 1988.

Rydell, Robert W., and Nancy E. Gwinn. *Fair Representations: World's Fairs and the Modern World.* Amsterdam, 1994.

Silverman, Deborah L. "The 1889 Exhibition: The Crisis of Bourgeois Individualism." *Oppositions* 8, no. 1 (1977): 71–89.

Stoklund, Bjarne. "The Role of International Exhibitions in the Construction of National Cultures in the 19th Century." *Ethnologia Europaea* 24, no. 1 (1994): 35–44.

Tenorio-Trillo, Mauricio. *Mexico at the World's Fairs: Crafting a Modern Nation.* Berkeley, Calif., 1996.

Williams, Rosalind H. *Dream Worlds: Mass Consumption in Late Nineteenth-Century France.* Berkeley, Calif., 1981.

ANTHONY SWIFT

WUNDT, WILHELM (1832–1920), German psychologist.

Wilhelm Maximilian Wundt was the leading institution builder for the modern discipline of experimental psychology. He wrote the first effective textbook for the new field—*Grundzüge der physiologischen Psychologie* (1874; Principles of physiological psychology)—and in 1879 he established a laboratory and institute at the University of Leipzig to which students could come for the explicit purpose of conducting Ph.D. research in experimental psychology. In 1881 he founded *Philosophische Studien,* a journal that despite its title published the results of the research conducted in Wundt's institute, thus becoming the first in the world to be explicitly devoted to experimental psychology. Wundt and his institute attracted students from around the world, many of whom returned to their home countries to establish similar psychology laboratories and programs there; by 1900 there were more than one hundred of them worldwide, and psychology was widely recognized as an important new academic discipline.

Wundt was born near Mannheim, Germany, on 16 August 1832, into an academic family, his paternal grandfather having been a professor of history at Heidelberg, and his uncle Philipp Friedrich Arnold (1803–1890) a physician and professor of physiology. Young Wundt followed his uncle first to Tübingen and then to Heidelberg, where he completed his medical degree in 1856. As a student he published two physiological papers in the start of a prodigiously prolific career. Attracted more to research than to medical practice, he briefly worked at Johannes Müller's (1801–1858) celebrated Physiology Laboratory in Berlin before returning to Heidelberg as a *Privatdozent* in physiology. At that time the famous Hermann Helmholtz (1821–1894) arrived to establish a Physiology Institute, and Wundt was named his assistant. Although Helmholtz identified himself as a physiologist, he was also among the vanguard of those mid-nineteenth-century scientists who challenged Immanuel Kant's (1724–1804) influential characterization of psychology as an intrinsically nonexperimental, primarily philosophical discipline, on the grounds that psychological phenomena could not be experimentally manipulated or subjected to mathematical analysis. Helmholtz had shown that many aspects of conscious sensation and perception could be accounted for via mechanistic analysis of the physiological systems involved in vision and audition. His demonstration of the finite and measurable speed of the nervous impulse had led to experimental research on "reaction times" and "mental chronometry." Also in 1860, Gustav

Fechner (1801–1887) pioneered the field of "psychophysics," showing how the "just noticeable difference" in perceived stimulus intensity—clearly a psychological variable—could be measured and subjected to mathematical analysis.

The young Wundt contributed in a small way to the field of mental chronometry in 1861, with a study showing that the psychological act of switching attention from an auditory to a simultaneously occurring visual stimulus required a measurable one-tenth of a second. More consequentially, he concluded that the growing body of research at the boundary between psychological experience and its physiological underpinnings provided material for a discrete discipline of experimental psychology, an idea he introduced in his 1862 book, *Beiträge zur Theorie der Sinneswahrnehmung* (*Contributions to the Theory of Sensory Perception*), and then developed and illustrated more fully twelve years later in his *Principles of Physiological Psychology* (1874). The latter book greatly enhanced Wundt's visibility and led to his appointment as full professor in philosophy, first at Zurich in 1874 and then at Leipzig the following year.

Most of the experimental research conducted by Wundt's students at the Leipzig institute fell into the general categories of psychophysics and mental chronometry, augmented by introspective analyses of immediately conscious experience into categories of sensations and feelings. Significantly, however, even as he promoted these studies Wundt also argued that experimental methods were only applicable to those psychological phenomena lying close to the border of physiology, and not to the "higher" mental processes including memory and thinking. The latter, he argued, involved supraindividual, communal processes such as language and custom, which had to be studied by comparative and historical methods rather than laboratory manipulations in a separate discipline he called *Völkerpsychologie.* Wundt also described his overall approach to psychology as "voluntaristic," because it stressed that the higher mental processes occurring at the center of consciousness entailed an inherently unpredictable and sometimes creative process he called "apperception" (as opposed to simple perception), unbound by the mechanistic laws of association.

An ardent German nationalist, Wundt fell out of vogue in English-speaking countries during

World War I, and only fragments of his voluminous works have been translated. Further, a later generation of psychologists spearheaded by Hermann Ebbinghaus (1850–1909), who invented "nonsense syllables" as a vehicle for the experimental investigation of memory, vigorously challenged Wundt's assumptions regarding the limitations of experimental methods. Modern cognitive science routinely investigates many phenomena that Wundt would have considered out of bounds. But still, legitimate debate continues about the ultimate limitations of mechanistic and experimental analysis, as in the discussions about strong versus weak Artificial Intelligence. Since the 1970s a small but growing number of anglophone historians have called attention to the contemporary relevance of many of Wundt's works.

See also **Helmholtz, Hermann; Psychology.**

BIBLIOGRAPHY

Primary Sources

Wundt, Wilhelm. *Elements of Folk Psychology: Outlines of a Psychological History of the Development of Mankind.* Translated by Edward Leroy Schaub. London, 1916. Translation of parts of Wundt's ten-volume *Völkerpsychologie.*

———. *Principles of Physiological Psychology.* Translated by Edward Bradford Titchener. Reprint, New York, 1969. Translation of portions of the fifth German edition (1902) of *Grundzüge der physiologischen Psychologie,* criticized by some historians as providing a misleading picture of Wundt's overall psychology.

Secondary Sources

Bringmann, Wolfgang G., and Ryan D. Tweney, eds. *Wundt Studies: A Centennial Collection.* Toronto, 1980. Several important articles on Wundt prepared to mark the centennial of his first laboratory in Leipzig.

Fancher, Raymond E. "Wilhelm Wundt and the Establishment of Experimental Psychology." In his *Pioneers of Psychology,* 3rd ed., 145–185. New York, 1996.

Rieber, Robert W., and David K. Robinson, eds. *Wilhelm Wundt in History: The Making of a Scientific Psychology.* New York, 2001. Presents important aspects of the modern reevaluation of Wundt's work.

RAYMOND E. FANCHER

YEATS, WILLIAM BUTLER (1865–1939), Irish poet.

"I had three interests," William Butler Yeats wrote in 1919, "interest in a form of literature, in a form of philosophy, and a belief in nationality." Throughout a long life of exceptional creativity, Yeats was to try and hammer these thoughts into a unity. Drawing on his ancient Irish culture, he strove after a uniquely modern image of artistic, political, and spiritual wholeness. His heroic commitment to his task obliged Yeats to engage with his times as both a public and a private man. In so doing, the Irishman created some of the most important European poetry of the late nineteenth and early twentieth centuries.

Yeats's interest in nationality places him against Ireland's struggle to find its political independence from imperial England as well as its own unique cultural identity. In his youth, Yeats was greatly influenced in these matters by the commanding figure of John O'Leary (1830–1907), who, at Dublin's Contemporary Club, offered Yeats the influential notion of an elite Irish intelligentsia steeped in traditional values and strongly anti-bourgeois in its sentiments.

O'Leary also opened his library to Yeats, where the poet began to find in his Celtic inheritance the ideals and images that could foster a sense of nationhood. This initiative, called for its dreamy qualities the Celtic Twilight, led to Yeats's exploring versions of Irish folklore, to the recovery of mythical Irish heroes in *The Wanderings of Oisin* (1889) and, most fruitfully perhaps, to the lyrics gathered in that early masterpiece of the Irish Literary Renaissance: *The Wind among the Reeds* (1899). These poems, inspired by a sense of magical Ireland and hopes for the mystical transformation of loathed Victorian materialism—ideas nurtured by such mentors in London as William Morris (1834–1896) and Oscar Wilde (1854–1900)—lead to a consideration of Yeats's occult interests.

Yeats lost his Christian faith as a boy, but his naturally spiritual temperament was homesick. He would soon turn to occultism, the belief that the supernatural can be approached through ritual and incantation. A profound study of the English Romantic poet William Blake (1757–1827) showed Yeats the importance of a spiritual life rooted in the imagination, and he joined Madame Blavatsky's Theosophists in London before becoming a member of the Hermetic Order of the Golden Dawn. Drawing on the widest traditions of the occult and defiantly opposed to materialism, the Order's rituals appeared to offer its members a shared, instinctual, and numinous experience of life that could be felt as spiritual release. Such impulses inform the lyrics of *The Rose* (1893), which also contains Yeats's most famous and popular evocation of romantic Ireland, "The Lake Isle of Innisfree." In this poem, the exquisitely subtle vowel sounds create a mood of dreaming and escape into a redemptive world of vividly realized natural beauty as the poet imagines living alone in the "bee-loud glade." Here is Yeats's early style of Celtic Twilight at its finest.

Among the members of the Golden Dawn was the woman who was to dominate much of Yeats's life: the wildly beautiful and politically radical Maude Gonne (1866–1953), whose passionate commitment to Irish independence further inflamed Yeats's own. Their long, often painful relationship is deeply woven into Irish nationalist history, nowhere more vividly than when, in 1902, Gonne played the eponymous heroine of Yeats's play *Cathleen ni Houlihan,* a drama which examines the ruthless demands made by nationalism.

Yeats was greatly aided in the writing of this play by another woman friend: Lady Isabella Augusta Gregory (1852–1932), a patrician Anglo-Irish widow who, in middle age, was discovering her own formidable literary talent. Together they founded the Abbey Theatre, which had an incalculable influence on the flowering of Irish drama, not least through promoting Yeats's own dramatic works and above all the plays of J. M. Synge (1871–1909). Meanwhile, the life at Lady Gregory's house at Coole moved Yeats's own thought in an ever more aristocratic direction, impulses deepened by his reading of Friedrich Nietzsche (1844–1900). These influences led to a greater firmness and directness in Yeats's poetic style and subject matter, qualities to be seen in "To a Wealthy Man who Promised a Second Subscription to the Dublin Municipal Gallery if It Were Proved the People Wanted Pictures."

Celtic Twilight was fading before a horror of mass society, and Yeats now excoriated the majority of Dubliners as philistines unworthy of his ideal Ireland. He was caught unawares, however, by the Easter Uprising against the British and so by the deep, unflinching, reckless nationalism of men such as Patrick Henry Pearse (1879–1916). In his great poem on the subject, "Easter 1916," Yeats, deeply stirred, attempted a mixture of impartiality and wonderment as he realized how from this event, futile although it appeared, "a terrible beauty is born." Yeats's poetry—inspired by the occult, honed in its vigor, and politically informed—was beginning to stare at the ineluctable violence that lies at the heart of the twentieth century.

See also **Blake, William; Ireland; Morris, William; Wilde, Oscar.**

BIBLIOGRAPHY

Primary Sources

Yeats, William Butler. *Autobiographies.* London, 1955.

———. *The Variorum Edition of the Poems of W. B. Yeats.* Edited by Peter Allt and Russell K. Alspach. New York, 1957.

———. *The Variorum Edition of the Plays of W. B. Yeats.* Edited by Russell K. Alspach. London, 1966.

Secondary Sources

Coote, Stephen. *W. B. Yeats: A Life.* London, 1997.

Ellmann, Richard. *Yeats: The Man and the Masks.* Rev. ed. London, 1979.

Finneran, Richard, ed. *Yeats: An Annual of Critical and Textual Studies.* Ann Arbor, Mich., 1983–.

Foster, Roy. *W. B. Yeats: A Life.* 2 vols. Oxford, U.K., 1997–2003.

Harper, George Mills. *The Making of Yeats's "A Vision."* 2 vols. London, 1987.

Henn, T. R. *The Lonely Tower: Studies in the Poetry of W. B. Yeats.* London, 1950.

STEPHEN COOTE

YOUNG CZECHS AND OLD CZECHS.

Following the suppression of the 1848 revolutions in the Habsburg lands, political activity was outlawed, but the failures of this "neoabsolutist" system, especially the losses in the Italian War of 1859, caused Emperor Francis Joseph to change course. As a result, the so-called constitutional era in the Austrian Empire was launched in 1860, and provincial diets reappeared, an imperial parliament (the Reichsrat) was established in Vienna, and political parties were founded. In Prague, Czech leaders, led by František Palacký and his son-in-law František L. Rieger, created the Czech National Party, whose goals were the political autonomy of the Bohemian crown lands of the empire on the basis of the traditional state rights of the old Kingdom of Bohemia, and greater rights for Czech language and culture. Because elections were carried out according to a restrictive curial system, which weighted votes in favor of wealthy landowners and urban elites, the party made a tactical alliance with the conservative great landowners, who shared their desire for provincial autonomy. Although the 1867 Ausgleich (compromise), which created the new country of Austria-Hungary out of the old empire, expanded political and individual rights in the Bohemian crown lands, it represented a setback for the Czech program because it established German dominance in the western, or "Austrian," half of the monarchy. In response, the National Party launched a program of passive resistance, refusing to participate in the local diets and the imperial parliament.

From its origins, the National Party had incorporated two factions, the conservative Old Czechs and the progressive Young Czechs—the name of the latter reflecting not the age of its members, but rather its initial identification with liberal nationalist movements such as "Young Germany" and "Young Poland" that had been inspired by the Italian ideologue, Giuseppe Mazzini. The split in the Czech national camp became apparent in a debate over the Polish revolt against Russia in 1863. The more conservative wing around Palacký and Rieger, although critical of tsarist policies, continued to support Russian leadership of the Slavic world, whereas liberals condemned the Russians as oppressors, and a small group of radical polonophiles sought to aid the Poles directly. In addition, the Young Czechs questioned the need for an alliance with the landed aristocrats, and developed an interpretation of Bohemian state rights that de-emphasized its feudal aspects. They combined their demands for greater democracy with a program of strident nationalism and occasional anticlericalism designed to appeal to the broad masses.

Chafing under the restrictions of passive resistance, the Young Czechs broke with the National Party, establishing a new party, the National Liberal Party, in 1874, and resuming participation in the government. In 1878 the Old Czechs also abandoned passive resistance and made an agreement with the Young Czechs to promote the national agenda. This coalition, led by the Old Czechs, supported the government of Austrian Minister-President (prime minister) Eduard Taaffe, which came to power in 1879, in return for concessions on national issues. The diminishing returns of this agreement caused the Young Czechs to end their cooperation with the Old Czechs in 1888. Following a controversial agreement negotiated by the Old Czechs in 1890 that gave significant concessions to the Bohemian Germans, the Young Czechs unseated their rivals in the 1891 elections to the imperial parliament. The Young Czech victory was in many ways a protest against the Old Czechs, and it transformed the party from a small radical nucleus into a broad coalition encompassing disparate segments of Czech society.

Once in power, party leaders lost touch with the more radical elements that had brought them to victory. As a result, several new, mostly small, parties, advocating a variety of progressive reforms, emerged to challenge the Young Czechs. At the same time, the expansion of the franchise opened the way for a transfer of political power away from parties of notables such as the Old and Young Czechs to mass-based parties of interest, such as the Social Democrats and the Agrarian Party. The Young Czechs lost their leading role in Czech politics in 1907, following the first elections to the imperial parliament on the basis of universal male suffrage. They continued to exert significant influence in provincial and municipal politics, where the curial system remained in effect. Increasingly identified as the party of business and banking interests, the Young Czechs emerged after the fall of the empire as the Czechoslovak National Democratic Party, one of the five influential parties that set the political course in the interwar Czechoslovak Republic.

See also **Austria-Hungary; Bohemia, Moravia, and Silesia; Masaryk, Tomáš Garrigue; Palacký, František.**

BIBLIOGRAPHY

Garver, Bruce M. *The Young Czech Party, 1874–1901, and the Emergence of a Multi-party System.* New Haven, Conn., 1978.

Šolle, Zdeněk. *Století české politiky: Počátky moderní české politiky od Palackého a Havlíčka az po realisty Kaizla, Kramáře a Masaryka.* Prague, 1998.

Vojtěch, Tomáš. *Mladočeši a boj o politickou moc v Čechách.* Prague, 1980.

CLAIRE E. NOLTE

YOUNG HEGELIANS. The Young or Left Hegelians were the radical disciples of Georg Wilhelm Friedrich Hegel who formed a rather amorphous school in Germany between the late

1830s and the mid-1840s. They flourished in the middle of the period between the (successful) Revolution of 1830 in France, when the reactionary Charles X (r. 1824–1830) was deposed, and the (unsuccessful) wave of revolutions that swept Europe in 1848. The Young Hegelians were thus both the product and the producers of the potent mixture of religion, philosophy, and politics that fermented in Germany during that seminal period. Their leading members were David Friedrich Strauss, Arnold Ruge, Bruno and Edgar Bauer, August Cieszkowski, Ludwig Feuerbach, Max Stirner (Johann Kaspar Schmidt), Moses Hess, Karl Marx, and Friedrich Engels.

It is impossible to speak of a "movement" before about 1840, when the increasingly radical position of the *Hallische Jahrbücher,* their principal organ, provided a rallying point. They were at the beginning exclusively preoccupied with religious questions, and, as Ruge later remarked, the extent to which the origins of the Hegelian School were theological can be measured by the fact that it was the purely theological *Das Leben Jesu* (1835; Life of Jesus) by Strauss that had the most influence on its development. Apart from art and literature, religion was the only field where different alignments and relatively free debate were possible. Because of the censorship almost all newspapers were merely pale reflections of the government's views. Genuinely political arguments among the Young Hegelians did not appear before about 1840, when the accession of Frederick William IV (r. 1840–1861) and the attendant relaxation of press censorship opened the newspapers for a short time to their propaganda.

The focal point of the Young Hegelians was the University of Berlin. Almost all of them—Bruno and Edgar Bauer, Cieszkowski, Feuerbach, Stirner, Marx, and Engels—had studied philosophy in Berlin. Hess and Ruge were the only important exceptions. Several of them—Bruno and Edgar Bauer, Feuerbach, Ruge—had followed the example of Hegel in beginning their studies with theology, only later switching to philosophy. All came from well-to-do, middle-class families, such as could afford to send their sons to a university. For the Young Hegelians were an extremely intellectual group for which a university education was essential, Hess being the only self-educated member.

Apart from Hess and Engels—both to some extent autodidacts in philosophy since their fathers wished them to go into the family business—all the Young Hegelians wished to go on to teach in some form or another, most of them in universities, though Stirner taught in a high school. Their misfortune was that, owing to their unorthodox ideas, the universities were gradually closed to them and they found themselves without jobs and cut off from society.

With this background it is not surprising that the Young Hegelians should put such emphasis on the role of ideas and theory. They were essentially a philosophical school and their approach to religion and politics was always intellectual. Their philosophy is best called a speculative rationalism; for to their romantic and idealist elements they added the sharp critical tendencies of the *Aufklärung* (Enlightenment) and an admiration for the principles of the French Revolution. The second half of Feuerbach's *Das Wesen des Christenthums* (1841; Essence of Christianity) was full of the old *Aufklärung* arguments against religion; Bruno and Edgar Bauer made long historical studies of the French Revolution, as did Marx also; and the Young Hegelians in general were very fond of comparing themselves either to the "mountain" or to individual revolutionaries of that time. They believed in reason as a continually unfolding process and conceived it their task to be its heralds. They radicalized still further Hegel's conception of religion as a prelude to philosophy by denying the possibility of any supernatural revelation.

Like Hegel, they believed that this process would achieve an ultimate unity, but they tended—especially Bruno Bauer—to believe that it would be immediately preceded by an ultimate division. This meant that some of their writings had an apocalyptic ring, for they thought it their duty by their criticism to force divisions to a final rupture and thus to their complete resolution.

The sometimes fantastic views of the Young Hegelians, views that Marx was later led to call mockingly "pregnant with world revolution," were helped, firstly, by their impression that they lived in an age of transition and at the dawn of a completely new era. Their apocalyptic tendencies were increased by their position as jobless intellectuals on the margin of society. Having no roots in the society that they were criticizing, they could allow their ideas to range at will. Second, the Young Hegelians placed great faith in the power of ideas; here again Bauer was the most outstanding example. The German poet and critic Heinrich Heine (1797–1856) had already said that thought preceded action as lightning did thunder. It was precisely in this "trailblazing" that the Young Hegelians were engaged. Marx echoed this thought in his first piece of serious writing, the doctoral dissertation of 1841, when he wrote, following Bruno Bauer, that even the practice of philosophy was itself theoretical. Even when some of the Young Hegelians began to express their ideas in purely political terms, this idea of the independence and primacy of theory still held sway. Their watchword was "critique"—of religion, philosophy, and politics. They echoed the famous declaration of the young Mikhail Bakunin, at the time himself in contact with several of the Young Hegelians, that "the joy of destruction in itself is a creative joy." This implacably critical impulse led through a rejection of any form of Christianity and an idealized aspiration toward democracy to the solipsistic anarchy of Max Stirner.

Although the Young Hegelians had ceased to exist as a coherent force by 1844, they acted as a matrix in which several of the most important elements of European thought gestated. Strauss and Bruno Bauer began a radical critique of the New Testament that continues to this day in biblical studies, as does Feuerbach's humanist reading of religion in contemporary "death of God" theologies. Stirner's ne plus ultra of egoism in his book *Der Einzige und sein Eigentum* (1844; The ego and its own) has been seen as one of the founding documents of anarchism and a precursor of, and possible influence on, Friedrich Wilhelm Nietzsche (1844–1900). And, of course, in the evolution of Marx's ideas, a radical interpretation of Hegel was an essential addition to French socialism and English economics. Thus the influence of the Young Hegelian secularization of Christian eschatology has proved more influential and lasting than many at the time would have expected.

See also **Bakunin, Mikhail; Berlin; Engels, Friedrich; Hegel, Georg Wilhelm Friedrich; Revolutions of 1848.**

BIBLIOGRAPHY

Brazill, William J. *The Young Hegelians.* New Haven, Conn., 1970.

McLellan, David. *The Young Hegelians and Karl Marx.* London, 1969.

Stepelevich, Lawrence S., ed. *The Young Hegelians: An Anthology.* Cambridge, U.K., 1983.

DAVID MCLELLAN

YOUNG ITALY. Young Italy, a secret political association, was founded by Giuseppe Mazzini (1805–1872) in Marseilles in July 1831 to promote the fight for Italian independence and unity. Mazzini had taken up residence in the French port city to avoid serving a sentence of confinement for his political activities. At the time of his departure from Italy, the success of revolution of July 1830 in France encouraged Italians to expect a similar outcome on their country. Mazzini founded Young Italy after attempts at revolution in Italy were put down with the help of Austrian intervention. Young Italy recruited in Italy and among political exiles abroad in competition with other patriotic societies. The name indicated Mazzini's faith that the young would succeed where radicals of the older generation had failed, and his disappointment with the revolutionary tactics of the Carboneria, the secret society behind the unsuccessful revolutions of 1820–1821 and 1830–1831. But although Young Italy targeted those between the ages of twenty and thirty-five, it excluded no one on the basis of age or sex.

Mazzini hoped that Young Italy would serve as an umbrella organization for patriots who accepted its basic principles of republicanism, social justice, faith in the people, and in Italy's revolutionary mission. Its membership was secret out of necessity, but unlike other secret societies that kept their aims and programs shrouded in mystery, Young Italy proclaimed its intentions openly, recruited broadly, and disseminated its message in print and by word of mouth.

Young Italy's religious ethos reflected Mazzini's conviction that commitment requires a firm religious basis. Its members were called apostles, held to high standards of personal conduct, enjoined to appeal to ideals and principles rather than material interests, and to bring the word to the masses, without whose support no revolution could succeed. A firm believer in the importance of political education, Mazzini published the journal *Giovine Italia* and saw to it that copies were smuggled into Italy. But Young Italy did not confine itself to long-term political education. It also conspired to promote revolution and guerrilla warfare based on the theories developed by Mazzini's close collaborator, Carlo Bianco di Saint-Jorioz (1795–1843), in the book *Della Guerra nazionale d'insurrezione per bande* (1828; On the national war of insurrection by bands). Members of Young Italy pledged to destroy tyrants and keep ready a dagger, a gun, and fifty rounds of ammunition for action on short notice.

Young Italy was a remarkable achievement considering the difficulties that it faced. Funds were not a serious problem, for its activities were bankrolled by well-off Lombard exiles. But that created another problem for Mazzini, for the same exiles demanded a voice in decisions that he did not want to share.

Other secret societies regarded Young Italy as a rival and sabotaged its work. The reformed Carboneria, headed by the old Jacobin Filippo Michele Buonarroti (1761–1837) and the society Veri Italiani (True Italians), both advocating a materialistic philosophy abhorrent to Mazzini, were Young Italy's most formidable rivals in the political underground. Spies infiltrated its ranks and police crackdowns disrupted its operations. Rapid communication and coordination of efforts in the Italian states, France, and Switzerland, where Young Italy was active, presented insurmountable problems. Wildly inflated estimates put Young Italy's membership at around 140,000 in 1833, but even a membership of no more than a few thousand would have been a remarkable achievement under the circumstances. Whatever the numbers, Young Italy attracted the most idealistic and best educated Italians and constituted the first broadly based revolutionary movement in Italy.

In 1833 and 1834 Young Italy suffered a series of reverses that destroyed its effectiveness, the last and most severe setback occurring in February 1834 when armed incursions into Savoy from France and Switzerland failed to spark the popular uprising on which Mazzini counted for success. Mazzini revived Young Italy in London in the 1840s. This new version, which is sometimes referred to as the second Young Italy, differed from the first in paying less attention to political conspiracy and more to political education. It was particularly popular among Italian students, who did not remember the failures of the first Young Italy and revered the name of Mazzini. It was flanked by a workers' union and had branches in North America and South America. It contributed to the political climate that led to the revolutions of 1848, but played no direct role in the revolutions; it was replaced by other Mazzinian organizations after 1848. The name was replicated by other militant democratic movements, including Young Ireland in the 1840s and Young America in the 1850s.

See also **Carbonari; Mazzini, Giuseppe; Nationalism.**

BIBLIOGRAPHY

Hales, Edward E. Y. *Mazzini and the Secret Societies: The Making of a Myth*. New York, 1956.

Sarti, Roland. *Mazzini: A Life for the Religion of Politics*. Westport, Conn., 1997.

ROLAND SARTI

YOUNG TURKS. Between 1828 and 1867, the phrase *Young Turk* was used to denote those Ottoman intellectuals and statesmen advocating liberal reforms and a constitutional regime for the Ottoman Empire. Specifically, when a number of leading Ottoman intellectuals fled the Ottoman capital to organize an opposition movement in Paris financed by the Egyptian prince Mustafa Fâzıl (1829–1875) the European press called them Young Turks. Turkish historiography labels this group the Young Ottomans. Later on, British and French diplomatic correspondence used the terms *Young Turk* and *The Young Turkey Party* to refer to those statesmen who supported the movement for a constitution.

Following the end of the short-lived constitutional regime in 1878, both Ottomans and Europeans referred in general to the opponents of the regime of Sultan Abdülhamid II (r. 1876–1909) as the Young Turks. It was the Ottoman Freemasons who, in 1893, first formally named their political branch The Committee of Young Turkey at Constantinople. Then, in 1895, the main opposition group, the Ottoman Committee of Union and Progress, advertized its French journal as "Organe de la Jeune Turquie."

From this point on, the phrase *Young Turk* was used among Ottoman subjects (of all religions) to denote opposition organizations dominated by Muslim dissidents.

YOUNG TURK MOVEMENT: IDEAS AND POLICIES

The Young Turk movement took place in Europe and British-ruled Egypt between 1878 and 1908. Members of this movement founded a host of political parties, committees, and leagues to topple the absolutist regime of Abdülhamid II and replace it with a constitutional monarchy. Although their European contemporaries and many scholars commonly labeled the Young Turks liberals and constitutionalists, these traits were promoted by a small minority in the movement. Members of the major Young Turk organizations did not adopt liberal ideas and viewed constitutionalism merely as a device to stave off great-power intervention in the Ottoman Empire.

The initial activities of the Young Turks did not go further than the publication of a few journals. In 1889, the major Young Turk organization was established in the Royal Medical Academy, which originally called itself the Ottoman Union Committee. After protracted negotiations between the original founders and Ahmed Rıza (1859–1930), who led the Young Turk movement intermittently between 1895 and 1908, the name was changed to the Ottoman Committee of Union and Progress. This new title reflected the staunch positivism of Ahmed Rıza, who had unsuccessfully proposed naming the group "Order and Progress," after the famous aphorism of philosopher Auguste Comte (1798–1857). This committee, which remained the most

important Young Turk organization until the end of the movement, was a loose umbrella organization until 1902. While some branches supported the gradual reform program of the positivists, others advocated revolution; still others were dominated by the ulema, the Muslim learned establishment.

In 1902, a schism developed in Paris at the First Congress of Ottoman Opposition Parties. The majority party, led by the sultan's brother-in-law Mahmud Celâleddin Pasha and his two sons Sabahaddin and Lûtfullah Beys, allied itself with Armenian and Albanian committees. They promoted the idea of a coup with British assistance. This willingness to work with foreign powers sparked the opposition of the minority party, under the leadership of Ahmed Rıza. It adopted a Turkist policy, demanding a leadership role for Turks, and categorically rejecting any foreign intervention in Ottoman politics. The majority party reorganized itself in 1905 under Sabahaddin Bey's leadership; in that year Sabahaddin Bey also founded the League of Private Initiative and Decentralization, and he worked toward creating a mutual understanding with the non-Muslim organizations. Also in 1905, the minority party, under the leadership of Bahaeddin Şakir, reorganized itself under the new name, the Ottoman Committee of Progress and Union. In 1907 this new organization merged with the Ottoman Freedom Society, which had been established by army officers and bureaucrats in Salonica in 1906. From this point on, the Young Turk movement spread deeply among the Ottoman officer corps in European Turkey. In July 1908, the Ottoman Committee of Progress and Union carried out the Constitutional Revolution, which marked both the end of Abdul-Hamid II's regime and the Young Turk movement. Some European historians call the new administration "the Young Turk government." This usage is misleading, because actually both regime and opposition after 1908 came from former Young Turks.

Because all members of organizations dominated by the Muslim opponents of the sultan and their sympathizers in the empire were called

Young Turks, this phrase does not necessarily refer to individuals who shared similar ideas. For instance, ulema and ardent positivists worked together in various Young Turk organizations as members. In the early stages of the movement, many Young Turks, including the original founders of the Ottoman Committee of Union and Progress, were adherents of mid-nineteenth-century German materialism and admirers of Ludwig Büchner (1824–1899). Social Darwinism also deeply influenced many Young Turks. Positivism, too, was advanced by various Young Turk leaders, and the French organ of the Ottoman Committee of Union and Progress used the positivist calendar for a while. Interestingly, French social scientist Gustave Le Bon (1841–1931) and his theories on crowd psychology made a strong impact on almost all members of the movement. Le Bon's ideas shaped the elitism promoted by the Young Turks. For their part, Sabahaddin Bey and his followers were deeply influenced by the Science sociale movement, particularly by Edmond Demolins (1852–1907). (The Science sociale movement aimed at turning social research into a branch of science through scientific research and creating a truly scientific method of study and analysis of social phenomena.) Following the reorganization of the Ottoman Committee of Progress and Union, these ideas receded to the background. Practical political ideas took their place. For instance, a proto-nationalism emerged. It stressed a dominant role for ethnic Turks in the empire, while resisting European economic penetration and political intervention in the Ottoman Empire.

See also **Nationalism; Ottoman Empire.**

BIBLIOGRAPHY

Hanioğlu, M. Şükrü. *The Young Turks in Opposition.* New York, 1995.

———. *Preparation for a Revolution: The Young Turks, 1902–1908.* New York, 2001.

Petrosian, Iu. A. *Mladoturetskoe dvizhenie: vtoraia polovina XIX-nachalo XX v.* Moscow, 1971.

M. ŞÜKRÜ HANIOĞLU

ZASULICH, VERA (1849–1919), Russian revolutionary.

Born 8 August (27 July, old style) 1849 into a family of impoverished lesser nobility and raised by well-to-do relatives in Smolensk province of imperial Russia, Vera Zasulich first encountered radical ideas when she began attending boarding school in Moscow in 1866. The radicals of the 1860s, critical of the social, political, and cultural order associated with serfdom, regarded gender differences as irrelevant to the struggle against it, and welcomed the participation of women. Yekaterina, the eldest Zasulich sister, introduced Vera to members of the radical Ishutin circle who remained at liberty after Dmitri Karakozov's attempted assassination of the tsar, Alexander II. In the summer of 1868, Vera Zasulich settled in St. Petersburg, where she participated in work collectives and then taught in an evening literacy school for workers. There she met the notorious revolutionary Sergei Nechayev, whom she served briefly as a go-between, her only oppositional act thus far. It led to her arrest in April 1869. Released two years later, she was imprisoned again in the summer of 1872, then sent into exile.

These years, a time of deprivation and suffering, cemented Zasulich's commitment to the destruction of the state. Following her release in September 1875, Zasulich went to Kiev, where she joined the revolutionary Southern Insurgents, and assumed an illegal existence. In the group she met and became involved with Lev Deich, with whom she lived whenever circumstances permitted until Deich's arrest in 1884. In December 1876 Zasulich returned to St. Petersburg; joined the recently established group Land and Liberty, devoted to peasant revolution; and worked in its underground press and at planning comrades' prison escapes. In July 1877 she learned of the flogging of a political prisoner, Arkhip Bogolyubov, ordered by Fyodor Trepov, the governor-general of St. Petersburg, and, outraged, vowed retribution for an act she deemed immoral.

Zasulich's attempted assassination of Trepov the following January won her fame in Russia and abroad. Although she shot at close range, Zasulich only wounded Trepov; then, prepared to accept the consequences of her action, she made no effort to defend herself or flee. Promptly arrested, she was tried and acquitted by a jury at the end of March, then released. Zasulich's acquittal brought the end of jury trials for political crimes. To avoid being arrested again on government orders, she escaped to Geneva, where she remained until 1905 except for two brief, clandestine trips to Russia and three years spent in London.

Liberals and radicals in Russia and Europe applauded Zasulich's acquittal. Russian radicals understood it to indicate widespread popular sympathy for their aims, and it encouraged exponents of terrorism among the fracturing populist movement. Zasulich was not among them. Instead, she rejected terrorism as a political tactic. In August 1879, during a brief visit to Russia, she joined the short-lived Black Repartition, which favored the revival of agitation among the peasantry. Abroad, she gradually moved from a peasant-oriented to a Marxist view of social transformation. In September 1883 Zasulich became one of the founders of Russia's first Marxist organization, the Emancipation of Labor Group. It took seven more years, however, before she fully abandoned her faith in the peasant commune and Russia's ability to bypass capitalism, and became convinced that only the proletariat, a group just emerging in Russia, could make a socialist revolution. Her views were congruent with those known as Menshevism after 1903: the proletariat would assume its historical role only after an extended period of maturation and preparation by radical intellectuals.

Reserved and self-effacing, Zasulich never sought visibility or political authority, despite the level of respect she garnered from the Left. During her years abroad, she established links with European socialists; wrote political analyses and historical/biographical studies; edited émigré publications, most notably the Marxist periodical *Iskra* (The spark); worked to assist revolutionaries in Russia; and devoted considerable energy to preserving unity in the fractious émigré movement. When the Russian Social Democrats split in 1903, Zasulich sided with the Mensheviks. Eager to be on the scene, she returned to Russia in the fall of 1905; the failure of the Revolution of 1905 marked the end of her active participation in revolutionary politics. When World War I broke out in 1914, Zasulich supported Russia's participation against Germany, because she considered German imperialism a threat to international socialism. Following the revolution of February 1917, Zasulich backed the Menshevik policy of collaboration with liberals in the Provisional Government; in her view, the October Revolution perverted Marxism. Her health was seriously failing by then, weakened by the tuberculosis she had contracted in 1889, and from which she had suffered since. Zasulich died of pneumonia on 8 May 1919.

See also **Mensheviks; Nechayev, Sergei; Populists; Socialism.**

BIBLIOGRAPHY

Primary Sources

Koni, A. F. *Vospominaniia o dele Very Zasulich.* Moscow, 1933.

Zasulich, Vera. "Vera Zasulich." In *Five Sisters: Women against the Tsar,* edited and translated by Barbara Alpern Engel and Clifford N. Rosenthal, 59–94. New York, 1975. Translation of *Vospominaniia* (1931).

Secondary Sources

Bergman, Jay. *Vera Zasulich: A Biography.* Stanford, Calif., 1983.

BARBARA ALPERN ENGEL

ZIONISM. First used in public on 23 January 1892 by Nathan Birnbaum, *Zionism* is the term used for the main Jewish nationalist movement that originated in central and eastern Europe in the last quarter of the nineteenth century. Zionism's main ideological claim was that the Jews were not simply an ethnic or religious minority group but were rather a distinct, if dispersed, people—a nation. As such, Jews could never be fully integrated into their host societies, and indeed should not; instead they needed, and had a right to, their own state, in their national homeland, Palestine, or, as most Zionists came to call it, *Eretz Israel* (Hebrew for "Land of Israel"). Zionism therefore rejected the main integrative, assimilationist strategy of the movement for Jewish emancipation that started in the late eighteenth century. Zionism's relation to this movement was, however, highly ambivalent, for while many Zionists insisted on a distinct cultural and national identity for Jews, many others, including its founding figure and initial leader, Theodor Herzl, also saw the movement as a means of integrating the Jews into the rest of civilized society, but on a national rather than individual level. Jews were to be, therefore, a "normal" nation, but they were also to be a model "normal" nation: pioneers in technology, culture, progressive social causes, and pluralist tolerance, and at the center of world civilization. Zionism, therefore, rather than "solving" the Jewish Question, as was claimed for it, came to reflect the complex, dialectical relationship between particularism and universalism that marked Jewish emancipation and indeed modern Jewish history generally.

JEWS AND NATIONALISM

Zionism differed markedly from almost all other European nationalisms in the period, even diasporic nationalisms such as that of the Greeks, by having only a marginal overlap between people and territory. There were some Jews in the Jewish "homeland" in Palestine, but Jews were far from being a majority in the area, and had no political control or recognized claim to the territory. The vast bulk of Jews lived outside of Palestine: the Sephardic Jews were scattered mainly across the lands, current and former, of the Ottoman Empire as well as parts of western Europe and the Americas; the Ashkenazi Jews were concentrated in central and eastern Europe, especially the area of the Russian Empire known as the Pale. This discrepancy between people and territory was an accepted part of premodern, traditional Jewish life and thought. Jews thought of themselves as a people, living as they did in autonomous communities, apart from, and usually discriminated against by, the surrounding societies. Yet they did not see themselves in modern nationalist terms, and their dispersion was explained, and justified, in religious terms, with an ingathering of the Jewish people to the homeland in Palestine seen almost exclusively in connection with the coming of the Messiah.

This situation became untenable with the onset of the modern state and its concomitant, secular nationalism, in the late eighteenth century. Jewish autonomy was abolished as part of the centralization of state power, and the spread of secular nationalism, associated most strongly with the French Revolution, was a direct challenge to the Jews' traditional group identity.

The modernizers within western and central European Jewry, including the neo-Orthodox, initially responded by defining Jewish identity exclusively in individual religious terms, thus denying any secular Jewish group (i.e., national) identity. Many even removed any vestigial mention in the liturgy of the wish to return to Zion as an outdated confusion that might hamper the full identification of Jews with their respective nations, whether French, German, or any other. This "assimilationist" strategy was effective as long as the national identity in question was inclusive, civic, and not seriously challenged by competing national identities. Where the nation gained an ethnic or racial, hence exclusive, definition, or where nationalities competed for regional supremacy, as in the empires of central and eastern Europe, the strategy's success was not so clear: Jews were not accepted as members

of the nation because of their different ethnicity and traditional prejudices against them. It was also unclear to which national group Jews should try to belong: in Bohemia, for instance, German, Czech, or "Austrian"? In this way, Jews often became caught in the crossfire between competing nationalisms.

JEWISH NATIONALISM

There was also a more positive possibility arising from the Jewish confrontation with nationalism. In areas such as the Russian Pale, where Jews were in sufficient numbers to retain a strong group identity, the option presented itself of Jews imitating the other groups around them by themselves forming their own "nation." Hence Russian Jewish intellectuals, led by Perez Smolenskin, developed in the 1860s their own brand of secular Jewish nationalism, alongside all the others.

Initially, however, most of the proponents of this secular Jewish national identity thought it could be realized in Europe in deterritorialized form. Most saw no need for the apparently impossible project of mass immigration of Jews to Palestine. There were, admittedly, calls from the early nineteenth century from various sources, including several British Christian evangelicals and Benjamin Disraeli, for the Jews' return to their biblical homeland, and the connection between the rediscovery of Jewish identity and the reclaiming of Zion was the centerpiece of George Eliot's novel *Daniel Deronda,* published in 1876. A prominent German Jewish intellectual, Moses Hess, once an avowed supporter of total Jewish integration in a socialist society, in his book *Rome and Jerusalem* (1862), also lent his voice to the call for recognition of Jewish nationhood and the restoration of a Jewish state in Palestine. Until the very end of the 1870s, however, very few held this view. In western and central Europe the strategy of assimilation, or at least integration, remained dominant among Jews, and even those, largely in eastern Europe and Russia, who supported a secular Jewish nationalism denied that this necessitated a Jewish state in Palestine.

THE LOVERS OF ZION

The radicalization of European nationalism around 1880 brought a sea change in Jewish attitudes. In central Europe the emergence of "anti-Semitism" as a formal political movement began to sow doubts in the minds of some supporters of assimilation; and in eastern Europe the success of Slav liberation movements against the Turks led to the rapid growth in Russian elites of Pan-Slavism. The effect of this on Jews was twofold. Some, such as Eliezer Ben-Yehuda, were inspired by Slav nationalist success to demand that the Jews also realize their national identity. In Ben-Yehuda's view this meant that Jews should speak Hebrew, which in turn necessitated their living in their own land, which meant immigrating to Palestine, as he recommended in 1879. Others were dismayed at the ethnonationalist nature of Pan-Slavism, which threatened the status of Jews within the Russian Empire. Their fears were confirmed in 1881 when the assassination of the relatively liberal Tsar Alexander II was followed by a spate of pogroms and a reactionary crackdown under Alexander III.

After the pogroms of 1881 most Jewish nationalists, including Smolenskin, became supporters of mass Jewish immigration to Palestine. In many of Russia's Jewish population centers they formed groups, under the general rubric of *Hovevei Ziyyon* (Lovers of Zion), to promote this goal. The new rationale of the movement was articulated by Leo Pinsker's *Auto-Emanzipation* (1882), which identified anti-Semitism as a psychic disease that was incurable and would bar the acceptance of Jews by European societies. Hence Jews needed to emancipate themselves, and form their own state. Ironically, Pinsker was not at all convinced that this state should be in Palestine, thinking North America a preferable site, but the vast majority of secular Jewish nationalists, with their more ethnocultural understanding of Jewish identity, could recognize only Palestine as the goal of emigration.

The new movement gained some unity of purpose at the Kattowitz Conference of 1884, received some financial backing from such figures as Edmond de Rothschild, and did see some land purchases and immigration to Palestine, the "First *Aliyah*" (literally "Going Up"). Overall, however, the Lovers of Zion suffered from a lack of organization, persecution by the Russian authorities, and conflict between the secular and religious factions. Although the pressure to emigrate remained, this could be relieved more easily by settling in America than in Palestine. By the early 1890s, with its initial impetus long gone, the movement was almost defunct.

THEODOR HERZL AND "POLITICAL ZIONISM"

The intervention of a Viennese journalist with no previous connection to Zionism, Theodor Herzl (1860–1904), revived the movement's fortunes. A fairly typical product of Vienna's assimilated Jewish liberal bourgeoisie, Herzl had been a liberal German nationalist in his youth, and he held quite a negative opinion of the parvenu Jewish society around him. Increasing concern about anti-Semitism in France (where he was the correspondent of the *Neue Freie Presse* in Paris from 1891 to 1895) and Austria, and the negative effects of the new, social "ghetto" in which assimilated Jews found themselves as a result, eventually led him to question the wisdom of assimilation. In June 1895, in the wake of the Dreyfus trial in France and, more crucially, the electoral triumph of the anti-Semitic Christian Socials in April that year in Vienna, Herzl came to the radical conclusion that the only way to solve the Jewish Question was for the Jews to recognize that they were a separate people, and should leave Europe to settle in a state of their own, as agreed to by the international community.

After failing to win over the western and central European Jewish elite, Herzl started appealing to the Jewish masses, and his plan was published as a pamphlet, *Der Judenstaat: Versuch einer modernen Lösung der Judenfrage* (The Jewish state: An attempt at a modern solution of the Jewish Question), in February 1896. His call met with an enthusiastic response not among western and central European Jews (at which it was aimed), but rather among eastern European Jews, in the pre-existing Zionist movement of which Herzl had been unaware. While in many respects simply repeating the core ideas of Pinsker, Herzl's plan was more detailed, Herzl himself had a higher prestige, as a "Western" intellectual, and he brought to the "Jewish cause" a remarkable political and organizational flair and energy. Very soon he became the leader of the movement, with Max Nordau, another highly prestigious "Western" intellectual, as his deputy.

The initial results of Herzl's leadership were dramatic: in 1897 he convened the First Zionist Congress in Basel, Switzerland, and he managed in a very short space of time to create the institutional structures and the *appearance* of a legitimate, substantial Jewish nationalist movement that firmly anchored Zionism in the international political world. His brand of "political Zionism" laid great stress on securing international recognition of and hence legitimacy for the goal of a Jewish state, and the resulting diplomatic campaign saw Herzl meet many of Europe's heads-of-state, including William II of Germany. This made Zionism respectable and gave it a high profile that was indispensable for its later success.

STRUGGLE FOR THE JEWISH FUTURE

Zionism, however, remained weak, and was soon in deep crisis. The movement convinced only a small minority of western and central European Jewry of the need to give up the strategy of integration into European society. Even in eastern Europe, Zionism had to compete with other models of Jewish modernization, such as the socialist Bundists, and within Zionism there were several competing visions of how to proceed. Herzl's political Zionism, for all its diplomatic glamour, had achieved hardly any success in pursuit of the movement's main goal: securing the right to a Jewish homeland in Palestine. Its neglect of a distinct, ethnoculturally Jewish content for the new state of the Jews also antagonized the "cultural Zionists," such as Asher Ginzberg (also known under the pseudonym Ahad Ha'am) and Martin Buber. Herzl's main goal for his Jews' state was to act as a refuge from anti-Semitism and to transform Jews into "real humans" by making them fully responsible citizens—of their own country. He had (like Pinsker) initially not seen Palestine as the necessary and sole site for his state, and even when he accepted this need, his Zionist vision, as articulated in the novel *Altneuland* (1902; Old new land), remained one with a progressive, liberal, universalist, pluralist, and humanist character (as befitted his central European Jewish background), rather than one with an identifiably, ethnically Jewish one. Cultural Zionists, in contrast, were intent on promoting a particular, culturally Jewish national identity (especially involving Hebrew as the national language), and saw a Jewish homeland more as a means to that end, rather than as a site for the "normalization" of Jews. "Practical Zionists" also differed from the political Zionists in insisting on the need to pursue colonization of Palestine even before international agreement on this (especially from the Turkish government that ruled Palestine) had been achieved.

The conflict over the movement's future culminated in the Uganda Crisis of 1903, when the (largely Russian) opposition protested vehemently at Herzl's agreement to pursue the prospect of a Jewish colony in British East Africa ("Uganda"), seeing this as a fatal detour from the goal of Palestine. Herzl achieved a compromise with the rebels, but very soon thereafter, on 3 July 1904, he died of heart disease. In the aftermath of the leader's death, the movement regrouped, but with power shifting to the "Russians." The supporters of the idea behind the Uganda project, of a territory that could be a "night shelter" for Jews fleeing anti-Semitism, broke away in 1905 and formed the Jewish Territorial Organization. David Wolffsohn became the new leader and continued the political Zionist strategy of Herzl, negotiating with Turkey for more Jewish rights in Palestine. Meanwhile, however, the goals of the cultural and practical Zionists, to further Jewish educational and economic development, and Jewish settlement, in Palestine, were also pursued. The combination of diplomatic activity and practical activity on the ground, named "synthetic Zionism" by its leading practitioner, Chaim Weizmann, became the dominant trend in the movement, especially after Wolffsohn's resignation in 1911, and Nordau's subsequent self-imposed absence.

By 1914, Zionism presented a complex and ambivalent picture. On the one hand, it remained riven by factional disputes, with political, cultural, and synthetic Zionists being accompanied by other factions, such as the religious-Orthodox Mizrahi, and the socialist Poale Zion. On the other, however, many of these disputes were taking place in Palestine as well as in Europe because the Second *Aliyah*, after 1905, had brought a substantial number of Jews to Palestine, and various educational, cultural, and economic institutions had been founded and financed, much of it under the skillful direction of Arthur Ruppin at the Palestine Office of the Jewish National Fund. Moreover, the evident weakness of Turkish rule in the area had led to renewed hopes of a diplomatic breakthrough, which was indeed to occur with the Balfour Declaration of 1917.

What remained quite unclear in 1914, and almost entirely unaddressed, was the question of how—assuming its future success—the nascent Zionist colony in the Jewish homeland of Palestine would deal with the fact of the Arab population that already lived there.

See also Anti-Semitism; Herzl, Theodor; Jews and Judaism; Minorities; Nationalism.

BIBLIOGRAPHY

Primary Sources

Hertzberg, Arthur, ed. *The Zionist Idea: A Historical Analysis and Reader.* Garden City, N.Y., 1959.

Herzl, Theodor. *Old New Land.* Translated by Lotta Levensohn. New York, 1960.

———. *The Jewish State.* Translated by Harry Zohn. New York, 1970.

Secondary Sources

Avineri, Shlomo. *The Making of Modern Zionism: Intellectual Origins of the Jewish State.* New York, 1981.

Beller, Steven. *Herzl.* 2nd ed. London, 2004.

Frankel, Jonathan. *Prophecy and Politics: Socialism, Nationalism, and the Russian Jews, 1862–1917.* Cambridge, U.K., 1981.

Laqueur, Walter. *A History of Zionism.* New York, 1972. Reprint, with a new preface by the author, New York, 1989.

Vital, David. *The Origins of Zionism.* Oxford, U.K., 1975.

———. *Zionism: The Formative Years.* Oxford, U.K., 1982.

STEVEN BELLER

ZOLA, ÉMILE (1840–1902), French novelist who founded the naturalism movement in literature.

The second half of the nineteenth century in France was less prolific of great creative artists who made their presence felt in the realm of politics. A notable exception was Émile Zola.

Born in Paris on 2 April 1840, Zola grew up in Aix-en-Provence where his father, an expatriate Italian engineer, had been engaged to build the dam and canal that now bear his name. Zola's father died in 1847, shortly before construction began, leaving his family in straitened circumstances. Swindled of shares in the canal company, his widow, Emilie, initiated a lawsuit that lasted for years and haunted her son's childhood and adolescence. Zola attended the Collège Bourbon on a scholarship. His classmates there included Paul Cézanne (1839–1906), with whom he formed a close friendship.

After Emilie Zola's case was done inching through provincial courts, she followed it to a higher tribunal in Paris. The year was 1857. Zola completed secondary school up north, at the lycée Saint-Louis, in a troubled state of mind. Wanting a literary career but burdened with expectations that he would imitate his father, he failed the baccalaureate examination. This calamity, which coincided with the final, disappointing adjudication of Emilie's suit, proved to be a blessing in disguise, for in 1862 Zola found employment at the publishing house of Hachette and by 1866 had become its publicity director.

Zola's four years at Hachette shaped his future. He came under the influence of a house author, the philosopher Hippolyte-Adolphe Taine (1828–1893), whose seminal work, *Histoire de la littérature française* (1862–1863), propagated the idea that cultural traits, works of art, and even metaphysical pieties, far from being independent of nature, belong to the material world and warrant material analysis. Epitomized in a celebrated formula—*race, milieu, moment* (race, environment, historical moment)—this view of human affairs would imbue Zola's fiction when, during the 1860s, he began to write novels. His animus against literary conventions extended to the realm of fine art, where the École des Beaux-Arts held sway, exercising its academic custodianship through the annual state exhibition, the Salon. In 1865, Zola, guided by Cézanne, took up the cudgels for avant-garde painting in a long article on Edouard Manet (1832–1883), later published under separate cover.

Distinctly unconventional was Zola's first important work of fiction, *Thérèse Raquin* (1867), which reflected his preoccupation with the theories of heredity that abounded in midcentury France. Ten years after the imperial regime had prosecuted Gustave Flaubert (1821–1880) for his "assault on public morals" in *Madame Bovary* (and lost), it thought better of bringing similar charges against Zola, but *Thérèse Raquin* nonetheless enjoyed a *succès de scandale*, with one critic citing it as a prime example of crude realism, or what he dubbed *la littérature putride*.

One year later, Zola drafted the outline of a saga that was eventually to fill twenty volumes and bear the comprehensive title *Les Rougon-Macquart: Histoire naturelle et sociale d'une famille sous le second Empire*. Work on it began in great earnest after the Franco-Prussian War (1870–1871).

Émile Zola. Portrait by Edouard Manet, 1868. MUSÉ D'ORSAY, PARIS, FRANCE, LAUROS/GIRAUDON/BRIDGEMAN ART LIBRARY

Zola's purposes in *Les Rougon-Macquart* were to trace the ramification of a single family through the whole of French society between 1851 and 1870, to describe the various milieux its members inhabit, and to show heredity manifesting itself in the ghosts that pursue them. While earning his livelihood in journalism, he found time to compile for each novel a file or *dossier préparatoire* often bulkier than the novel itself. His motto, *nulla dies sine linea,* served him well. "No day without a line" resulted in few years without a novel. Journalism supported him until 1876, when the seventh installment of his saga, *L'Assommoir*—a story that unfolds in a Paris slum—achieved commercial success. Zola's powerful portrayal of the dissoluteness to which poverty lends itself went hand in hand with his exploitation of working-class argot. Thenceforth, every work he produced was a bestseller.

Fame attracted followers. Since 1872 Zola had been a reverent confrere of Flaubert, at whose flat he joined Ivan Turgenev (1818–1883), Alphonse Daudet (1840–1897), and Edmond de Goncourt

(1822–1896) every Sunday afternoon during the winter season. Now he became a *maître à penser* in his own right, marshalling his entourage, which included Guy de Maupassant (1850–1893) and Joris-Karl Huysmans (1848–1907), under the banner of naturalism. Well-schooled in publicity, he favored slogans that linked his aesthetics to scientific thought of the day. Claude Bernard's *An Introduction to the Study of Experimental Medicine* (1865) is evoked throughout his critical work, where "naturalism," "physiology," and "experimental" recur with the obsessiveness of a mantra. This jargon did not please all his protégés—least of all Maupassant, who chafed at wearing labels. More importantly, it slighted the imaginative brilliance of his own work. During the last few decades of the twentieth century literary scholars, hostage no longer to Zola's polemical gloss, elucidated the art of his fiction and the mythic structures that demonstrate his affinity to the Romantic generation of French writers.

Zola's politics were no less complex than his artistic personality. He gave an excellent account of himself as a parliamentary reporter after the Franco-Prussian War, but came to hate political debate for distracting the public from literary conversation. He wrote stories that exposed the misery of the working class but excoriated the Communards of 1871. Zola the literary baron who fancied himself a captain of industry in his own domain (and a worthy heir of François Zola, who would have acquired great wealth had he lived long enough) idealized Fourierist utopianism in a late novel, *Le Travail.* Attacked by the Right as a saboteur of venerable institutions and by the Left for describing rather too vividly the moral degradation of slum dwellers, he contributed to liberal papers and conservative alike.

Of his devotion to the Republic there was never any doubt, however. When, in 1896, two years after the trial of Alfred Dreyfus (1859–1935) and his transportation to Devil's Island, a journalist named Bernard Lazare (1865–1903) asked Zola to join the small party of Dreyfusards in their campaign to exculpate the captain, he agreed with the alacrity of a man eager as much to avenge the unjust verdict of his mother's trial as to unmask the military establishment. The Dreyfus affair truly became an Affair when *L'Aurore*

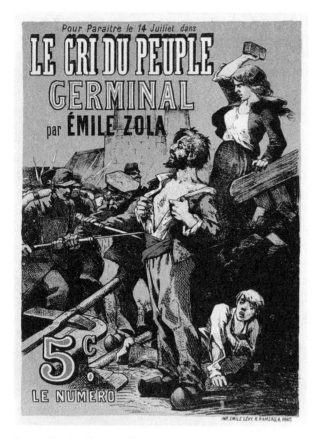

Cover illustration for the leftist periodical **Le Cri du Peuple** advertising its forthcoming publication of **Germinal.** MUSÉE DE LA VILLE DE PARIS, MUSÉE CARNAVALET, PARIS, FRANCE/BRIDGEMAN ART LIBRARY/ARCHIVES CHARMET

BIBLIOGRAPHY

Primary Sources

Zola, Émile. *Oeuvres complètes.* 15 vol. Paris, 1966–1969. The two principal editions of the *Rougon-Macquart* are in the Bibliothèque Pléiade (5 vols., edited by Henri Mitterand; Paris, 1960) and in the Bouquins series (3 vols., edited by Colette Becker; Paris, 1991).

———. *Correspondance de Émile Zola.* 12 vols. Edited by B. H. Bakker. Montreal, 1978–1995. Compiled by a team of French and Canadian scholars.

Secondary Sources

Becker, Colette. *Les Apprentissages de Zola.* Paris, 1993.

Becker, Colette, Gina Gourdin-Servenière, and Véronique Lavielle. *Dictionnaire d'Émile Zola.* Paris, 1993. A useful reference work.

Borie, Jean. *Zola et les mythes; ou, De la nausée au salut.* Paris, 1971.

Bredin, Jean-Denis. *The Affair: The Case of Alfred Dreyfus.* New York, 1986. Offers a wide perspective on the Dreyfus affair.

Brown, Frederick. *Zola: A Life.* New York, 1995.

Hemmings, F. W. J. *Emile Zola.* Oxford, U.K., 1953.

Levin, Harry. *The Gates of Horn: A Study of Five French Realists.* Oxford, U.K., 1966.

Mitterand, Henri. *Zola. L'Histoire et la fiction.* Paris, 1990.

———. *Zola.* Paris, 1999–2002.

Pagès, Alain. *Emile Zola, un intellectuel dans l'Affaire Dreyfus.* Paris, 1991. The most thorough account of Zola's role in the Dreyfus affair.

Serres, Michel. *Feux et signaux de brume, Zola.* Paris, 1975.

FREDERICK BROWN

published Zola's celebrated indictment, "J'accuse," on the front page of its 13 January 1898 issue. Only then did the cause gain adherents all over France, indeed, throughout Europe. Vilified by the anti-Republican, anti-Semitic opposition, Zola fled to England rather than risk imprisonment for slander and lived in hiding outside London until June 1899, when evidence supporting his allegations came to light. The Dreyfus affair inspired *La Vérité,* the fourth novel of his unfinished tetralogy, *Les Quatres Évangiles.*

Zola died in 1902 of asphyxiation from a defective flue. Suspicions linger to the present day that he was the victim of an anti-Dreyfusard conspiracy. Six years after his death, his remains were reinterred in the Pantheon, alongside those of Victor Hugo (1802–1885).

See also **Anti-Semitism; Cézanne, Paul; Dreyfus Affair; Flaubert, Gustave; Goncourt, Edmond and Jules de; Huysmans, Joris-Karl; Paris; Paris Commune; Realism and Naturalism; Republicanism.**

ZOLLVEREIN. The image of the German Zollverein (customs union, formed in 1834 between the members of the German Confederation) has been heavily influenced by two nineteenth century authors. The famous economist Friedrich List (1789–1846) as early as the 1830s spoke of the Zollverein and the railways as the Siamese twins of German economic modernization, thus stressing the importance of market integration for the Industrial Revolution. The famous historian Heinrich von Treitschke (1834–1896) a half a century later linked the foundation of the German Zollverein in 1834 to the battle of Königgrätz (1866), drawing a direct line from the beginnings of the customs union to national unification under Otto von Bismarck (1815–1898). While more recent authors are quite skeptical about either claim, the economic consequences of market integration and nation building still dominate the literature on the German Zollverein.

FOUNDATION OF THE ZOLLVEREIN AND ITS ECONOMIC IMPORTANCE

While the post-Napoleonic German Confederation proved unable to agree upon a common trade policy, the still more than forty German states after 1815 at least began to abandon the internal tariff borders running through their territories. In the following years—and after difficult negotiations—agreements between some German states were reached so that by the late 1820s three customs unions transcending the borders of single German states had been founded. In the south Bavaria and Württemberg had formed an alliance, while in the north Hesse-Darmstadt had joined Prussia. Partly as a reaction to the latter, and with support from the Austrian government, Hanover, Hesse-Cassel, Saxony, and a number of smaller states formed a Middle German Commercial Union later that year (1828). The tension between its character as an anti-Prussian bulwark and its conception as a tariff union clearly diminished its economic attractiveness. The initiative thus fell to the customs union dominated by Prussia, which as early as 1829 reached a first agreement with the southern customs union of Bavaria and Württemberg. A further decisive step on the way to the German Zollverein was taken when Hesse-Cassel joined the customs union dominated by Prussia in 1833, thus bridging the territorial gap between the eastern and western provinces of Prussia. The same year saw Bavaria and Württemberg as well as Saxony and a number of smaller states joining, so that the name of a German Zollverein, which quickly gained currency, was justified for the system of tariff contracts coming into force on 1 January 1834. While most German states in the south that had remained outside the Zollverein in 1834 joined during the following years, the refusal of Hanover, Hamburg, and Bremen to do so deprived the Zollverein of direct access to the North Sea for several decades to come.

Why was the Prussian-dominated customs union so successful, and what were the motives of those who joined it? For one, already Prussia's tariff law of 1818 had served as a model for a compromise between divergent economic interests. Immediate neighbors often had no choice but to join because they depended on Prussia for their exports. Others profited from the enormous rise in the efficiency of the new system. The costs of securing the tariff borders and of tariff administration—which had eaten up about 100 percent of tariff incomes in Hesse-Darmstadt and Hesse-Cassel before 1830—were drastically reduced. The importance of tariff income for the budgets, especially of many smaller states, grew accordingly. This was more than merely a fiscal question because income raised through tariffs was not subject to the parliamentary control that had been established in the mostly constitutional German states after 1815. The motives for joining thus were manifold, and by no means exclusively economic. But although economic interests differed from one state to the next, economic interest groups often lobbied for joining the Zollverein. Saxony for example, certainly the most developed industrial region in the 1830s, could hardly do without the Prussian market. But many other states such as Württemberg realized as well that their commercial activity was oriented toward the north and the west rather than the south. This had, among other things, to do with the construction of the railway system since the mid-1830s that strengthened the ties between Baden, Württemberg, and Bavaria and the northern parts of Germany.

The Zollverein thus fostered the economic integration of its territory without being the sole driving force behind this process. But while market integration was certainly advantageous for the industrial development that gained considerable pace from the mid-1840s onward, the Zollverein can hardly be credited with causing the German Industrial Revolution. Economic historians tend to agree that it was not even a necessary prerequisite of industrial development. With the Industrial Revolution under way, however, the renewable contracts constituting the Zollverein increasingly reflected the more and more industrial character of its member states. Thereby the gap between the Zollverein and Austria widened. It was not only that the Habsburg Monarchy as a whole retained a far more agrarian character, but even its more

EUROPE 1789 TO 1914

industrial regions fell behind during the 1850s and 1860s. Thus while the economic integration fostered by the Zollverein did not cause the German Industrial Revolution, it intensified enormously the economic integration of its territory, turning the Zollverein into an ever sharper weapon within the Austro-Prussian struggle over supremacy within the German Confederation.

TRADE POLICY AND NATION BUILDING

Thus, while the Zollverein originally was not designed to be a means of isolating Austria within the German Confederation, it increasingly became one. The political public of the 1840s discussed intensely the Zollverein's unifying potential, which became more and more obvious from the 1850s onward. While the economic and administrative integration of the Zollverein progressed, a commercial treaty between Austria and Prussia in February 1853 seemed to open up the possibility of Austrian membership in the future. The treaty stipulated that negotiations were to begin no later than 1860. Thus by 1865, when the renewed Zollverein contracts were due to run out, a central European customs union including Austria would have been possible. That this possibility remained a mere chimera had to do with Prussian policy as well as with different economic structures and interests. It proved all too easy for Rudolph Delbrück (1817–1903), who directed Prussian trade policies, to advocate a free trade course that was unacceptable to the protectionist Austrian economy. Politically the Prussian quest for hegemony thus was hardly concealed. And while this provoked considerable opposition in many member states of the Zollverein, it soon turned out that these states could hardly afford economically to leave the Zollverein behind. Petitions by chambers of commerce and political campaigns made that abundantly clear.

Thus in 1861, rather than working toward the integration of Austria into the Zollverein, Prussia was negotiating a commercial treaty with France that aimed at the equal treatment of Prussian imports to France with those from Britain or Belgium, and which meant a considerable lowering of tariffs. Against considerable opposition from the non-Prussian members of the Zollverein, Prussia not only signed the treaty on 2 August 1862, but

in December 1863 terminated the Zollverein contracts that were running out in 1865. Prussian officials knew only too well that this put its Zollverein partners in an extremely difficult spot. While most of them objected to the hegemonic role claimed by Prussia, they needed the Prussian market and were attracted by the enlarged trade zone opened up by the French-Prussian treaty. Ultimately they had to pay the price of accepting Prussia's arbitrary behavior for a renewal of the Zollverein.

Economic interests thus weighed heavily. This is not to say, however, that they determined the political outcome (i.e., German unification). After all, Austria in 1866 successfully called for the mobilization of the non-Prussian troops of the German Confederation after Prussia had invaded Holstein. The following war thus saw Prussia fighting not only against Austria but against non-Prussian members of the Zollverein as well. Since its outcome was by no means a foregone conclusion, it would be farfetched to regard the economic integration of the Zollverein as the anticipation of the German nation state. But if it was not determinative, it was nevertheless crucially important, which can be gauged from its continued operation during the war. Neither the Austro-Prussian War of 1866 nor the Franco-Prussian War of 1870–1871 meant the end of the economic integration of Germany fostered by the Zollverein, however. Hamburg and Bremen did not become part of the German tariff area until 1888.

See also **Germany; Hamburg; List, Georg Friedrich; Nationalism; Prussia; Trade and Economic Growth.**

BIBLIOGRAPHY

Böhme, Helmut. *Deutschlands Weg zur Großmacht. Studien zum Verhältnis von Wirtschaft und Staat während der Reichsgründungszeit 1848–1881.* Cologne, 1966.

Hahn, Hans-Werner. *Geschichte des Deutschen Zollvereins.* Göttingen, 1984.

Henderson, W. O. *The Rise of German Industrial Power, 1834–1914.* Berkeley, Calif., 1975.

Lenger, Friedrich. *Industrielle Revolution und Nationalstaatsgründung.* Stuttgart, 2003.

FRIEDRICH LENGER

SYSTEMATIC OUTLINE OF CONTENTS

This outline provides a general overview of the conceptual scheme of the encyclopedia, listing the titles of each entry. Because the section headings are not mutually exclusive, certain entries in the encyclopedia may listed in more than one section. Under each heading, relevant articles are listed first, then biographies.

Stendhal (Marie-Henri Beyle)
Stevenson, Robert Louis
Strachey, Lytton
Strauss, Johann
Stravinsky, Igor
Strindberg, August
Symonds, John Addington
Tchaikovsky, Peter
Tennyson, Alfred
Tolstoy, Leo
Toulouse-Lautrec, Henri de
Turgenev, Ivan
Turner, J. M. W.
Van Gogh, Vincent
Verdi, Giuseppe
Verga, Giovanni
Verne, Jules
Wagner, Richard
Wells, H. G.
Wilde, Oscar
Wordsworth, William
Yeats, William Butler
Zola, Émile

2. CONCEPTS AND IDEAS

Anarchism
Anarchosyndicalism
Carlism
Civilization, Concept of
Conservatism
Degeneration
Eugenics
Eurasianism
Feminism
Imperialism
Jingoism
Liberalism
Nationalism
Pacifism
Pan-Slavism
Phrenology
Primitivism
Race and Racism
Radicalism
Republicanism
Secularization
Socialism
Spiritualism
Utopian Socialism
Westernizers

2.1. BIOGRAPHIES
Bakunin, Mikhail
Bely, Andrei
Blanc, Louis
Cabet, Étienne
Dohm, Hedwig
Fourier, Charles
Galton, Francis
Herzen, Alexander
Herzl, Theodor
Kropotkin, Peter
Maurras, Charles

3. ECONOMIC HISTORY

Agricultural Revolution
Artisans and Guilds
Banks and Banking
Business Firms and Economic Growth
Capitalism
Coal Mining
Colonies
Combination Acts
Commercial Policy
Consumerism
Continental System
Corn Laws, Repeal of
East India Company
Economic Growth and
    Industrialism
Factories
Industrial Revolution, First
Industrial Revolution, Second
Krupp
Labor Movements
Luddism
Machine Breaking
Monetary Unions
Protectionism
Rothschilds
Sewing Machine
Strikes
Syndicalism
Trade and Economic Growth
Zollverein

9. PLACES

10. POLITICAL HISTORY

11. RELIGION

Millet System
Missions
Papacy
Papal Infallibility
Pilgrimages
Protestantism
Roman Question
Russian Orthodox Church
Salvation Army
Separation of Church and State
(France, 1905)
Socialism, Christian
Zionism

11.1. BIOGRAPHIES
Agassiz, Louis
Drumont, Édouard
Leo XIII
Maistre, Joseph de
Manning, Henry
Newman, John Henry
Pius IX
Schleiermacher, Friedrich
Soloviev, Vladimir
Wilberforce, William

12. REVOLUTIONS
Counterrevolution
French Revolution
Paris Commune
Revolution of 1905 (Russia)
Revolutions of 1820
Revolutions of 1830
Revolutions of 1848
Secret Societies
Socialist Revolutionaries

12.1. FRENCH REVOLUTION
Committee of Public Safety
Directory
Estates-General
Federalist Revolt
French Revolution
Girondins
Jacobins
Levée en Masse
Reign of Terror
Sister Republics

12.2. BIOGRAPHIES
Danton, Georges-Jacques
Engels, Friedrich
Fouché, Joseph
Gouges, Olympe de
Jelačić, Josip
Kuliscioff, Anna
Lafayette, Marquis de
Ledru-Rollin, Alexandre-Auguste
Lenin, Vladimir
Luxemburg, Rosa
Marat, Jean-Paul
Marie-Antoinette
Marx, Karl
Michel, Louise
Nechayev, Sergei
Paine, Thomas
Robespierre, Maximilien
Sieyès, Emmanuel-Joseph
Zasulich, Vera

13. SCIENCE
Chemistry
Electricity
Engineers
Evolution
Physics
Science and Technology
Statistics

13.1. MEDICINE
Cholera
Disease
Nurses
Psychoanalysis
Public Health
Red Cross
Smallpox
Syphilis
Tuberculosis

13.2. BIOGRAPHIES
Adler, Alfred
Bernard, Claude
Braille, Louis
Cajal, Santiago Ramón y

15. SOCIAL HISTORY

14. SOCIAL CLASSES AND ORDERS

15.1. BIOGRAPHIES

RIGHT: *A Nurse.* Painting by Nikolai Alexandrovich Yaroshenko, 1886. Previously performed largely by untrained volunteers, the role of the nurse became professionalized in Europe during the mid-nineteenth century under the guidance of Florence Nightingale. Yaroshenko's nurse wears the emblem of the Red Cross, founded in Switzerland in 1864. Ivanovo Museum of Art, Ivanovo, Russia/Bridgeman Art Library

BELOW: *Women in a Canning Factory.* Painting by Max Liebermann, 1879. The idea of preserving food through the use of special containers originated in France at the beginning of the nineteenth century and quickly gained popularity throughout Europe. As with much light industry in the nineteenth century, the work was often performed by women. Erich Lessing/Art Resource, NY

LEFT: **Poster for May Day celebrations, Italy, 1902.** The first day of May was adopted as a holiday for laborers by the Second Socialist International in 1889. PRIVATE COLLECTION /BRIDGEMAN ART LIBRARY/ARCHIVES CHARMET

BELOW: *Plowing in Ukraine.* Painting by Leon Wyczolkowski, 1892. Hampered by physical isolation and, in many cases, by retrogressive government policies, farmers in eastern Europe lagged behind their western counterparts in realizing the benefits of mechanized farming in the late nineteenth and early twentieth centuries. NATIONAL MUSEUM IN CRACOW, POLAND/BRIDGEMAN ART LIBRARY

16. TRANSPORTATION AND COMMUNICATION

DIRECTORY OF CONTRIBUTORS

JOHN J. ABBATIELLO
United States Air Force Academy
Dreadnought

HENRY ABRAMSON
Touro College South, Miami Beach, Florida
Pogroms

ELINOR ACCAMPO
University of Southern California
Feminism
Roussel, Nelly

HAZARD ADAMS
University of Washington
Blake, William

HOLGER AFFLERBACH
Emory University
Congress of Berlin

JOHAN ÅHR
Hofstra University
Denmark
Sweden and Norway

ANDREW AISENBERG
Scripps College
Body
Syphilis

JOHN H. ALCORN
Trinity College, Hartford, Connecticut
Sicilian Fasci

ANN TAYLOR ALLEN
University of Louisville
Bäumer, Gertrud
Otto, Louise

JAMES SMITH ALLEN
Southern Illinois University, Carbondale
Freemasons

ADEL ALLOUCHE
Yale University
Mahmud II
Millet System
Tunisia

KATHRYN AMDUR
Emory University
Anarchosyndicalism

OLOV AMELIN
Independent Scholar
Nobel, Alfred

FRANS C. AMELINCKX
University of Louisiana at Lafayette
Chateaubriand, François-René

MARGARET LAVINIA ANDERSON
University of California—Berkeley
Windthorst, Ludwig

ANTONY ANGHIE
University of Utah
Berlin Conference

MARK ANTLIFF
Duke University
Bergson, Henri
Cubism

CELIA APPLEGATE
University of Rochester
Music

JULIAN ARCHER
Drake University
First International

JOHN H. ARNOLD
Birkbeck College, University of London, U.K.
History

WALTER ARNSTEIN
University of Illinois at Urbana-Champaign (emeritus)
Victoria, Queen

SUSAN A. ASHLEY
Colorado College
Umberto I
Victor Emmanuel II

NICHOLAS ATKIN
University of Reading
Catholicism, Political

JEFFREY A. AUERBACH
California State University
Crystal Palace

JOSEPH AUNER
State University of New York at Stony Brook
Schoenberg, Arnold

LEORA AUSLANDER
University of Chicago
Furniture

MICHAEL R. AUSLIN
Yale University
Japan
Russo-Japanese War

TIMOTHY BAHTI
Claviers, France
Hölderlin, Johann Christian Friedrich

DUDLEY BAINES
London School of Economics
Emigration

DAVID E. BARCLAY
Kalamazoo College
Frederick William IV

ELAZAR BARKAN
Claremont Graduate University
Primitivism

MARGARET BARNETT
University of Southern Mississippi
Roentgen, Wilhelm

RICHARD BARNETT
Wellcome Trust Centre for the History of Medicine at University College London, U.K.
Lister, Joseph

VINCENT BARNETT
Birmingham University, U.K.
Humboldt, Alexander and Wilhelm von
Pavlov, Ivan

SAMUEL H. BARON
University of North Carolina (emeritus)
Plekhanov, Georgy

TIMOTHY JOHN BARRINGER
Yale University
Pre-Raphaelite Movement

H. ARNOLD BARTON
Southern Illinois University at Carbondale (emeritus)
Bernadotte, Jean-Baptiste

JOHN BATCHELOR
University of Newcastle upon Tyne, U.K.
Conrad, Joseph
Ruskin, John

JOERG BATEN
Eberhard Karls University of Tuebingen, Germany
Trade and Economic Growth

SIGRID BAUSCHINGER
University of Massachusetts
Lasker-Schüler, Else

JONATHAN BEECHER
University of California, Santa Cruz
Fourier, Charles
Utopian Socialism

JOHN BELCHEM
University of Liverpool, U.K.
Cobbett, William
Cobden, Richard
Lovett, William

STEVEN BELLER
Independent Scholar, Washington, D.C.
Adler, Victor
Ferdinand I
Francis I
Francis Ferdinand
Francis Joseph
John, Archduke of Austria
Rudolf, Crown Prince of Austria
Vienna
Zionism

ALAIN BELTRAN
Institut d'Histoire du Temps Présent (CNRS, France)
Electricity

EDWARD BERENSON
New York University
Caillaux, Joseph

MAXINE BERG
University of Warwick, U.K.
Industrial Revolution, First

GUNTHER BERGHAUS
University of Bristol
Futurism

SUSAN BERNSTEIN
Brown University
Liszt, Franz

DAVID CARSON BERRY
Univ. of Cincinnati
Stravinsky, Igor

PATRICK BESNIER
University of Maine, Le Mans-Laval, France
Jarry, Alfred

EUGENIO F. BIAGINI
University of Cambridge
Gladstone, William
Great Britain

JOHN W. BICKNELL
Drew University
Stephen, Leslie

PATRICK KAY BIDELMAN
The Ringling School of Art and Design and the University of South Florida
Deraismes, Maria
Richer, Léon

EMILY D. BILSKI
Liebermann, Max

RUDOLPH BINION
Brandeis University
Andreas-Salomé, Lou

JOHN T. BLACKMORE
Independent Scholar (emeritus University of Vienna, Tsukuba University, Japan)
Mach, Ernst

MARK E. BLUM
University of Louisville
Kafka, Franz

JUDIT BODNAR
Central European University, Budapest
Budapest

LLOYD BONFIELD
Tulane University
Napoleonic Code

MATTIE BOOM
Rijksmuseum, Amsterdam
Photography

JAMES A. BOON
Princeton University
Frazer, James

LAIRD BOSWELL
University of Wisconsin—Madison
Alsace-Lorraine

PATRICE BOURDELAIS
Ecole des Hautes Etudes en Sciences Sociales, Paris
Cholera

PETER BOWLER
Queen's University of Belfast, U.K.
Evolution

JOSEPH BRADLEY
University of Tulsa
Civil Society

J. DANIEL BREAZEALE
University of Kentucky
Fichte, Johann Gottlieb

GREGORY BREDBECK
University of California, Riverside
Carpenter, Edward
Wilde, Oscar

CHRISTOPHER BREWARD
Victoria & Albert Museum, London
Clothing, Dress, and Fashion

MICHAEL BROERS
Oxford University
Napoleonic Empire
Piedmont-Savoy
Sister Republics

TED R. BROMUND
Yale University
Olympic Games

ERIC DORN BROSE
Drexel University
Frederick William III

DANIEL R. BROWER
University of California, Davis
Central Asia

FREDERICK BROWN
State University of New York at Stonybrook
Zola, Émile

MICHAEL BROWN
University of Kent, U.K.
Jenner, Edward

ROBERT W. BROWN
University of North Carolina, Pembroke
Degas, Edgar
Monet, Claude
Pissarro, Camille

LOGAN DELANO BROWNING
Rice University
Cruikshank, George

ALMUTH BRUDER-BEZZEL
Alfred Adler Institute, Berlin
Adler, Alfred

JULIA BRUGGEMANN
DePauw University
Augspurg, Anita
Dohm, Hedwig

ANTHONY BRUNDAGE
California State Polytechnic University, Pomona
Chadwick, Edwin

JOHN BUCKLEY
University of Wolverhampton, U.K.
Airplanes

PHILLIP BUCKNER
University of New Brunswick (emeritus)
Canada

JANE BURBANK
New York University
Intelligentsia

RICHARD W. BURKHARDT JR.
University of Illinois at Urbana-Champaign
Cuvier, Georges
Lamarck, Jean-Baptiste

SIMON BURROWS
Leeds University, U.K.
Press and Newspapers

JUNE K. BURTON
University of Akron
Champollion, Jean-François

JOSEPH CADY
New York University School of Medicine
Symonds, John Addington

PETER CAIN
Sheffield Hallam University, U.K.
Hobson, John A.

WILLIAM M. CALDER III
University of Illinois, Urbana-Champaign
Mommsen, Theodor

CRAIG CALHOUN
New York University
Sociology

JANE CAMERINI
Independent Scholar
Wallace, Alfred Russel

NICHOLAS CAPALDI
Loyola University New Orleans
Mill, John Stuart

MARIE CARANI
Laval University, Canada
Cézanne, Paul
Rodin, Auguste

TERRELL CARVER
University of Bristol, U.K.
Communism
Engels, Friedrich
Marx, Karl

JORDI CAT
Indiana University
Maxwell, James Clerk

LAMAR CECIL
Washington and Lee University
William II

JEAN-FRANÇOIS CHANET
University of Lille-3, France
Jaurès, Jean

CHRISTOPHE CHARLE
Universite de Paris I—Pantheon Sorbonne
Universities

RACHEL CHRASTIL
Xavier University
Cobden-Chevalier Treaty
Lesseps, Ferdinand-Marie de
Red Cross

PETRA TEN-DOESSCHATE CHU
Seton Hall University
Courbet, Gustave

CLIVE H. CHURCH
University of Kent, U.K.
Revolutions of 1830

GREGORY CLAEYS
Royal Holloway, University of London, U.K.
Owen, Robert
Socialism

CHRISTOPHER CLARK
St. Catherine's College, London
Prussia

RICHARD CLOGG
St. Antony's College, University of Oxford
Greece

JOHN CLUTE
Independent Scholar
Verne, Jules

JEAN CHRISTOPHE COFFIN
University of Paris 5 René Descartes
Bernard, Claude

JUDITH G. COFFIN
University of Texas, Austin
Consumerism
Sewing Machine

GARY B. COHEN
University of Minnesota, Twin Cities
Prague Slav Congress

ANDREA COLLI
Bocconi University, Milan, Italy
Business Firms and
Economic Growth

MARY SCHAEFFER CONROY
University of Colorado at Denver
Stolypin, Peter
Witte, Sergei

FREDERICK COOPER
New York University
Colonialism

SANDI E. COOPER
College of Staten Island and The Graduate Center, City University of New York
Pacifism
Suttner, Bertha von

STEPHEN HUGH COOTE
Naresuan University, Thailand
Yeats, William Butler

ROGER COOTER
Wellcome Trust Centre for the History of Medicine, University College London
Gall, Franz Joseph

FRANK J. COPPA
St. John's University
Concordat of 1801
Leo XIII
Papacy
Pius IX

PHILIP COTTRELL
University of Leicester, U.K.
Banks and Banking
Brunel, Isambard Kingdom
Cockerill, John

MAURA COUGHLIN
Brown University
Barbizon Painters

KRISTA COWMAN
Leeds Metropolitan University, U.K.
Butler, Josephine

JAMES CRACRAFT
University of Illinois at Chicago
St. Petersburg

RICHARD CRAMPTON
University of Oxford
Albania

TRAVIS L. CROSBY
Wheaton College
Chamberlain, Joseph
Lloyd George, David

MARGARET L. CRUIKSHANK
University of Maine
Macaulay,
Thomas Babington

HUGH CUNNINGHAM
University of Kent, U.K.
Jingoism

JAMES CURRIE
State University of New York at Buffalo
Brahms, Johannes
Mahler, Gustav

ROBERT CUSHMAN
The National Post, Canada
Shaw, George Bernard

MARY E. DALY
University College, Dublin, Ireland
Dublin

JOHN A. DAVIS
University of Connecticut
Carbonari
Kingdom of the Two Sicilies
Risorgimento (Italian Unification)
Rome

ALEXANDER DE GRAND
North Carolina State University
Carducci, Giosuè

ALEXANDER DE GRAND
North Carolina State University
D'Annunzio, Gabriele
Giolitti, Giovanni
Kuliscioff, Anna
Turati, Filippo

ISTVÁN DEÁK
Columbia University
Deák, Ferenc
Kossuth, Lajos

PATRICE DEBRE
Université Pierre et Marie Curie, Paris, France
Pasteur, Louis

ROBERT K. DEKOSKY
University of Kansas
Rutherford, Ernest

BERNARD DELPAL
Secularization

SELIM DERINGIL
Bogazici University, Turkey
Black Sea
Bosphorus
Jadids

DIMITRIJE DJORDJEVIC
University of California, Santa Barbara
Belgrade

DEIRDRE DONOHUE
International Center of Photography, New York
Nadar, Félix

SEYMOUR DRESCHER
University of Pittsburgh
Tocqueville, Alexis de

LAURENT DUBOIS
Michigan State University
Caribbean
Haiti

BERNARD DUCHATELET
University of Brest
Rolland, Romain

JACALYN DUFFIN
Queen's University, Kingston, Canada
Laennec, René

CHRISTOPHER DUGGAN
University of Reading, U.K.
Crispi, Francesco

JEAN-NOËL DUMONT
Collège Supérieur, Lyon, France
Péguy, Charles

PASCAL DUPUY
University of Rouen, France
Sade, Donatien-Alphonse-François de

STEVEN F. EISENMAN
Northwestern University
Gauguin, Paul

GEOFFREY ELLIS
Hertford College, Oxford University
Continental System

CLIVE EMSLEY
Open University, U.K.
Crime
Fouché, Joseph
Police and Policing

BARBARA ALPERN ENGEL
University of Colorado
Zasulich, Vera

JENS IVO ENGELS
University of Freiburg, Germany
Environment

LAURA ENGELSTEIN
Yale University
Revolution of 1905 (Russia)

STEVEN ENGLUND
Independent Scholar
Barrès, Maurice

Drumont, Édouard
Napoleon

MICHAEL EPKENHANS
Otto-von-Bismarck-Stiftung,
Germany
Tirpitz, Alfred von

ROBERT M. EPSTEIN
U.S. Army Command and
General Staff College
Leipzig, Battle of

EDWARD J. ERICKSON
International Research Associates,
LLC.
Adrianople
Eastern Question

AHMET ERSOY
Bogazici University
Istanbul

THOMAS ERTMAN
New York University
Opera

CHARLES J. ESDAILE
University of Liverpool, U.K.
Carlism
Ferdinand VII
Peninsular War

ANDREAS ETGES
Free University of Berlin, Germany
Anneke, Mathilde-Franziska

WILLIAM EVERDELL
Saint Ann's School
Cajal, Santiago Ramón y
De Vries, Hugo

CATHERINE EVTUHOV
Georgetown University
Soloviev, Vladimir

RAYMOND E. FANCHER
York University
Galton, Francis
Wundt, Wilhelm

GIOVANNI FEDERICO
European University Institute,
Florence, Italy
Commercial Policy
Protectionism

WILFRIED FELDENKIRCHEN
University of Erlangen-
Nuremberg, Germany
Siemens, Werner von

NIALL FERGUSON
Harvard University
Rothschilds

GEOFFREY G. FIELD
Purchase College, State University
of New York
Chamberlain, Houston
Stewart

K. FLEMING
New York University
Abdul-Hamid II
Mediterranean

RICHARD FLOYD
Washington University,
St. Louis, MO
Poor Law

MARK FOLEY
Independent Scholar
Barry, Charles
Nash, John
Pugin, Augustus Welby

SUSAN K. FOLEY
Victoria University of Wellington,
New Zealand
Gambetta, Léon-Michel
Michel, Louise
Roland, Pauline
Tristan, Flora

JOHN FOOT
University College London
Milan

EVA FORGACS
Art Center College of Design,
Pasadena, CA
Avant-Garde

ALAN FORREST
University of York, U.K.
Directory
Levée en Masse

GILLIAN FORRESTER
Yale Center for British Art
Turner, J. M. W.

JOHN FORRESTER
University of Cambridge, U.K.
Psychoanalysis

WILLIAM FORTESCUE
University of Kent, Canterbury,
U.K.
Lamartine, Alphonse
Ledru-Rollin, Alexandre-
Auguste
Paris Commune
Talleyrand, Charles Maurice de
Thiers, Louis-Adolphe

RICHARD FREEBORN
University of London
Belinsky, Vissarion

GREGORY L. FREEZE
Brandeis University
Russian Orthodox Church

UTE FREVERT
Yale University
Dueling

JULIA FREY
Independent Scholar
Toulouse-Lautrec, Henri de

CATHY A. FRIERSON
Univesity of New Hampshire
Great Reforms (Russia)

PETER FRITZSCHE
University of Illinois, Urbana
Champaign
Nietzsche, Friedrich

JACK FRUCHTMAN JR.
Towson University
Paine, Thomas

RACHEL G. FUCHS
Arizona State University
Population, Control of
Welfare

THOMAS W. GALLANT
York University, Canada
Athens

NIKOLAS GARDNER
*European Studies Research
Institute, University of Salford,
U.K.*
Fashoda Affair

ALICE GARNER
*University of Melbourne,
Australia*
Seaside Resorts

IAIN GATELY
Independent Journalist
Tobacco

PETER GAY
Freud, Sigmund

RICHARD S. GEEHR
Bentley College
Lueger, Karl

ROBERT P. GERACI
University of Virginia
Civilization, Concept of

CHRISTOPHER H. GIBBS
Bard College
Schubert, Franz

MARY GIBSON
*John Jay College, City University
of New York*
Lombroso, Cesare
Mozzoni, Anna Maria
Prostitution

RICHARD L. GILLIN
Washington College
Shelley, Percy Bysshe

CHARLES C. GILLISPIE
Princeton University
Marat, Jean-Paul

HALINA GOLDBERG
*Indiana University—
Bloomington*
Chopin, Frédéric

RICHARD E. GOODKIN
University of Wisconsin, Madison
Bernhardt, Sarah
Flaubert, Gustave

DANA GOOLEY
Case Western Reserve University
Paganini, Niccolò

JOEL GORDON
*University of Arkansas,
Fayetteville*
Suez Canal

RAE BETH GORDON
University of Connecticut, Storrs
Méliès, Georges

BORIS B. GORSHKOV
Kennesaw State University
Serfs, Emancipation of

LIONEL GOSSMAN
Princeton University
Burckhardt, Jacob

GIOVANNI GOZZINI
University of Siena
Poverty

CHRISTOPH GRADMANN
*Ruprecht-Karls-Universität
Heidelberg, Germany*
Koch, Robert

KENNETH W. GRAHAM
University of Guelph, Canada
Godwin, William

ARTHUR L. GREIL
Alfred University
Sorel, Georges

**PATRICIA GUENTHER-
GLEASON**
Independent Scholar
Schleiermacher, Friedrich

SUZANNE GUERLAC
University of California, Berkeley
Hugo, Victor

PETER J. GURNEY
University of Essex, U.K.
Cooperative Movements

SARA HACKENBERG
San Francisco State University
Dickens, Charles

HEATHER HADLOCK
Stanford University
Offenbach, Jacques

HAEJEONG HAZEL HAHN
Seattle University
Posters

W. SCOTT HAINE
*University of Maryland University
College*
Alcohol and Temperance

LESLEY A. HALL
*Wellcome Library for the History
and Understanding of Medicine/
University College London*
Ellis, Havelock

RICHARD C. HALL
*Georgia Southwestern State
University*
Balkan Wars
Bulgaria

G. M. HAMBURG
Claremont McKenna College
Herzen, Alexander
Westernizers

MAURA E. HAMETZ
Old Dominion University
Trieste

CYRUS HAMLIN
Yale University
Schinkel, Karl Friedrich
Schlegel, August Wilhelm von

MICHAEL HANAGAN
Vassar College
Capitalism
Class and Social Relations
Economic Growth and
Industrialism

IAN HANCOCK
University of Texas
Romanies (Gypsies)

M. ŞÜKRÜ HANIOĞLU
Princeton University
Young Turks

ALASTAIR HANNAY
University of Oslo
Kierkegaard, Søren

PAUL R. HANSON
Butler University
Counterrevolution
Estates-General
Federalist Revolt
Girondins
Reign of Terror

ROBERT HARMS
Yale University
Africa

STEVEN L. HARP
University of Akron
Automobile
Tourism

MARK HARRISON
University of Oxford, U.K.
Smallpox

JANET HARTLEY
London School of Economics and
Political Science
Alexander I

HEINZ-GERHARD HAUPT
European Unversity Institute
Artisans and Guilds

STEVEN C. HAUSE
Washington University, St. Louis,
Missouri
Auclert, Hubertine
Delcassé, Théophile
Ferry, Jules
Norton, Caroline
Popular and Elite Culture
Protestantism
Separation of Church
and State
(France, 1905)
Suffragism
Waldeck-Rousseau, René

JAMES L. HAYNSWORTH
Independent Scholar
Toussaint Louverture

LEO HECHT
George Mason University
Mussorgsky, Modest
Tchaikovsky, Peter

JAMES A. W. HEFFERNAN
Dartmouth College
Coleridge, Samuel Taylor
Constable, John

MICHAEL HEIDELBERGER
University of Tübingen, Germany
Helmholtz, Hermann von

DAVID S. HEIDLER
University of Southern Colorado—
Pueblo
War of 1812

JEANNE T. HEIDLER
U. S. Air Force Academy
War of 1812

JOHN HEILBRON
Yale University
Planck, Max

JAMES HEINZEN
Rowan University
Lenin, Vladimir
Nechayev, Sergei

REINHOLD HELLER
University of Chicago
Munch, Edvard

DAVID V. HERLIHY
Cycling

HOLGER H. HERWIG
University of Calgary
Bethmann Hollweg,
Theobald von
Germany
List, Georg Friedrich

CARLA HESSE
University of California, Berkeley
Gouges, Olympe de

COLIN HEYWOOD
University of Nottingham
Childhood and Children

DAVID HIGGS
University of Toronto
Landed Elites

ANNE HIGONNET
Barnard College, Columbia
University
Morisot, Berthe

KEITH HITCHINS
University of Illinois at Urbana-
Champaign
Romania

ADAM HOCHSCHILD
Independent Scholar
Leopold II

DIRK HOERDER
Université de Paris 8, Saint Denis
   Immigration and Internal Migration

STEFAN-LUDWIG HOFFMANN
University of Bochum
   Associations, Voluntary

MICHAEL HOLQUIST
Yale University
   Chekhov, Anton

NILES R. HOLT
Illinois State University
   Darwin, Charles

ELIZABETH L. HOLTZE
Metropolitan State College of Denver
   Grimm Brothers

SUNGOOK HONG
Seoul National University, South Korea
   Physics

GAIL TURLEY HOUSTON
University of New Mexico
   Bentham, Jeremy
   Mill, James

R. A. HOUSTON
University of St. Andrews, Scotland
   Scotland

ALAN HOUTCHENS
Texas A&M University
   Dvořák, Antonín

RICHARD G. HOVANNISIAN
University of California, Los Angeles
   Armenia

LINDSEY HUGHES
University College London
   Paul I

MADELEINE HURD
Södertörn University College, Sweden
   Hamburg

JOHN HUTCHESON
York University
   Economists, Classical

PATRICK H. HUTTON
University of Vermont
   Blanqui, Auguste
   Secret Societies

PAULA E. HYMAN
Yale University
   Jews and Judaism

WILLIAM D. IRVINE
York University, Toronto
   Boulanger Affair

GERALD N. IZENBERG
Washington University in St. Louis
   Kandinsky, Vasily

JO ELLEN JACOBS
Milliken University
   Mill, Harriet Taylor

DALE JACQUETTE
The Pennsylvania State University
   Brentano, Franz
   Husserl, Edmund

CHRISTOPHER JANAWAY
University of Southampton, U.K.
   Schopenhauer, Arthur

KONRAD H. JARAUSCH
University of North Carolina at Chapel Hill
   Professions

MAYA JASANOFF
University of Virginia
   Curzon, George
   Egypt
   India

PETER JELAVICH
Johns Hopkins University
   Cabarets

RUTH Y. JENKINS
University of California State at Fresno
   Nightingale, Florence

RICHARD JENKYNS
Lady Margaret Hall, University of Oxford
   Philhellenic Movement

JEREMY JENNINGS
Queen Mary, University of London
   Intellectuals

AUSTIN JERSILD
Old Dominion University
   Shamil

CHRISTOPHER H. JOHNSON
Wayne State University
   Cabet, Étienne

ROBERT E. JOHNSON
University of Toronto
   People's Will

BRIAN JOHNSTON
Carnegie Mellon University
   Ibsen, Henrik

PHILIP T. A. JOHNSTON
University of Illinois at Urbana-Champaign
   Nijinsky, Vaslav

CHRISTOPHER JONES
   Spain

COLIN JONES
University of Warwick, U.K.
   Marie-Antoinette

GRETA JONES
University of Ulster
   Tuberculosis

H. S. JONES
University of Manchester, U.K.
Constant, Benjamin
Saint-Simon, Henri de

MAX JONES
University of Manchester
Baden-Powell, Robert

DAVID JORAVSKY
Northwestern University
Schnitzler, Arthur

DAVID P. JORDAN
University of Illinois at Chicago
Haussmann, Georges-
Eugène
Louis XVI
Paris
Robespierre, Maximilien

PIETER M. JUDSON
Swarthmore College
Austria-Hungary

FREDERICK W. KAGAN
U. S. Military Academy
Austerlitz
Borodino
Nicholas I
Ulm, Battle of

J. F. V. KEIGER
Salford University, U.K.
Poincaré, Raymond

MALCOM KELSALL
Cardiff University
Byron, George Gordon

PETER KEMP
The Johann Strauss Society of Great Britain
Strauss, Johann

SUSAN KINGSLEY KENT
University of Colorado at Boulder
Davies, Emily
Fawcett, Millicent Garrett

JOSEPH A. KESTNER
University of Tulsa
Doyle, Arthur Conan

ALAN J. KIDD
Manchester Metropolitan University, U.K.
Manchester

BEN KIERNAN
Yale University
Indochina

ESTHER KINGSTON-MANN
University of Massachusetts, Boston
Populists

KONSTANTINE KLIOUTCHKINE
Pomona College, Claremont, CA
Goncharov, Ivan

JANE KNELLER
Colorado State University
Novalis (Hardenberg, Friedrich von)

JOVANA L. KNEŽEVIĆ
Yale University
Black Hand
Bosnia-Herzegovina
Montenegro
Serbia

ALEXANDRA KOENIGUER
University Paris X—Nanterre
Atget, Eugène

DIANE P. KOENKER
University of Illinois at Urbana-Champaign
Bolsheviks

PATRICIA KOLLANDER
Florida Atlantic University
Frederick III
William I

MARTTI KOSKENNIEMI
The Academy of Finland
Brussels Declaration

Geneva Convention
International Law

DALE KRAMER
University of Illinois, Urbana-Champaign
Hardy, Thomas

LLOYD KRAMER
University of North Carolina, Chapel Hill
Lafayette, Marquis de

SARAH A. KRIVE
Independent Scholar
Tolstoy, Leo
Turgenev, Ivan

SHERYL KROEN
University of Florida
Louis XVIII
Restoration

THOMAS KSELMAN
University of Notre Dame
Anticlericalism
Catholicism
Pilgrimages

MARY HAYNES KUHLMAN
Creighton University
Gaskell, Elizabeth

BRIAN LADD
University of Albany, State University of New York
Berlin
Cities and Towns

ANDREW LAMBERT
King's College, London
Crimean War
Navarino

HUGO LANE
Polytechnic University of Brooklyn
Pan-Slavism

COLIN LANG
Yale University
Modernism

CHARLES LANSING
University of Connecticut
   Treitschke, Heinrich von

DAVID CLAY LARGE
Montana State University,
Bozeman
   Louis II
   Wagner, Richard

BARBARA LARSON
University of West Florida
   Symbolism

DAVID LAVEN
University of Reading, U.K.
   Venice

KEITH LAYBOURN
University of Huddersfield, U.K.
   Hardie, James Keir
   Labour Party

DAVID LEARY
University of Richmond
   Psychology

RENE LEBOUTTE
University of Luxembourg
   Coal Mining

RICHARD A. LEBRUN
University of Manitoba
   Maistre, Joseph de

SIMON LEE
University of Reading, U.K.
   David, Jacques-Louis

LYNN HOLLEN LEES
University of Pennsylvania
   London

MICHAEL V. LEGGIERE
Louisiana State University
   Hundred Days
   Larrey, Dominique-Jean
   Waterloo

FRIEDRICH LENGER
University of Giessen, Germany
   Zollverein

YVES LEQUIN
Université-Lumière-Lyon 2,
France
   Lyon

KATHARINE ANNE LERMAN
London Metropolitan University
   Bismarck, Otto von

SOPHIE LETERRIER
Université d'Artois, France
   Ravel, Maurice

FRED LEVENTHAL
Boston University
   Fabians

MATTHEW LEVINGER
Lewis and Clark College
   Hardenberg, Karl August
     von
   Stein, Heinrich Friedrich Karl
     vom und zum

E. JAMES LIEBERMAN
George Washington University
   Rank, Otto

HARRY LIEBERSOHN
University of Illinois at Urbana-
Champaign
   Ranke, Leopold von

ANDRE LIEBICH
Graduate Institute of
International Studies, Geneva
   Martov, L.
   Mensheviks

DOMINIC LIEVEN
London School of Economics and
Political Science
   Aristocracy

ALBERT LINDEMANN
University of California, Santa
Barbara
   Anti-Semitism

TESSIE P. LIU
Northwestern University
   Citizenship

JAMES LIVESEY
University of Sussex, U.K.
   Republicanism

NANCY LOCKE
Pennsylvania State University
   Manet, Édouard
   Renoir, Pierre-Auguste

OLIVER LOGAN
University of East Anglia,
Norwich, U.K.
   Papal Infallibility
   Papal State
   Roman Question

PETER MELVILLE LOGAN
Temple University
   Eliot, George

DAVID LOMAS
University of Manchester, U.K.
   Picasso, Pablo

NANCY LOPATIN-LUMMIS
University of Wisconsin—Stevens
Point
   George IV

JENNIFER LORCH
University of Warwick, U.K.
   Wollstonecraft, Mary

PATRICIA M. E. LORCIN
University of Minnesota, Twin
Cities
   Algeria

ANNE LOUNSBERY
New York University
   Gogol, Nikolai

BRIGID LOWE
Trinity College, Cambridge
   Brontë, Charlotte and Emily

DAVID S. LUFT
University of California, San
Diego
   Hofmannsthal, Hugo von
   Musil, Robert

JESPER LÜTZEN
University of Copenhagen
Hertz, Heinrich

DOUGLAS P. MACKAMAN
*The University of Southern
Mississippi*
Leisure

EMMA MACLEOD
University of Stirling, U.K.
Fox, Charles James

PAOLO MACRY
University of Naples "Federico II"
Garibaldi, Giuseppe
Naples

STEVEN E. MAFFEO
*U.S. Air Force Academy and U.S.
Joint Military Intelligence College*
Nelson, Horatio

DRISS MAGHRAOUI
*Al Akhawayn University, Ifrane,
Morocco*
Morocco

LOIS N. MAGNER
Purdue University
Curie, Marie

ROGER MAGRAW
University of Warwick, U.K.
Working Class

OLGA MAIOROVA
University of Michigan
Eurasianism

DAN MALAN
Independent Scholar
Doré, Gustave

FRANCES MALINO
Wellesley College
Jewish Emancipation

PHILLIP MALLETT
University of St. Andrews, U.K.
Kipling, Rudyard

BRENT MANER
Kansas State University
Virchow, Rudolf

JO BURR MARGADANT
Santa Clara University
Louis-Philippe

MARTIN F. MARIX EVANS
Independent Scholar
Majuba Hill

STEVEN G. MARKS
Clemson University
Siberia
Vladivostok

ERIC MASSIE
University of Stirling, U.K.
Stevenson, Robert Louis

GIOVANNI MATTEUCCI
University of Bologna
Dilthey, Wilhelm

PATRICK MAUME
Queen's University, Belfast, U.K.
Parnell, Charles Stewart

MARY JO MAYNES
University of Minnesota
Marriage and Family

PAUL MAZGAJ
*University of North Carolina,
Greensboro*
Maurras, Charles

PAULINE M. H. MAZUMDAR
University of Toronto
Eugenics

DAVID MCDONALD
University of Wisconsin, Madison
Holy Alliance
Münchengrätz, Treaty of
Nicholas II
Unkiar-Skelessi, Treaty of

IAN C. MCGIBBON
*New Zealand Ministry for
Culture and Heritage*
New Zealand

JOHN P. MCKAY
*University of Illinois, Urbana-
Champaign*
Michelet, Jules

STEVEN MCLEAN
Nottingham Trent University
Wells, H. G.

DAVID MCLELLAN
*Goldsmiths College, University of
London*
Young Hegelians

DARRIN M. MCMAHON
Florida State University
Conservatism

JAMES F. MCMILLAN
University of Edinburgh, U.K.
Durand, Marguerite

PETER MCPHEE
*University of Melbourne,
Australia*
Committee of Public Safety
French Revolution
Jacobins

NEIL MCWILLIAM
Duke University
Rude, François

R. DARRELL MEADOWS
Independent Scholar
Housing

CHRISTINE MEHRING
Yale University
Klimt, Gustav

EVAN M. MELHADO
*University of Illinois at Urbana-
Champaign*
Chemistry

WILLIAM E. MELIN
Lafayette College
Berlioz, Hector

ANNE K. MELLOR
University of California, Los Angeles
Shelley, Mary

BRUCE W. MENNING
U.S. Army Command and General Staff College
Mukden, Battle of
Russo-Turkish War
San Stefano, Treaty of

LESLIE ANNE MERCED
Benedictine College
Generation of 1898

CAROL P. MERRIMAN
Independent Scholar
Art Nouveau
Schiele, Egon

JOHN MERRIMAN
Yale University
Captain Swing
Charles X
France
Ravachol (François Claudius Koenigstein-Ravachol)

MARK S. MICALE
University of Illinois
Absinthe
Charcot, Jean-Martin
Eiffel Tower
Romanticism

ELISA R. MILKES
Horace Mann School
Brougham, Henry
Castlereagh, Viscount (Robert Stewart)
Combination Acts
Corn Laws, Repeal of
Palmerston, Lord (Henry John Temple)
Wellington, Duke of (Arthur Wellesley)

MARTIN A. MILLER
Duke University
Kropotkin, Peter

MONSERRAT MILLER
Marshall University
Markets

NICHOLAS MILLER
Boise State University
Gaj, Ljudevit
Jelačić, Josip
Karadjordje

PAVLA MILLER
Royal Melbourne Institute of Technology, Australia
Education
Montessori, Maria

BARRY MILLIGAN
Wright State University
Drugs

MARGARET MINER
University of Illinois at Chicago
Baudelaire, Charles

JOEL MOKYR
Northwestern University and University of Tel Aviv
Industrial Revolution, Second
Science and Technology

ANNIKA MOMBAUER
The Open University, U.K.
Alliance System
Moroccan Crises
Schlieffen Plan

JOHN WARNE MONROE
Iowa State University
Spiritualism

DANIEL MORAN
Naval Postgraduate School
Clausewitz, Carl von
Jomini, Antoine-Henri de

MICHAEL MORTON
Duke University
Herder, Johann Gottfried

PETER MORTON
Flinders University, Adelaide, Australia
Gissing, George

NORMAN H. MURDOCH
University of Cincinnati (emeritus)
Salvation Army

WILLIAM MURRAY
Latrobe University, Australia
Football (Soccer)

SCOTT HUGHES MYERLY
Independent Scholar
Beards

GLENN MYRENT
Independent Scholar
Lumière, Auguste and Louis

ISABELLE H. NAGINSKI
Tufts University
Sand, George

WILLIAM NASSON
University of Cape Town
Boer War
Kitchener, Horatio Herbert
Omdurman
Rhodes, Cecil
South Africa

MICHAEL S. NEIBERG
University of Southern Mississippi
Armies

CATHARINE THEIMER NEPOMNYASHCHY
Barnard College
Pushkin, Alexander

SUSAN VANDIVER NICASSIO
University of Louisiana at Lafayette
Puccini, Giacomo

RICHARD NOLL
DeSales University
Haeckel, Ernst Heinrich

CLAIRE E. NOLTE
Manhattan College
Masaryk, Tomáš Garrigue
Palacký, František
Young Czechs and Old
Czechs

DEBORAH EPSTEIN NORD
Princeton University
Webb, Beatrice Potter

SHERWIN B. NULAND
Yale University
Semmelweis, Ignac

ROBERT A. NYE
Oregon State University
LeBon, Gustave
Masculinity
Sexuality

LYNN K. NYHART
University of Wisconsin, Madison
Museums

DAVID O'BRIEN
University of Illinois at Urbana-Champaign
Canova, Antonio
Delacroix, Eugène
Géricault, Théodore

CAROL OCKMAN
Williams College
Ingres, Jean-Auguste-Dominique

RALPH O'CONNOR
University of Aberdeen, U.K.
Lyell, Charles

ROBERT OLBY
University of Pittsburgh
Mendel, Gregor

ROBERT WILLIAM OLDANI
Arizona State University
Rimsky-Korsakov, Nikolai

PAUL O'LEARY
University of Wales, Aberystwyth, U.K.
Wales

HARRY OOSTERHUIS
University of Maastricht
Krafft-Ebing, Richard von

SHANE O'ROURKE
York University, U.K.
Cossacks

MICHAEL R. ORWICZ
University of Connecticut
Millet, Jean-François

ROBERT J. PARADOWSKI
Rochester Institute of Technology
Einstein, Albert
Lavoisier, Antoine

JONATHAN PARRY
Pembroke College, University of Cambridge
Disraeli, Benjamin

ALLAN H. PASCO
University of Kansas
Balzac, Honoré de

KEVIN PASSMORE
Cardiff University
Action Française

ALICE K. PATE
Columbus State University
Socialist Revolutionaries

SILVANA PATRIARCA-HARRIS
Fordham University
Leopardi, Giacomo
Manzoni, Alessandro
Verga, Giovanni

MARTA PETRUSEWICZ
City University of New York and Universitá della Cabria, Italy
Peasants
Sismondi, Jean-Charles
Leonard de

ROD PHILLIPS
Carleton University, Ottawa
Wine

DANIEL PICK
Birbeck College, University of London
Degeneration

MARY PICKERING
San Jose State University
Comte, Auguste

PAUL A. PICKERING
The Australian National University
O'Connor, Feargus
Peel, Robert

PAMELA PILBEAM
Royal Holloway, University of London
Blanc, Louis
Bonapartism
Bourgeoisie
Bureaucracy
Deroin, Jeanne
Guizot, François

TERRY PINKARD
Georgetown University
Hegel, Georg Wilhelm
Friedrich

STEPHEN C. PINSON
New York Public Library
Daguerre, Louis

LEON PLANTINGA
Yale University
Beethoven, Ludwig van

JANET POLASKY
University of New Hampshire
Brussels
Leopold I

HILARY PORISS
University of Cincinnati
Rossini, Gioachino
Verdi, Giuseppe

BERNARD PORTER
University of Newcastle upon Tyne, U.K.
Colonies
Imperialism

BRIAN PORTER
University of Michigan
Czartoryski, Adam
Endecja
Nationalism
Polish National Movement
Warsaw

DOROTHY PORTER
University of California San Francisco
Disease
Public Health

THEODORE M. PORTER
University of California, Los Angeles
Quetelet, Lambert Adolphe Jacques

LARRY L. PORTIS
Université Paul Valéry (Montpellier 3)
Durkheim, Émile

CAROLYN J. POUNCY
University of Maryland
Pavlova, Anna

PETER C. POZEFSKY
The College of Wooster
Chaadayev, Peter
Nihilists

JENIFER PRESTO
University of Oregon
Silver Age

RADO PRIBIC
Lafayette College
Dostoyevsky, Fyodor

ROGER PRICE
University of Wales, Aberstwyth, U.K.
Napoleon III
Phylloxera
Railroads
Transportation and Communications

CHRISTOPHER J. PROM
University of Illinois, Urbana Champaign
Smiles, Samuel

JUNE PURVIS
University of Portsmouth, U.K.
Pankhurst, Emmeline, Christabel, and Sylvia

JOHN W. RANDOLPH JR.
University of Illinois at Urbana-Champaign
Bakunin, Mikhail

CHARLES REARICK
University of Massachusetts at Amherst
Fin de Siècle

ALAN J. REINERMAN
Boston College
Diplomacy
Metternich, Clemens von
Revolutions of 1820

LUCY RIALL
Birkbeck College, University of London
Sicily

NATHALIE RICHARD
Universite Paris I—Pantheon, Sorbonne
Renan, Ernest

ANGELIQUE RICHARDSON
University of Exeter, U.K.
Spencer, Herbert

BERNHARD RIEGER
University College, London
Krupp

DANIEL RINGROSE
Minot State University
Engineers

DAVID D. ROBERTS
University of Georgia
Croce, Benedetto

SUSANNE ROBERTS
Yale University Library
Libraries

HARLOW ROBINSON
Northeastern University
Meyerhold, Vsevolod

JUDITH ROHRER
Emory University
Gaudí, Antonio

BERNICE GLATZER ROSENTHAL
Fordham University
Berdyayev, Nikolai

RONALD J. ROSS
University of Wisconsin—Milwaukee
Center Party
Kulturkampf

NICOLAS ROUSSELLIER
Institut d'études politiques, Paris
Liberalism

EDWARD ROYLE
University of York, U.K.
Chartism

HELEN M. ROZWADOWSKI
University of Connecticut, Avery Point Campus
Oceanic Exploration

JAMES H. RUBIN
State University of New York, Stony Brook
Impressionism
Painting

PENNY RUSSELL
University of Sydney
Manners and Formality

MICHAEL A. RUTZ
University of Wisconsin—Oshkosh
Explorers
Missions

JAMES SACK
University of Illinois, Chicago
Tories

ROBERT E. SACKETT
University of Colorado, Colorado Springs
Frankfurt Parliament

MICHAEL SALER
University of California, Davis
Decadence

BRITT SALVESEN
University of Arizona, Tucson
Seurat, Georges

JEFFREY L. SAMMONS
Independent Scholar
Heine, Heinrich

MAURICE SAMUELS
University of Pennsylvania
Stendhal (Marie-Henri Beyle)

JOSHUA SANBORN
Lafayette College
Portsmouth, Treaty of

ROLAND SARTI
University of Massachusetts, Amherst
Cavour, Count (Camillo Benso)
Charles Albert
Italy

Mazzini, Giuseppe
Young Italy

BENJAMIN C. SAX
University of Kansas
Fontane, Theodor
Goethe, Johann Wolfgang von

JEAN-FRÉDÉRIC SCHAUB
Ecole des hautes etudes en sciences sociales (Paris)
Madrid

WIELAND SCHMIED
Akademie der Bildenden Kuenste, Munich
Friedrich, Caspar David

BARBARA SCHMUCKI
University of York, U.K.
Subways

FREDERICK C. SCHNEID
High Point University
Congress of Troppau
Congress of Vienna
French Revolutionary Wars and Napoleonic Wars
Sieyès, Emmanuel-Joseph

JANE SCHNEIDER
City University of New York
Mafia

PETER SCHNEIDER
Fordham University
Mafia

KATRIN SCHULTHEISS
University of Illinois at Chicago
Nurses

JERROLD SEIGEL
New York University
Flâneur

SUDIPTA SEN
University of California, Davis
East India Company

CHANDAK SENGOOPTA
Birkbeck College, University of London
Weininger, Otto

ALFRED E. SENN
University of Wisconsin
Lithuania

SONU SHAMDASANI
Wellcome Trust Centre for the History of Medicine, University College London
Jung, Carl Gustav

BARRY M. SHAPIRO
Allegheny College
Danton, Georges-Jacques

DENNIS SHOWALTER
Colorado College
Addis Ababa, Treaty of
Austro-Prussian War
Concert of Europe
Danish-German War
Franco-Austrian War
Franco-Prussian War
Hague Conferences
Moltke, Helmuth von
Shimonoseki, Treaty of
Trafalgar, Battle of

NICHOLAS SHRIMPTON
Lady Margaret Hall, University of Oxford
Arnold, Matthew

MICHAEL SIBALIS
Wilfrid Laurier University
Homosexuality and Lesbianism

LISA Z. SIGEL
De Paul University
Pornography

DAVID SILBEY
Alvernia College
Asquith, Herbert Henry
Edward VII

LISA SILVERMAN
University of Sussex, U.K.
Herzl, Theodor

MARC SMEETS
Raboud University Nijmegen, The Netherlands
Huysmans, Joris-Karl

BONNIE G. SMITH
Rutgers University
Gender

CROSBIE SMITH
University of Kent
Kelvin, Lord (William Thomson)

DOUGLAS SMITH
University of Washington
Catherine II

SUSAN SMITH-PETER
College of Staten Island/City University of New York
Speransky, Mikhail

FRANK SNOWDEN
Yale University
Malatesta, Errico

TIMOTHY SNYDER
Yale University
Mickiewicz, Adam
Poland
Ukraine

REBA N. SOFFER
California State University, Northridge
Acton, John

LAWRENCE SONDHAUS
University of Indianapolis
Naval Rivalry (Anglo-German)

CHARLES SOWERWINE
University of Melbourne, Australia
Boulangism
Dreyfus Affair

Pelletier, Madeleine
Syndicalism

REBECCA L. SPANG
University College, London
Restaurants

JONATHAN SPERBER
University of Missouri
Revolutions of 1848

MATTHIAS STADELMANN
University of Erlangen-Nuremberg, Germany
Glinka, Mikhail

ADAM C. STANLEY
Univerity of Wisconsin, Platteville
Staël, Germaine de

PETER STANSKY
Stanford University
Morris, William

ALESSANDRO STANZIANI
Centre national de recherches scientifiques, Paris
Statistics

JAMES D. STEAKLEY
University of Wisconsin, Madison
Hirschfeld, Magnus
Ulrichs, Karl Heinrich

BIRGITTA STEENE
Sweden
Strindberg, August

GARY P. STEENSON
California Polytechnic State University, San Lois Obispo
Bebel, August
Kautsky, Karl
Lassalle, Ferdinand
Liebknecht, Karl
Second International

MANFRED B. STEGER
Royal Melbourne Institute of Technology, Australia
Bernstein, Eduard

SUSIE L. STEINBACH
Hamline University
Austen, Jane

JONATHAN STEINBERG
University of Pennsylvania
Switzerland

MARK D. STEINBERG
University of Illinois at Urbana-Champaign.
Gorky, Maxim

CHRISTOPHER H. STERLING
George Washington University
Telephones

JANET STEWART
University of Aberdeen
Loos, Adolf

RICHARD STITES
Georgetown University
Diaghilev, Sergei
Struve, Peter

MELISSA K. STOCKDALE
University of Oklahoma
Kadets
Milyukov, Pavel

CHRIS STOLWIJK
Van Gogh Museum, Amsterdam
Van Gogh, Vincent

DANIEL STONE
University of Winnipeg, Canada
Kosciuszko, Tadeusz

JUDITH F. STONE
Western Michigan University
Clemenceau, Georges
Radicalism

TYLER STOVALL
University of California, Berkeley
Minorities

CARL J. STRIKWERDA
The College of William and Mary
Belgium
Socialism, Christian

ROB STUART
University of Western Australia
Guesde, Jules

CLAUDE J. SUMMERS
University of Michigan—Dearborn
Forster, E. M.

JOHN SUTHERLAND
*University College London
(emeritus)*
Scott, Walter

RICHARD SWEDBERG
Cornell University
Simmel, Georg
Weber, Max

DENNIS SWEENEY
*University of Alberta, Edmonton,
Alberta, Canada*
Labor Movements
Strikes

ANTHONY SWIFT
University of Essex, U.K.
World's Fairs

JULIE ANNE TADDEO
University of California, Berkeley
Strachey, Lytton

EMILE J. TALBOT
*University of Illinois at Urbana-
Champaign*
Goncourt, Edmond and
Jules de

HENK TE VELDE
Leiden University, Netherlands
Netherlands

**PETRA TEN-DOESSCHATE
CHU**
Seton Hall University
Corot, Jean-Baptiste-Camille
Realism and Naturalism

THIERRY TERRET
University of Lyon, France
Sports

CYRIL THOMAS
Université de Paris Nanterre
Fauvism
Matisse, Henri

JAMES THOMPSON
University of Bristol
Bagehot, Walter

ROBERT W. THURSTON
Miami University
Moscow

JOHN GEOFFREY TIMMINS
University of Central Lancashire
Factories

MARIA TODOROVA
*University of Illinois at Urbana-
Champaign*
Ottoman Empire

JANIS A. TOMLINSON
*University Museums, University of
Delaware*
Goya, Francisco

DAVID G. TROYANSKY
*Brooklyn College of the City
University of New York*
Death and Burial
Old Age

ALEX TYRRELL
La Trobe University
William IV

HANS RUDOLF VAGET
Smith College (emeritus)
Mann, Thomas

CYRUS VAKIL
*Mahindra United World College
of India*
Malthus, Thomas Robert

**ELIZABETH KRIDL
VALKENIER**
Columbia University
Repin, Ilya

BARBARA VALOTTI
Marconi, Guglielmo

ETIENNE VAN DE WALLE
University of Pennsylvania
Demography

JOHN VAN WYHE
Cambridge University
Phrenology

LIANA VARDI
*State University of New York,
Buffalo*
Agricultural Revolution

STEPHEN VELLA
Yale University
Carlyle, Thomas
Manning, Henry
Newman, John Henry
Pater, Walter
Sepoy Mutiny
Tennyson, Alfred
Whigs

BRIAN VICK
University of Sheffield
Gagern, Heinrich von

ELOINA VILLEGAS
University of Colorado, Boulder
Barcelona

DAVID VINCENT
The Open University
Literacy

K. STEVEN VINCENT
North Carolina State University
Anarchism
Proudhon, Pierre-Joseph

ARON VINEGAR
Ohio State University
Viollet-le-Duc, Eugène

IGOR VISHNEVETSKY
*St. Sava Serbian Orthodox School
of Theology, Libertyville, Illinois*
Bely, Andrei

THIERRY L. VISSOL
European Union
Monetary Unions

GREGORY VITARBO
Meredith College
Kutuzov, Mikhail

MICHIEL F. WAGENAAR
University of Amsterdam, The Netherlands
Amsterdam

PETER WALDRON
University of Sunderland, U.K.
Alexander II
Russia

ANDRZEJ WALICKI
University of Notre Dame
Slavophiles

BARBARA WALKER
University of Nevada, Reno
Alexandra

SCOTT WALTER
Henri-Poincaré Archives (CNRS) and University of Nancy, France
Poincaré, Henri

KATHRYN A. WALTERSCHEID
University of Missouri—St. Louis
Coffee, Tea, Chocolate
Diet and Nutrition

JAMES WALVIN
University of York, U.K.
Race and Racism
Slavery

GEOFFREY WAWRO
University of North Texas
Military Tactics

STEWART WEAVER
University of Rochester
Luddism
Machine Breaking

R. K. WEBB
University of Maryland, Baltimore County (emeritus)
Martineau, Harriet

JUDITH WECHSLER
Tufts University
Daumier, Honoré

THEODORE R. WEEKS
Southern Illinois University at Carbondale
Alexander III

ROBERT WEINBERG
Swarthmore College
Bund, Jewish

DORA B. WEINER
University of California, Los Angeles
Pinel, Philippe

JOAN WEINER
Indiana University
Frege, Gottlob

GABRIEL P. WEISBERG
University of Minnesota
Guimard, Hector

ERIC D. WEITZ
University of Minnesota
Luxemburg, Rosa

ANGELIKA WESENBERG
Nationalgalerie, Berlin
Menzel, Adolph von

JAMES L. WEST
Middlebury College
Octobrists

TIMOTHY C. WESTPHALEN
State University of New York, Stony Brook
Blok, Alexander

ZINA WEYGAND
Conservatoire National des Arts et Metiers, Paris
Braille, Louis

STEPHEN WHEATCROFT
University of Melbourne, Australia
Exile, Penal

DOUGLAS L. WHEELER
University of New Hampshire, Durham
Portugal

KEVIN WHELAN
Keough Notre Dame Centre, Dublin, Ireland
Ireland
O'Connell, Daniel

CHARLES WHITE
U.S. Army Forces Command, Fort McPherson, Georgia
Jena, Battle of

PAUL WHITE
Cambridge University
Huxley, Thomas Henry

SARAH WHITING
Princeton University
Parks

STEVEN M. WHITING
University of Michigan
Satie, Erik

JAMES WHITMAN
Yale University
Law, Theories of

CRAIG WILCOX
Independent Scholar
Australia

ALAN WILLIAMS
Rutgers University
Cinema

JOHN WILLIAMS
Colorado College
Nanking, Treaty of

GEORGE S. WILLIAMSON
University of Alabama
Carlsbad Decrees
Schelling, Friedrich von

ROLF WINAU
Charite-Universitatsmedizin
BerlinDavis
    Ehrlich, Paul

NANCY M. WINGFIELD
Northern Illinois University
    Bohemia, Moravia, and Silesia
    Prague

MARY PICKARD WINSOR
University of Toronto
    Agassiz, Louis

ALISON WINTER
University of Chicago
    Mesmer, Franz Anton

ROBERT WOKLER
Yale University
    Bonald, Louis de
    Burke, Edmund
    Utilitarianism

GAIL HILSON WOLDU
Trinity College
    Debussy, Claude

J.R. WOLFFE
Open University, U.K.
    Wilberforce, William

SUSAN J. WOLFSON
Princeton University
    Wordsworth, William

BRADLEY D. WOODWORTH
University of New Haven
    Finland and the Baltic
    Provinces

T. R. WRIGHT
University of Newcastle, U.K.
    Positivism

GUOQI XU
Kalamazoo College
    Boxer Rebellion
    China
    Opium Wars

LINDA GERTNER ZATLIN
Morehouse College
    Beardsley, Aubrey

INDEX

Page references include both a volume number and a page number. For example, **5:**2409–2411 refers to pages 2409–2411 in volume 5. Page numbers in **boldface** type indicate references to complete articles. Page numbers in *italic* type indicate illustrations, tables, and figures.

B

C

Champollion, Jean-François, **1:**406–407

Champs Elysees (Paris), **2:***869*; **4:**1735

Chance (Conrad), **2:**536

Chancery Court (Britain), **1:**303

Chandelle verte, La (Jarry), **3:**1214

Chandler, Alfred, **2:**711

Changarnier, Nicolas-Anne-Theoduke, **3:**1318

"Channel Firing" (Hardy), **2:**1045

Chansons des rues et des bois, Les (Hugo), **2:**1094

Chansons madécasses (Ravel), **4:**1945

Chanteuse, La (Degas), **1:***336*

Chants du Crépuscule, Les (Hugo), **2:**1093

Chanute, Octave, **4:**2115

Chapman, Maria Weston, **3:**1459

Chaptal, Jean-Antoine, **4:**1790

Chapters on Socialism (J. S. Mill), **3:**1514

Charbonnerie conspiracy, **1:**337, 361

Charcot, Jean-Martin, **1:**407–411, *409*; **3:**1665; **4:**1908, 2255

 Freud and, **2:**639; **4:**1904

Charcot's joints, **1:**408

Chardin, Jean-Baptiste-Siméon, **3:**1474

Charenton (French prison/asylum), **4:**2074

"Charge of the Light Brigade" (Tennyson), **1:**95, 244

Charging Chasseur (Géricault), **2:**955

Charigot, Aline, **4:**1956

charity

 African colonization and, **1:**222

 Belgian Catholic relief work and, **1:**203

 Catholic poverty relief as, **1:**383

 fundraiser poster, **4:***1853*

 Malthusian opposition to, **3:**1425–1426

 nursing and, **3:**1649

 poor relief and, **4:**1847, 1849, 1850, 1851, *1852*, 1854; **5:**2450, 2451

 unemployed workers and, **5:**2454

 voluntary associations and, **1:**119

 See also welfare

Charity Organization Society (London), **2:**769; **4:**1851

Charivari, Le (French journal), **2:**621, 622

Charlatans modernes, Les (Marat), **3:**1443

Charles I, king of England, **4:**1738, 1958

Charles VIII, king of France, **4:**2300

Charles X, king of France, **1:**411–413; **2:**1029; **3:**1442; **4:**2038

 abdication of, **1:**270, 457; **2:**566, 640; **3:**1301, 1303; **4:**1984; **5:**2310

 accession of, **2:**847–848

 Algeria and, **3:**1389

 Bonald's hostility to, **1:**269

 brother Louis XVIII and, **3:**1386

 Chateaubriand and, **1:**421

 counterrevolutionary program of, **3:**1387

 French Revolution and, **2:**843; **3:**1386, 1403

 grandson of, **2:**855

 July Ordinances (1830) and, **1:**412; **3:**1387, 1388

 Louis-Philippe and, **3:**1388

 Restoration and, **4:**1968–1969, 1970

 Revolution of 1830 and, **1:**412, 413; **3:**1393; **4:**1983–1984; **5:**2512

 Rossini opera and, **3:**1671

 suffrage and, **4:**2277

 Talleyrand and, **5:**2306

Charles VI, Holy Roman emperor, **5:**2354

Charles III, king of Spain, **1:**336; **2:**809; **4:**2227, 2229

 Naples and, **3:**1191, 1580

Charles IV, king of Spain, **4:**2225

 Carlist coup and, **1:**366, 367

 David commission from, **2:**624

 French Revolutionary War and, **2:**899

 Goya as court painter to, **2:**997, 999

 Napoleon and, **2:**902; **4:**1763–1764

 son Ferdinand VII and, **2:**808, 809, 998; **4:**1763

Charles V (self-proclaimed), king of Spain, **1:**367, 368; **2:**809

Charles XIII, king of Sweden, **1:**226

Charles XIV John, king of Sweden and Norway. *See* Bernadotte, Jean-Baptiste

Charles XV, king of Sweden, **4:**2283

Charles IV, king of the Two Sicilies. *See* Charles III, king of Spain

Charles XII (Strindberg), **4:**2286

Charles, archduke of Austria, **1:**132, 133; **2:**860, 901, 902; **5:**2374

Charles Albert, king of Sardinia-Piedmont, **1:**413–414; **3:**1195; **4:**1969; **5:**2409

 constitution of, **1:**414; **3:**1196, 1197

 Risorgimento (Italian unification) and, **4:**2002, 2003

 Venice and, **5:**2403–2404

Charles Baudelaire (Deroy), **1:***187*

Charles Emmanuel II, king of Piedmont-Savoy, **4:**1786

Charles Felix, king of Piedmont-Savoy, **1:**413, 414; **2:**539; **4:**1786, 1969

Charles of Hohenzollern-Sigmaringen. *See* Carol I, king of Romania

Charles University (Prague), **3:**1469; **4:**1858

Charlotte, princess of Great Britain, **3:**1334–1335, 1336; **5:**2411

Charlotte, queen consort of Great Britain, **3:**1224

Charlottenburg (Berlin suburb), **1:**217, 218

Charlton, D. B., **1:**228

Charnock, Harry, **2:**834

Charpentier, Charlotte, **4:**2123

Charpentier, Georges, **4:**1955

Charterhouse of Parma, The (Stendhal), **4:**2253

Charter of 1814 (France), **1:**270, 457; **3:**1387; **4:**1969, 1971, 1984

Charter of 1826 (Portugal), **4:**1839, 1839–1840

Charter of Amiens (1906), **1:**60

Charter of the Nobility (Russia, 1785), **4:**1747; **5:**2370

Chartism, **1:**271, 290, **414–419**, 459; **2:**1006; **3:**1286; **4:**1991

 artisans and, **1:**111; **3:**1286

 Carlyle and, **1:**371

 cooperatives and, **2:**555

 Corn Laws repeal campaign and, **2:**559

 Engels and, **2:**754

 influence of, **1:**417–418

 Ireland and, **3:**1657–1658

 Lovett and, **1:**414, 416, 418; **3:**1390–1391

 Manchester and, **3:**1430

 O'Connor and, **1:**415, 416–417; **3:**1657–1658; **4:**2277

 Peel government and, **4:**1759

 platform of, **1:**414; **2:**1003, 1009; **3:**1286, 1657

 police and, **4:**1814

 public education and, **2:**720

 Punch cartoon on, **1:***416*

 repression of, **2:**1004, *1004*

 republicanism and, **4:**1963

 Smiles and, **4:**2199

 sources of, **1:**414–415

 strikes and, **1:**416–417; **4:**2265

 suffragism and, **4:**2277; **5:**2487

 temperance movement and, **1:**36

 utilitarianism and, **5:**2394

D

républicaine dans un grand pays (Constant), **2:**545
"Fragment of an Analysis of a Case of Hysteria:`Dora" (Freud), **4:**1905
Fragment on Government (Bentham), **1:**210; **5:**2393
Fragment on Mackintosh (J. Mill), **3:**1510
Fragments on Recent German Literature (Herder), **2:**1061
Fragments Written for Hellas (P. B. Shelley), **4:**2170
franc (French monetary unit), **3:**1538, 1586
France, **2:840–860**
  absinthe and, **1:**2–4
  Action Française and, **1:**4–5
  African colonies and, **1:**18, 19, 20, 21, 43–47, 500; **2:**812; **3:**1122, 1389, 1548, 1549
  African trade commodities and, **1:**15
  Agadir Crisis and, **3:**1546
  agriculture and, **1:**24, 28; **2:**762; **3:**1305
  airplanes and, **1:**30, 31, *31*
  alliance system and, **1:**41, 47–50; **2:**1013
  Alsace and Lorraine and, **1:**50–52
  American Revolution and, **2:**840–841, 884; **3:**1385
  anarchists and, **1:**56, 57, 59, 60, 62; **2:**857; **3:**1497
  anticlericalism and, **1:**67–69, 70, 380, 389, 410–411, 479; **2:**540, 689, 812; **4:**1929, 1969
  anti-Semitism and, **1:**4, 5, 74–77, 97, 184, 185, 383; **2:**540, 542, 683–686, 688–690, 816, 1068; **3:**1233, 1338; **5:**2489, 2520
  architecture in, **4:**2030
  aristocracy in, **1:**80, 81
  army system of, **1:**93–94, 95, 96, 97, 98, 99, 100–101, 271; **3:**1222
  artisans in, **1:**104–105, 106, 459
  art nouveau and, **1:**109–112, 152; **2:**815
  Atget and, **1:**123–125
  Austria and, **4:**1937, 2001; **5:**2305, 2306, 2374, 2442
  Austrian war with. *See* Franco-Austrian War
  Austro-Prussian War and, **1:**236
  automobile industry and, **1:**148–150; **5:**2352
  avant-garde and, **1:**151–158; **3:**1675; **4:**1706–1709
  Balzac and, **1:**166–169

  banking and, **1:**170, 171, 173, 174, 175, 176
  banquet campaigns and, **4:**1990
  Barbizon painters and, **1:**176–180
  Barrès and, **1:**184–185; **4:**1705
  baths and spas and, **5:**2327
  Baudelaire and, **1:**186–188
  beards as fashion in, **1:**191
  Becquey Plan and, **5:**2348
  Belgian immigrants in, **1:**201
  Belgian neutrality and, **2:**566–567
  Belgium and, **1:**199, 200, 201
  belle époque of, **2:**817
  Bentham and, **5:**2393–2394
  Bergson and, **1:**213–215
  Berlin Conference and, **1:**221
  Berlioz and, **1:**224–225
  Bernhardt and, **1:**229–230
  Blanc and, **1:**247–248
  Blanqui and, **1:**248–249
  Boer support by, **5:**2502
  Bonapartism and, **1:**269–271
  Boulanger affair and, **1:**279–281
  Bourbon restoration and. *See* Restoration
  bourgeoisie in, **1:**106, 283–291, 471
  Boxer Rebellion and, **1:**292, *293*
  Braille and, **1:**296–298
  British free trade treaty with, **1:**491–492; **3:**1537
  British naval agreement with, **3:**1546
  bureaucracy in, **1:**320–322; **2:**846; **3:**1387
  business firms in, **1:**329
  cabarets in, **1:**335
  Cabet and, **1:**337–338
  Caillaux and, **1:**338–340
  canals in, **2:**757–758; **5:**2347–2348, 2350
  Carbonari and, **4:**2130–2131
  Caribbean colonialism and, **1:**363, 364; **2:**1035, 1036–1037
  Catholicism in, **1:**278–279, 377, 378–379, 380, 381, 383, 384, *384,* 385, 386–388; **3:**1648; **4:**1721, 1929, 2030, 2031, 2136–2137; **5:**2305, 2488
  Catholic nursing care in, **3:**1648, 1649–1650
  Catholic political parties in, **1:**388, 389
  Cavour and, **1:**390, 391–392
  censorship in, **4:**1869
  Charbonnerie conspiracy in, **1:**337, 361

  Charter of 1814 and, **4:**1969, 1971, 1984
  chauvinism in, **3:**1235
  chemistry in, **1:**424–425, 427; **3:**1153
  child abandonment in, **5:**2454–2455
  child labor in, **1:**429, 430, *430;* **4:**1830
  China and, **1:**432, 434–435; **3:**1579, 1679–1680
  chocolate and, **1:**496
  cholera epidemics and, **1:**436, *437,* 438; **2:**669; **4:**1915
  Chopin and, **1:**439, 440
  Christian Democrats in, **4:**2209
  Christian Socialism in, **4:**2208
  church-state separation in. *See* separation of church and state
  cinema in, **1:**440, 441, 442, 443; **3:**1396–1398, 1482–1484; **4:**1824
  citizenship and, **1:**456, 458
  civilizing mission of, **1:**462–463, 464
  civil society and, **1:**466
  Clemenceau and, **1:**479–480
  coal mining in, **1:**485, 486, 487, 488; **4:**1936
  coffee consumption in, **1:**494
  colonialism and, **1:**339, 498, 499, 501; **2:***504,* 507–508, *507,* 508, 642, 859; **3:**1114, 1151, 1154; **5:**2330, 2332–2333, 2363
    See also Algeria; Indochina
  colonial wars and, **2:**505
  commercial policy and, **2:**512, 514, 516, 517
  commodity transport by, **5:***2350*
  Comte and, **2:**522–524; **4:**1844
  Congress of Berlin and, **2:**530, 812; **5:**2363
  Congress of Vienna and, **2:**532–534, 565
  conservatism and, **2:**537–538, 541–542
  Constant and, **2:**545–546
  consumerism and, **2:**548, 549
  contraception legislation and, **4:**2042
  cooperative movements in, **2:**555–557
  Corot and, **2:**560–562
  corporations in, **1:**354
  cotton production in, **1:**329
  counterrevolutionists in, **1:**268–269; **2:**563–568, 567
  Courbet and, **2:**568–569
  Crimean War and, **1:**38–39, 94, 244, 271, 278; **2:**577–580, 866; **3:**1592; **4:**2048, 2051; **5:**2410

H

I

Lourdes, **1:**411; **2:**1104; **4:**1826
  Marian shrine at, **4:**1788–1789, *1789,* 1790
Lourié, Arthur, **4:**2262
Louvel, Louis-Pierre, **1:**412
Louvet de Couvray, Jean-Baptiste, **2:**973, 974
Louvre (Paris), **1:**287, 407; **2:**737, 1047; **4:**1726, 1727, 1729; **5:**2327
  as high-art cultural museum, **3:**1562; **4:**1825
  Ingres ceiling painting for, **3:**1165
  photographs of, **4:**1772
love, **4:**2026, 2028, 2029
Love (Munch), **3:**1559; **4:**2294
Love and Mr. Lewisham (Wells), **5:**2458
Love for Three Oranges (Prokofiev), **3:**1496
Lovejoy, Arthur, **4:**2031
love letters, **4:**2029
love poetry, **1:**249
Lovers of Wisdom (Russia), **2:**772
Lovers of Zion, **5:**2519–2520
Love Ruling the World (Rude), **4:**2044
Loves Coming of Age (Carpenter), **1:**372
love songs, **4:**2029
Lovett, William, **1:**414, 416, 418; **3:**1286, **1390–1391**
Low Countries. *See* Belgium; Netherlands
Löwenthal, Elsa Einstein, **2:**740
Lower Depths, The (Gorky), **2:**993
lower middle class, **1:**472–473
  conservative leanings of, **1:**204
  consumerism and, **2:**550
Löwith, Karl, **1:**320
Luanda Empire, **1:**15–16, 19
Luang Prabang, **3:**1142
Lubin, Georges, **4:**2084, 2085
Lucca, **3:**1191; **4:**1970
Lucchesi, Police Commissioner, **4:**2174
Lucerne, electric lighting and, **2:**741
Lucia di Lammermoor (Bellini), **3:**1671
Lucien Leuwen (Stendhal), **4:**2253
Lucinde (Schlegel), **4:**2097
Lucknow, **3:**1133, 1135
Lucrèce Borgia (Hugo), **2:**1093
Ludd, Ned ("King" or "General"), **1:**358; **3:**1391, 1392, 1410; **4:**1821
Luddism, **1:**358; **2:**511; **3:1391–1392**
  machine breaking and, **3:**1410, 1411

Ludlow, Fitz Hugh, **2:**687
Ludlow, John, **4:**2208
Ludwig II, king of Bavaria. *See* Louis II
Ludwig Feuerbach and the End of Classical German Philosophy (Engels), **2:**756
Lueger, Karl, **2:**1068; **3:1392–1396,** *1394;* **4:**2282
  anti-Semitism and, **1:**73, 75, 77; **2:**689, 816; **3:**1233, 1393–1395
  mass politics and, **3:**1395
  Vienna and, **5:**2420–2421
Lugard, Frederick (Lord Lugard), **1:**20; **2:**507
Luis I, king of Portugal, **4:**1841
Luisa Miller (Verdi), **5:**2406
Luis Filipe, prince of Portugal, **4:**1841
Lukács, György, **2:**830; **3:**1253; **4:**2186
Lumière, Auguste and Louis, **1:**441, 442; **3:1396–1398,** *1397,* 1414; **4:**1774, 1824
  Méliès contrasted with, **3:**1482
Lumière Company, **3:**1396
Lumír (Czech journal), **4:**1857
Lunacharsky, Anatoly, **1:**267
Luna Park Scenic Railway (Paris), **4:***1825*
Luncheon of the Boating Party (Renoir), **4:**1955
Lunda Empire, **1:**13
Lundbye, Johan, **2:**647
Lunéville, Treaty of (1801), **2:**860, 901; **5:**2305
Luppe River, **3:**1320
lupus, **2:**649
Lutezia (Heine), **2:**1056
Lûtfullah Bey, **5:**2515
Luther, Martin, **2:**959; **5:**2447
Lutheranism, **1:**51; **4:**1890, 1891
  Baltic provinces and, **2:**821
  as established church, **4:**1895
  northern German population of, **4:***1892*
  Sweden and, **1:**226
  temperance and, **1:**36
Luxe, calme, et volupté (Matisse), **2:**797; **3:**1474; **4:**1710
Luxembourg
  peasant revolt in, **4:**1755
  Schlieffen Plan and, **4:**2098
  slave trade ban and, **1:**308
  telephone service in, **5:**2308
  welfare initiatives in, **5:**2452
Luxembourg Commission (France), **2:**849–850; **3:**1287
Luxembourg gardens (Paris), **2:**1048

Luxembourg Gardens at Twilight (Sargent), **1:***289*
Luxemburg, Rosa, **2:**707; **3:**1248, **1398–1401,** *1399;* **4:**1811, 2205
  assassination of, **3:**1401
  attack on Bernstein by, **1:**231; **3:**1399–1400
  Liebknecht and, **3:**1356
luxury goods
  Asian trade and, **3:**1151–1152, 1153
  automobiles as, **1:**149–150
  Brussels production of, **1:**305
  consumers of, **2:**547, 548, 551
  fashion and, **1:**481
  London production of, **3:**1373–1374
  Lyon and, **3:**1404
Luzán y Martínez, José, **2:**996
Lüzen, Battle of (1813), **2:**903
Luzzatti, Luigi, **2:**971; **5:**2364
LWMA. *See* London Working Men's Association
Lyell, Charles, **3:1401–1403;** **4:**2133
  as Darwin influence, **2:**615; **3:**1402
Lyell, Mary Horner, **3:**1402
Lyon, **3:1403–1406**
  Catholicism and, **3:**1404–1405
  federalist revolt in, **2:**799, 800, 844; **3:**1403
  Lumière brothers in, **3:**1396, 1398
  miners protests in, **3:**1272
  nursing school in, **3:**1650
  Paris Commune and, **4:**1736
  population of, **3:**1404
  radical press in, **4:**1870
  Reign of Terror in, **2:**800, 894; **3:**1403
  silk manufacture in, **3:**1153, 1404, 1405
  silkworkers' rebellion in, **2:**848, 849; **3:**1284, 1404
  urban redevelopment ind, **2:**1088; **3:**1404
  waterway transport and, **5:**2348
  worker housing in, **2:**1089
Lyrical Ballads (Coleridge and Wordsworth), **1:**496, 497; **2:**543; **5:**2482
Lytton, Edward Robert Bulwer-Lytton (Lord Lytton), **2:**674; **4:**2237

M

Mably, Abbé, **4:**1958
Macaire, Robert, **2:**621

Monnier, Henry, **2**:586
Monod, Gabriel-Jean-Jacques, **2**:1073, 1074
monogamy, **1**:287
Monologen (Schleiermacher), **4**:2097
Monophysites, **3**:1687
monopoly, **4**:1961
  African trade and, **1**:221, 222, 223, 303
Monroe Doctrine (1823), **3**:1174
Mon Salon (Zola), **1**:397
Monstre, Le (film), **3**:1483
montage techniques, **2**:593
Montagnards, **2**:799, 800, 851, 973–974; **4**:1960
Montagne Sainte-Victoire, La (Cézanne), **3**:1132–1133
Montagu, Mary Worley, **3**:1223
Montalembert, Charles de, **1**:387
Mont Blanc, **3**:1324–1325
"Mont Blanc" (Shelley), **4**:2170
Mont des Arts (Brussels), **1**:306
Montenegro, **3**:1539–1542
  Albania and, **1**:32, 33
  Balkan League and, **1**:32
  Balkan wars and, **1**:34, 163, 164, 165, 166; **2**:704–705; **3**:1541, 1691; **4**:2149
  Bosnia-Herzegovina and, **1**:273, 275–276; **3**:1541
  independence of, **2**:530; **3**:1173, 1541, 1689
  nationalism and, **1**:163, 166; **3**:1540–1541
  Ottoman Empire and, **1**:2; **3**:1541
  population of, **3**:1539
  San Stefano Treaty and, **4**:2069, 2085
  Serbia and, **1**:242; **3**:1539, 1541, 1546; **4**:2148, 2149
  soldiers, **3**:*1540*
Montesquieu, baron de (Charles-Louis de Secondat), **1**:376, 432; **2**:522, 994; **4**:2007, 2192, 2212; **5**:2448
  conservative rationale and, **2**:537–538
  mechanization concerns of, **3**:1411
Montesquiou, Robert de, **2**:*1082*
Montessori, Maria, **2**:947; **3**:1542–1543
Montez, Lola, **2**:961; **3**:1382, 1383; **4**:1834
Montgolfier, Joseph-Michel and Jacques-Étienne, **1**:30
Montherlant, Henri-Marie-Joseph de, **1**:184; **3**:1475
Month in the Country, A (Turgenev), **5**:2365

Monthly Repository (Unitarian periodical), **3**:1458, 1459, 1509
Monticelli, Adolphe, **5**:2400
Montmartre (Parisian quarter), **2**:590; **4**:1709, 1735, 1737
  Picasso and, **4**:1782
  as Toulouse-Lautrec subject, **4**:1846
Montreal, **1**:343
Montreuil, Madame de, **4**:2073–2074
Montreuil, Renée-Pélagie Cordier de, **4**:2073, 2074
Mont Sainte-Victoire, **1**:398; **3**:1530
Mont Sainte-Victoire, Seen from Bellevue (Cézanne), **4**:1710
Monumenta Germaniae Historica, **2**:1072; **3**:1533; **4**:2252
Moore, George Augustus (Irish novelist), **3**:1109
Moore, George Edward (English philosopher), **3**:1514; **4**:2258
Moore, Hannah, **1**:36
Moore, James, **2**:600, 614
Moore, John, **4**:1764, 2227
Moore, Thomas, **5**:2403
Moorish "horseshoe" arch, **1**:109
Moral Education League (Britain), **2**:769
moral improvement associations, **1**:115, 119, 120
morality
  Nietzsche on, **3**:1631–1633, 1634, 1635
  positivism and, **4**:1844
  Protestant political leadership and, **4**:1896
  Schopenhauers theory of, **4**:2105
  sexuality and, **4**:2161
  Soloviev's (Vladimir) view of, **4**:2216
  Stephen on, **4**:2254
Morand, Paul, **5**:2503
Morant Bay uprising (1865), **1**:365, 371
  British writers debate on, **1**:371
Moravia. *See* Bohemia, Moravia, and Silesia
Moravian Boys' School, **2**:834
Moravian Brethren, **4**:2096
Moravian Compromise of 1905, **1**:262
Moravian Duets (Dvořák), **2**:701
Moravianism, **3**:1527; **4**:1895
Mordaunt case (1870), **2**:730
More, Thomas, **1**:26, 337; **2**:520; **4**:2200
Moréas, Jean (pseud.), **2**:633; **4**:2294
Moreau, Gustave, **2**:795–796; **3**:1474; **4**:1865, 2292
Moreau, Victor, **2**:901

Moreau de Tours, Jacques-Joseph, **2**:687
Morel, Bénédict Augustin, **1**:37; **2**:636, 637
Morel, E. D., **1**:205
Moret y Prendergast, Sigismundo, **4**:2231
Morgan, C. Lloyd, **4**:1908
Morgan, Lady Sydney, **3**:1300
Morisot, Berthe, **3**:1126, 1128, 1433, 1534, **1543–1545**; **4**:1955, 2156
  portraits of daughter Julie by, **3**:1544, *1544*
Morisot, Edma, **3**:1543–1544
Morley, John, **3**:1513
Morley-Minto Reforms (1909), **3**:1137
Morning Chronicle (London newspaper), **2**:716
Morning Leader Group (Britain), **4**:1871
"Morning Mood" (Grieg), **4**:2287
Mornings on the Seine (Monet), **3**:1536
Morning Star of Croatia, Slavonia, and Dalmatia The (newspaper), **2**:925
Moroccan Crises (1905, 1911), **2**:527, 663; **3**:1545–1546, 1549
  Agadir Crisis and, **1**:49, 339; **3**:1370, 1545–1546, 1549
  Bethmann Hollweg and, **5**:2312
  Entente Cordiale and, **1**:49; **2**:795; **3**:1545; **4**:2098
Morocco, **1**:18, 49, 339; **3**:1546–1549
  Delacroix visit to, **2**:641
  French influence over, **2**:795; **3**:1545–1546, 1549
  Ottoman Empire and, **5**:2361
  population of, **3**:1547
  Spain and, **4**:2231
  Tangier marketplace, **1**:*19*
  tourism and, **5**:2330
  world's fair displays and, **5**:2497
  See also Moroccan Crises
Morozov, Savva, **1**:287
Morozov family, **1**:284
Morpeth, Lord (George Howard), **4**:*1913*
morphine, **2**:686, 688
morphological types, **2**:1102
Morris, Philip, **5**:2314
Morris, William, **3**:1549–1551
  aesthetic movement and, **5**:2464
  art nouveau and, **1**:109
  Arts and Crafts movement and, **1**:152; **3**:1550
  chrysanthemum wallpaper design of, **3**:*1550*

O

Odi barbari (Carducci), **1**:362

O'Donnell, Leopoldo, **4**:2229, 2230

Odyssey (Homer), **3**:1165, 1675

Oedipus at Colonus (Sophocles), **3**:1663

Oedipus complex, **4**:1770, 1904

Oedipus Tyrannus (Sophocles; Hölderlin translation), **2**:1078

Oeri, Jacob, **1**:318

Oersted, Hans, **2**:741; **4**:2109

Oeuvre, L' (Zola), **1**:398

Oeuvres (Bergson), **1**:213

Oeuvres (Gouges), **2**:994

Offen, Karen, **2**:801, 806

Offenbach, Jacques, **3**:1414, **1660–1662**, 1672

  Manet and, **3**:1432

  Strauss (Johann) and, **4**:2260–2261; **5**:2420

officer corps, **1**:96, 97, *98*, 99–100

Official Nationality (Russian concept), **3**:1626; **4**:2048

Of Population (Godwin), **2**:981

Ogarev, Nikolai, **2**:1064; **3**:1613

Ohlin, Bertil Gotthard, **2**:752; **5**:2334

Ohm, Georg Simon, **3**:1162

oil industry, **1**:88; **3**:1161

Oken, Lorenz, **2**:615

Okin, S. M., **3**:1514

Okinawa, **3**:1211

Oku, Yasutaka, **3**:1557

Olbrich, Joseph Maria, **1**:112, 113, 152; **3**:1260, 1381

old age, **1**:408; **3**:1662–1665

old-age insurance. *See* pensions

Old Believers, **4**:2062, 2257

Old Calabar, **1**:15

Old Catholic Church, **4**:1723, 1798

Old Church Slavonic, **4**:1716

Old Closes and Streets of Glasgow (Annan), **4**:*2119*

Old Confederation (Switzerland), **4**:2288

Old Curiosity Shop, the (Dickens), **2**:656

Old Czechs. *See* Young Czechs and Old Czechs

Oldenburg, house of, **4**:2287

Old Etonians (football team), **2**:831

old-folks homes, **5**:2455

Old Guitarist, The (Picasso), **4**:1781

Old Hegelians, **3**:1464

Old Poor Law. *See* Poor Law

Old Regime and the Revolution, The (Tocqueville), **3**:1342; **5**:2316, 2317–2318

Old Serbia. *See* Serbia

Oldsmobiles (cars), **1**:149

Old Town Square (Prague), **4**:1858

Old World and the New, The (political cartoon), **2**:*749*

"Old-World Landowners" (Gogol), **2**:988

O'Leary, John, **5**:2509

Olga, princess of Russia, **3**:1627

oligarchy, **1**:457

Oliveira de Martins, Joaquim Pedro, **4**:1840

Oliver Cromwell's Letters and Speeches (Carlyle), **1**:371

Oliver Twist (Dickens), **2**:573, 575, 656

  Cruikshank illustrations, **2**:585

  as New Poor Law critique, **4**:1820, 1848

Olivier, Fernande, **4**:1782, 1783–1784

Olivier, Sydney, **5**:2444

Ollivier, Émile, **2**:853–854

Olmstead, Alan, **5**:2337

Olmütz, Battle of (1805), **1**:132

Olmütz, Punctuation of (1850), **2**:962; **4**:1902

Olson, Mancur, **2**:516

Olsson, Ulf, **4**:2269

Olympia (Manet), **2**:940; **3**:*1432,* 1433; **4**:1707–1708, 1954

Olympic Games, **3**:1665–1668, *1666*

  Athens and, **1**:126; **3**:1665, 1667, *1667*

  football (soccer) and, **2**:834

  Greece and, **4**:2244

  masculinity and, **3**:1473

  sites of, **4**:2246; **5**:2592

Oman, Charles, **4**:1766

Oman, sultan of, **1**:16

Omani Empire, **1**:16

Omar Pasha, **1**:244

Omdurman (1898), **2**:734, 794; **3**:1125, 1258, **1668–1669**, *1669*

Ömer Pasha Latas, **1**:274; **3**:1541

omertà, **4**:2174

"On Agitation" (Martov and Kremer), **3**:1460

Onatario, **1**:345

On Crimes and Punishment (Beccaria), **3**:1371; **5**:2393

"On Diligence in Several Learned Languages" (Herder), **2**:1061

On Dramatic Art and Literature (Schlegel), **4**:2095

O'Neill, Eugene, **4**:2269

On Germany (Staël), **4**:2247

On Heroes, Hero Worship, and the Heroic in History (Carlyle), **1**:371

On Kulikovo Field (Blok), **1**:250; **2**:774

On Liberty (J. S. Mill), **2**:1006; **3**:1509, 1513; **5**:2394

"On Narcissism" (Freud), **2**:907–908

On Religion: Speeches to Its Cultured Despisers (Schleiermacher), **4**:2097

On the Basis of Morality (Schopenhauer), **4**:2104

"On the Basis of our Belief in Divine Governance of the World" (Fichte), **2**:813

On the Conception of Aphasias (Freud), **2**:904

On the Concept of Irony with Continual Reference to Socrates (Kierkegaard), **3**:1250

On the Conservation of Force (Helmholtz), **2**:1057

On the Constitution of the Church and State (Coleridge), **1**:497

On the Development of the Monistic Conception of History (Plekhanov), **4**:1801

On the Eve (Turgenev), **5**:2365

On the Fourfold Root of the Principle of Sufficient Reason (Schopenhauer), **4**:2103

On the Freedom of the Will (Schopenhauer), **4**:2104

"On the Fundamental Laws of the State" (Speransky), **4**:2236

On the Genealogy of Morals (Nietzsche), **3**:1631

On the Inequality of Human Races (Gobineau), **1**:403

On the Limits of State Action (W. Humboldt), **2**:1097

"On the Modern Element in Literature" (Arnold), **1**:102

"On the Necessity and Possibility of New Principles in Philosophy" (Kireyevsky), **4**:2195

On the Origin of Species (Darwin), **2**:613, 614, 615, 616–618, 637, 776, 777, 1031, 1102; **3**:1302, 1426, 1563; **4**:1908, 2234, 2255

On the Penitentiary System in the United States and Its Application to France (Tocqueville and Bonninière), **5**:2316

"On the Probable Futurity of the Working Classes " (H. T. Mill), **3**:1509

"On the Proper Sphere of Government" (Spencer), **4**:2233

On the Sensation of Tone as a Physiological Basis for the Theory of Music (Helmholtz), **2**:1057

"On the Spiritual in Art" (Kandinsky), **3**:1244, 1245

On the Turf Bench (Repin), **4**:1956

"On the Uses and Disadvantages of History for Life" (Nietzsche), **3**:1635

Ontogenie (Jarry), **3**:1213

divorce scandal and, 2:978, 1011;
3:1181–1182; 4:1742

Parnok, Sofia, 4:2183

Parr, Samuel, 2:981

Parricide, A (cartoon), 4:*1870*

Parsifal (Wagner), 3:1571, 1674,
1675; 5:2431

Parsons, Charles Algernon, 3:1161

Parthenon (Athens), 1:125; 3:1376,
1562

Parthenopean Republic (Naples),
3:1192, 1581, 1597;
4:2186–2189

Parthe River, 3:1320

Parti Ouvrier (France), 1:127; 2:1025;
4:2205

Parti Socialiste Unifie (France), 2:859

Partitions of Poland. *See* Poland,
partitions of

Partito Populare Italiano, 1:389

Partridge, Ralph, 4:2259

Party of Order (France), 1:271

Party of People's Freedom (Russia). *See*
Kadets

Party of the People's Will (Russia). *See*
People's Will

Pascendi Dominici Gregis (encyclical,
1907), 4:1721

Pas d'acier (Prokofiev), 2:655

Paseo de Gracia (Barcelona), 1:181

Pashalik of Belgrade. *See* Serbia

pashas, 5:2362

Pašić, Nikola, 1:242, 243; 4:2145

Passage to India, A (Forster), 2:836

Passanante, Giovanni, 5:2377

Passant, Le (Coppée), 1:229

Passeig de Colom (Barcelona), 1:183

Passy, Frédéric, 4:1695, 1697

Past and Present (Carlyle), 1:373;
4:2206

Pasternak, Boris, 4:2182, 2183

Pasteur, Louis, 2:659; 4:*1742–1745*,
1744, 2110, 2113
anthrax and, 4:1744–1745
as cultural hero, 2:738; 4:1882
disease decline and, 2:628, 644
fermentation and, 4:1743; 5:2477
germ theory and, 3:1358; 4:1743,
1744, 2135
Koch's critique of, 3:1263
public health and, 4:1914

Pasteur Institutes, 1:438; 4:1745

pasteurization, 2:628, 645, 659;
3:1164; 4:1742, 1743; 5:2361,
2477

Pastor Aeternus (papal bull, 1870),
4:1895–1896
See also papal infallibility

"Pastoral" (Sixth) Symphony
(Beethoven), 1:197

pastoral poetry, 4:1756

Pastrone, Giovanni, 1:443

Pastry Cooks' revolt (1843), 1:181

pataphysics (absurdist idea), 3:1213

patent medicines, 2:686

patents, 4:2111
bicycle, 2:600
scientific discoveries, 2:595
Siemens and, 4:2179
wireless telegraphy, 3:1444

Patents and Designs Act of 1907
(Britain), 3:1369

Pater, Walter, 2:632; 4:*1745–1747*,
1770

paternalism
industrial, 1:446; 2:793, 1087,
1088; 3:1275
private poor relief and, 4:1851, 1854

paternity suits, 4:1886

Pathé, 3:1483

Pathé, Charles and Emile, 2:551;
3:1397

Pathé Frères, 1:442

Pathetique (Tchaikovsky), 5:2307

pathological anatomy, 3:1297, 1298;
4:2135

Pathological Institute (Berlin), 5:2425

pathology, 5:2425

Patience (Gilbert and Sullivan), 5:2464

Patkanian, Raphael, 1:88

Patmore, Coventry, 2:943

patriarchy
bourgeois family as, 1:287
Dohm feminist writings against,
2:675
fin de siècle challenges to, 2:816
French Revolutionary ideals and,
2:941; 3:1595
masculinity and, 3:1470
Napoleonic Code and, 3:1595
Russian autocratic system and,
2:1017

Patrie, La (Parisian newspaper),
4:1866

Patrimonium Petri, 4:1723, 1724,
1725, 1726

Patriotica (Struve), 4:2271

patriotism
conservatism and, 2:540
jingoism and, 3:1234–1235
nationalism and, 4:1826

Patriot League (France), 1:282;
4:2243

Patriots (Netherlands), 3:1616

patrolman. *See* police and policing

Patten, Simon Nelson, 4:2235

Patterson, Julia (Jenny), 4:2166

Pauk, Fritz, 1:427

Paul, Jean (Jean Paul Friedrich
Richter), 1:296; 2:873

Paul I, emperor of Russia, 1:375;
3:1265; 4:*1747–1748*, 2049
assassination of, 4:1748
Czartoryski and, 2:603
Napoleonic Wars and, 2:901
parentage of, 1:375; 4:1747, 1748
son Alexander I and, 1:37; 4:1748

Paul Sacher Foundation, 4:2263

Paulze, Marie Anne, 3:1312

paupers. *See* poverty

Pausanias Description of Greece
(Frazer), 2:872

"Pauvre Belgique!" (Baudelaire),
1:188

Pavane pour une infante défunte
(Ravel), 4:1944

Pavía y Lacy, Manuel, 4:2231

Pavillon d'Armide (ballet), 3:1642

Pavlov, Ivan, 4:*1748–1749*, 1908

Pavlova, Anna, 2:655; 3:1642;
4:*1749–1751*, *1750*

pawnshops, 2:550, 571; 3:1582

Pax Britannica, 5:2321

Paxton, Joseph, 2:587, 589; 4:1738

Paxton, Robert, 5:2494

Payne-Townshend, Charlotte, 4:2166

Paysage aux arbre rouge (Vlaminck),
2:796

Paysans au XIXe siècle, Les
(Bonnemère), 4:1753

Peace—Burial at Sea (Turner), 4:*1704*

Peace Law of 1886 (Prussia), 3:1279

peace movements. *See* pacifism

Peace of Paris. *See* Paris, Treaty of

Peacock Skirt, The (Beardsley), 1:*193*

peanut oil, 1:15

peanuts, 1:20, 21

Pearse, Patrick, 3:1181, 1185; 5:2510

Pearson, Cyril, 1:159

Pearson, Karl, 2:770, 927; 3:1409;
4:2248, 2249

Peary, Robert, 2:783

peasant art, 1:112

Peasant Land Bank (Russia), 4:2257

peasant revolts, 1:376; 2:669;
4:*1754–1755*, 2067
Poland and, 4:1755
populist incitement of, 4:1831–1832
Russia and, 1:376; 2:669; 3:1328;
4:1755, 1831–1832
Sicilian Fasci and, 4:2173–2175
Sicily and, 3:1414, 1415

peasants, 1:475–476; 4:*1751–1757*

Malthusianism and, **2**:715; **3**:1425, 1426

Mill (J.S.) view of, **2**:718

Scotland and, **4**:2119; **5**:2452

Speenhamland System and, **1**:358, 359, 1425; **2**:709; **4**:1819

Swing riots and, **1**:359

Poor Law Act of 1845 (Scotland), **4**:2119

Poor Law Amendment Act of 1834 (Britain). *See* New Poor Law of 1834

poor relief. *See* poverty; welfare

Poovey, Mary, **5**:2481

pop art, **2**:593

Pope, Alexander, **4**:2027, 2254

popes. *See* papacy; papal infallibility; *names of specific popes*

Popkin, Jeremy, **4**:1869

Poplars on the Epte (Monet), **3**:1536

Poplawski, Jan Ludwik, **2**:752

Popolo d'Italia, Il (Mussolini newspaper), **3**:1504

Popova, Lyubov, **3**:1496

Popp, Adelheid, **1**:431; **3**:1456

Populaire, Le (French weekly), **1**:337, 338

popular and elite culture, **4**:1820–1827

artisans and, **1**:104

avant-garde and, **1**:151–158

Berlin and, **1**:215, 219–220; **3**:1412

Bernhardt and, **1**:229–230

blending of, **4**:1824–1825

body and, **1**:252–254

Bohemian Lands and, **1**:261–262

Bonapartism and, **1**:270

bourgeoisie and, **1**:287–288

British aristocracy and, **1**:86

Brussels and, **1**:307

Catalanism and, **1**:182

cinema and, **1**:440–443; **4**:1824

cities and, **1**:445, 447–448, 455; **3**:1412

consumerism and, **2**:549–550, 551

cycling and, **2**:599–602; **4**:1824

death and, **2**:628–629

diversity of, **4**:1821–1822

Doré and, **2**:277–278, 676

Dublin and, **2**:693

fin de siècle and, **2**:815–817

furniture and, **2**:912–915

German nationalism and, **2**:960–961

landowning elite and, **1**:469

leisure and, **3**:1322–1325; **4**:1824

libraries and, **3**:1350–1352

London and, **3**:1376–1378

Madrid and, **3**:1414

mesmerism and, **3**:1490–1491; **4**:1822

Milan and, **3**:1504

Moscow and, **3**:1551–1552

museums and, **3**:1561–1564

music and, **3**:1565–1573

national thinking and, **3**:1608

"New Journalism" and, **4**:1870–1871

old age representations and, **3**:1663–1664

opera and, **3**:1669–1677

Paris and, **4**:1727, 1732–1733

photography and, **4**:1772

phrenology and, **4**:1774–1776, 1822

piano and, **1**:439; **3**:1566

pleasure parks and, **4**:1738

pornography and, **4**:1833–1836

racism and, **4**:1927

regionalism and, **4**:1821

restaurants and, **4**:1964–1967

St. Petersburg and, **3**:1552; **4**:2079

seaside resorts and, **4**:2125

secularization and, **4**:1893–1894

Serbia and, **5**:2147–2148

spiritualism and, **3**:491; **4**:2237–2239, 14901

sports and, **4**:1824, 2240–2241, 2244, 2245

tobacco use and, **5**:2314

tourism and, **5**:2325–2331

voluntary associations and, **1**:115–122

wine and, **5**:2475

See also folk culture

Popular Front (Spain), **1**:62

popular journalism, **4**:1870–1871

popular sovereignty, **1**:456, 457

Guizot's denunciation of, **4**:1971–1972

republicanism and, **4**:1962

Popular Union. *See* Catholic Action

population. *See* birthrate; demography; fertility rate; population, control of; *specific cities and countries*

population, control of, **4**:1827–1831

abortion and, **4**:1762, 1827, 1829

abstinence and, **4**:1827, 1829

contraceptives and, **2**:645–646, 805, 947; **4**:1827, 1829–1830, 1836

degeneracy theme and, **2**:639

emigration and, **2**:503, 960, 1005

eugenics and, **2**:239, 769

fertility decline and, **4**:1829–1831

Godwin on, **2**:981

Malthusian theory and, **2**:615, 616, 714–715, 777; **3**:1425–1427; **4**:1827

marital age and, **4**:1827–1828

migration and, **2**:646

mortality and, **4**:1829

neo-Malthusians and, **4**:1762

peasants and, **4**:1753

Pelletier and, **4**:1762

Philosophic Radicals and, **3**:1512

population growth (1750–1850) and, **4**:1827–1829

population growth in selected countries (1800–1913) and, **2**:644

women's changed role and, **2**:947

populism

Bonapartism and, **1**:269, 271

French anti-Semitic socialists and, **1**:184

German anti-Semitism and, **1**:82; **2**:542

See also Chartism

populists (Russian intelligentsia), **4**:1831–1833, 2052, 2053, 2132

anarchist theory and, **1**:62

nihilists and, **3**:1640–1641

People's Will and, **4**:1767–1768, 1800

Plekhanov's view of, **4**:1800, 1801

revolutionary right and, **2**:542

as socialist revolutionaries, **4**:2209–2210

Struve and, **4**:2270

in Ukraine, **5**:2371, 2373

Zasulich and, **5**:2517

porcelain

China and, **3**:1151, 1152, 1678

Denmark and, **2**:647

Rosenthal, **1**:192

Wedgwood, **2**:547; **3**:1153

Porche du mystère de la deuxième vertu (Péguy), **4**:1760

pornography, **2**:941; **3**:1471; **4**:1833–1837

bibliography of, **4**:1836

origins of, **4**:2029

Sade and, **4**:2074

Schiele's jailing related to, **4**:2090

sex manuals seen as, **4**:2163

porphyria, **5**:2470

Porta, Giambattista della, **3**:1580

Port Arthur (China), **1**:292; **3**:1212, 1507, 1628; **4**:1837

Ireland and, 3:1180
Italy and, 3:1192
Jacobins and, 3:1205–1206
liberalism and, 3:1343, 1344
Lovett and, 3:1390–1391
Lyon and, 3:1405
Marx and, 3:1464
Marxism and, 1:264–265
Nechayev and, 3:1613–1614
nihilists and, 3:1638–1641
Paine and, 4:1700
Paris Commune and, 4:1735–1737
peace movements and, 2:1034
People's Will and, 4:1767–1768
police surveillance of, 4:1815
populists and, 4:1831–1832
pornography and, 4:1834
revolutionary right and, 2:542
Revolutions of 1830 and, 4:1986
Revolutions of 1848 and, 4:1988,
    1995
Robespierre and, 2:610
Russia and, 4:1975–1978, 2053
Switzerland and, 4:1990, 2289, 2291
Westernizers and, 2:1064
women's movements and,
    1:127–128, 129; 2:805
See also socialism
Radical Manifesto of 1885, 4:2136
Radical Party (Britain), 5:2444
Radical Party (France), 1:339, 480;
    2:540, 642, 858, 859
Radical Party (Serbia), 4:2145–2146
Radical Republican Party (France),
    2:698
radical right (France). *See* New Right
Radical-Socialist Party (France), 1:279;
    2:697, 698
radioactivity, 2:595; 4:2070–2071
radio speaker, 3:1398
radio waves, 3:1163, 1444, 1445;
    4:1780
Radishchev, Alexander, 1:376;
    2:1014–1015; 3:1170,
    1551–1552
radium, 2:595, 596
Radium Institute (France), 2:596
Radium Institute (Warsaw), 2:596
Radonjić family, 3:1539, 1540
Radowitz, Joseph Maria von,
    2:876, 877
Radziwill, Elise, 5:2467
Raeder, Linda, 3:1514
Raeff, Marc, 2:540
Raevsky Redoubt, 1:273
Raffalovich, Marc-André, 2:1082

Raffi, 1:88
Raft of the Medusa (Géricault),
    2:955–956; 4:1705
"ragged schools," 2:*722*
Raglan, Lord, 2:577, 579
ragtime, 4:2087
Raiffeisen, Friedrich Wilhelm, 1:111;
    2:960
Railroad, The (Manet), 3:1433
railroads, 4:1930–1938, *1935*;
    5:2349–2350
  African colonization and, 1:18, 20,
    21, *21*
  Amsterdam and, 1:53
  army use of, 1:96; 2:580; 3:1506
  Austria-Hungary and, 1:142, 144
  bank financing of, 1:170, 174
  Belgium and, 1:201, 305; 2:764;
    3:1335
  Belgrade and, 1:206
  Berlin and, 1:217
  Bohemian Lands and, 1:261
  bridge design, 2:*759, 760*
  Britain and, 1:303, 304
  broad gauge and, 1:304
  Brunel and and, 1:303, 304
  Brussels and, 1:305, 306
  capitalist bourgeosie and, 1:284
  Central Asia and, 1:395, 396
  cities and, 1:452
  coal production and, 1:486
  construction of, 4:1931–1934
  crime and, 2:576
  Denmark and, 2:647
  Dublin and, 2:691
  Egypt and, 2:732
  engineers and, 2:757, 758, 760
  environment and, 2:764
  France and, 4:1932, 1933, 1934;
    5:2349
  German nationalization of, 2:965
  Hamburg and, 2:1039
  impact of, 4:1934–1937
  as impressionist subject, 3:1128
  India and, 3:1135
  Industrial Revolution (second) and,
    1:329–330; 3:1305
  Istanbul and, 3:1188
  Italy and, 1:390; 2:764; 3:1195,
    1200
  Japan and, 3:1210, 1212
  leisure travel and, 1:288; 4:1824
  List's lobbying for, 3:1357
  London and, 3:1372, 1373, 1374
  Madrid and, 3:1413

  Manchester and, 3:1428
  migration and, 2:646
  Milan and, 3:1502
  militarization of, 2:580; 3:1506
  Netherlands and, 1:201, 305;
    3:1335, 1617; 4:1933, 1934,
    1936, 1937
  newspaper delivery by, 4:1866
  New Zealand and, 3:1624
  Paris and, 4:1729
  passenger traffic (1913), 4:*1937*
  pilgrimages and, 4:1789
  Portugal and, 4:1840
  Prussia and, 1:147; 2:876
  refrigeration wagons and,
    5:2340–2341
  as revolution in travel time, 1:353
  Revolutions of 1848 and, 4:1988
  Rothschilds and, 4:1933, 2040
  Russia and, 4:1933, 1936, 1937,
    1975, 2064, 2172–2173; 5:2426,
    2427, 2478, 2479, 2503
  seaside resorts and, 4:2124, 2125
  Serbia and, 4:2147
  social benefits of, 4:1930, *1931*
  steam locomotive, 4:*1932*
  steel and, 3:1158, 1159, 1274
  suburbanization and, 2:1087
  Sweden and, 4:2285
  tourism and, 5:2328–2329, 2330
  track length and use (1913), 4:*1934*
  trade and, 5:2340–2342
  Trieste and, 5:2355
  vacations and, 3:1324
  Vienna and, 4:1933; 5:2418
  Wales and, 5:2434, 2437
  warfare and, 2:580
  wine and, 5:2476
  worker typhus epidemics and, 2:670
  workforce for, 1:473
*Railroads and American Economic
    Growth* (Fogel), 4:1930
Raimund, Ferdinand, 5:2418
Raj (India), 3:1135–1137
Rakes Progress, The (Stravinsky),
    4:2262
Rakovski, Georgi, 3:1687
Raleigh Cycle Company, 2:602
Rama III, king of Siam, 3:1139
Rambler, The (periodical), 1:6
*Rambles in Germany and Italy in 1840,
    1842, and 1843* (Shelley), 4:2169
Ramdohr, Basilius von, 2:910–911
Ramey (sculptor), 4:2043
Rampolla del Tindaro, Mariano,
    3:1331

St. Petersburg State University,
4:1976, 2075
St. Peter's Square (Rome), 4:*1720*
St. Rollox chemical complex, 4:2117
saints
 canonization and, 1:385
 shrines of, 4:1788–1789
Saint-Saëns, Camille, 3:1572, 1675;
 4:1750, 1751
Saint-Simon, Henri de, 1:151, 459,
 491; 2:930; 4:**2080–2082**, 2200,
 2212
 as Comte influence, 2:522–523
 feminism and, 2:803, 946
 as Heine influence, 2:1056
 as Herzen influence, 2:1064
 Mill (John Stuart) and, 3:1513
 Romanticism and, 4:2031
 socialism and, 3:1286
 utopian socialism and, 5:2395, 2396
Saint-Simonism, 2:650; 3:1337;
 4:2081–2082, 2202–2203, 2204
 on egoism, 5:2396
 Roland and, 4:2013
 secret societies and, 4:2131
 Tristan and, 5:2357
 utopian socialism and, 5:2396
St. Thomas's Hospital (London),
 2:1102; 3:1649
Saisons Russes, 4:1750
Sakhalin Island, 4:1837, 2064, 2065
Şakir, Bahaeddin, 5:2515
salacious literature. *See* pornography
Salammbô (Flaubert), 2:827, 828
Salandra, Antonio, 2:972;
 3:1202–1203
Salburger grosse Welttheater, Das
 (Hofmannsthal), 2:1077
Saleilles, Raymond, 3:1315
Salic Law, 4:2229
Salieri, Antonio, 4:2106
Salis, Rodolphe, 1:335
Salisbury, Lord (Robert Cecil), 1:308,
 404; 2:1009; 5:2322, 2414
 program of, 2:1010–1011, 1013
Salisbury Cathedral, 4:1705
Salle River, 3:1319
Salmerón y Alonso, Nicolás, 4:2230,
 2231
Salmon, André, 2:590; 4:1782
Salo de Cent de Barcelona, 1:182
Salomé (Wilde), 2:633; 3:1377;
 5:2466
 art nouveau imagery and, 1:108
 Beardsley illustrations, 1:109, 192, *193*
Salomé, Louise. *See* Andreas-Salomé,
 Lou

Salon (Paris), 2:544; 4:1946
 avante-garde and, 1:153, 155
 Corot and, 2:561
 Courbet and, 2:568, 569
 Daguerre and, 2:605
 Daumier and, 2:621
 Degas and, 2:634
 Delacroix and, 2:640
 of 1830s, 1:178
 Géricault and, 2:955
 impressionists excluded from,
  3:1126, 1127–1128, 1535
 Ingres and, 3:1165
 Manet and, 3:1431, 1432, 1433
 Monet and, 3:1535
 rejections by, 3:1432
 Renoir and, 4:1954, 1955
 Rodin and, 4:2008, 2009
 Rude and, 4:2043
salon cubists, 2:590–591, 592–593
Salon d'Art Idéaliste, 4:2295
Salon d'Automne (Paris), 1:399;
 3:1474
 avant-garde and, 1:153, 155
 cubism and, 2:590
 fauvism and, 2:795
Salon des Indépendants (Paris), 2:590;
 3:1474
Salon des Refusés (Paris), 3:1432,
 1433, 1530; 4:1707
Salonika, 1:1, 32, 163; 2:704; 3:1482
Salon of the King (France), 2:640
salons
 aristocratic women and, 1:469
 Berlin and, 1:215, 316; 2:675
 Chopin's performances in,
  1:439, 440
 Durand and, 2:696
 Enlightenment and, 4:2029
 Parisian republican, 2:649
 Rossini and, 4:2038
Salons of the Rose + Cross, 4:2295
Šaloun, Ladislav, 4:1858
Salpêtrière Hospice (Paris), 4:1791,
 1959
salvarsan, 2:736
Salvation Army, 1:36; 4:1886,
 2082–2083
Salvemini, Gaetano, 3:1277
Salzburg, 2:958
Salzburg Festival, 2:1076, 1077
Samarin, Yuri, 4:2154, 2196
Samaritaine, Le (Paris department
 store), 2:548
Sambre River, 486

samedi soirs, 4:2038
same-sex desire. *See* homosexuality and
 lesbianism
Sammlung architektonischer Entwürfe
 (Schinkel), 4:2093
Samori Empire, 1:20
Samson et Delilah (Saint-Saëns),
 3:1675
"Samuel Johnson" (Macaulay),
 3:1408
samurai (daimyo), 3:1208, 1209, 1210
San (Bushmen), 4:2219
sanatoriums, 5:2360–2361
Sand, George, 1:162, 168; 2:828;
 3:1662, 1680; 4:1706, 1757,
 2083–2085, *2084*
 Chopin relationship with, 1:439;
  4:2029, 2084
 feminism and, 2:802
 Liszt and, 3:1360
 Nadar and, 3:1578
 as against women's suffrage of, 2:651
 on women's superior sensibility,
  2:945–946
Sand, Karl, 1:369; 2:959
Sandeau, Jules, 1:168
Sandhurst. *See* Royal Military Academy
San Domingo, 1:14
Sandžak of Novi Pazar, 3:1541
San Fernando Academy (Madrid),
 4:1781
Sangiorgi, Ermanno, 3:1416
San Giuliano, marquis di (Antonio
 Paternò Castello), 3:1202, 1203
Sangnier, Marc, 1:389
San Ildefonso alliance (1796), 2:901
sanitation, 1:251, 253
 Berlin and, 1:218, 219
 Chadwick and, 1:401–402
 cholera and, 1:437, 438, 450; 2:658,
  668, 669, 765
 clean water's importance and, 2:658,
  667, 670
 death rates and, 2:628, 644
 Hamburg and, 2:1040
 London and, 3:1372, 1373, 1380;
  4:*1911*
 London sewer construction and,
  2:*758;* 3:1379
 Madrid and, 3:1412
 municipal reforms and, 1:450, 451
 Paris sewer system and, 2:1049;
  4:1731, *1774*
 slum housing and, 1:453, *454;*
  2:670; 4:*1912*
 water pollution and, 2:764; 4:*1912,*
  1914

V

wheat. *See* grain
Wheaton, Henry, **3**:1175
Wheeler, Anna, **2**:650, 803; **3**:1288; **4**:2201
When We Dead Awaken (Ibsen), **3**:1107, 1109
Where Angels Fear to Tread (Forster), **2**:835
Where Do We Come From? What Are We? Where Are We Going? (Gauguin), **1**:152; **2**:941
Whewell, William, **3**:1477, 1654
Whigs, **1**:416; **2**:1004; **4**:1984; **5**:2321, 2367, 2385, 2412, 2457, **2460–2462**
  Brougham and, **1**:302, 303
  Corn Laws repeal and, **2**:559, 1005; **4**:1759
  Fox and, **2**:1001
  liberalism and, **3**:1343, 1347, 1348
  newspapers and, **4**:1872
  parliamentary reform and, **2**:1001
  Pitt and, **2**:101
  Poor Law and, **4**:1819–1820
  trade policies and, **2**:517
  William IV and, **5**:2461, 2471
  See also Liberal Party
Whirlpool, The (Gissing), **2**:975
whiskey. *See* alcohol and temperance
Whistler, James Abbott McNeill, **1**:109, 191; **4**:1874, 2294
Whitbread, Samuel, **5**:2461
Whitbread brewery, **1**:284
White Army (anti-Bolshevik), **3**:1520; **4**:1803
Whiteboys, **3**:1657
Whitechapel (London), **3**:1373, 1375, 1376
white-collar crime, **2**:571
white-collar workers, **1**:352, 355, 473; **4**:1879
White Company, The (Doyle), **2**:681
White Fathers (Society of Missionaries of Africa), **3**:1528, *1528*
Whitehall Mystery, The: Discovering the Mutilated Trunk (engraving), **2**:*576*
Whitehead, Alfred North, **1**:214
White Horse, The (Gauguin), **2**:941
Whiteley, William, **3**:1378
White Mountain, Battle of (1620), **1**:259
Whites (Polish moderates), **4**:1809
white slave trade, **4**:1884
White Terror of 1815 (France), **2**:565, 847
Whitman, Walt, **1**:372; **4**:2296, 2297
Wholesale Salvation (social reform programs), **4**:2083

whooping cough, **2**:667
Whydah (African trading port), **1**:14, 15
Why I Am a Communist (Cabet), **2**:521
"Why We Paint Ourselves: A Futurist Manifesto" (Larionov and Zdanevich), **1**:157
Wide Streets Commission (Dublin), **2**:691
Widowers' Houses (Shaw), **4**:2165
widows, **1**:287; **5**:2452, 2455
Wiehl, Antonín, **4**:1858
Wielopolski, Aleksandr, **4**:1809
Wiener Werkstätte, **1**:112, 153, 336; **3**:1260, 1261
Wieniawski, Henri, **4**:1700
Wiese, Leopold von, **4**:2215
Wigram, Clive, **3**:*1136*
Wilberforce, Samuel, **2**:614, 1102; **4**:1896
Wilberforce, William, **1**:36; **2**:510; **5**:2462–2463
Wild Duck, The (Ibsen), **3**:1108
Wilde, Jane, **5**:2464
Wilde, Oscar, **2**:951; **4**:2182, 2255; **5**:2464–2466, *2465*
  Beardsley's illustrations and, **1**:109, 192, *193*
  censorship and, **3**:1377
  cigarette smoking and, **5**:2315
  Decadence and, **2**:632, 633
  degeneration and, **2**:639
  fin de siècle and, **2**:816
  hashish reference by, **2**:687
  homosexuality of, **2**:241, 633, 1070, 1084; **3**:1184; **4**:2258, 2297; **5**:2465–2466
  as Ibsen enthusiast, **3**:1109
  Pater and, **4**:1746, 1747
  Yeats and, **5**:2509
Wilde, William, **5**:2464
Wilhelm Braumüller (publisher), **5**:2449
Wilhelmina, queen of the Netherlands, **3**:1619
Wilhelm Meister's Apprenticeship (Goethe), **2**:985, 987; **4**:2095
  Carlyle translation, **1**:370
Wilhelm Meisters Lehrjahre (Goethe), **2**:985, 987; **4**:2095
Wilhelm Meisters theatralische Sendung (Goethe), **2**:984
Wilhelmstrasse (Berlin), **1**:217
Wilhelm Tell (Schiller), **4**:2288
Wilhelm zu Wied, prince of Albania, **1**:34
Wilkinson, James, **5**:2440

will, the, **4**:2103, 2104–2105
Willemfonds (Belgium), **1**:202
Willette, Adolphe, **1**:335
William I, emperor of Germany and king of Prussia, **1**:234, 235; **3**:1394, 1533; **5**:2325, **2467–2468**
  alliance system and, **1**:48
  anarchist assassination attempts on, **2**:966
  Austro-Prussian War and, **1**:147, 148
  Bismarck and, **1**:238–239, 240; **2**:962–963, *963*, 964
  brother Frederick William IV and, **2**:877
  German unification and, **2**:964; **3**:1383; **4**:1902
  gerontocracy and, **3**:1664
  Krupp and, **3**:1274
  Menzel painting of, **3**:1489
  as regent, **2**:962
  son Frederick III and, **2**:874, 966
William II, emperor of Germany and king of Prussia, **2**:966–969, 1068; **5**:2467, **2468–2470**, *2469*
  accession to throne of, **1**:240; **2**:966
  alliance system and, **1**:48, 49; **2**:663, 664
  authoritarianism of, **2**:862
  Bismarck and, **5**:2468, 2474
  Bismarck's dismissal by, **1**:233, 240–241; **2**:663, 967
  on Boxer Rebellion, **1**:292
  British policies and, **2**:1013
  cabaret satire of, **1**:336
  Chamberlain's (Houston) racial theories and, **1**:403
  conservatism of, **2**:874, 967
  Eulenburg affair and, **2**:1071, 1084
  father, Frederick III, and, **2**:873, 874
  Herzl and, **5**:2521
  Moroccan Crises and, **3**:1545, 1549
  musical taste of, **1**:219
  naval buildup and, **3**:1609, 1610
  popularity of, **3**:1347
  Prussia and, **4**:1903
  Rudolf (crown prince) and, **4**:2045
  Russia and, **3**:1628
  technical colleges and, **5**:2382
  Tirpitz and, **3**:1610; **5**:2312
  Victoria and, **5**:2415, 2468, 2471
  World War I and, **1**:232; **2**:663, 664
  World War II and, **1**:232
William III, king of Great Britain, **3**:1407

For Reference

Not to be taken from this room